AMERICAN EDUCATION 1945-2000

Carl Kaestle

AMERICAN EDUCATION 1945-2000

A HISTORY AND COMMENTARY

GERALD L. GUTEK
Loyola University, Chicago

WAVELAND
PRESS, INC.
Prospect Heights, Illinois

For information about this book, write or call:

Waveland Press, Inc.
P.O. Box 400
Prospect Heights, Illinois 60070
(847) 634-0081
www.waveland.com

Cover photo: Reproduction from the collections
of the Library of Congress

Printed in the United States of America

7 6 5 4 3 2 1

This book is dedicated
to those who were my teachers
at St. Mary's School and Streator Township High School
in Streator, Illinois.

Contents

Acknowledgments

Throughout my teaching career I have benefitted from the association and advice of my colleagues and from the insights provided by my students at Loyola University, Chicago; Northern Michigan University; and the University of Glasgow, Scotland. In doing the research for this book, I had the opportunity to use the archives of the Eisenhower Library, the Gerald Ford Library, and the Lyndon B. Johnson Library. I was greatly aided by the professional assistance and courtesy of the archivists at these presidential libraries. To all of you I am deeply indebted.

In addition, my thanks go to Neil Rowe, publisher at Waveland Press, for his sustained interest in my work on the book. Special thanks go to Jeni Ogilvie, my editor, at Waveland Press, for her editorial expertise and guidance into turning a manuscript into a finished product. To my wife, Patricia, I give my thanks for her meticulous work in making the index for the book. Pat has always been there to encourage my research and writing.

Finally, I want to thank the administration and search committee at Otterbein College, Westerville, Ohio, for selecting me as the Visiting Humanities Scholar for the spring quarter, 2000. I hope to gain additional insights into the history of education from the faculty and students at Otterbein College.

1

Society, Politics, and Education: 1945–1950

T he enthusiastic victory celebrations that swept the nation with the news that Japan's surrender had ended World War II brought a euphoria that the dawn of a new peaceful world was here at last. The organization of the United Nations in San Francisco promised the possibility of a world without war.[1] Americans believed that the United States, the world's exclusive atomic power, could be counted on to maintain that peace. While there was a surface euphoria, there were still unresolved fears remaining from the Great Depression of the 1930s. Would the prosperity generated by the wartime economy continue after the war, or would the country slip back into economic depression? Developments in education in the immediate postwar period need to be considered in the context of what was a massive readjustment. Such a readjustment called for changing the war-driven economy to a peace-time economy. It meant readjusting the national and individual psyche from the sense of mobilization in a common cause against clearly identified foreign enemies to the pursuit of happiness American style. Would this readjustment be accompanied by the cynical withdrawal from world responsibilities to the isolationism that followed World War I?

While these questions were of serious magnitude, the speed of postwar readjustment was so rapid that events rather than intellectual musing answered them. What was real about the post–World War II situation were the major changes that had occurred. The limited geographical horizons and localism of prewar America had been eroded by the massive movement of people, especially military personnel, that the war had caused. Further, there was great desire to buy those consumer products, such as radios and automobiles, which had been so scarce during the war. Perhaps nothing symbolized the great postwar transformation as the disappearance of the icebox and its replacement by the refrigerator. The transformation would unleash the era of unabashed consumerism, national economic growth, and significant demographic changes. The following sections of the chapter examine: (1) situating American education in the postwar decade, (2) the enactment of the GI Bill, and (3) the U.S. educational role in occupied Germany and Japan.

Situating American Education

As often occurs, the nation's educators and teachers were responding to the changes engendered by postwar readjustment rather than anticipating and leading them. The reigning philosophy for many educators in the late 1940s continued to be progressivism, the educational philosophy that had originated during the Progressive Movement of the early twentieth century. Political progressives such as Theodore Roosevelt and Woodrow Wilson had supported legislation to curb the economic power of business corporations, to conserve natural resources, and to safeguard the public's health by inspection of food and drugs. Progressives in education, influenced by John Dewey's experimentalism, used methods that featured problem solving according to the scientific method and group-centered learning activities. During the depression of the 1930s, the progressivism of the twentieth century's earlier decades was infused with the liberal reformism of Franklin Roosevelt's New Deal. When the United States entered World War II, progressive educators, inclined to liberalism, emphasized education for democracy as an ideological antithesis to Nazi and Fascist totalitarianism. With the end of World War II, these liberal currents, fused with earlier progressive impulses, continued to motivate many educators. The war, however, had generated new scientific and technological developments as well as major social changes that needed to find their way into the schools. For educators, an important question was—would progressivism prove to be an adequate educational philosophy in the postwar reality? (The progressives are also discussed in chapter 4.)

The Condition of U.S. Schools

In 1945, the U.S. Senate Committee on Education and Labor conducted hearings that revealed the condition of the nation's schools. In the early 1940s, the nation's big-city schools were generally regarded as quantitatively superior in terms of tax base, revenues generated, facilities, professional administrative and teaching staffs, and curriculum to those in small towns and rural areas. Rural schools, particularly in the South, showed the greatest quantitative weaknesses—inadequate funding, overaged buildings, and outdated curricula.[2] What was made clear in the Senate's hearings was the long-standing but unaddressed problem of the inequalities in American schools, especially urban/rural differentials. The emerging role that suburbia would play in American society and education was not yet apparent because migration to the suburbs was still in its beginning stages.

Generally, the schools, like other institutions, were recovering and readjusting from wartime restrictions on construction and renovation. Only a few new schools had been built during the war, primarily in areas impacted by the military and defense industries. Further, needed repairs and renovations to schools' physical plants had been delayed due to shortages of material and labor. While school buildings throughout the country needed to be constructed or modernized, the needs of the South were most acute. A further complication was that Southern and many border states had erected and maintained dual school systems based on legal racial segregation. Although the *Plessy v. Ferguson* decision in 1896 gave legal sanction to the separation of the races, the doctrine of "separate but equal" held that facilities, while segregated, were to be equal. In fact, however, educational facilities were not equal when the Supreme Court made its pronouncement, nor were they ever equal. Schools attended by white students uniformly enjoyed better buildings, an enlarged curriculum, and more professionally qualified teachers. Schools attended by African Americans were often rundown and neglected, overcrowded, and offered a limited curriculum. While the schooling of the South's white and black pupils was quantitatively unequal, the per pupil expenditure for students in the South was less than that spent on children in the North. The educational situation in 1945, like that in earlier and later years, revealed sharp regional and racial inequalities.

The Senate committee heard testimony and gathered evidence that indicated that the country's schools were seriously overcrowded and understaffed. Teachers' salaries, especially at the elementary level, had always been low and, with the postwar period's rising inflation, were growing desperately low. Further, the Senate committee heard that many teachers were inadequately prepared academically and professionally.[3] The issue of the deficiency in the number of trained teachers available and their low salaries was almost directly attributable to historic circumstances surrounding the teaching profession and the law of supply and demand. During the depression of the 1930s, teachers' salaries had fallen as the tax base of the states and local districts

An elementary school class, which was typical in the 1940s. (Reproduction from the National Archives, photo #83-G-41598.)

declined. Fiscal retrenchment in education occurred throughout the country during the 1930s. While schools continued to function during the depression, the length of the school year and the salaries of administrators and teachers were reduced in many cases. While their salaries improved somewhat during World War II, teachers' economic gains were modest. Further, the birthrate had declined during the depression period. Large class sizes, used as an economy measure, and a smaller student population reduced the demand for teachers. At the war's end in 1945, the supply of teachers being prepared in normal schools and teachers colleges was inadequate to meet accelerating demands. As the birthrate increased and the school-age population grew after the war, the demand for teachers also increased.

While there were obvious indicators of quantitative deficiencies in American education, less visible but equally real signs of qualitative weaknesses were present. Historically, the school curriculum generally has lagged behind and has been slow to adapt to social and economic change. In the post–World War II era, especially its first decade, the problem of curricular lag had become particularly acute. School districts customarily reviewed curriculum—books and materials—on a cyclical basis, often every five years. The result was a "normal" institutional lag in reviewing and replacing outdated books and materials. The depression and the war compounded the time lag affecting curricular revision. During the depression, many school districts, out of economic necessity, could not afford to replace old books and materials. Then the war, immediately following the depression, limited the publication of new books and materials because of military and defense priorities. In 1945–46, some school districts were still using books and materials published in the 1930s.

In addition to the effects of the conventional time lag for curriculum review and revision and the restrictions of depression and war, the curriculum had become seriously dated in key areas, particularly in incorporating the international changes and scientific and technological innovations of the war years. The United States' entry into World War II drastically altered Americans' perceptions of their nation's international role. Before the entry of the United States into World War II, a fierce national debate was waged between "America First" isolationists and those seeking to aid the allies, especially Great Britain, against Nazi aggression. The Japanese attack on Pearl Harbor on December 7, 1941, dramatically ended the debate as the United States, with its allies, waged a war on a global scale in Africa, Europe, and Asia. When the war ended, the United States was an undisputed global power, a role it would exercise throughout the twentieth century. The inherited curriculum and textbooks in history and the social studies were inadequate in introducing American students to their country's new world role. Textbooks needed to be rewritten and revised to reflect the new international reality.

If the school curriculum did not adequately reflect the changing role of the United States internationally, there was even a greater gap between what had happened in science and technology during the war and what was being taught in science courses and laboratories. World War II had a major impact on developments in science and technology. There were new developments in medicine, such as the invention of sulfa and penicillin. In the war's last year, the German's use of V-1 and V-2 rockets, although too late to change the war's course, began the age of missiles that would affect not only the military but would contribute to space exploration in the coming decades. The splitting of the atom and President Truman's decision to drop atomic bombs on the Japanese cities of Hiroshima and Nagasaki ushered in the atomic and nuclear age. These scientific and technological developments had occurred so quickly and dramatically that the school curriculum was in urgent need of revision and updating to catch up.

The general conclusions from the Senate committee's hearings on education were clear: (1) educational opportunities, based on both quantitative and qualitative indicators, were unequal; (2) sharp educational disparities existed between the North and the South and urban and rural areas; (3) immense inequalities existed in the Southern and border states' racially segregated schools, which were disadvantageous to the education of African-American children; (4) the schools' physical plants were inadequate and needed expansion; (5) teacher shortages were looming, a problem exacerbated by large numbers of inadequately prepared teachers.

While the parameters of the postwar problems facing American education were becoming focused, what remained unclear was the answer to the question: who was responsible for remedying the country's educational situation? With only a very few exceptions in America's historic pattern, education issues had been reserved for the states and local school districts. Was the same historic pattern to apply in the postwar reality? Would the federal government play a new and major role? Did the federal government have a responsibility in equalizing educational opportunities, in dealing with racial segregation, and in encouraging curricular revision? Or, were these issues best left to the states and local school districts? While the questions were easy to frame, they raised a debate that would continue throughout the twentieth century. (Chapter 2 examines the federal aid to education issues in the late 1940s and early 1950s.)

The Nature and Purpose of Secondary Schooling

While the issues facing education were found throughout the system from elementary through secondary to higher education, they seemed to have their greatest impact on secondary institutions—the country's high schools. In addition to the rather clearly defined needs to update and modernize the school curriculum to reflect new international, scientific, and technological realities, other developments in American education were also having their impact on the public and on professional educators' perceptions and responses. The institution where the challenges of a new era would have their greatest impact was on the high school and its curriculum.

A larger cohort than ever before was attending secondary schools. The number of students enrolled in secondary schools had increased from 80,000 in 1870 to 7,000,000 in 1940, the last year before the war.[4] While the comprehensive high school remained the favored and dominant institution of secondary education, the secondary school population had grown increasingly diverse. Students from formerly underrepresented groups were being retained and tending to complete their secondary school education. Progressive educators, in the 1920s and 1930s, had responded to this growing diversity in the secondary school population in two ways: (1) by emphasizing the high schools' "comprehensiveness," that is, providing a learning environment for students of varied socioeconomic backgrounds regardless of their

An architect's design for a public high school, typical of the late 1940s. (Reproduction from the National Archives.)

future educational goals, as the appropriate institutional mix to educate American adolescents, and (2) by devising a range of curricular options or tracks that reflected the students' varying educational needs, expectations, and career destinations. The progressives were responding to the issue: if access is increased and the socioeconomic backgrounds of high school students become more mixed, what is the best way to satisfy the educational needs of a more diverse high school population? Should not the high school curriculum also become more diversified? The response of educational progressives, especially the professional educators in schools of education, was to argue that the key to educating a varied school population was to diversify the curriculum to meet distinct student needs. The path they took was to diversify the high school curriculum into multiple tracks and courses. A large remaining issue was that of a common core. The critics of curricular diversity within a comprehensive institution were mainly academicians who argued for retaining the high school's traditional academic function as a college preparatory institution. Throughout the twentieth century, there would be major debates over the nature of American secondary schooling.

Related to the issues of the role and function of American secondary schooling were those associated with higher education. Should colleges and universities continue to be selective institutions serving an elite minority of the general population? Or should higher education institutions be opened, like the high schools, to a larger and more representative student population? Connected to these big questions were the issues that derived from them, especially those of a mass versus a selective system and attended matters of quantity and quality.

Finding a Direction

At the federal level from 1945 to 1952, the years of the Truman administration, paradoxically the country moved in new directions that would change education forever but also remained mired in old patterns that were difficult to break. While the GI Bill brought dramatic and irreversible growth to higher education, initiatives for federal aid for elementary and secondary education were bogged down in the swamps of racism, sectarianism, and localism. Where possible to act, Truman was decisive. When blocked by a recalcitrant or hostile Congress, he created special commissions whose investigations, reports, and recommendations paved the way for reforms.

Although the fight for freedom throughout the world fueled patriotic rhetoric during the war, the war had little effect in ending the patterns of racial discrimination in housing, transportation, employment, and education. From 1945 until the *Brown vs. the Board of Education* decision in 1954, the schools of the South and the border states were racially segregated by law. Gunnar Myrdal, in his classic sociological study, *An American Dilemma*, which investigated racial relationships in the United States, pointed out the major discrepancy in American life between its stated belief in equality and its practice of discrimination. Myrdal found that American behavior, especially of white people, showed a gulf between the general ethic of individual equality and the practice of racial discrimination. Despite his rather stark findings, Myrdal noted a glimmer of hope—he believed that particular individual behavior was moving slowly in the direction of conformity with the more generalized ethic of human equality and individual rights.[5]

While Myrdal investigated racism in the realm of sociological theory, the actual political situation during the first five years after the war was definitely not favorable to legislatively mandated change. The racial situation was aggravated by the inherited political situation, especially in the South where the Democratic Party was dominant. With only very rare exceptions, the South, since the end of Reconstruction, voted solidly Democratic. Its congressional delegations were exclusively made up of Democrats. Based on the seniority system, Southern Democrats, chairing key Senate and House committees, had the power to "bottle up" any legislation that threatened the region's racially segregated status quo.

Truman inherited a fragile Democratic coalition of diverse groups, interests, and geographic sections that his predecessor, Franklin D. Roosevelt, had put together during the Great Depression of the 1930s. In this coalition were the big cities with their ethnic populations, the labor unions, and the traditionally Democratic South. Also included was the vast majority of African Americans who had switched party loyalty from the Republicans, the party of Lincoln, to the Democrats, the party of Roosevelt, because of the depression. Since most of the African Americans in the South were disenfranchised by restrictive voting laws, those who could vote lived primarily in Northern big cities. Any of President Truman's actions on civil rights had to navigate through these complicated political seas.[6]

Truman, though from the border state of Missouri, soon showed his support for civil rights. By executive order, he ended racial segregation in the armed services. In 1946, Truman appointed the President's Committee on Civil Rights. The committee investigated discrimination in such sensitive political areas as employment, voting, education, and the armed services. The committee made sweeping recommendations to: (1) enact a federal antilynching law; (2) abolish the poll tax; (3) strengthen the civil rights section of the Justice Department; (4) federally protect voting rights; (5) end discrimination in the armed forces; (6) ban segregation and discrimination in employment, housing, health care facilities, interstate transportation, and public accommodations; (7) cut off any federal aid to racially segregated schools; and (8) prohibit discrimination in the admission of students based on race, color, creed, or national origin, except in religious denominational schools. The last two recommendations would have initiated powerful change in American education.[7] It remained until later in the twentieth century for this change to occur.

Truman, on February 2, 1948, sent a special message to Congress that incorporated the recommendations of the committee on civil rights. Civil rights legislation, however, was blocked by a coalition of conservative Republicans and Southern Democrats. On July 26, 1948, Truman issued an executive order that ended racial segregation in the armed forces and banned discrimination in federal housing.[8]

During Truman's administration, the direction that American education would take was impacted by several unresolved strains in American life: (1) racially segregated schools in the Southern and border states; (2) the role of Roman Catholic and other private schools in any future federal aid to education programs; (3) the appropriate relationships of federal, state, and local governments in education.

The GI Bill: Servicemen's Readjustment Act

While the educational situation at the beginning of the postwar era called for long-term solutions, the immediate, urgent problem was to readjust and reintegrate 20,000,000 members of the armed forces returning to civilian life. The enactment of the Servicemen's Readjustment Act of 1944, the "GI Bill," a quick but highly significant response, would have a sustained impact on American higher education and on the country. Although historic precedents existed for limited and specific federal assistance to higher education, the GI Bill signaled an important watershed in U.S. educational history. The federal government, through the Morrill Land Grant Act of 1862, which granted federal land to the states for agricultural and mechanical schools, had stimulated higher education's growth and movement in a more technologically applied direction. The Servicemen's Readjustment Act would change higher education by making it more accessible to what had been historically underrepresented groups. The GI Bill was a key development in making American higher education more inclusive of the general population.

The nation's political leaders realized that the country faced a momentous challenge with the return of millions of military personnel to domestic life. A massive human resources mobilization had turned the U.S. armed services into one of the world's most powerful fighting forces and now an equally rapid demobilization was anticipated. There were lingering doubts about the economy's ability to absorb millions of returning veterans. Indeed, there was some foreboding that the specter of dreaded economic depression might return. Further, the nation's politicians as well as the public still remembered the debacle when World War I veterans, determined to be paid their bonuses, marched on Washington, D.C., only to be ejected forcibly by U.S. Army troops, commanded by Chief-of-Staff, General Douglas MacArthur.

As early as 1942, with the United States just entering the war, President Franklin D. Roosevelt asked the National Resources and Planning Board (NRPB) to develop proposals for demobilizing the armed forces and for the adjustment to a peacetime economy. Under NRPB auspices, the Post-War Manpower Conference (PMC), chaired by Floyd W. Reeves, a staff member of the American Council on Education and a professor at the University of Chicago, was formed to develop proposals. The PMC's report, "Demobilization and Readjustment," issued in 1943, outlined a plan for the government-subsidized education and training of returning veterans. The report's thrust was to provide job retraining and continuation of the education of those military personnel whose education had been interrupted by wartime service.[9] The PMC report was referred to a new committee, the "Armed Forces Committee on Post-War Educational Opportunities for Service Personnel," chaired by Brigadier General Frederick Osborn. The Osborn committee generally reaffirmed the earlier report, moving the matter of veterans' assistance further in the direction of education and training. Concurrently, the American Council on Education (ACE) developed a plan that largely endorsed the Osborn committee's recommendations. The American Legion, a large national veterans' organization, generally supporting the Osborn recommendations, wanted even more comprehensive legislation. Not forgotten was the fact that the returning 20,000,000 veterans would be a powerful political force in future elections.

With the groundwork established, Congress in 1944 began to consider legislation when Senator Elbert D. Thomas introduced a military personnel's aid bill in the Senate and Representative John Rankin introduced a somewhat different one in the House. When differences between the two bills were resolved, Congress passed the Servicemen's Readjustment Act, which when signed by President Franklin D. Roosevelt, took effect on June 22, 1944.[10]

The Servicemen's Readjustment Act, which also provided loans for housing and business ventures, contained highly significant educational provisions that would revolutionize American higher education. It provided: (1) one year of federally aided education for veterans who were honorably discharged and had served at least ninety days and were not over twenty-five years of age when entering the service (the deletion of age restrictions in 1946 made all veterans eligible for benefits); (2) additional eligibility and duration of support, up to a maximum of four years of benefits, were determined by the recipient's time on active military duty; (3) benefits included tuition, books, fees, supplies, and a monthly living allowance.[11] The actual application and admission procedures to schools, colleges, and universities for veterans remained under the control of the institutions and the individuals, with little federal interference. The veteran, like any other prospective student, applied for admission to an institution; the institution determined either the acceptance or rejection.[12]

The influx of veterans and the tuition and fees that they brought with them helped to pull institutions out of financial doldrums. However, the cost of attending college was much less in the 1950s than in later decades, especially the 1980s and 1990s. Tuition and fees at the most expensive private colleges were about $400 a year. University-owned housing and food costs were also reasonable. Although the federal investment in veterans' education was costly, it was not prohibitive and was judged to be a reasonable investment in the nation's future.

The massive influx of veterans using GI Bill benefits rapidly transformed colleges and universities, which traditionally were slow to change. Institutions of higher education had suffered fiscal retrenchment policies during the depression. Further, their enrollments had fallen during the war years. With the entry of veterans, colleges and universities needed to improve and expand facilities, libraries, classrooms, and laboratories. They had to construct or arrange housing quickly for veterans and their families; many veterans came to campus with spouses and children.

The entry of veterans to colleges and universities introduced the concept of what came to be called, the "nontraditional" student. Before the war, the typical undergraduate was a recent high school graduate, age eighteen or nineteen. The new nontraditional students were older, more mature, and much less interested in campus social and athletic affairs.

Some institutions responded to the new students by modifying their entry requirements, policies, and curricula. Because some veterans who applied lacked high school diplomas, certain institutions made greater use of College Entrance Board Examinations. Some institutions gave preference to veterans in admissions and gave credit for equivalent experiences. Some institutions created refresher courses and developed general education divisions that provided basic courses. There were also adjustments in the school calendar, with greater use of summer school, since many veterans wanted to continue studies throughout the year.[13]

Along with curricular change, colleges and universities expanded their student personnel services from what once had been the small office of the dean of students. Institutions established veterans' counseling and guidance departments or services, which grew into general divisions of student personnel services dealing with housing, vocational guidance, and adjustment problems.[14]

Very few government officials or college and university administrators accurately projected the extensive use that veterans would make of their opportunity for higher education. In 1945, the number of veterans using benefits for higher education was a deceivingly low 88,000. In 1946, one year after the war's end, veterans' enrollments grew to 1,080,396, 51.9 percent of the total college population. In 1947, the figure reached 1,122,738, 48 percent of the total college population; in 1948, veterans' enrollments were 1,021,038, or 42.4 percent of the total college population. For the years 1946–1956, a total of 2,232,000 veterans, including 64,728 women, or 15 percent of all veterans, had attended college under the GI Bill.[15] During the decade from 1945 to 1955, an additional 3.5 million veterans engaged in some type of postsecondary training that was not at the college or university level. The total cost of the GI Bill for World War II veterans was estimated at $14,500,000,000.[16]

While most college and university administrators welcomed the veterans to their institutions, a few harbored serious initial reservations that the high tide of enrollments and the admission of academically unprepared students would erode academic standards. For example, Robert Hutchins, chancellor of the University of Chicago and a consistent opponent of vocationalism in higher education, admonished that higher education should not be used to avert mass unemployment. He warned that colleges and universities would admit academically unqualified veterans in order to increase their revenues.[17] James B. Conant, Harvard's president, also urging caution and maintenance of selectivity, feared that "the least capable" may be "flooding" colleges and universities.[18] The Readjustment Act, he initially believed, failed to distinguish between those who could and those who could not profit from higher education. Later, Conant publicly admitted that his initial reservations were unfounded as the returning veterans proved themselves to be serious and highly capable students.

The veterans, a new category of students, gave a generally impressive academic account of themselves. More likely to be married with children and holding part-time jobs, they changed higher education's character. Educators typically found that veterans were more mature, more serious, more highly motivated, and were pursuing more specific goals than traditional undergraduates. George MacFarland, director of the Veterans' Advisory Council at the University of Pennsylvania, found them to be time conscious and academically capable.[19] They were concerned with determining and fulfilling their personal futures, which the war had delayed. They wanted to "get with it," which meant fulfilling career objectives, rather than to be committed to larger social causes. Although there were few empirical studies that assessed the veterans' academic achievement, educators' anecdotal recollections refer to their strong motivation to succeed. This motivation probably came from a desire to recapture something that was missed earlier, either for self, family, or ancestors. Enlisted personnel, those who were the privates and sergeants during the war, had learned the importance that a college degree had made for their officers.

Among the empirical research on veterans' academic achievement was an Ohio State University study that compared 2,000 veterans with a nonveteran student population of 5,887. The veterans tracked in the Ohio State study were found to have a slightly superior academic grade point average, scoring 7 percent more grades of B or better than nonveterans.[20] The Fredericksen and Schrader study, financed by the Carnegie Foundation for the Advancement of Teaching in 1951, provided the most comprehensive and sophisticated comparison of the academic achievement of veterans and nonveterans. The findings showed that veterans received higher grades as freshmen. Further, those veterans who returned to college after their higher education had been interrupted by wartime service scored significantly higher than nonveterans.[21]

With some modifications in benefits, the GI Bill was extended to veterans of the Korean and Vietnam conflicts. A total of 2,391,000 Korean conflict veterans and 3,300,000 Vietnam veterans received benefits from the extended Servicemen's Readjustment Act.[22]

The Servicemen's Readjustment Act produced both short- and long-term consequences for higher education and for the nation. The greatly increased enrollments, which taxed existing physical plants, housing, classrooms, libraries, and laboratories, led to a massive expansion of college and university facilities. Class sizes became larger as did the ratio of students to professors. The larger lectures and discussion sections led to the use of more teaching assistants and instructors, a persistent trend in U.S. higher education. The need for more professors stimulated the growth of graduate studies, especially Ph.D. programs. College administrative roles grew and became more special-

slides over import of the extension (from crisis episode to regular aid to vets)

doesn't talk about import of grant going to individ not inst.

ized with greater separation between academic and student services, particularly in larger institutions, as student services began to incorporate housing, health, and other nonacademic functions.

For the nation, the GI Bill was an internal investment in human resources that paid large and continuing dividends. The bill created a large body of educated and trained people who contributed intellectual, managerial, and technical knowledge and skills for decades after they had completed their college degrees. Those educated by the GI Bill contributed to America's economic productivity and expansiveness throughout the next decades.

New Directions for Higher Education

The GI Bill brought about a major transformation of American higher education. Once-selective colleges and universities had now become massive institutions, serving a student body that was more representative of the nation as a whole. Higher education was now attracting more attention than ever before from a larger audience of citizens, many of whom had been to college and were familiar with it. Further, the influx of the veterans of World War II had an intergenerational spiraling effect. The veterans who attended colleges and universities, often the first of their families to do so, now had expectations that their children, too, would have a college education.

In 1946, President Truman appointed the President's Commission on Higher Education. The commission produced a series of reports, *Higher Education for American Democracy*, issued in 1947, that pointed to new directions for higher education. The general tone of the reports was that U.S. higher education should promote greater equality of opportunity in higher education. The reports, endorsing a quantitative expansion of institutions of higher education, called for the admission of larger numbers of qualified students. Indeed, they called for a doubling of student enrollments to 4.6 million by 1960. To advance general equality of opportunity, the commission condemned racial segregation and the use of quotas in admission.[23] The use of quotas in the late 1940s was very different from the affirmative action procedures of the 1960s, 1970s, and 1980s. Although not officially documented, some institutions, or departments within institutions, were believed to use a quota system that limited the number of minority students such as Jews, Roman Catholics, and African Americans.

The commission also made a series of specific recommendations, many of which would be implemented in the ensuing decades. Recognizing the key role of the states, the commission urged the states to establish planning commissions and to establish extensive community college systems. Both of these recommendations were implemented in the 1950s and 1960s.

Prior to the 1950s, higher education development was largely unplanned. In many of the states, state institutions were virtually autonomous on admissions, enrollments, curricula and programs, budgeting, and expansion. This kind of institutional autonomy had been highly prized, especially in the prewar years when institutions and enrollments were smaller. After the war, with the rapidly expanding enrollments caused by the GI Bill, higher education institutions expanded dramatically. Colleges and universities were now experiencing the general growth patterns that had occurred at the elementary and secondary school levels. The president's commission was urging the states to coordinate the growth, development, and expansion of their higher education systems. In the 1950s and 1960s, the thrust of planning was for orderly expansion. By the mid-1970s, the concept of planning was further refined into strategic planning. During the 1970s, strategic planning meant state-wide coordination of public higher education to avoid program duplication and contain rapidly escalating costs.

The mood of the 1950s and 1960s in higher education was one of expansion, coupled with greater equality of educational opportunity. The president's commission focused on the junior college as the principal institution that would make equality of educational opportunity a "close to home," inexpensive alternative for a student's first two years of higher education. Two-year junior colleges, which had existed since the early twentieth century, were typically upward extensions of high schools. Essentially, the junior colleges provided the first two years of basic courses of undergraduate education. Where junior colleges existed, students could live at home, attend classes, and transfer credits to four-year institutions. The president's commission urged an extensive development of two-year community colleges that would not only provide two years of undergraduate education but offer a wide range of vocational, technical, health care, and adult education programs. The commission's recommendations were prophetic for the large system of community colleges that were developed throughout the country in the following decades.

In addition, the commission recommended federal scholarships for undergraduates based on need and graduate fellowships based on academic ability. This recommendation pointed to the future enactment of federal loan and grant programs in higher education. It further anticipated racial desegregation by urging the repeal of racial segregation laws and the banning of discrimination in admissions and enrollment.

The changes that were taking place in American higher education were not unlike those that had occurred earlier in secondary education with the development of the comprehensive high school. Just as the high school had felt the pressure of new social and economic demands in earlier decades, these pressures were now reaching colleges and universities. Higher education faced the mixed motives and conflicting social demands generated by serving differing and more varied publics. It was expected to incorporate advances in science and technology, solve socioeconomic problems, and deal with larger global issues.

Military Occupation and Educational Reforms

skip

The earlier sections of chapter 1 discussed the educational situation relating to education domestically in the United States. This section examines the American role in education in the principal Axis nations, Germany and Japan, in which the United States had the status of being an Allied occupying power.

The end of World War II brought about some interesting challenges as the United States along with the victorious allies occupied the territory of its principal antagonists—Germany and Japan. As part of the process of demilitarization of these defeated Axis powers, the United States sought to inaugurate educational reforms. Among these reforms was the denazification of education in Germany and the demilitarization of education in Japan. Just as the schools in these countries had served the purposes of totalitarian dictatorship, the United States and other allies sought to reform the schools for democratic purposes.

The role that the United States played in reforming Japanese education is a fascinating episode in the interchange of educational ideas and structures from one country to another. In the case of occupied Japan, this educational borrowing was not really voluntary but rather imposed by U.S. military occupation authorities. It is especially fascinating in that the establishment of largely American imposed educational reforms in Japan contributed to what would be proclaimed in the 1970s and 1980s as the highly successful Japanese school system. Indeed, there were those critics who recommended that U.S. schools should imitate educational patterns found in modern Japan. We turn now to education in occupied Germany and Japan. We briefly treat Germany and then discuss Japan in more depth.

Education in Occupied Germany

After Germany's unconditional surrender in 1945, the country was divided into American, British, French, and Soviet military occupation zones. While each occupying power followed its own course, a general denazification of education occurred, as suspected and known

Nazis were purged from schools and universities. The purging of Nazis and their sympathizers was followed by the elimination of National Socialist racist ideology. Western versions of parliamentary democracy were taught in the schools in the French, British, and American zones which would eventually become the German Federal Republic (West Germany). The Soviets replaced Nazi totalitarianism with Communism in the Soviet zone destined to become the German Democratic Republic (GDR) or East Germany. The former Reich capital, Berlin, also was divided into four zones of occupation.[24]

During the four years of military occupation from 1945 to 1949, U.S. educational policy in Germany was driven by changing attitudes in American foreign policy. In its initial stage, from 1945–46, the U.S. military government's educational policy emphasized denazification and democratization. This first stage rested on long-held American premises regarding Hitler's rise to power and the Nazi regime in Germany. It was generally held that the Nazi regime had established a totalitarian monopoly over information by rigorous censorship of the media and by control of educational institutions. Not only were alternative opinions suppressed and punished but the Nazis had manipulated opinion through carefully orchestrated propaganda. The virulent racism, anti-Semitism, and extreme nationalism of the Nazi ideology had pervaded educational institutions. During the early occupation, American policy decisions rested on the question of guilt and complicity for the aggression and atrocities committed by German forces during the war. Were these crimes caused by Hitler and his Nazi henchmen or did the responsibility for these heinous deeds also fall on the shoulders of the German people? How this question was answered shaped American policy in the early postwar period.

In 1945–46, U.S. occupation authorities sought to purge known Nazis and Nazi sympathizers from the educational system. Educational agencies, under close American scrutiny, were instructed to inform the defeated Germans about the historic facts of German aggression and atrocities and emphasize the German people's guilt and complicity. The concept of collective complicity implied a general national guilt and responsibility for atonement.

Under U.S. and Allied auspices, German media and informal educational agencies covered the Nuremberg War Crimes Trial, which was extensively reported in German newspapers and magazines. As the scenario shifted to cold war concerns, the concept of collective guilt was revised to mean the guilt of the Nazi war criminals rather than the guilt of the German people as a whole.

By 1947–48, the early years of the cold war, U.S. educational policy, like American foreign policy, was responding to growing tensions with the Soviet Union, a former World War II ally. American military authorities, like their diplomatic counterparts, were now more concerned with containing the Soviet Union and stopping the spread of Communism in Europe. Anti-Communism now became the major focus of U.S. policy.

As the chief concern shifted to anti-Communism, U.S. policy sought to counter the Soviet allegation that the United States wanted to impose capitalism on Germany to benefit American economic interests. In 1948, General Lucius Clay announced a vigorous anti-Communist campaign. German media, in particular, under U.S. auspices, was to document clearly and thoroughly the differences between Communism as form of totalitarianism and democracy. The Soviet blockade of Berlin and the Berlin air lift in the late 1940s dramatically invigorated the anti-Communist campaign.

U.S. educational policy in Germany brought about more ideological changes than structural ones. The school system in the American, French, and British zones did not radically change but generally followed the pre–World War II structures of *grund schulen*, or common primary schools, and specialized types of secondary schools, which were closely tied to career destinations. In the Soviet zone, which became the German Democratic Republic (GDR), changes were structural as well as ideological. Schools in the Soviet zone and then in the GDR took on Soviet patterns with the variety of secondary schools collapsed into a unified school.

Education in Occupied Japan

Although there was formally an Allied Control Commission in Japan, the occupation was essentially under U.S. control under General Douglas MacArthur, the supreme commander. The dropping of two atomic bombs by the United States in August 1945 totally destroyed the Japanese cities of Hiroshima and Nagasaki and inflicted great loss of life. President Truman authorized the use of these bombs to end the war and save American lives from what was projected to be a bloody invasion of Japan's main islands. While the Japanese were allowed to retain their emperor, Hirohito, their surrender, like that of Germany, was unconditional. In many ways, MacArthur, with his flair for the dramatic, became something like a second emperor. An often contradictory figure, MacArthur had a long and distinguished military career, which began on World War I's battlefields, included his suppression of the bonus marchers during the depression of the 1930s, extended to his command of Allied forces in the Pacific during World War II, and now carried him to the role of supreme commander in occupied Japan. Known as a political conservative in the United States, MacArthur embarked on reforms to liberalize Japan's government and education. He encouraged women's rights, trade unions, and other democratic changes.

Quite early in the occupation, on September 22, 1945, the Civil Information and Education Section was established as a Special Staff Section of the General U.S. Military Headquarters. With the general mission to advise General MacArthur "on policies relating to public information, education, religion, and other sociological problems of Japan," the section was to

> make recommendations to effect the accomplishment of the information and educational objectives of the Allied Powers . . . to maintain liaison with the Japanese Ministry of Education, (and) Educational Institutions . . . to direct the initiation and production of such plans, materials and programs as are required to implement the information and education objectives of the Supreme Commander . . . to make recommendations to ensure the elimination of militarism and ultranationalism, in doctrine and practice, including military training, from all elements of the Japanese educational system, (and to ensure) the inclusion of such new courses of instruction in school curricula as are necessary to accomplish the mission of proper dissemination of democratic ideals and principles.[25]

U.S. military authorities ordered the Japanese Ministry of Education to:

1. suspend courses in morals (*shushin*), Japanese history and geography until a substitute program had been prepared and approved in these areas;
2. abolish government sponsorship of the state religion, *Shinto*, and forbid dissemination of *Shinto* doctrines in state-supported institutions;
3. eliminate *budo* (traditional martial arts) and military drill and training from physical education programs;
4. screen, investigate and remove ultranationalistic educational personnel from schools and other institutions.

As in Germany, school administrators, teachers, and educational personnel who had been ultra militaristic or nationalistic were purged. All military personnel were removed from educational institutions. Teachers, who had been dismissed because of political dissent by the Japanese government, were to be reinstated. Unwittingly, the U.S. military reinstated many Socialists and Communists who had been dismissed by the Japanese government before and during the war. The U.S. military also encouraged the formation of trade unions. The reinstated educators would give the Japanese Teachers Union a definite leftist political orientation in postwar Japan. To expedite the reorientation of Japanese teachers, a new teachers' manual and in-service program were developed to encourage teaching about democracy.

The U.S. Education Mission to Japan

In 1946, a group of leading American educators were called to Japan to examine the system and make recommendations for its reform. The mission, chaired by Dr. George D. Stoddard, then New York State commissioner of education and president-elect of the University of Illinois, included three college presidents, two university deans, three prominent members of educational organizations such as the National Education Association (NEA) and American Federation of Teachers (AFT), seven professors, two state superintendents in addition to Stoddard, and a member of the U.S. Office of Education who was also a school administrator.[26] Among the professors were two distinguished professors of education from Columbia University's Teachers College, George S. Counts and Isaac L. Kandel. Counts, a long-time progressive and former president of the AFT, was an expert on Soviet education. Kandel, the more conservative essentialist educator and a noted comparative scholar, had written definitive works on the impact of nationalism on education.

The report of the U.S. Educational Mission provides a thoroughly documented record of the intended educational reforms in Japan.[27] The report represents an interesting episode in educational history in which a victor, the United States, sought to tutor a conquered nation in the theory and practices of democratic education.

In briefing the mission about the situation in Japan prior to its departure from the United States, John Carter Vincent, a career State Department official, identified two major U.S. policy objectives—"one of them is that we shall insure ourselves that Japan cannot become a menace to peace, and (2) that we shall encourage the establishment of a government in Japan that is peacefully inclined and responsible."[28]

The U.S. mission was to meet periodically with a complementary working committee of Japanese educators. The complementary Japanese team included both Ministry of Education officials as well as those outside of official circles. Sensitive to the Japanese fear of "losing face," Vincent advised the American educators that it would be diplomatically prudent to persuade Japanese educators to accept the mission's recommendations without feeling forced to yield to their imposition.

Beginning its work by examining the aims and content of Japanese education, mission members, finding it based on outmoded nineteenth-century patterns, concluded it to be too highly centralized. Even if there had been no war and no defeat, the Japanese system needed American-style educational reforms.

The mission recommended the following general reforms: the new Japanese educational system should (1) replace imperialist militarism with democracy and conformist obeisance to centralized authority with individualism and local self-government; (2) end the overemphasis on passing examinations; (3) facilitate cooperative preparation of textbooks by educators rather than by Ministry of Education dictates; (4) replace the old history and geography that indoctrinated students in militarism with social studies that emphasize a sense of community; (5) remove military drills from courses in health and physical education.[29]

Basing their organizational and administrative recommendations on American local control antecedents, the mission urged decentralization of the highly centralized Japanese national system. Many prerogatives exercised by the centralized Ministry of Education, the *Mombusho*, were to be transferred to prefectural and local districts with elected boards. Like the U.S. system, the local board was to appoint a professional educator, a superintendent, to implement board policies. Further reflecting the American educational experience, the mission recommended establishing a foundation formula to fund schools from public revenues. As in U.S. school districts, teacher salary schedules were to be established by Japanese districts.

In terms of school structure and organization, the mission, again following American precedents, recommended a 6–6–4 pattern, consisting of six years of primary school, six years of secondary school, and four years of college. There would be a free and compulsory six-year primary school for ages six through twelve. Secondary schooling would be divided into two levels: a three-year lower secondary school for ages thirteen through fifteen that, as a transition stage, featured exploratory learning activities; and an upper secondary school of three years, for ages sixteen through eighteen, that offered academic college preparatory and vocational tracks.[30] Postsecondary education was to consist of four year colleges and universities. The Japanese government accepted the Americans' recommendations on school organization. The 6–6–4 educational system, based on the American model, was established and continues to be the organizational structure of Japanese schools. While local district control was implemented, it was discarded when the U.S. military occupation ended and the Japanese returned to their highly centralized national system of education, tightly controlled by the Ministry of Education.

The mission sought to disengage the group conformity that characterized Japanese education. In place of memorization and rote learning, it urged Japanese teachers to encourage curiosity, imagination, and problem-solving skills. Contrary to the Japanese adage that the "nail that stands up should be hammered down," the mission's educators advised Japanese teachers to respect individual differences. Students should be encouraged to ask questions, express their opinions, and engage in discussion.

The mission even went so far as to recommend a drastic reform in the Japanese language, which it found was a formidable obstacle to learning. It stated that the memorization of *kanji*, Japanese script, placed a time-consuming burden on students. It recommended that *kanji* be replaced with *romanji*, a phonetic roman alphabet.[31] Although General MacArthur thanked the mission for its suggestion in this area, the U.S. military government had no intention of implementing such a drastic recommendation.

In historical retrospect, the U.S. mission to Japan reveals two parallel trends: an American belief that the U.S. experience could be replicated elsewhere in the world and that the Japanese could adapt to the changes. Though consisting of experienced and often well-traveled educators, the mission's members tended to pay insufficient attention to the differences between the American and Japanese cultural contexts. The mission assumed that it was possible to transfer decentralization, local control, and other American educational structures and methods to Japan.

The Japanese, for their part, were ready to take advice from the American educators. Selective educational borrowing from other nations was not new to them. They had borrowed from other nations during the Meiji restoration during the 1870s. The organizational structure recommended by the Americans was easily transplanted to the Japanese educational environment. However, after the end of the occupation, the core values of the system would remain unmistakenly Japanese.

Conclusion

One of the profound readjustments in social and educational perspective that came in the early postwar years was an attitude that sustained the idea that growth was possible, indeed, was probable. Before the war in the midst of the Great Depression, there was the view that the United States had reached its limits of economic growth. Within these limits, America's social and educational possibilities would also be limited and perhaps even restricted by a poverty that would be a permanent condition for many. Though there were fears of a reversion to the economic limitations of the depression, the prosperity induced by the war effort continued onward from the late 1940s into the ensuing decades. The postwar prosperity, especially that of the 1950s and 1960s, gave a reaffirmation to capitalism, albeit a regulated capitalism with ample social services and welfare provisions.

With the reinvigorization of capitalism, there was also a sense that the United States, the world's most powerful country, had a mission. This reassertion of American exceptionalism did not rekindle the old isolation that had followed World War I. This time the victory had been won against the truly diabolical force of Hitler's Nazism rather than the archaic Kaiser's Prussian generals. The new affluent America could also be the democratic America. Victory in World War II showed the power of the good intentions of a good people. There was the assumption that the United States and the American people had something worth sharing with others in the world.

The GI Bill, in particular, signaled that U.S. education would be on an expansive course, particularly in higher education. However, elementary and secondary schools continued to face pressing problems as the 1940s came to a close. Chapter 2 examines the difficulties surrounding recommendations of federal aid.

Notes

[1] American reactions to World War II are examined in Michael C. C. Adams, *The Best War Ever: America and World War II* (Baltimore: Johns Hopkins University Press, 1993).

[2] Diane Ravitch, *The Troubled Crusade* (New York: Basic Books, 1983), pp. 3–5.

[3] Ibid., pp. 6–7.

[4] Ibid., p. 9.

[5] Gunnar Myrdal, *An American Dilemma: The Negro Problem and Modern Democracy* (New York: Harper and Bros., 1944).

[6] For commentaries on the Truman administration, see Michael J. Lacey, ed., *The Truman Presidency* (New York: Cambridge University Press, 1991).

[7] Ravitch, pp. 20–24.

[8] Ibid., p. 25.

[9] Keith Olson, *The GI Bill, the Veterans, and the College* (Lexington: University Press of Kentucky, 1974), pp. 4–10.

[10] Ibid., pp. 10–17.

[11] Thomas Bonner, "The Unintended Revolution in America's Colleges Since 1940," *Change* 28 (September–October 1986), p. 45.

[12] Ravitch, pp. 12–13.

[13] Olson, pp. 37–39.

[14] Jessie Overall, *Higher Education and the Servicemen's Readjustment Act of 1944* (Los Angeles: University of California Press, 1976), pp. 15–17.

[15] Ravitch, pp. 13–14.

[16] Harold Hyman, *American Singularity* (Athens: University of Georgia Press, 1987), p. 67; and Carman Johnson, "GI Educational and Job Training Benefits," *Occupational Outlook Quarterly* 15 (Spring 1971), p. 21.

[17] Donald Johnson, "A Quarter-Century of the Bill," *School and Society* 1048 (April 1970), pp. 226–28.

[18] Ravitch, p. 13.

[19] Julian Stanley, "Interaction of Intellectual Vacuum with GI Bill," *Theory Practice*, 8 (December 1969), p. 319.

[20] D. Johnson, p. 228.

[21] Overall, p. 27.

22 Sar Levitan and Joyce Zwicker, *Swords into Plowshares: Our GI Bill* (Salt Lake City: Olympus Publishing Co., 1973), p. 10 and William Steif, "GI Bill to Attract Vietvets," *College University Business*, 14 (September 1969), p. 63.

23 Ravitch, pp. 14–16.

24 For the U.S. policy in occupied Germany, see Jeffrey M. Diefendorf, Alex Frohn, and Hermann–Josef Rupiper, eds. *American Policy and the Reconstruction of West Germany, 1945–1955* (New York: Cambridge University Press, 1993).

25 "Part II: Allied Control of Japanese Education," undated. p. 1, in Collections of the Hoover Institution on War, Revolution, and Peace, Stanford, CA.

26 Department of State, Press Release (February 18, 1946) in Collections of the Hoover Institution on War, Revolution and Peace, Stanford, CA.

27 *Report of the United States Education Mission to Japan* (Washington, DC: U.S. Government Printing Office, 1946).

28 "Conference of Advisory Group on Education to Japan," February 18, 1946, p. 1, Collections of the Hoover Institution on War, Revolution and Peace, Stanford, CA.

29 *Report of the United States Education Mission in Japan*, pp. 7–19.

30 Ibid., pp. 24–31.

31 Ibid., pp. 20–23.

Further Reading

Adams, Michael C. C. *The Best War Ever: America and World War II*. Baltimore: Johns Hopkins University Press, 1993.

Diefendorf, Jeffrey M., Alex Frohn, and Hermann-Josef Rupiper, eds. *American Policy and the Reconstruction of West Germany, 1945–1955*. New York: Cambridge University Press, 1993.

Hogan, Michael J., ed. *Hiroshima in History and Memory*. New York: Cambridge University Press, 1996.

Hyman, Harold. *American Singularity*. Athens: University of Georgia Press, 1987.

Lacy, Michael J., ed. *The Truman Presidency*. New York: Cambridge University Press, 1991.

Levitan, Sar, and Joyce Zickler. *Swords into Plowshares: Our GI Bill*. Salt Lake City: Olympus Publishing Co., 1973.

Myrdal, Gunnar. *An American Dilemma: The Negro Problem and Modern Democracy*. New York: Harper & Bros., 1944.

Olson, Keith. *The GI Bill: The Veterans and the College*. Lexington: University Press of Kentucky, 1974.

Overall, Jessie. *Higher Education and the Servicemen's Readjustment Act of 1944*. Los Angeles: University of California Press, 1976.

Ravitch, Diane. *The Troubled Crusade: American Education 1945–1980*. New York: Basic Books, 1983.

2

Controversies over Federal Aid to Education, 1945–1955

*L*ike the general society, the signs were clear that American elementary and secondary schooling needed fundamental readjustment after World War II. Restrictions on labor and material during the war had limited school construction and renovation of existing facilities. While the most pressing needs were quantitative—new buildings, more classroom space, and more teachers, there were also qualitative needs—updating the curriculum to reflect the war-generated advances in science and technology. The condition of elementary and secondary education showed: (1) serious shortages of classrooms for a growing school-age cohort; (2) existing facilities in need of renovation; (3) an undersupply of trained teachers; (4) too many academically under-qualified teachers; (5) gross inequities in educational quality between urban and rural, Northern and Southern, and white and black schools; and (6) a need to update curriculum to incorporate political, social, economic, and especially scientific and technological change. While most people agreed that U.S. schools needed improvement, profound disagreements developed in the late 1940s and early 1950s on how these improvements were to be initiated, directed, and financed. This chapter examines the controversy surrounding federal aid to education. While the inability to agree on federal aid to education is a complex and fascinating story in itself, the general context of the debate reveals much about the United States at mid-twentieth century.

The Context of the Federal Aid Controversy

The conflicts over federal aid to elementary and secondary education occurred in a context shaped by history, race, politics, and religion. Since the U.S. Constitution did not address education as a federal power, the Tenth Amendment reserved it as a power of each state. Historically and constitutionally, each of the states had the paramount authority and responsibility for education.

Historical Precedents of Local Control

The dominant historical pattern for establishing common or public schools was based on precedents developed in mid-nineteenth century New England, with Horace Mann's Massachusetts model. In Massachusetts and other New England states, local districts, sanctioned by the state and with their own elected boards of education, had established and financed public schools. Despite some exceptions, especially in the South, most of the states emulated the New England pattern of establishing common schools. The state, as the government authority responsible for education, would delegate important functions to local districts and their boards of education. Significantly, local districts, through property taxation, generated most of the funding for schools. The states gradually began to provide some equalization between wealthy and poor districts through foundation grants, which gave financial aid to school districts. Historically, the predominant amount of school revenues came from local funding. While there were persistent criticisms of inequities in funding schools, efforts to change the basic pattern of school funding were generally sporadic and ineffectual.

Federal Aid: Limited Precedents

While there was periodic support for some kind of federal assistance to education, these efforts were limited. The Northwest Ordinances of 1785 and 1787, enacted under the Articles of Confederation, marked the earliest national government support for education. The ordinances reserved the sixteenth section, 640 acres, in each township in the Northwest Territory for educational purposes.[1] The Morrill Act, in 1862, setting an early precedent for federal assistance to higher education, provided federal land grants to establish agricultural and mechanical colleges and universities. Several failed attempts in the post-Reconstruction period—the Hoar Bill in 1870, the Pierce Bill in 1872, the Burnside Bill in 1879, and the Blair Bills in 1884, 1886, and 1888—sought to tie federal aid to the protection of African-American education in the South. A notable success in the history of federal aid to education was the Smith-Hughes Act, in 1917, that provided federal aid for vocational education. The Smith-Towner Bill, in 1919, which would have provided for assistance for teachers' salaries, failed to secure passage.[2] While there was no general aid to education during the depression of the 1930s, some school construction projects were assisted by funds from the Public Works Administration and some teachers' salaries were paid from Federal Emergency Relief Funds.[3]

In 1941, Congress enacted the Lanham Act, which provided federal aid for school construction and operating expenses in federally impacted areas, such as those located near military bases and installations where children went to public schools but whose families paid no property taxes. Then, in 1944, Congress passed the Servicemen's Readjustment Act, the GI Bill, which provided education and training for returning veterans of World War II (as mentioned in chapter 1). When federal aid was passed, generally it was designated for a specific category rather than for general assistance to elementary and secondary education. With the exceptions noted above, the federal government's role and its assistance to education were quite limited in comparison to other modern countries. The result was that educators in the immediate post–World War II era found their options for school rebuilding and renewal hampered by antiquated and often inadequate funding patterns.

These historical precedents of limited federal assistance to public schools rested on the long-standing foundation of local control. Proponents of federal aid to education could cite these precedents as well as the "general welfare" clause in the Constitution's preamble to build their case. Opponents, however, claimed that instances of federal aid were designed to meet unique, often emergency situations, rather than to lay the foundations for a more extensive federal role.

The pattern of public school governance and funding that developed in the nineteenth century was that of a partnership between the states and the local districts. The state-local district partnership, often crossing political party lines, had complex and often mixed political origins in Jacksonian democracy, Whig internal improvements, and Populism. The Jacksonian Democrats supported public schools but preferred them to be controlled locally with the states having only a limited role. Whigs, such as Horace Mann, saw public schools as a kind of internal improvement that would contribute to economic growth. The Whig orientation, which gave the states a larger role in encouraging and requiring the establishment of public schools, became the dominant model of public school governance and support. The Populists, an important third party in many Western states, saw the local school district and board as a kind of direct democracy. Though based on differing political orientations, local control became enshrined in the public school ideology. Defenders of local control insisted that public schools, as the "schools of the children of all the people," were best governed by the directly elected representatives of the people, friends and neighbors serving on local district school boards. For many supporters of public schools, the dictum of local control became an article of faith in an almost religious-like creed. Defenders of local control—school board members, parent groups, and some school administrators and teachers—were vigilant against any maneuver that imperiled this Populist prerogative and that gave federal bureaucrats in Washington, D.C., any control over local schools. In post–World War II America, it became part of the conservative ideological platform, particularly among Midwestern and Western Republicans. It also gained serious support from states' rights conservative Democrats in the South, determined to hold racial segregation's color line.

Racially Segregated Schools

Of the regions of the country, schools in the Southern states had the most severe quantitative and qualitative problems. In per pupil expenditures for public schooling, Southern states ranked at the bottom of the then forty-eight states. Compared to the North, schools in the South registered deficits in facilities, expenditures, and the number of qualified teachers with college degrees. Though schools throughout the region had problems, the most desperate situation was for those attended by African-American children. Throughout the Southern and border states, the system of *de jure* racial segregation, upheld in the *Plessy v. Ferguson* decision (discussed in chapter 6), was firmly in place. The political power structure in the South, then a one-party region, was firmly held by white Southern Democrats. Although the Democratic Party's Northern liberal wing supported civil rights, powerful Southern Democrats in Congress, buttressed by the seniority system that gave them control of key committees, were determined to block any initiatives weakening racial segregation. Again, the historically based pattern of race relations in the South complicated any federal funding of schools. Southern Democrats, often repeatedly reelected in the one-party region, successfully blocked legislation that might jeopardize racial segregation. While many Southern politicians wanted federal aid to rescue their schools, they favored it only on the condition that it did not alter the racially segregated status quo.

While Southern white politicians were a powerful force in blocking federal aid that threatened racial segregation, African Americans, civil rights organizations, and the liberal wing of the Democratic Party supported federal aid initiatives that would weaken, if not end, racial segregation in public schools. However, the history of U.S. politics and race relations had a significant impact on the proponents of federal aid. During the period from 1945 to 1950, African-American spokespeople for federal aid and desegregation were mainly from Northern big cities. Black voters in the South had been largely disenfranchised by the "Jim Crow" legislation of the 1890–1910 period that used the poll tax, special tests in which blacks had to explain the Constitution, or the "white primary," as well as physical and economic intimidation to keep African Americans from voting. Because of this disenfranchisement, the African-American political base in the South was weak and disorganized. National organizations such as the National Association for the Advancement of Colored People (NAACP) and the Urban League had long been engaged in the struggle against racial segregation, but their efforts would not reach a legal climax until the *Brown* case in 1954. The African-American leadership, although generally supporting federal aid, did not want this assistance to be used to reinforce the racially segregated dual school system.

Aid to Parochial Schools

Still another factor in the complex context surrounding federal aid to education in the late 1940s and early 1950s was historic tensions between proponents of public and private, primarily Roman Catholic, schools. Earlier in describing the context of the federal aid issue, reference was made to the historic precedents of local control. Equally powerful and highly emotional were the role of religion in public schools and government's role with regard to private schools. Even before Jefferson's failed attempt to create a secular state school system in Virginia, religion's role in the schools had been controversial. Horace Mann's compromise of the 1840s that common schools could teach a "common Christianity," agreeable to all denominations, never really was accepted by Roman Catholics. In the public schools of the 1840s, 1850s, and 1860s, "common Christianity" often meant teaching the commonalities of Protestantism. The "common Christianity" compromise was unacceptable to Roman Catholics who began to form a large minority group, especially with increased immigration from Ireland and Germany in the 1840s. Further, the Roman Catholic hierarchy, the bishops, steadfastly resisting public schooling as a form of Protestant schooling, were determined to create their own parochial parish schools.

In addition to Protestant-Catholic tensions over aid to private and church-related schools was the creation of a "wall of separation" between church and state in which the courts, particularly the U.S. Supreme Court, generally had ruled that state assistance to religious schools was unconstitutional. In the postwar period, Catholics tended to support federal aid when it included parochial schools and opposed it when they were excluded.

A class in a Roman Catholic parochial school, typical of the 1940s. Federal aid to private schools was a deeply controversial issue in the late 1940s. (Reproduction from the National Archives, #208-L6-41P-7.)

Adding to the complexity of the context surrounding federal aid to education was the key role played by the public school lobby, organizations having public education as their special interest. These organizations had long been active in promoting or blocking legislation that affected their interests both nationally and at the state level. Among them was the large and powerful National Education Association (NEA), the Organization of Parents and Teachers (OPT), the American Federation of Teachers (AFT), and the National Organization of School Boards, for example. These large and powerful organizations, with a grassroots base of professional educators and laypeople throughout the country, subscribed to the public school ideology. They believed that aid to education should be exclusively for public and not private or church-related schools. Further, federal aid should complement their efforts and not interfere with their specially defined roles in the public schools. Equally determined to have their say on pending federal aid legislation were smaller yet influential organizations that lobbied for vocational education, agricultural education, home economics education, libraries, and so on. While these groups supported federal aid, they wanted to preserve the special categories of aid that benefitted their interests.

The post–World War II context surrounding the schools' need for federal aid was a fearful political jungle of conflicting groups through which any prudent politician would have to tread lightly. A virtual political "mine field," it could ruin a political career if not traversed with utmost vigilance. Even the highly politically adroit Franklin D. Roosevelt had avoided the dangers of entering the federal aid to education field. In the postwar era, it fell to Harry S. Truman and his administration to negotiate the politically dangerous context through which a successful aid to education bill had to pass.

Strategic Considerations

Although the context related to federal aid to education was exceedingly complex and politically perilous, aid proposals surfaced in the late 1940s. There was a general consensus that the public schools were in crisis with teacher shortages, crowded and inadequate facilities, and funding inequalities between rich and poor states and rich and poor districts in a given state.

President Truman, well aware of the controversies surrounding federal aid to education, did not take a strong advocacy position in the first two years of his presidency, 1944–1946. Concerned with postwar readjustment, he sought to reaffirm a general commitment to his predecessor's New Deal programs. By 1948, Truman, more confident as president and advancing his own "Fair Deal," was moving to a more determined stand for federal aid. While opposing centralization of education in the federal government, he was now supporting federal assistance that would aid in equalizing educational opportunity, assist in school construction, and improve teachers' salaries. In his economic message, Truman urged Congress, controlled by Republicans, to enact a program to assist elementary, secondary, and higher education. Although President Truman supported federal aid, an administration bill was not introduced in Congress. The prospects for federal aid were highly uncertain in the Republican-controlled Eightieth Congress. The Democrats were divided into a more conservative segregationist Southern wing and a liberal Northern wing. The Republicans also had a more moderate division between Midwestern and Western conservatives and a moderately liberal Eastern wing. A successful federal aid bill would require considerable maneuvering across party lines. An

unexpected development occurred when Senator Robert A. Taft, a conservative and the Senate's Republican majority leader, came out in
support of federal aid. With President Truman, a Democrat, and Senator Taft, the leading Republican conservative, in favor, the prospects
for some kind of federal aid to education looked promising. However,
serious policy questions remained unanswered:

1. How would federal aid relate to local control and state
   authority?

2. Should racially segregated schools receive federal funding? Or
   should federal aid be used to change patterns of school segregation?

3. Should private and parochial schools, primarily Roman Catholic schools, be included in funding?[4]

Shifting Coalitions

In order for a federal aid to education bill to pass Congress, it
would have to command the support of a majority of members who
were keenly sensitive to the issues involved. The issues, in turn, were
being defined by large national groups with influential lobbies in Washington. These groups could be identified as the proponents of federal
aid, the opponents, and crucial swing groups. Firmly on the side of federal aid to public schools were the organizations that comprised the
highly influential public school lobby: the NEA and the National Congress of Parents and Teachers. While these groups favored federal aid,
they had strong reservations against including private schools. Other
groups that gave strong support to federal aid were the American Federation of Labor (AFL), the Congress of Industrial Organization (CIO)
and other trade and labor unions. The labor organizations tended to
support general federal aid and did not get entangled in the church-
state issues.

Strong opposition came largely from conservatives, especially in
the Republican Party, who traditionally opposed federal interference in
what they regarded as a local and state area of responsibility. Some
taxpayer associations and business groups such as the U.S. Chamber
of Commerce and the Investment Bankers Association opposed it for
fear of higher taxes.

Very important in the federal aid equation were "swing groups,"
whose support or opposition was conditional. White Southern Democrats, many from states with depressed schools, favored federal aid on
the condition that it not jeopardize the existing system of racially segregated schools. Some Southern Democratic senators and congressmen, recognizing the educational needs of their region, were willing to
support federal aid that equalized the condition of white and black

schools but left racial segregation intact. This kind of aid, they reasoned, would give support to the "separate but equal" doctrine, which was coming under greater attack.[5]

Many Roman Catholics, led by the bishops, favored general federal aid to elementary and secondary schools on the condition that parochial schools were included. Roman Catholic parochial schools were the largest nonpublic school system in the country, enrolling 13.2 percent of all elementary students. The Catholic hierarchy's position was generally stated by the National Catholic Welfare Conference (NCWC).[6] Claiming that both public and private schools were vital to the nation's welfare, the NCWC claimed that Catholics were bearing the brunt of "double taxation"—paying for their own schools while being taxed for public schools. It strongly opposed aid that excluded private and parochial schools, claiming it was discriminatory and unjust. In a rationale anticipating the call for vouchers for nonpublic schools, which would come in the 1980s, John McDonough argued that "the one-sided protectionism granted public schools through permitting state institutions a total monopoly . . . has resulted in a situation where our children are effectively compelled to attend these institutions. . ."[7] Catholics, contending that they were paying twice to educate their children, argued: (1) schools that fulfilled compulsory education laws and prepared students as citizens deserved government recognition; (2) when government enters education, it should serve all citizens equally and equitably; (3) equity could be achieved by sharing the tax funds.[8]

In addition to the "double taxation" argument, Catholics and other proponents of private schools were also beginning to base their arguments for federal and state aid on the "child benefit theory" that such assistance benefitted children rather than religious institutions. Child benefit aid would cover such expenses as nonreligious textbooks, health services, and transportation costs. The NCWC made the case that these benefits to children did not violate the Constitution's separation of church and state in that they did not directly support religious institutions. However, opponents countered that such assistance was an indirect form of subsidizing an establishment of religion in violation of the Constitution.

The Taft Legislation

Ohio Senator Robert Taft, the Senate's Republican majority leader and a staunch conservative, emerged as an unexpected champion of federal aid. Although he opposed federal assistance to education during much of his political career, Taft made a dramatic shift in 1948 when he sponsored aid legislation. Explaining his change from opponent to sponsor, he stated:

Four years ago, I opposed the bill on this subject; but in the course of that debate it became apparent that many children in the United States were left without education . . . that it was not the fault, necessarily, of the states where they lived . . . I could see no way of meeting the condition which now exists . . . without some federal assistance . . . I think the obligation of the federal government is . . . where . . . necessary to back up the states.[9]

Taft cosponsored the Taft-Thomas Bill for Federal Aid to Education. If enacted, the bill would have provided $300 million annually in federal assistance. Avoiding entanglement in the highly complex and cumbersome state funding programs, Taft's bill simply gave each public school pupil in each state a flat federal grant of five dollars. It avoided conflicts between rich and poor states over formulas and also preserved the state's educational rights since the funds would go to each state for distribution to public school districts. In an effort to defuse the potentially volatile religious issue, each state had the option to determine if federal funds would be distributed to nonpublic schools. To avoid the racial segregation issue, the bill provided an equitable distribution of funds between black and white schools, but the federal government was not to intervene in segregated school arrangements.[10] The Taft bill passed in the Senate but was held up indefinitely in the House Committee on Education and Labor.

Supreme Court Cases

In addition to the political intricacies of passing federal aid in the Congress, a body of judicial precedents had been building up on the issue of federal aid to nonpublic schools. These precedents provided an important background for the debates over federal aid.

The *Everson* Case

As federal aid was being debated in Congress, the U.S. Supreme Court made a highly important decision in *Everson v. the Board of Education of Ewing Township* in 1947.[11] The case dealt with the reimbursement of school bus transportation costs for children attending nonpublic schools. The town of Ewing, New Jersey, reimbursed parents for school bus transportation, regardless of whether the children attended a public or a nonpublic school. Everson, a taxpayer, challenged the policy, claiming it was unconstitutional to use public funds for church-related schools. In a close, five-to-four decision, the Court upheld the constitutionality of the town's transportation policy. Justice Hugo Black, giving the majority opinion, stated that the subsidy for school transportation was like any other government service such as police and fire protection. If a private school was burning, the municipal fire department was expected to fight the fire. Further, the First Amendment required the state to be neutral toward but not an adversary of religious groups. Supporters of aid to private and parochial schools were enthused by the decision, which appeared to give greater legal credence to their position.

The *Everson* decision was based on a very close vote, however. The dissenting opinion carried with it arguments that could be used to oppose aid to church-related schools. The dissent argued that the First Amendment created "a complete and permanent separation of the spheres of religious activity and civil authority by comprehensively forbidding every form of public aid or support for religion." The payment for transportation was the same as a tuition payment. The minority opinion further stated that denying the transportation payment to parochial school children was not discriminatory since they had the same right as everyone else to attend a public school.[12]

McCollum v. Board of Education

The Supreme Court's decision in *McCollum v. Board of Education*, a case regarding released time for religious instruction in public schools, generated considerable controversy.[13] The Court ruled, in 1948, that an Illinois law permitting released time for religious instruction in public schools during regular school was unconstitutional. According to the Court, the public schools could not be used "to aid any or all religious faiths or sects in the dissemination of their doctrines and ideals."[14]

Religious Controversies

The Supreme Court's decisions and the ongoing debates over federal aid to education generated deep religious tensions. While Roman Catholics were encouraged by the *Everson* decision, those opposed to aid to nonpublic schools feared that it threatened separation of church and state. In considering the intense religious conflicts surrounding federal aid, it should be noted that there were some divisions within the ranks of Catholics, Protestants, and Jews on the federal aid to education issue. The late 1940s and early 1950s, however, experienced sharp divisions among organizations that took a stand and appeared to speak for large groups. The bishops of the Catholic Church supported federal aid to education for Catholic schools. In 1948, a national organization, Protestants and Other Americans United for Separation of Church and State (POAU) was formed to oppose federal aid to parochial schools. Other Protestant organizations that opposed federal aid to nonpublic schools were the American Christian Foundation, the American Protestant Defense League, the National Association of Evangelicals, and the National Council of Churches.[15] Along with Protestants, some Jewish groups, too, opposed federal aid to parochial schools.

An interesting polemic in the debate was written by Paul Blanshard, whose book, *American Freedom and Catholic Power*, attacked the Roman Catholic church as antidemocratic and authoritarian. Blanshard claimed Catholic schools were separatist and encouraged intolerance.[16]

Spurred by the *Everson* decision, the Catholic position on federal aid was redefined as the "child benefit theory," according to which aid would be for children rather than institutions. The child benefit theory conceded that Catholic schools were constitutionally ineligible for public funds for facilities, tuition, or teachers' salaries. However, and most importantly, parochial students had equal rights for public subsidies for auxiliary services such as transportation, textbooks for secular subjects, and health services. These benefits, according to the theory, should be for all children in the land, regardless of the school they attended.[17]

Further Battles over Federal Aid

In 1948, President Truman, the Democratic incumbent, surprisingly won a four-way race between New York Governor Thomas E. Dewey, the Republican candidate, Henry Wallace, the Progressive candidate, and Strom Thurmond, the States' Rights Democrat. During the campaign, Truman warned that elementary and secondary schools, with "overworked" and "underpaid" teachers, faced "serious trouble" unless aid was provided.[18] Truman's State of the Union Address, in 1949, lamenting that "millions of our children are not receiving a good education," called for federal aid to education.[19]

The Barden Bill

The Senate in 1949 passed a federal aid bill based largely on the earlier Taft legislation. When the bill reached the House, a bitter controversy erupted in the Committee on Education and Labor that reflected the strong racial and religious divisions surrounding federal aid. On the House Committee, the aid bill was assigned to Graham A. Barden, a Southern Democratic congressman and former teacher, who supported federal aid only to public schools. Barden was determined to exclude any aid to parochial schools, which he believed violated strict separation of church and state.

Barden rejected the Senate version of federal aid and introduced his own legislation, the Barden bill. Barden's bill would have provided $300 million a year in aid but only for public schools. Rejecting the child benefit theory, Barden's bill excluded using federal funds for transportation and health services for nonpublic school students. Barden also removed the Senate bill's requirement that Southern states were to make a "just and equitable" distribution of funds to black and white schools. While winning support of white Southern Democrats, Barden's tactics enraged Northern liberals and African Americans. Barden's bill unleashed highly divisive controversy. While the NEA and the public school lobby supported the bill, the Catholic Church hierarchy attacked it. The leading Democratic congressmen, John W. McCormick, the House majority leader, and John Lesinski, the chair of the Education and Labor Committee, both of whom were Roman Catholics, attacked the bill as unfair to African Americans and Roman Catholics. New York City's ranking Roman Catholic prelate, Cardinal Francis Spellman, called Barden a "new apostle of bigotry."[20]

As hearings over the Barden bill continued, a national furor over federal aid occurred in summer 1949 between Mrs. Eleanor Roosevelt, widow of the former president, and Cardinal Spellman. Mrs. Roosevelt, in her column, "My Day," in the *New York World Telegram*, wrote, "we do not want . . . public education connected with religious control of schools, which are paid for by taxpayers' money." Cardinal Spellman, the archbishop of New York City, angrily responded on July 21, 1949, that Mrs. Roosevelt was acting from "misinformation, ignorance or prejudice" in a manner "unworthy of an American mother."[21] Despite some efforts at a public reconciliation, the widely reported, angry exchange between two respected Americans over aid to parochial schools aggravated already high tensions.

Conclusion

Truman continued to endorse federal aid for elementary and secondary education throughout the remainder of his term. Catholics, using the child benefit theory, continued to press for federal aid for students attending parochial schools. Congressman Barden became chairman of the House Committee on Education and Labor. Federal aid proposals were still locked in deep controversies over religion, race, and local control. Throughout most of the 1950s, federal aid to education was restricted to categorical aid to areas impacted by federal defense and military installations. It would take a dramatic event occurring elsewhere in the world, the Soviet launching of Sputnik, to unravel the intricate spider's web that imperiled federal aid in the past and that led to the enactment of the National Defense Education Act (NDEA) in 1958, during President Eisenhower's second term.

   With the notable exception of the NDEA, more general federal aid bills languished in Congress, falling victim to the maneuvers of conflicting groups and forces. It would not be until Lyndon Johnson's "Great Society" and "War on Poverty" programs in the mid-1960s that general federal aid legislation would be enacted.

Notes

[1] Sidney W. Tiedt, *The Role of the Federal Government in Education* (New York: Oxford University Press, 1966), p. 14.

[2] Ibid., pp 15–29.

[3] Carl F. Kaestle and Marshall S. Smith, "The Federal Role in Elementary and Secondary Education, 1940–1980," *Harvard Educational Review*, 52 (November 1982), pp. 388–89.

[4] Diane Ravitch, *The Troubled Crusade: American Education 1945–1980* (New York: Basic Books, 1983), p. 5.

[5] Ibid., p. 26.

[6] Frank J. Munger and Richard F. Fenno, *National Politics and Federal Aid to Education* (Syracuse, NY: Syracuse University Press, 1962), pp. 55–56.

[7] Daniel D. McGarry and Leo Ward, eds. *Educational Freedom and the Case for Government Aid to Students in Independent Schools* (Milwaukee, WI: Bruce Publishing Co., 1966), p. 124.

[8] Ibid., p. 186.

[9] *Federal Role in Education*, 2nd ed. (Washington, DC: Congressional Quarterly, Inc., 1967), p. 21.

[10] Ravitch, p. 28.

[11] *Everson v. the Board of Education of Ewing Township*, 330 US 1 (1947).

[12] Ravitch, p. 29.

[13] *McCollum v. Board of Education*, 333 US 203 (1948).

[14] Ravitch, p. 32.

[15] Munger and Fenno, p. 63.

[16] Paul Blanshard, *American Freedom and Catholic Power* (Boston: Beacon Press, 1949).

[17] Ravitch, p. 30.

[18] Robert J. Donovan, *Conflict and Crisis: The Presidency of Harry S. Truman, 1945–1948* (New York: W. W. Norton & Co., 1977), p. 393.

[19] Ibid., p. 123.

[20] *Federal Role in Education*, p. 124.

[21] Ravitch, pp. 36–37.

Further Reading

Bernstein, Barton J., and Allen J. Matuson. *The Truman Administration: A Documented History*. New York: Harper & Row Publishers, 1966.

Brickman, William E., and Stanley Lehrer, eds. *Religion, Government, and Education*. New York: Society for the Advancement of Education, 1961.

Chafe, William H. *The Unfinished Journey: America Since World War II.* New York: Oxford University Press, 1995.

Donovan, Robert J. *Conflict and Crisis: The Presidency of Harry S. Truman, 1945–1948.* New York: W. W. Norton & Co., 1977.

Donovan, Robert J. *Tumultuous Years: The Presidency of Harry S. Truman, 1945–1953.* New York: W. W. Norton & Co., 1982.

Lee, Gordon C. *The Struggle for Federal Aid.* New York: Bureau of Publications, Teachers College Press, 1949.

McGarry, Daniel D., and Leo Ward, eds. *Educational Freedom and the Case for Government Aid to Students in Independent Schools.* Milwaukee, WI: Bruce Publishing Co., 1966.

Munger, Frank J., and Richard F. Fenno, Jr. *National Politics and Federal Aid to Education.* New York: Syracuse University Press, 1962.

Quattlebaum, Charles A. *Federal Educational Policies, Programs and Proposals.* Washington, DC: Library of Congress, 1968.

Ravitch, Diane. *The Troubled Crusade: American Education, 1945–1980.* New York: Basic Books, 1983.

Smith, Gilbert E. *The Limits of Reform: Politics and Federal Aid to Education, 1937–1950.* New York: Garland Publishing Co., 1982.

Steel, Ronald. *Federal Aid to Education.* New York: H. W. Wilson Co., 1961.

Tiedt, Sidney W. *The Role of the Federal Government in Education.* New York: Oxford University Press, 1966.

3

The 1950s: Postwar Changes

The 1950s have often-conflicting historical characterizations. They have been labeled as the decade of: "quiet conformism," the heightened cold war, the atomic age and the bomb shelter, suburbia, McCarthyism, interstate highways, and an affluent America. If they were these things, they were also marked by the legal end of racial segregation, scientific and technological advances, the polio vaccine, the advent of television, and the development of the computer.

The 1950s was a decade of economic prosperity and rising expectations, population growth, and significant demographic changes. Beneath the quiet surface of what seemed to be a conformist America came several important tendencies that would change American life: the growth of suburbia, the full realization of the nuclear age, the development of an interstate highway system that linked the nation, and the advent of television as a major source of entertainment and information. Three of these forces—television, interstates, and suburbia—while at first glance disconnected, heralded highly significant socioeducational changes.

While pockets of poverty, largely ignored by politicians and policymakers, existed in inner cities and neglected rural areas, the country enjoyed good times economically. Fears of the depression's return, so evident immediately after the war, dissipated as the post–World War II boom, which began in the late 1940s, continued into the 1950s. The GNP, $285 billion in 1950, climbed to $501 billion when the decade ended. Unthreatened by foreign competition and industrial change, manufacturing generated an income of $76 billion in 1950, which would reach $126 billion in 1960. The service sector, which would continue to grow throughout the twentieth century's second half, standing at $22 billion in 1950, more than doubled to reach $44.5 billion in 1960. Employment rates stayed high, with unemployment at a low 4 percent. Further, real earnings were protected by a low rate of inflation of less than 2 percent annually.[1]

While not as dramatic as those in the 1960s, there were changes in popular and youth cultures that had an impact on education. Television had entered homes throughout the country. In 1950, 3,900,000 households had a television set; in the 1960s, the number had skyrocketed to 46,000,000.[2] TV news coverage of fast-breaking events, such as the Kefauver crime hearings, the McCarthy hearings, and General MacArthur's "Old Soldiers Never Die" speech, were a dramatic replacement for the newspaper "extra." It also created a framework of popular culture and values, which in the 1950s seemed to reinforce the "Dick and Jane" perspective on how Americans should live. The 1950s brought with them Elvis Presley, "rock and roll," and the "Beat Generation." It also brought the concept of maladjusted youth, juvenile delinquents.

Along with rising economic expectations, the 1950s were marked by a steadily rising birthrate. With the generation of the "baby boomers," the U.S. population grew from 152 million in 1950 to 181 million in 1960. In the early 1960s, 35 percent of the country's population was under age eighteen.[3] Significant demographic shifts began the process of the resettlement of Americans, creating new and leaving old population centers. The traditional big-city population centers in the industrial East and Middle West reached their population peak and began to decline. The inner cities of the large urban centers accelerated in their racial and ethnic change as African Americans, many migrating from the South, and Hispanics located in them. White ethnics began their move to the cities' fringes and to the new suburban communities that ringed them. The growth of suburbia was made possible not only by the new economic affluence and the climate of rising expectations but also by changes in home building and ownership—the mass construction of relatively inexpensive tract homes.

Another important development during the 1950s was the creation of an interstate federally subsidized highway system of transcontinental proportions. The new highway system, linking cities across the country, reduced geographical isolation and made for a highly mobile society. The movement to the Sunbelt states of the South and West began in earnest. These movements in the nation's population held momentous implications for education. Further, the Eisenhower administration's large federal subsidies for interstate highway construction facilitated the growth of the suburban community. The material changes resulted in largely unanticipated psychic changes in American life—the daily commute from home in the sub-

urbs to a job in the large city, the American love affair with the automobile, and eventually the rush hour traffic jam.

Suburbia

Although suburbs had existed before their burgeoning growth in
the 1950s, the general U.S. demographic pattern could have been
described as big city, small town, and rural. There were the very large
cities, New York, Chicago, and Philadelphia, for example, which incorporated business centers, industries, and residential neighborhoods.
These large Northern cities in the late nineteenth and early twentieth
centuries generally had been the places where immigrants first located
and many neighborhoods represented concentrations of particular
ethnicities. The basic educational organization pattern in the large cities was the large urban school district that encompassed the public
elementary and secondary schools under the jurisdiction of a single
board and superintendent of schools. When World War II ended, these
large urban schools were often judged to be the strongest sectors of
American public education, particularly in terms of facilities, richness
of curricular offerings, and size of administrative-teaching professional
staffs. However, this would begin to change in the early 1950s. The
changing demographics in the large city core areas and the movement
of industry from them saw a declining urban tax base and declining
schools. The inner-city needs, which would not be addressed until the
1960s, saw a new school population with different educational needs.

The small towns and rural areas of the nation represented the
other inherited nineteenth-century demographic pattern in the United
States. Some of these rural areas still had single school, one-room, districts, but these were rapidly disappearing. Rural schools were being
consolidated into larger, supposedly more efficient, modern districts.

During the 1950s, the basic demographic patterns in the United
States experienced a major shift. There was a large-scale migration of
white middle-class families from the large cities to the suburbs that
ringed these cities. The result was the creation of what could be called
metropolitan areas, which consisted of large cities, such as New York,
Chicago, Philadelphia, Los Angeles, and so forth, and their suburbs.
While some older suburbs had existed since the late nineteenth and
early twentieth centuries, hundreds of new suburbs were established
throughout the country. Each of these suburbs had its own local
municipal government and its own elementary and secondary school
districts. The new demographic and housing pattern was large cities,
surrounded by concentric rings of suburban communities, extending
out for miles from the central big city core. The emergence of these
suburbs in the 1950s marked a new and permanent feature on the

American socioeconomic and educational landscape.

The new suburbs were the most rapidly growing, most dynamic demographic and residential pattern in the country. Often they were called "bedroom communities" because wage earners who commuted and worked in the large city retreated to them at night in what became the daily commute of the workweek. In the 1950s, most of this work-force consisted of males; women had left their wartime jobs to become homemakers. Though some suburbs were settled by members of the upper-socioeconomic class and some by particular ethnic groups, the new trend was a large middle-class exodus from city apartments to the single family home that the suburbs promised. Suburbia was becoming a white ethnic middle-class "melting pot." As new housing developments with similar and rather standardized houses sprung up in suburbia, so did the need for new schools and more teachers. The suburbs, settled by young and growing families, produced large school-age cohorts. The elementary-age school cohort, ages five to eleven, increased from 24,300,000 in 1950 to 35,500,000 in 1960.

The response was to usher in what has been called the "brick and mortar" period of school construction in American educational history. Successful school administrators were those who presided over large building programs, creating the classroom space needed to educate suburban children. The Eisenhower administration, following the traditional Republican ideology of local control, was reluctant to enter the aid-to-education area except for supporting federal aid for school construction.

The Eisenhower Administration

President Truman was succeeded by Dwight David Eisenhower, the Republican nominee, who defeated Adlai Stevenson, the Democratic candidate in the election of 1952. Eisenhower, a popular war hero, had a distinguished career as allied supreme commander in Western Europe in World War II, president of Columbia University, and commander of NATO.[4] Eisenhower defeated Stevenson again in 1956, thus serving as president of the United States, from 1953 to 1961. The opposing candidates in the two presidential contests of the 1950s, in many ways, revealed the continuities and tensions of what was called by some historians, the quiet decade.

Stevenson, the articulate, urbane, intellectual governor of Illinois, was a liberal, but a moderate one, likely to carry on Roosevelt's New Deal and Truman's Fair Deal policies. A moderate, middle-of-the-road Republican, Eisenhower did not attempt to reverse the major trends set in motion by the New Deal. As the cold war escalated and hardened into a bipolar world standoff between the United States and the USSR, the cautious but firm Eisenhower was a commanding, reassuring father-figure to a nation living with the threat of nuclear war.

Eisenhower, who saw himself as a moderate Republican, made no significant revisions in the inherited New Deal laws. He presided, like a chairman of the board or a chief executive officer of a corporation, over a nation experiencing thorough-going modernization.[5] The Eisenhower years, from 1953 to 1961, were generally economically prosperous and affluent, especially for the growing middle class.

In foreign policy, Eisenhower continued and developed the policy to contain the Soviet Union which was inaugurated by his predecessor, Truman. Eisenhower, who had a broad military and foreign affairs experience based on his role as supreme commander in Europe during World War II, pursued a delicately poised foreign policy. His military and diplomatic policy rested on two major premises: (1) avoiding

Dwight D. Eisenhower, U.S. Supreme Commander in Europe during World War II, with Winston Churchill, Prime Minister of the United Kingdom. (Courtesy Dwight D. Eisenhower Library.)

the catastrophe of nuclear war and (2) maintaining national security through nuclear deterrence.[6]

As mentioned in chapter 2, though Truman was unsuccessful in securing the enactment of federal aid legislation, he believed that the federal government had a role to play in advancing education. Eisenhower, in contrast, believed that education was appropriately a province of the states and local districts. He did not believe that the federal government had a large role to play in education. Firmly convinced that education was a state and local matter, Eisenhower tried to stay clear of educational controversies. While he often acknowledged that the schools faced serious problems, he just as frequently stated, "I do not accept the simple remedy of federal intervention."[7] He wanted to limit federal assistance to facilities' maintenance and construction in federally impacted areas.

Despite Eisenhower's reluctance to enter the field of education, he was drawn into the area on several occasions: (1) the establishment of the Department of Health, Education, and Welfare, in 1953; (2) the Supreme Court ruling that racial segregation in public schools was unconstitutional in 1954; (3) the Little Rock, Arkansas, controversy over school desegregation (discussed further in chapter 5); (4) the enactment of the National Defense Education Act (NDEA) in 1957 as a reaction to Sputnik.

National Defense Education Act

Despite President Eisenhower's general reluctance to become involved in federal aid to education controversies, the highly significant NDEA was enacted during his administration. Although there had been sustained debates over federal aid, educational goals, and curriculum throughout the late 1940s and the 1950s, the intense cold war rivalry with the Soviet Union generated the rationale for the NDEA. The immediate catalyst for federal aid came on October 4, 1957, when the Soviet Union successfully launched Sputnik, a space satellite that orbited the earth. The Soviet success in space generated widespread criticism of American education, especially in mathematics, sciences, and technology. Like the comparative claims of the 1980s that American students were deficient in mathematics and sciences that led to *A Nation at Risk* (discussed in chapter 11), the educational controversy surrounding *Sputnik* was internationally driven. Critics alleged that declining academic rigor in American mathematics and science curricula and instruction had allowed the USSR to take the lead in the space race. A greater and more rigorous concentration on mathematics and science in U.S. schools would allow Americans to reverse the deficits and reclaim the lead.

Eisenhower, his predecessor Truman, and his successors Kennedy, Johnson, Nixon, Ford, Carter, Bush, and Reagan, all were preoccupied with the Soviet and Communist threat. Instead of using the conventional arguments for federal aid, Congress responded with the enactment of the National Defense Education Act, which gave assistance to science, mathematics, and foreign language instruction and to guidance programs. Congressional action was based on the premise that the federal government had an interest in these areas of education that were specifically related to the national defense. While the NDEA provided categorical aid, it pointed to possibilities that, despite Eisenhower's disinclination, the federal government might have a more general and sustained role to play in education.[8] Eisenhower signed the act, claiming it "would do much to strengthen our American system of Education" and advance the country's "basic national security."[9]

The NDEA led to new curricular developments, especially in mathematics and science, that would lead to the "new math," "new chemistry," "new physics," and other subjects. Indirectly, it stimulated changes in social studies as well. An important feature of the NDEA were teachers' institutes that brought classroom teachers to college and university campuses, during the summers, to work with professors who were regarded as academic innovators in their fields.

With the notable exception of the NDEA, more general federal aid bills languished in Congress, falling victim to the maneuvers of conflicting groups and forces. It would not be until Lyndon Johnson's "Great Society" and "War on Poverty" programs in the mid-1960s that more general federal aid legislation would be enacted.

While the growth of suburbia, the space race, and the enactment of the NDEA were noteworthy developments of the 1950s, civil defense and civil defense education were rather unique signs of the era.

The Atomic Age, Cold War, and Civil Defense

The dropping of atomic bombs on the Japanese cities Hiroshima and Nagasaki in August 1945, with massive loss of life, forced Japan's surrender, ending World War II. The post–World War II era was haunted by the indelible image of the mushroom shaped cloud that signalled atomic explosion. As the cold war became part of postwar life so did the threat of nuclear war. The Soviet Union, detonating its own atomic bomb in 1949, ended the U.S. atomic monopoly. Then, both the United States and the USSR began a race to create a super bomb, a hydrogen bomb. The United States detonated a hydrogen bomb in 1952, followed nine months later by the Soviets. Throughout the cold war from the 1950s until its end in 1990, nuclear weapons proliferated

The mushroom cloud of a U.S. atomic bomb test. (Reproduction from the Collections of the Library of Congress.)

and reached escalating heights of destructiveness, with a potential for global holocaust.

Although war in the atomic age carried the threat of annihilation of the human race, much of the thinking that framed the cold war's early context, especially in the 1950s, was shaped by World War II. Postwar historical interpretations claimed that World War II came because of the willingness to appease dictators and because of the democracies' military unpreparedness to defend themselves. It was the Western democracies' attempts to appease Hitler that enlarged the dictator's appetite. If an earlier stand had been made, then the Nazi, Fascist, and Japanese aggression could have stopped much earlier. Now, for Americans, the new aggressor was, without doubt, the Soviet Union, the bearer of atheistic Communist totalitarianism. World War II also demonstrated that war in the future would be total, involving civilians as well as military personnel. National security and U.S. military preparedness had to be accompanied by civilian defense. Not only was the general ideological reaction based on assumptions from World War II but so were the practical plans for civilian defense. The Detroit public schools, for example, instituted a civil defense program similar to the one followed during World War II, but it was modified because of "new methods of attack, especially the atom bomb."[10]

The Japanese attack on Pearl Harbor on December 7, 1941, was a grim memory of how war would come in the future—an unannounced secret attack coming when least expected. The Soviet Union, which had successfully exploded an atomic device on August 29, 1949, was such a potential aggressor. For U.S. policymakers, the struggle against the Soviet Union was ideological as well as military. In the battle to win the hearts and minds of men and women, education for democracy had to play a crucial role. This time, however, education for democracy included civil defense education. President Truman in 1949 stated, "Education is our first line of defense. In the conflict of principle and policy which divides the world today, America's hope, our hope, the hope of the world is education." Truman created the Federal Civil Defense Administration (FCDA) in January 1951 to encourage and coordinate the nation's civil preparedness. The U.S. Education Policies Commission in *Education and National Security*, in 1951, reiterating Truman's words, called on schools to "educate for moral and spiritual values."[11]

Dana B. Roblee, a school relations officer of the FCDA, stated that educationally "functional civil defense" was a form of "protective citizenship." Roblee identified four major emphases of civil defense education as: (1) creating an "intensified sense of social interdependence and group solidarity;" (2) broadening "understandings of interpersonal responsibilities;" (3) improving knowledge of contemporary "political currents" and "modern social and scientific power;" (4) mastering the "skills which enable mankind to meet adequately the dangers and tensions of emergency situations."[12] Like Roblee, civil defense educators often began with broad goals and then moved toward specific procedures to be used in case of national emergency, in this case atomic attack.

Leading the federal effort, the FCDA was a national center for civil defense, mobilizing state and local agencies for the cause. Identifying schools as a set conduit for diffusing information throughout the country, it produced educational materials about civil defense. Many in the educational establishment, such as the U.S. Office of Education, state departments of education, schools of education, and school administrators and teachers, took up the challenge to develop and promote civil defense education. Most state departments of education prepared civil defense strategies and materials for use in schools. Representative examples were New York's *Civil Defense and the Schools*, Colorado's *Organizing Colorado Schools for Civil Defense*, Michigan's *Civil Defense in the Classroom: A Handbook for Teachers*, and Indiana's *Civil Defense for the Schools of Indiana*.[13] Schools were identified as key agencies and teachers as key people in civil defense.

Curriculum and Instruction for Civil Defense

Curricular developments related to civil defense education need to be interpreted in terms of the atomic era, the cold war, and the anti-

Communist context of the 1950s and 1960s. (See chapter 5 and anti-Communism and McCarthyism for a further discussion of this topic.) The U.S. Atomic Energy Commission assisted in developing workshops and institutes for teachers. Frequently schools of education conducted special civil defense education programs. For example, Harvard, the University of Illinois, New York University, Stanford, and other institutions had such programs.

Information about atomic energy tended to be infused into the curriculum as units in existing science or social studies courses rather than as separate courses. There are many examples of efforts to develop materials for teaching about atomic energy. Idaho's State Department of Education sponsored intensive training courses to develop teaching materials on atomic energy as part of a state-wide project to familiarize teachers with the fundamentals of peacetime applications of atomic energy. Nebraska's State Department of Public Instruction developed a unit, "Facing the Facts of Atomic Energy." The Iowa State Department of Education published a comprehensive set of curriculum guides for elementary, secondary, college, and adult education. Elementary pupils incorporated atomic energy into their reading and writing assignments. For example, a second grader wrote an essay about "good atoms":

> Everything is made of atoms. When we learn more about how valuable these atoms are, people will be very happy. We will know more about mecticine [sic] to keep people well. The farmer will know how to have better crops. The business man will have machines and better things to sell. Everybody will be happier." Mary H. 2-C.[14]

High school science courses incorporated units on atomic energy. While the more ambitious secondary programs featured Geiger counters, scintillation counters, and models of atoms and electrons, most included references to the power and danger of atomic energy. The title of The North Central Association of Colleges and Secondary Schools' unit, "Atomic Energy, Double-Edged Sword of Science," reveals the cold war's educational tensions.[15] While atomic energy education emphasized the atom's positive energy potentials, civil defense education took a strongly precautionary stance about its powers of massive destruction.

The dangers of atomic weaponry were related to the menace of Communism versus democracy and to the Soviet threat to the United States. History and the social studies included more coverage of the rise of Communism and the Soviet system, by contrasting Soviet totalitarianism with American freedom and democracy. Just as they prepared materials for instruction in atomic energy and civil defense education, state departments of education developed units, for teachers and classrooms, on the rise of Communism as part of the worldwide threat posed by the Soviet Union. Also, information about atomic and nuclear fission and energy was making its way slowly into science and social studies texts. Much of the impact of civil defense in schools came in the way of safety education, atomic bomb drills, and changes in school architecture as well as through the formal curriculum. Anti-Communism, information about the Soviet threat and nuclear developments, and civil defense, however, were all related parts of cold war education in the United States.

Civil defense education included teacher in-service programs and the development of materials for use in the schools. Among films used were *Inside the Atom, Our Cities Must Fight,* and *Survival under Atomic Attack.* Filmstrips included *How to Live with the Atom* and *You and the Atom.* One of the most popular and widely used set of instructional materials for classroom use was the live action and animation film *Duck and Cover* in which Bert the Turtle, a friendly cartoon character, ducks and covers, in turtle-like fashion, during an atomic attack. Following Bert's example, the film showed school children "ducking and covering" during an attack.[16]

The civil defense administrator, Clara P. McMahon, in the *Elementary School Journal* advised teachers that the "threat to our national security" made it imperative that schools adjust the curriculum to incorporate the "qualities and characteristics" needed in such an emergency. She listed nine desired skills and abilities that pupils were to acquire:

1. To carry out automatically the rules of effective self-protection

2. To recognize and obey air-raid signals

3. To act without panic in an emergency

4. To be able to administer simple first aid

5. To think critically about the social, political, economic, and moral problems and issues created by the release of atomic energy

6. To read with understanding materials that deal with atomic energy, civil defense, and related areas

7. To gain increased knowledge of world affairs and the critical issues confronting mankind

8. To work well with peer groups on solving problems arising from the study of civil defense

9. To evaluate the impact of civil defense on society[17]

McMahon's list of skills followed the conventional pattern used in many "practical" articles on education. Her list, however, combined progressive concepts of critical thinking, problem solving, and group work with what was then regarded as skills needed in the event of atomic attack.

In typical style, school administrators sought to involve parents and community in civil defense education, often forming district-wide coordinating committees. John W. Pritchard, secretary for civilian defense of the Detroit Public Schools, pointing out the importance of community involvement, stated: "We realized from the outset that the effectiveness of our preparation depended on close working ties with the city office of civilian defense and its cooperating agencies, such as the police, fire, health and welfare departments (the last being concerned with post disaster shelter and feeding."[18] School districts sent letters about civil defense home with their children. Parents were advised to talk about atomic attack with their children. Attempting to reassure parents against feeling hopeless in the case of an atomic attack, one letter stated that "relatively slight obstacles" provided protection and that "construction used in our schools is a definite item in our favor."[19]

The National Parent-Teachers Association (PTA) in 1951 advised members to develop a "positive mental health program" and not "become unduly emotional" to alleviate children's anxieties about an atomic attack. Parents and teachers were advised that such anxieties could contribute to panic in the event of an attack and might cause neuroses in children. Parents and teachers were urged to be calm and "transmit a feeling of assuredness" so children could be prepared to "meet squarely" future emergencies, even atomic attack.[20]

School Preparedness Procedures

After establishing districtwide guidelines, many schools implemented civil defense preparedness procedures and actual atomic bomb drills. Then, as now, the responsibility for the smooth implementation of disaster preparedness measures was delegated to building principals. In the Detroit public schools, a directive, "Protection of School Children in the New Emergency: Preliminary Guide for Immediate Action," gave the steps each principal was to take immediately. Principals were to: (1) develop a school protection plan; (2) appoint a school defense director; (3) organize school personnel to maintain discipline, carry out evacuations, apply first aid, and deal with parents coming to the school in an emergency; (4) select a refuge area, preferably in the basement or a protected corridor; (5) inventory supplies needed for emergency; (6) inservice teachers and staff on air raid warnings; (7) begin air raid drills; (8) urge parents to place identification on children by marking garments with indelible ink; (9) prepare a limited evacuation plan; (10) explain drills to children and parents so that they know their "real potential value" without causing "undue fear."[21]

Detroit, regarded as a high-profile target city due to its automobile industry, took serious precautions. A telephone-warning system was set up to reach all schools rapidly. The public school radio station, WDTR, was in a state of readiness to broadcast attack alerts. First aid kits were issued to all schools, and teachers were inserviced in their use.

For children attending schools in the 1950s, the threat of nuclear war was an important formative part of their childhood and school experiences. Conducted by principals and teachers, often following state-mandated guidelines, bomb drills sought to teach students how to hide and protect themselves from atomic attack.[22] Atomic attack drills remain vivid memories. Remembering these drills, a teacher recalled that the alarm would sound and "teachers would tell everybody to get under the desks." Recalling "the tension" as pupils at first fearfully whispered and then became silent, she stated, "You never knew if it was a drill—a test—or the real thing."[23]

Drills

A U.S. Office of Education study indicated that 95 percent of 437 elementary schools, sampled in cities of 50,000 or more, taught civil defense education as did most secondary schools. The first school districts to begin atomic air raid drills were those in the large target cities. New York City, Los Angeles, Chicago, Detroit, Milwaukee, Fort Worth, San Francisco, and Philadelphia began drills in the school year 1950–51.[24] Drills typically were conducted each month. Los Angeles, in 1951, held weekly drills. Small towns in rural areas had them sporadically.[25]

Schools conducted three types of drills during the 1950s: no advanced warning, advanced warning, and dispersal. No advanced warning drills called "duck and cover," were most common. On the teacher's signal, pupils were to fall to the floor, crawl under their desks, and assume "the atomic head clutch position." Their backs were to "windows, faces buried between their knees, hands clasped on the backs of their necks, ears covered with their arms and eyes closed . . . to protect them from the bomb flash, flying glass, and falling timbers. . . ."[26]

Advance working drills, or "shelter drills," assumed that teachers and pupils had sufficient time to hide in the school's basement, halls, or other sheltered areas believed strong enough to withstand a bomb blast. In these drills, the principals sounded the alarm and then teachers would give the order for students to stand, lining up in orderly fashion, and move to the designated shelters where everyone sat as close as possible to the walls.[27]

The less commonly used dispersal drill presumed that when an attack was anticipated there would be enough time for pupils to be dismissed and reach home before it occurred. Dispersal drills were usually conducted at the end of the school day. Teachers instructed their pupils that an attack was expected and that they should go home as quickly as possible and take shelter at home or other areas. Dispersal drills were most frequently attempted in New York City and other large Eastern cities.[28] It was soon realized, however, that dispersal drills provided little control over students' movements. For this reason, they did not become a standard part of the civil defense education repertoire.

Based on the British experience during World War II when children were evacuated from the large cities to the countryside, some school districts developed similar evacuation plans for American children in the event of atomic attack. In 1955, Mobile, Alabama, and Atlanta and Savannah, Georgia, conducted school evacuation exercises to transport children to rural areas. Coordination proved to be so difficult that these evacuation plans were abandoned.

Along with atomic attack drills, some school districts began issuing identification tags, modeled after GI dog tags, to students. For example, New York City, with the most extensive program, by 1952 had spent $159,000 to produce and distribute 2,500,000 dog tags for public, parochial, and private school children. Other school districts followed suit. In San Francisco, the board of education provided them and in Seattle the program was managed by the PTA.[29]

Impact on Children

The cold war's first two decades, the 1950s and 1960s, were a period of fear of the inevitability of nuclear war. "Nuclear stockpiles," "deterrent," "balance of terror," and "the missile race" were terms commonly used by the press and television to describe America's nuclear competition with the Soviet Union. With television sets in virtually every American home, children could not escape the general atmosphere of the nuclear age. By the mid-1950s, knowledge about the hydrogen bomb and the immense dangers of radiation raised doubts about the adequacy of civil defense in the schools and caused some administrators to develop more comprehensive strategies. W. Gayle Starnes, director of training and education, of the Federal Civil Defense Administration in Battle Creek, Michigan, sought to alert school boards to the heightened dangers of nuclear attack posed by the hydrogen bomb and intercontinental ballistic missiles. Starnes warned, our children "cannot remain in our school buildings if they lie within the potential target area of an H-bomb. No school building could possibly withstand the terrific blast. Therefore they must be taken to safe areas as quickly as possible."[30] Starnes then advised school boards to weigh possibilities open to schools. If children were sent in mass to safe areas, it might be days before they could be reunited with their families. If sent home, it could only be hoped that they would reach their families in time to begin evacuation. While not proposing a specific solution, Starnes advised boards to work quickly to resolve this problem. While anxiety about nuclear attack was generalized throughout these decades, the most intense period was the crisis over Soviet placement of missiles in Cuba in 1962.

Psychiatrists, counselors, early childhood and other educators were uncertain about the effects of civil defense programs, especially atomic bomb attack drills on children. The general tone was to attempt to reduce anxiety by presenting civil defense as another kind of safety precaution. Atomic bomb drills were often compared to fire drills with which teachers and pupils were generally familiar. Teachers often made the drills into both a routine and a game in which the prize was to determine which class moved in the most orderly and rapid fashion. John Pritchard, of the Detroit public schools, warned against "slackening" the effort after the initial enthusiasm that typically came with the introduction of new school programs. Pritchard found the educators' challenge too "psychologically tricky." They had to implement a "minimum protection program" immediately and then develop it "smoothly and dynamically, possibly for many years, without letdown and also without undue buildup."[31] He warned against inculcating "permanent defensive" attitudes of abject fear, "huddling helpless attitudes," in children. He encouraged teachers to do their job in this "time of crisis" in the right way so that we can come "up out of the basement . . . fit for work and full of fight."[32]

A New York psychiatrist warned against fostering a climate of "atomic jitters" in children and the Pennsylvania Council of Civil Defense advised, teach children the "essential facts and procedures for self protection . . . *without frightening them*."[33] Some educators reported that children were frightened by atomic bomb drills; others found them handling them well, if properly conducted. According to New Jersey Assistant Commissioner of Education Thomas Durrell, "Many children in the kindergarten and primary grades have been upset by mismanaged air raid drills, some of them to such an extent that they were afraid to go to school."[34]

School Architecture

The era of the early cold war coincided with the movement of people from large cities to suburbs where new schools were being built to accommodate growing student populations. In some cases, school architects, mindful of civil defense needs, sought to design schools that could serve the dual purpose of being educationally functional and providing maximum shelter in event of nuclear attack. The dual purpose architectural design focused on preserving some elements of the building style that followed progressive designs. However, one element that was eliminated was the large banks of exterior windows, which maximized light and ventilation. In the event of nuclear attack, these banks of windows were likely to shatter into dangerous shards of broken glass. Thus, there was an emergence of new designs that reduced the number and size of windows, provided solid exterior walls, and sometimes included bomb curtains. Architects argued that these designs would protect children and teachers not only from nuclear attack but also from natural disasters such as tornadoes and hurricanes. An emergency post in the basement of Detroit's Emerson Elementary School was described as an "ideal air raid shelter," with "reinforced concrete ceilings and walls, where air is mixed for ventilation."[35] Further, schools built with civil defense in mind could be community shelters for the larger population.[36]

A Retrospective on Civil Defense Education

As arsenals of nuclear weapons grew larger and delivery systems became more sophisticated and efficient, the time for civilian defensive preparation grew shorter. School and other civil defense procedures against nuclear attack lost their credibility.

In a larger sense, however, the "duck and cover" drills of school civil defense programs had a larger significance. They continued a pattern, found in American educational history, that education and schools were valuable components of national security. During World Wars I and II, schools were called upon to play their part. The U.S. Office of Education and state departments of education encouraged schools and teachers to use classrooms to protect democracy and the American way of life against foreign and domestic threats. During the cold war, especially its first two decades, they played a familiar and similar role. The civil defense programs, even when they no longer seemed creditable, developed a readiness to believe that schools were part of the larger national security program.

In October 1957, the USSR successfully orbited *Sputnik* into space. The small silvery sphere orbiting the earth launched a national comparative education debate about the quality of American education versus that of the Soviet Union. The debate confirmed the importance of civil defense education. The debate led to the swift passage of the National Defense Education Act, which in 1958 made the school curriculum part of the nation's defense arsenal. As JoAnne Brown astutely commented, "Educators adapted schools to the national security threat of atomic warfare and claimed a proportionate federal reward for their trouble."[37]

Conclusion

In the 1950s, the United States moved in two major directions. The affluence of the postwar economy brought about significant social and educational change as an important demographic development occurred with the migration to and growth of suburbs. The development of an extensive suburban school system marked a new dimension in American education. The 1950s also saw the cold war taking its long hold on American life and thought. The atomic era and the ever-present fear of nuclear conflict with the Soviet Union led to a preoccupation with civil defense education. In addition to these developments, the 1950s witnessed debates about the American school curriculum, a pervasive climate of anti-Communism that led to McCarthyism, and the U.S. Supreme Court's momentous decision in 1954 to rule racial segregation in schools unconstitutional. These important developments are discussed in the next three chapters. Chapter 4 examines the curricular debates. Chapter 5 discusses the anti-Communist and antisubversive investigations of the McCarthy period. Chapter 6 analyzes racial relations in American education in the wake of the Supreme Court's *Brown* decision.

Notes

[1] Harold G. Vatter, *The U.S. Economy in the 1950s* (New York: Norton, 1963), pp. 15, 73.

[2] U.S. Bureau of the Census, *Historical Statistics of the United States, Colonial Times to 1957* (Washington, DC: U.S. Government Printing Office, 1960), p. 488. Also, see U.S. Bureau of the Census, *Historical Statistics of the United States, Colonial Times to 1957; Continuation to 1962 and Revisions* (Washington, DC: U.S. Government Printing Office, 1965).

[3] Landon Y. Jones, *Great Expectations: America and the Baby Boom Generation* (New York: Coward, McCann and Geoghegan, 1980), p. 337.

[4] For Eisenhower's account of World War II, see Dwight D. Eisenhower, *Crusade in Europe* (Baltimore: Johns Hopkins University Press, 1997).

[5] For Eisenhower's administrative style, see Fred I. Greenstein, *The Hidden-Hand Presidency: Eisenhower as Leader* (Baltimore: Johns Hopkins University Press, 1994).

[6] For an analysis of Eisenhower's military and foreign policy, see Robert R. Bowie and Richard H. Immerman, *Waging Peace: How Eisenhower Shaped an Enduring Cold War Strategy* (New York: Oxford University Press, 1998).

[7] *Federal Role in Education*, 2nd ed., (Washington, DC: Congressional Quarterly, Inc., 1967), p. 25.

[8] Hugh Davis Graham, *The Uncertain Triumph: Federal Education Policy in the Kennedy and Johnson Years* (Chapel Hill, NC: University of North Carolina Press, 1984), pp. 4–5.

[9] *Federal Role in Education*, p. 26.

[10] John W. Pritchard, "Disaster from the Air," *The Nation's Schools*, 47 (April 1951), p. 35.

[11] Michael J. Carey, "The Schools and Civil Defense: The Fifties Revisited," *Teachers College Record*, 84, No. 1 (Fall 1982), p. 118.

[12] Dana B. Roblee, "What Schools Are Doing About Civil Defense," *School Life*, 35 (September 1953), pp. 152–54, 159.

[13] New York State Civil Defense Commission, *Civil Defense and the Schools* (Albany: New York State Civil Defense Commission, 1953); Colorado State Department of Education, *Organizing Colorado Schools for Civil Defense* (Denver: Colorado State Department of Education, 1953); Michigan Department of Public Instruction, *Civil Defense in the Classroom: A Handbook for Teachers* (Lansing: Michigan Department of Public Instruction, 1955); Indiana Department of Public Instruction, *Civil Defense for the Schools of Indiana* (Indianapolis: Indiana Department of Public Instruction, 1952).

[14] George L. Glasheen, "What Schools Are Doing in Atomic Energy Education," *School Life*, 35 (September 1953) pp. 152–54.

[15] Ibid., p. 154.

[16] Carey, pp. 117–18.

[17] Clara P. McMahon, "Civil Defense and Educational Goals," *Elementary School Journal*, 53 (April 1953), p. 442.

[18] Pritchard, p. 34.

[19] National Education Association, National Commission on Safety Education, *Civil Defense Plans for School Systems* (Washington, DC: National Education Association, 1951), p. 11 as quoted in Carey, p. 120.

[20] From "A Civil Defense Program for Parent-Teacher Associations," *National Parent-Teacher*, 45 (June 1951), pp. 21, 34-35, as quoted in JoAnne Brown, "A Is for Atom, B is For Bomb": Civil Defense in American Public Education, 1948-1963," *The Journal of American History*, 75, No. 1 (June 1988), p. 76.

[21] Pritchard, p. 35.

[22] Carey, p. 115.

[23] Ibid., p. 115.

[24] Brown, p. 80.

[25] Carey, p. 116.

[26] Ibid., p. 116.

[27] Ibid., pp. 116–17.

[28] Ibid.

[29] Brown, p. 81.

[30] W. Gayle Starnes, "Schools and Civil Defense," *American School Board Journal*, 135 (August 1957), p. 22.

[31] John W. Pritchard, "Detroit's Plan for Coping with possible Disaster from the Air," *The Nation's Schools*, 47 (April 1951), p. 36.

[32] Ibid., p. 37.

[33] Pennsylvania State Council on Civil Defense, *Civil Defense for Schools* (Harrisburg: Pennsylvania State Council for Civil Defense, 1952), p. 8 as quoted in Carey, p. 121.

[34] State of New York, "Proceedings of the Institute on Mental Health Aspects of Civil Defense," June 21, 1951, p. 48 as quoted in Carey, p. 121.

[35] Pritchard, p. 34.
[36] Brown, pp. 87–89.
[37] Ibid., p. 68.

Further Reading

Bernhard, Nancy E. *US Television News and Cold War Propaganda, 1947–1960*. New York: Cambridge University Press, 1999.

Bernstein, Barton J., and Allen J. Matuson. *The Truman Administration: A Documented History*. New York: Harper & Row Publishers, 1966.

Bowen, Ezra, ed. *This Fabulous Century, 1950–1960*. New York: Time-Life Books, 1970.

Bowie, Robert R., and Richard H. Immerman. *Waging Peace: How Eisenhower Shaped an Enduring Cold War Strategy*. New York: Oxford University Press, 1998.

Brickman, William E., and Stanley Lehrer, eds. *Religion, Government, and Education*. New York: Society for the Advancement of Education, 1961.

Brown, JoAnne. "A Is for Atom, B Is for Bomb": Civil Defense in American Public Schools, 1948–1963," *The Journal of American History*, 75, No. 1 (June 1988), pp. 68–90.

Carey, Michael J. "The Schools and Civil Defense: The Fifties Revisited," *Teachers College Record*, 84, No. 1 (Fall 1982), pp. 115–27.

Carter, Paul A. *Another Part of the Fifties*. New York: Columbia University Press, 1983.

Chafe, William H. *The Unfinished Journey: America Since World War II*. New York: Oxford University Press, 1995.

Colorado State Department of Education. *Organizing Colorado Schools for Civil Defense*. Denver: Colorado State Department of Education, 1953.

Detroit Public Schools and Wayne University Joint Committee on Civil Defense. *Civil Defense in the Schools*. Detroit, MI: Board of Education, 1956.

Donovan, Robert J. *Conflict and Crisis: The Presidency of Harry S. Truman, 1945-1948*. New York: W.W. Norton & Co., 1977.

Donovan, Robert J. *Tumultuous Years: The Presidency of Harry S. Truman, 1945-1953*. New York: W.W. Norton & Co., 1982.

Eisenhower, Dwight D. *Crusade in Europe*. Baltimore: Johns Hopkins University Press, 1997.

Goulden, Joseph C. *The Best Years: 1945–1950*. New York: Athenaeum 1976.

Greenstein, Fred I. *The Hidden-Hand Presidency: Eisenhower as Leader*. Baltimore: Johns Hopkins University Press, 1994.

Jones, Landon Y. *Great Expectations: America and the Baby Boom Generation*. New York: Coward, McCann and Geoghegan, 1980.

Lee, Gordon C. *The Struggle for Federal Aid*. New York: Bureau of Publications, Teachers College Press, 1949.

McGarry, Daniel D., and Leo Ward, eds. *Educational Freedom and the Case for Government Aid to Students in Independent Schools*. Milwaukee, WI: Bruce Publishing Co., 1966.

Miller, Douglas T., and Marion Nowak. *The Fifties: The Way We Really Were*. Garden City, NY: Doubleday, 1977.

Munger, Frank J., and Richard F. Fenno, Jr. *National Politics and Federal Aid to Education*. Syracuse: Syracuse University Press, 1962.

National Education Association, National Commission on Safety Education. *Civil Defense Plans for School Systems*. Washington, DC: National Education Association, 1951.

New York State Civil Defense Commission. *Civil Defense and the Schools*. Albany: New York State Civil Defense Commission, 1953.

Perrett, Geoffrey. *A Dream of Greatness: The American People, 1945–1963*. New York: Coward, McCann and Geoghegan, 1979.

Quattlebaum, Charles A. *Federal Educational Policies, Programs and Proposals*. Washington, DC: Library of Congress, 1968.

Russell, Louise B. *The Baby Boom Generation and the Economy*. Washington, DC: Brookings Institution, 1982.

Satin, Joseph, ed. *The 1950s: America's "Placid" Decade*. Boston: Houghton Mifflin, 1960.

Sayre, Nora. *Previous Convictions: A Journey through the 1950s*. New Brunswick, NJ: Rutgers University Press, 1995.

Smith, Gilbert E. *The Limits of Reform: Politics and Federal Aid to Education, 1937–1950*. New York: Garland Publishing Co., 1982.

Steel, Ronald. *Federal Aid to Education*. New York: H.W. Wilson Co., 1961.

Stone, I. F. *The Haunted Fifties*. New York: Random House, 1963.

Tiedt, Sidney W. *The Role of the Federal Government in Education*. New York: Oxford University Press, 1966.

Vatter, Harold G. *The U.S. Economy in the 1950s*. New York: Norton, 1963.

4

The Curricular Controversies of the 1950s

As the nation moved into the postwar era, a long-standing debate in American education resurfaced over the nature and content of the school curriculum. While many of the arguments and counterarguments had been heard before, the curricular debates of the 1950s took place in a changing national context. As discussed in chapter 3, the country was experiencing economic affluence, suburbia was rapidly becoming a significant feature of American politics and society, and the United States was locked in an unrelenting cold war with the USSR. The school-centered debates of the 1950s reflected this changing national context but also educational continuities from the earlier progressive era.

Historical Context

Throughout the history of the American school curriculum, at least in modern times, there appears to be two long-standing tensions. In fact, it is possible to speak of a curricular pendulum that relates to the schools' basic nature and function. At one pole of the pendulum is the belief that the school is primarily a place for students to learn academic subjects and skills and at the other pole is the assumption that the school is primarily a place for children's development through experiences and activities.

The view that the school is primarily an academic institution sees the curriculum as consisting of organized academic skills, such as reading, writing, arithmetic, and civility, and basic subjects such as history, mathematics, science, and foreign languages. The opposing perspective contends that the school is a multifunctional institution for child and adolescent development and socialization through activities and experiences, some of which are academic in nature and others that are not.

In educational reality as distinct from educational theory, schools in the United States have incorporated both the academic and the multifunctional aspects in their curricula. However, as the curriculum pendulum swings to and fro, either the primarily academic view or the multifunctional socialization orientation has prevailed. In the literature of professional education, authorship has been preponderantly on the side of a loosely labeled progressivism that has emphasized the development of the "whole child" through a variety of activities, such as those involving hands-on learning, collaboration, and constructivism. While the professional education literature has encouraged a departure from the academic orientation to curricular multifunctionalism, the view that schools have a primarily academic mission, function, and role has had pronounced staying power in the school curriculum, particularly at the secondary school level. The view that schools are primarily academic generally has enlisted academicians, especially professors of the arts and sciences, and a body of educational critics and commentators who are generally external to what is called professional education.

Historically, there have been periods when the trend to multifunctionalism has been most evident and then periods when the trend has been reversed in favor of the ascendancy of traditional academic skills and subjects. Hence, the curricular pendulum can be said to swing back and forth, to and fro, throughout the history of American education. For example, the National Education Association's Committee of Ten in 1893 endorsed a basically academic subject-matter curriculum for the high school. The NEA Commission on the Reorganization of Secondary Schools took a decided multifunctional perspective in 1918, arguing that the high school curriculum should be organized around personal, social, and economic needs. In the period from the end of World War II to the present, there have been such swings of the curricular pendulum. During the late 1940s, strong currents of progressive education were still operative, particularly in the life adjustment movement in education, whereby high school curricula dealt with the real problems of living, not just preparation for college. By the mid-to-late 1950s, life adjustment had been soundly criticized and academic skills and subjects rose to the ascendancy. The enactment of the National Defense Education Act (1958) marked this swing back to academic skills and subjects. In the first half of the 1960s the movement to the structure of disciplines showed the academic ascendancy. However, by the mid- to late 1960s, the pendulum had swung back in the other direction with a variety of multifunctional approaches pushing back the academic view. Congruent with Lyndon Johnson's Great Society this move was toward compensatory education as part of the War on Poverty. Other critics lashing out at the "mindlessness of traditional schooling" called for more open and humanistic curricula. By the late 1970s and early 1980s, academic proponents had launched a concerted counterattack with the call for "basic education." By the 1980s, during the Reagan and Bush administrations, the movement to basic education had reached a high point with the assertion of *A Nation at Risk*.

The shifts of the curricular pendulum also can be interpreted as reflecting the political mood or climate of the country. When the country's mood leans toward liberalism, social reform, and change, the curriculum reflecting that ideological and political climate tends to be multifunctionalism; when the political climate is conservative and leans toward preserving the status quo or is in a period of consolidation rather than change, the curriculum takes on a more academic orientation. While the view that the school curriculum is tied to the nation's ideological and political orientation holds up fairly well, the generalization, though having some explanatory power, is also flawed. For example, certain educators, such as Robert Hutchins and Arthur E. Bestor Jr., while academically conservative were politically liberal.

In addition to the presence of the curricular pendulum swinging throughout educational history, a second generalization is also operative. That is, the higher institution and its curriculum exerts a power over the lower institution and its curriculum. Graduate and professional schools, through their entry requirements and examinations, exert a power over the college curriculum, which prepares their graduates for advanced programs; in turn, college entry requirements and examinations exert a power over secondary schools and their curricula; secondary institutions, such as high schools, prepare students to meet the entry requirements and to pass the examinations for college admission. While junior high schools, middle schools, and elementary schools prepare students for high school, the power of the higher institution over the lower one is lessened in their case. These schools, lower in the chain or ladder of institutions, have more freedom to deviate from the curricular requirements of the higher institution. Historically, they have been the locations of the greatest change and innovation. The institutions where the trends from the lower schools and the institutions of higher education meet, and often conflict, are high schools. It was in the high schools and their curricula that the greatest controversies occurred in the post–World War II period. The era of the 1950s

was interesting for the curricular debates that brought these issues
into clear focus.

The Legacy of Progressivism

In addition to the generalizations about the curricular pendulum
and the power of higher institutions to shape the curricula of lower
institutions, the 1950s' curricular debates also need to be interpreted
in terms of the impact of progressivism on the school curriculum.
Such an interpretation involves the critics of progressivism called
"essentialists."

The history of progressive education, both as part of the broader
progressive movement in politics and society as well as a development
within schooling, is complex. While the whole history of progressivism
in education is too varied and complex to be treated in detail here, certain broad features of progressivism in education are useful in interpreting the debates of the 1950s. In Western education, the origins of
progressivism can be traced back to such major figures as Johann
Amos Comenius, Jean-Jacques Rousseau, and Johann Heinrich
Pestalozzi. These educational thinkers challenged traditional European conceptions of schooling that were book-centered, emphasized
religious indoctrination, stressed memorization of factual content, and
frequently coerced or repressed children as a form of discipline. In
contrast, the naturalist educational reformers, who anticipated child-
centered progressivism, believed that education should be congruent
and parallel with children's natural development. For them, education
should begin with children's needs, interests, and curiosity; should be
based on sense experience rather than the memorization of books; and
should emphasize the dignity and importance of childhood as a crucial
stage of human development. It is important to note that Comenius,
Rousseau, Pestalozzi, and other like-minded figures from the past
were the characters who were featured in books on the history and philosophy of education and treated as hero figures or reformers who did
battle against traditionalism. Part of the prospective teachers' preparation was to study these hero figures as models of educational reform.

While the Western educational reformers were included in the
pantheon of educational heroes, an equally and perhaps more powerful formative force came from the progressive movement in American
politics and economics, society, and education. In American politics
and economics, key political figures, such as Theodore Roosevelt,
Woodrow Wilson, Robert LaFollette, and others championed the progressive reform of political institutions and processes to remove the
influence of corporate monopolies and corrupt bosses. Journalists
such as Lincoln Steffens, Ida Tarbell, Upton Sinclair, and Herbert

Croly championed investigative reporting into a range of issues such as corrupt politics, unsafe food and drugs, and economic monopoly. Settlement-house workers such as Jane Addams worked to make the burgeoning urban areas into more hospitable and humane places to live. In education, the mood of progressive reform also was felt. Schools should be free from political control, should instill a progressive civic spirit, and should be connected to broad social issues and change rather than being exclusively academic places of learning.

Perhaps John Dewey and his pragmatic experimentalism best characterized the larger social view of educational progressivism. In Dewey's view, the schools of the future were to be centered in the community and intimately connected to the people they served. Rather than being organized into discrete and separate subjects, the school curriculum should begin with the children's direct experiences and then, extending these experiences in space and time, should lead to the larger social concerns of human life. Education's only purpose, Dewey claimed, was an ever-broadening human experience, or growth for its own sake. In many ways, Dewey's pragmatic philosophy provided the theory of progressivism in education that came to dominate educational theory and teacher education. Leading progressive disciples of Dewey, such as William H. Kilpatrick, Harold Rugg, George S. Counts, and Boyd H. Bode, occupied premier positions in colleges of education, were the editors of and contributors to important journals, and wrote the books that tilted the ideology of professional education in a definitely progressive direction. Kilpatrick's project method emphasized cooperative, collaborative group work on projects as the heart of the curriculum and method of teaching. Counts, arguing that schools should originate rather than reflect society in *Dare the School Build a New Social Order?*, sought to reconnect schools to major social issues.[1] Rugg, interestingly, argued for both a progressive child-centeredness as well as a social reformist direction. Other educational progressives, often from independent and private schools, developed a child-centered orientation that emphasized the child's interests and needs and the freedom to learn without coercion.

The progressive curricular legacy from these diverse sources contained areas of mutual agreement as well as areas of disagreement. Progressives were generally united in their opposition to traditional book-centered, teacher-dominated instruction. For them, the child should be the focus of classroom activity and instruction should be based on children's interests and needs rather than externally imposed goals. Teachers in such situations should be directors of research and inquiry, who establish a classroom environment conducive to children's growth and development. While progressives agreed in their opposition to traditional school practices, they disagreed on the nature of and degree of children's freedom. Dewey, himself, in *Experience and*

Education, had challenged the notion of making children's freedom into an educational absolute divorced from society.[2] However, child-centered progressives feared that their socially impelled colleagues might be leaning toward imposing a particular sociopolitical ideology on children. It was this mixed legacy of progressivism in education that was being felt by the schools at the end of the 1940s and early 1950s.

The Essentialist Critique of Progressives

While the progressives had dominated educational thought in the 1920s, 1930s, and 1940s, they had been challenged by a small group of educators who called themselves essentialists. The essentialist critique is worth commenting on because it was, in many ways, germinal and similar to later attacks on progressive education, especially the critique of life adjustment education during the 1950s. While many progressive educational leaders such as Kilpatrick, Counts, and Rugg were professors of education at Columbia University's highly influential Teachers College, among their colleagues at the same institution were such skilled adversaries as William C. Bagley and Isaac Kandel. Rejecting much of progressivism, the essentialists stressed that education, rather than relying on children's interests and needs or being used to direct deliberate social change, should transmit a fund of human skills and knowledge from the adult generation to the society's children. Further, this knowledge should be arranged cumulatively and sequentially in a carefully articulated curriculum.

The highly articulate Bagley, using polar opposites, outlined the "crux of the conflict" between progressives and essentialists.[3] While progressives emphasized children's interests in learning, essentialists stressed the need for effort in mastering lessons; while progressives stressed freedom to learn, essentialists argued that discipline was needed; while progressives exalted individual experience, essentialists prized the experience of the human race over time. Further, progressives emphasized the psychological organization of the curriculum in contrast to the essentialists' emphasis on its logical organization. Finally, progressives emphasized learning through activities while essentialists maintained the need for subject-matter organization. After outlining the polar opposites, Bagley then sought to reconcile them with an Hegelian-like synthesis. He argued that while interest may lead children to problems, they need effort to pursue them to their solutions. Further, not all interests were equally important. Some were more important than others because they led to matters of permanent concern. The view that some areas of the curriculum were related to permanent cultural matters was a real point of difference between progressives and essentialists. Still another serious difference was Bagley's argument that the teacher, as an adult representative of the culture, was responsible for guiding learning to a definite goal rather than to the prized progressive "open-endedness."[4]

Bagley and his essentialist conferees' identification of educational deficiencies in late-1930s' America would re-echo in the twentieth century. Among these educational deficits was the charge that American children, in contrast to their European counterparts, did not have high rates of academic achievement. Further, the essentialists charged that the progressives' abandonment of the logical, chronological, and systematic in curricular organization had caused the decline of academic standards in the United States. The progressive overemphasis on incidental or concomitant learning and the neglect of exact subjects had weakened academic standards and had led to social promotion policies that left students unprepared. The essentialists argued that there was an essential curriculum that all students should pursue: reading, writing, and arithmetic, the skills that reproduced the human race's achievements in recording, computing, and measuring, as well as history, health, natural sciences, fine arts, and industrial arts. Bestor and the critics of the 1950s and the proponents of *A Nation at Risk* in the 1980s would mount similar arguments. While later subject-matter proponents had an even more prescribed view of the curriculum than the essentialists, their arguments followed a similar logic. They would make comparisons between the achievement of American students with those of other countries; find defects in the educational system, usually attributable to progressive education; and then call for a uniform subject-matter curriculum for all students.

Residues of Progressivism

In the late 1940s, progressivism was still the regnant educational theory among professional educators, especially among teacher educators, curriculum specialists, and school administrators. For example, teacher education programs emphasized Deweyite themes such as "educating the whole child," "learning by doing," and Kilpatrick's project method. The curriculum, too, reflected the progressive impulse: in the elementary school, the traditional reading, writing, and arithmetic had been reorganized into an integrated language arts approach; the conventional history and geography, too, had been restructured into a multidisciplinary social studies. Progressivism also had reshaped the secondary school curriculum: courses in practical mathematics were an alternative to the traditional algebra and geometry, and courses in integrated natural science combined features of the traditional biology, botany, and chemistry. Administrative progressives, prepared in "modern" programs of educational administration, sought to combine the "progressive" curriculum with new organizational, scheduling, and even architectural designs that stressed "bigness" and efficiency. While these progressive tendencies were dominant throughout professional education, it should not be assumed that all schools, in their day-to-day instruction, had been transformed into progressive institutions. Many schools, perhaps even the majority of schools, remained quite traditional in curriculum and instruction. Indeed, many administrators and teachers were examples of a classic pattern of dualism in that while their theories were progressive, their practices were traditional.

Life Adjustment Education

In 1945, with the nation at the beginning of its readjustment from war to peacetime, Charles Prosser, a highly respected leader in vocational education introduced a resolution that inaugurated what was called the "life adjustment" movement. Life adjustment would enlist many professional educators and develop a momentum that would quickly influence national, state, and local policymakers and educators. While striking a sympathetic chord among many professionals, it also generated a determined opposition, especially among academicians. The following section examines the life adjustment controversy in American education.

Prosser's Resolution

Charles Prosser, an educational administrator, had earned distinction in professional education. He had been a classroom teacher, a principal, a superintendent and then went on to play a national role as secretary of the National Society for the Promotion of Industrial Education. During World War I, he was director of the Federal Board for Vocational Education and was instrumental in lobbying for and drafting vocational education legislation. Among his publications were *Vocational Education in a Democracy* (1925), *Vocational Education and Changing Conditions* (1934), and *Secondary Education and Life* (1939). Prosser was a highly respected voice in vocational education who throughout his career had pressed for a wider public and professional acceptance of vocational education as a integral part of secondary education.

Prosser introduced his resolution, launching the life adjustment education movement on June 1, 1945, at a conference in Washington, D.C., of the consulting committee that was reviewing the draft of a U.S. Office of Education bulletin, *Vocational Education in the Years Ahead*. Noting that 20 percent of secondary students were enrolled in college preparatory academic programs and 20 percent in vocational education programs, Prosser stated:

We do not believe that the remaining 60 per cent of our youth of secondary school age will receive the life adjustment training they need and to which they are entitled as American citizens—unless and until the administrators of public education with the assistance of vocational education leaders formulate a comparable program for this group.[5]

Prosser then urged the U.S. commissioner of education to call conferences to consider and resolve the problem that left 60 percent of students underserved by public schools.[6] To remedy this glaring inequity in secondary education, Prosser recommended a total restructuring of secondary schools and curriculum. An important motivation for Prosser as well as many who supported life adjustment was the need to reduce the drop out rate of high school students by providing a more relevant curriculum, supported by greater guidance and counseling services.

Although the elder statesman of the nation's vocational education establishment, Prosser was doing more than arguing that vocational studies should get a larger share of the high school curriculum. He based his recommendation on what he considered to be a serious appraisal of the condition of post–World War II education. Since the early years of the twentieth century, the American high school population was growing larger. As its size increased, its student population was becoming increasingly diverse in ethnicity, race, and socioeconomic class. Professional educators, particularly those in the public school establishment, had emphasized equality of educational opportunity but reasoned that equality would best be obtained by reducing standardized subject-matter curriculum into more varied secondary offerings that corresponded to the differing needs and interests of a highly diverse secondary school population. In particular, it was important to relax the grip that colleges had on the high school curriculum. The academic, college preparatory, curriculum should no longer dominate the secondary curriculum. In addition to this trend to diversify the curriculum and reduce the dominance of the college preparatory program, the post–World War II era also generated new demands on the high school. Powerful social changes were at work. Just as the economy and society were readjusting from war to peace, so the American family was undergoing change. A time of change was unsettling personally and psychically as well as socially, economically, and politically. As the nation moved to readjustment, there were social strains and imbalances. The nation's secondary school-age youth, too, were experiencing these changes, evidenced by the new phenomenon of juvenile delinquency.[7] Secondary education needed to be redesigned to aid adolescents on their path to maturity.

The term "adolescence" was not unique to the postwar era. Psychologists such as the pioneering G. Stanley Hall and a later host of

developmental child and adolescent psychologists had been building
the case that the adolescent years, like childhood, was a special and
unique stage of human development. Progressive educators had long
argued that the elementary school was a place for children's exploration of the environment, growth, and development. Should not the
same developmental criteria be applied to adolescents? Life adjustment educators believed that large numbers of high school students
had disengaged themselves from academic programs which they found
irrelevant to their lives. Instead of being exclusively an institution to
prepare for college entry by studying strictly academic subjects, should
not the high school become an institution for the growth and development of adolescents, American "teenagers"? For Prosser and his like-
minded colleagues, the time was ripe to restructure the high school
into a broad-based institution where adolescent growth and development were tied to the saleable vocational skills that would lead to a
socially satisfying and economically productive adulthood.

The Life Adjustment Movement

Based on the Prosser Resolution, life adjustment was launched
and took off like a bandwagon. It quickly gained the support of the U.S.
Department of Education, state departments of education, and leading
organizations of professional educators.

With the professional educational establishment largely endorsing the life adjustment concept, the focus turned to developing and
implementing a life adjustment curriculum in the schools. With
unusual rapidity, a strategy was designed for the transformation of
American secondary education via the concept of life adjustment education. With U.S. Department of Education support, regional conferences took place during 1946 in New York City, Chicago, Cheyenne,
Sacramento, and Birmingham. The general consensus coming out of
the regional conferences was that:

1. Public secondary schooling was failing to "provide adequately"
   for the life adjustment of a major percentage of students.

2. A public movement needed to be generated for life adjustment
   education.

3. Educational experiences should reflect the "diverse individual
   needs" of secondary school aged youth.

4. Teacher preparation curriculum should manifest a "genuine
   desire" to serve all youth.

5. "Functional experiences in the areas of practical arts, home
   and family life, health and physical fitness, and civic compe-

tence" as well as "supervised work experience" were to be components in secondary programs.

6. Comprehensive and continuous guidance and pupil personnel services were indispensable elements in life adjustment efforts.[8]

The regional conferences culminated in a national conference in Chicago, May 8–10, 1947. At the Chicago conference, Prosser, rewording his initial resolution, eliminated percentages used in the 1945 statement. Now, more generally stated, his revised resolution reiterated that the "ideal of secondary education for all youth" was an American principle. To realize this ideal, the high school needed to "serve an increasing number of youth for whom college preparation or training for skilled occupations is neither feasible nor appropriate." The schools, he admonished, needed to devise a "suitable educational program" for this underserved majority of secondary students.[9]

After the Chicago conference, the U.S. commissioner of education, John W. Studebacker, appointed a National Commission on Life Adjustment Education for Youth. The commission's members included representatives from the country's leading educational organizations: the American Association of School Administrators, the American Association of Junior Colleges, the National Association of State Directors for Vocational Education, the National Association of High School Supervisors and Directors of Secondary Education, the National Association of Secondary-School Principals, the National Catholic Welfare Conference, the National Council of Chief State School Officers, and the National Education Association.[10] A second national commission was appointed in 1950. Despite the tensions over federal aid to private schools, a number of Catholic educators joined the life adjustment movement.[11] The life adjustment strategy developed by the commissions involved: (1) building a base of organizational support in the U.S. office and the state offices of education: (2) enlisting the support of the media in gaining national coverage; (3) enlisting the support of the national professional education organizations; (4) developing curricular programs by encouraging the contributions of leading teacher educators, curriculum specialists, and educational administrators in colleges and schools of education; (5) encouraging school districts to implement the life adjustment curriculum and provide in-service to teachers.

Much of the life adjustment strategy was designed to bring about a major restructuring of the American secondary school curriculum. An important strategic change in the movement was that life adjustment education was now promoted as the ideal for all students, not only the underserved minority initially identified by Prosser. A U.S. Office of Education publication stated:

Life adjustment education is designed to equip all American youth to live democratically with satisfaction to themselves and profit to society as home members, workers, and citizens. It is concerned especially with a sizable proportion of youth of high-school age (both in school and out) whose objectives are less well served by our schools than the objectives of preparation for either a skilled occupation or higher education. . . .

Many high schools, however, continue to be dominated by traditional curriculum patterns which emphasize verbal and abstract learning or place undue emphasis on specialized courses useful to a relatively small number of pupils. As a result many pupils unable to benefit from either of these types of instruction are left to flounder or leave the school as soon as the compulsory education laws will permit.[12]

A feature of the momentum of the movement was to create an alternative to the primacy of the college preparatory academic curriculum over secondary education. For the life adjustment proponents, a more relevant experience-based curriculum would reduce the drop out rate and retain more students in high school. The emphasis on academic subjects would be replaced by a different curricular lynch pin— students' personal, social, and economic needs. Some proponents of life adjustment urged its infusion throughout the curriculum. Instead of adding new courses, existing courses, including academic subjects, were to be reconfigured to prepare all youth functionally in all areas of living. Thus, curricular specialists, departing from locating the core of the secondary curriculum in academic subjects, reintroduced a multi-functionalist argument. Like the earlier essentialists, critics of the movement in the 1950s, such as Bestor, would charge life adjustment advocates with displacing intellectualism with functionalism. As the curriculum revisions were launched, there was much to indicate that life adjustment would succeed. It was geared to dealing with the large impersonal forces of postwar social and economic change in a way that was highly personal and student-centered. The linking of social and psychological adjustment with vocational productivity appealed to the ingrained American sense of functional practicality. Finally, the movement put professional educators, rather than their academic colleagues and often rivals, in a potentially powerful position.

After conducting many need surveys and holding many conferences and meetings, a national conference in Washington, D.C., in October 1948 specified life adjustment's guiding principles as: (1) respect for students' individual worth and personality; (2) the enrollment and retention of all youth; (3) required courses to be concerned with the problems of living; (4) an emphasis on direct experience; (5) the planning, organization, implementation, and administration of schools to be democratic; (5) students' records and data to be used constructively; (6) evaluation to effect desirable changes in students' behavior.[13] Several of the principles reiterated progressive educational concepts. For the life adjustment educators, cumulative student records were to be used for individual student self-appraisal and placement purposes, to improve instruction, and to counsel with parents and pupils. The emphasis on using student records constructively to bring about desired changes in pupil behavior was prophetic of the individualized pupil plans used in later decades for students with special needs and the emphasis on portfolio assessment (this topic is discussed in chapter 12).

The life adjustment curriculum began to take shape. It was determined that the new curriculum was to be based on an areas-of-living approach. All problems of youth would fall into four broad areas: (1) personal; (2) personal-social; (3) social-civic; (4) economic. The four broad areas, however, were not capable of being neatly defined into subject compartments as was the case with the traditional curriculum's history, mathematics, foreign languages, chemistry, and physics. Indeed, the life adjustment proponents wanted curricular integration rather than subject compartmentalization. The movement created a terminology that included progressive-sounding phrases such as "common learnings," "the functional core curriculum," "pupil-centered" and "experienced-centered" schools.[14] Rather than identifying subjects, the life adjustment curriculum-makers concentrated on developing a series of objectives such as:

1. interpersonal skills needed to live a socially and personally satisfying life with others—in school, in the local community, in the state, in the nation, and in the world;

2. life skills that contributed to physical and mental health;

3. life skills that contributed to effective personal living in the family and the group, including the skill in being an effective consumer and producer of goods and services;

4. recreational skills for the effective use of leisure;

5. skills for assimilating and communicating information and ideas;

6. interests, language, and skills for continuing citizenship, home life, wellness, vocations, and personal development.

With the areas of living identified, it was then possible to become more specific in laying out a life adjustment curriculum. However, a major enlargement in the scope of life adjustment occurred. While Prosser had initially identified the 60 percent of the secondary school population underserved by the college preparatory and vocational education curricula, the life adjustment goal was enlarged from the 60 percent cohort to the entire secondary school age population. Proponents of life adjustment identified its major goal as assisting all secondary students to achieve effective adjustability. An appropriately designed curriculum, including graduation requirements, would ensure that all students were being prepared for all areas of living.

State Initiatives

The U.S. Office of Education and the National Commission on Life Adjustment Education enlisted the support of the state departments of education to promote the life adjustment curriculum. Each state department was encouraged to appoint a statewide coordinating committee to develop programs to be implemented in selected schools. States were advised to build broad-based constituencies for life adjustment that included representatives from teachers', secondary school principals', and parents' associations. State departments were encouraged to sponsor conferences, provide consultative services, and sponsor in-service sessions about life adjustment education. In turn, the U.S. Office of Education and National Commission on Life Adjustment would diffuse information about exemplary programs throughout the county.[15]

Although there were many variations from state to state and district to district, certain common themes ran through the life adjustment curriculum. The entire secondary school curriculum, reflecting the common needs of all adolescents, was to be a program in all the areas of living—it would be a complete taxonomy of adjustment to the here and now as well as to the future. Life adjustment advocates said that new curriculum would bring transformational rather that additive change to schools. Life adjustment did not mean that a new course called "life adjustment" was to be merely added to the traditional curriculum. It meant that life adjustment was to be at the heart, at the vital center, of the secondary school curriculum. The term "infusion" became popular in life adjustment circles. Infuse life adjustment into the entire curriculum, they said. Implementing the new curriculum would require modifying existing courses and creating new courses. All existing courses, including language, mathematics, science, and history, would need to be revised so that they dealt with the real problems of living rather than academic preparation for college. Further, new courses were to be developed around the common needs theme. For example, a course, dealing with physical, mental, and emotional health would include units on personal adjustment, a balanced diet, developing good health habits, knowing how to provide first aid, exercises for physical development, skills in developing poise in difficult situations, and learning to understand and control personal emotions.

The life adjustment advocates were also bent on tearing down the walls that separated school from the community. Building on the progressive legacy that the school should be part of society, they attacked what they derisively labeled the "four walls" traditional model of the school, which identified the institution in exclusively academic terms. The life adjustment curriculum would require student involvement in social and community service. It would include time for students to work in local businesses and service agencies.

With the curriculum so broadened to include all the areas of life, then the nature of the school and the role of the teacher would need to be expansively reconceptualized. The school was to be a total agency that addressed all areas of human life, including but not exclusively limited to the academic one. The school of the future would deal with education in very broad terms that were social, personal, civic, and economic, as well as academic. Further, since the concept of adjustment involved much that was psychological and emotional as well as intellectual, the life adjustment school had to become completely multifunctional. It had to deal with the students' total adjustment, especially the psychological modes of adjustment. This meant that schools and teachers, becoming more psychologically therapeutic, would need to offer extended guidance and counseling services to students. Repeatedly, the proponents of life adjustment stated that the life adjustment school would be experimental and open to change, particularly the change needed for healthy adjustment. As an experimenting institution, the school was to be a place of continuous formative evaluation in which the school administration and staff would be in a situation of continuous adjustment.

Reaction against Life Adjustment

The 1950s and early 1960s saw the publication of numerous books about the condition of American education. Many of these books were written by persons who were outside of the professional education establishment and were openly critical of U.S. public schools, typically finding them insufficient in academic standards. James D. Koerner's *The Case for Basic Education* (1959), attacking progressive education, called for an emphasis on basic skills and subjects. Other noteworthy critical books were Mortimer Smith's *And Madly Teacher* (1949); Bernard Iddings Bell's *Crisis in Education* (1949); Albert Lynd's *Quackery in the Public Schools* (1950); and Robert Hutchins's *The Conflict in Education* (1953).[16] The voices of three other critics influenced the direction that life adjustment would take. We will now examine the strong views of these critics.

Arthur E. Bestor Jr. One of the leading critics of life adjustment education was the historian, Arthur E. Bestor Jr. The son of Arthur E. Bestor Sr., the director of the famed Chautauqua Institution in New York, Bestor was a scion of a distinguished academic family. At the time of his major critiques of American education, Bestor was a history professor at the University of Illinois in Urbana, where he taught courses in American history, historical methods, and U.S. constitutional history. Though his educational philosophy tended toward academic conservatism, Bestor, like Hutchins, was a liberal in matters of academic freedom, civil rights, and freedom of expression. He was a member of the American Civil Liberties Union, serving on its Illinois board of directors, and was also a member of the National Association for the Advancement of Colored People. In addition, he was one of the founders of the Council for Basic Education, serving as the organization's first president in 1956–57. His most noteworthy educational critiques were *Educational Wastelands* (1953) and *The Restoration of Learning* (1955).[17]

In *The Restoration of Learning*, Bestor made a strong argument that the school has a primary purpose: it is an academic institution, a place of thorough and disciplined intellectual development. He argued that life adjustment proponents and other "professional educationists" had encouraged an anti-intellectual ideology that set forth "trivial" educational purposes that divorced schools from "the disciplines of science and scholarship."[18] He fired his salvos at the "professional educationists," who controlled schools and at state departments of education, which he alleged, set an anti-intellectual agenda for schools.

Bestor's educational philosophy based on academic disciplines ran counter to the progressive orientation that schools were multipurpose, multifunctional agencies that served personal, social, and economic as well as intellectual needs. Though he did not oppose the school's recognition of socialization, health, and other nonintellectual needs, he was adamant that these "ancillary functions" should not interfere with the school's primary intellectual function. His argument, though cogently delivered, was in many respects a retrospective of the Committee of Ten's emphasis on academic subjects. It also anticipated by thirty years the "new basics" recommended by *A Nation at Risk*, in 1983. In his rationale for an academic subject-matter curriculum, Bestor, much like the earlier essentialists, argued:

> An indispensable function of education . . . is to provide sound training in the fundamental ways of thinking represented by history, science, mathematics, literature, language, art, and other disciplines evolved in the course of mankind's long quest for usable knowledge, cultural understanding, and intellectual power.[19]

Bestor, like the earlier essentialists, identified reading, writing, and arithmetic as the indispensable studies of elementary schooling; science (biology, chemistry, and physics), mathematics (algebra, geometry, trigonometry, calculus), history (particularly political and constitutional), English (composition, grammar, and literature), and foreign languages formed the essentials of the secondary school curriculum. He strongly opposed the progressive tendency to correlate and fuse subjects into large interdisciplinary blocks such as social studies or life sciences. In terms of teaching methods, Bestor opposed the progressive inclination to fuse various kinds of subjects and materials into undifferentiated problems or projects. He argued that "clear thinking is systematic thinking" and requires the logical or chronological organization of knowledge.[20] The curriculum, therefore, was to be systematic and sequential, organized as separate subjects.

Bestor's charges that "professional educationists" had contributed to the decline of American educational standards evoked a strong counterattack by leading professors of education. The debates at Bestor's own institution, the University of Illinois, were particularly bitter. Harold C. Hand and Charles W. Sanford, of the university's College of Education, contended that Bestor's evidence was flawed in that he isolated statements out of context and ignored arguments that educators had used for the liberal arts.[21] Other educators charged that Bestor's academic proposals ignored the growing diversity of students in public high schools. Bestor, in turn, responded that equality meant that the same curriculum should be provided to all students rather than different ones for different groups.

Max Rafferty. Still another critic who gained national attention was Max Rafferty, a school administrator and conservative Republican, who was elected California State superintendent of public instruction in 1962. Lacking Bestor's scholarly credentials and intellectual erudition, Rafferty's attacks on progressivism and life adjustment were often vehement. In many respects, Rafferty epitomized a rising neoconservatism, surfacing in the Western states that, beginning with Goldwater's unsuccessful contest against Johnson in 1964, eventually would lead to Reagan's defeat of Carter in 1980. Rafferty's *What Are They Doing to Your Children?* (1964) was a frontal attack on educational progressivism and political liberalism, two forces that he believed were eroding American academic standards and patriotism.

Rafferty's attacks on progressivism, life adjustment, and liberalism need to be interpreted in terms of the climate of the 1950s and 1960s. Both decades were characterized by a strong anti-Communism sentiment, fear of Communist China and the Soviet Union, and Senator Joe McCarthy's investigations of alleged Communist subversives. McCarthy and other anti-Communist investigators alleged that Communists had infiltrated the public schools and state universities. (See chapter 5 for a discussion of McCarthyism.) Also contributing to the climate of fear was the military stalemate in Korea, where South Korean and U.S. military forces struggled against North Korean and Chinese armies. During the Korean conflict, 1950–1952, some U.S. prisoners of war made radio broadcasts in which they accused their own country of aggression. Critics such as Rafferty and others attributed the decline in military personnel's morale to progressive education that had sapped and weakened their patriotism.

Despite his unrestrained attacks on progressivism, Rafferty called for reforms, which, while generally not acted upon in the 1950s and 1960s, became standard items in the neoconservative educational agenda ushered in by *A Nation at Risk* in the 1980s. Rafferty argued for a return to the basic subjects of English, mathematics, science, and history. He urged that the states set minimum standards for promotion and graduation. He also argued that school administrators should pass cultural tests and prospective teachers should pursue a rigorous academic curriculum.

Rafferty, in his political campaigns and public statements, condemned the "four deadly sins" that were eroding the moral and patriotic foundations of American society—violence, pornography, drugs, and lawlessness. He called for the return of law and order to society and schools. In addition to fearing Communism, Rafferty and like-minded conservatives feared the rise of juvenile delinquency and violence. He attacked what he called the "cult of the slob, . . . side-burned, ducktailed, unwashed, booted, leather-jacketed slobs."[22]

Admiral Hyman G. Rickover. A U.S. Navy officer and a persistent national critic of American education, Admiral Rickover faulted American schools for their failures in mathematics and science. Nationally known as the "father of the atomic submarine," Rickover had supervised the scientists and engineers who planned and developed the first U.S. nuclear powered submarine, the *Nautilus*.[23] Like the earlier essentialists, Rickover, comparing U.S. schools to those in other countries such as Switzerland, Germany, and the Soviet Union, found American students lacking the mathematical and scientific knowledge needed for application to technology. While American high school students were being taught life adjustment courses, European secondary students were studying history, mathematics, and the sciences. By the end of their secondary schooling, many European students, in contrast to American students, had mastered their own vernacular and were conversant in one or two foreign languages.[24] For example, Rickover found Soviet students were required to master the Russian language and literature, a foreign language, algebra, geometry, physics, chemistry, and history. Testifying before congressional committees, Rickover

Admiral Hyman Rickover, a critic of U.S. education during the 1950s, testifying before a congressional committee. (Reproduction from the Collections of the Library of Congress.)

warned of the dangers to national security posed by American educational deficits.[25]

Rickover believed that American public secondary schools were inadequate on several counts, including (1) they were failing to provide a foundation in the basic academic subjects, especially in mathematics and science; (2) they were not providing an academically challenging education for gifted and talented students.[26] Rickover's proposal to establish demonstration schools for the top 20 percent of academically talented students diametrically countered Prosser's life adjustment argument to reorient the secondary school curriculum to met the needs of the 60 percent that were underserved students. Comparing

Swiss and American schools, Rickover commented that Swiss schools succeeded by concentrating on academic subjects and not life adjustment. It was the Swiss family that provided the personal and social manners and other practical skills, which life adjusters proposed to replace the academic curriculum.[27]

Like Bestor and Hutchins, Rickover was a prominent national spokesman for a subject-matter curriculum, based on the liberal arts, as a necessary background for the educated person.[28] His attacks on life adjustment education used a range of persuasive arguments. Namely, that the inadequacies of American secondary education were related to national security and were placing the nation in a dangerous lag behind the Soviet Union. American educators, should jettison life adjustment and emphasize mathematics and science, which were foundational to technological development. Further, there was much that the United States could learn from Europe about the education of academically talented students.

The Decline of Life Adjustment

As the 1950s came to an end, life adjustment educators were clearly on the defensive. Their critics had continually lambasted them, ridiculing their proposals as anti-intellectual fun and games. The Soviet orbiting of *Sputnik* in 1957 and the passage of the National Defense Education Act the next year put a close to the often polemical debates over the curriculum. Federal government funding for mathematics, science, and foreign languages gave educators a powerful incentive to abandon life adjustment for the subjects that were regarded as necessary to defending the nation.

Conclusion

Life adjustment education is often interpreted as a failure that led to the decline, if not demise, of progressive education. The life adjustment movement supplied the ammunition that critics of progressivism had been looking for. Leading progressives such as Archibald Anderson, the editor of *Progressive Education* and a respected historian of education, challenged the interpretation that life adjustment was truly progressive. According to Anderson, the progressive orientation, especially Dewey's view, was that the problem-solving mode of Dewey's complete act of thought was transformative in that both the person and the environment were changed as a result of using the scientific method. In contrast, life adjustment was simply a mode of adjusting persons to the status quo. Something a true progressive would oppose.

Despite Anderson's interpretation, critics of the movement saw it as a variant of progressivism that was largely anti-intellectual.

It appeared that the victory over the curriculum went to the critics of the life adjustment movement. The post-Sputnik era, especially the late 1950s and early 1960s saw an emphasis on mathematics, science, and foreign language. As Bestor had urged, academic scholars and scientists in the arts and science became involved in and often directed the development of new curricula—the new mathematics and new science that emphasized the structure of disciplines and the mode of inquiry used in the discipline. Like most curricular trends, the emphasis on subject matter, too, would wane by the late 1960s. However, it would reappear in the 1980s in the aftermath of *A Nation at Risk.*

Though life adjustment disappeared as a dominant movement, it left its impact on secondary education, especially in the growing middle schools. The middle school orientation emphasized that pupils should be introduced to the range of human careers rather than being specifically trained for them vocationally. Many middle schools also stressed the experiential mode of learning that life adjustment educators commended. Further, the ancillary support services found in secondary schools—guidance and counseling—increased.

Notes

[1] George S. Counts, *Dare the School Build a New Social Order?* (New York: John Day Co., 1932). Also, see Gerald L. Gutek, *The Educational Theory of George S. Counts* (Columbus: Ohio State University Press, 1970) and Gutek, *George S. Counts and American Civilization: The Educator as Social Theorist* (Macon, GA: Mercer University Press, 1984).

[2] John Dewey, *Experience and Education: The 60th Anniversary Edition* (West Lafayette, IN: Kappa Delta Phi, 1998).

[3] William C. Bagley, "What is the Crux of the Conflict between the Progressives and Essentialists?" *Educational Administration and Supervision,* 26 (1940), pp. 508–11.

[4] Ibid., pp. 508–9.

[5] Harl R. Douglass, ed., *Education for Life Adjustment: Its Meaning and Implementation* (New York: Ronald Press Co., 1950), pp. 3–4.

[6] U.S. Office of Education, *Life Adjustment for Every Youth* (Washington, DC: Government Printing Office, 1947), pp. 4, 19. Also see, Charles Franzen, "Life Adjustment Education: Basic Concepts, Antecedents, and Later Manifestations," (Unpublished Ph.D. Dissertation, Duke University, 1961), and Dorothy E. Broder, "Life Adjustment Education: An Historical Study of a Program of the United States Office of Education, 1945–54," (Unpublished Ph.D. Dissertation, Teachers College, Columbia University, 1976).

[7] For a treatment of juvenile delinquency, see James Gilbert, *A Cycle of Outrage: America's Reaction to the Juvenile Delinquent in the 1950s* (New York: Oxford University Press, 1986).

[8] Douglass, pp. 4–5.

9 Ibid., p. 5.

10 U.S. Office of Education, *Vitalizing Secondary Education* (Washington, DC: Government Printing Office, 1951), p. 31.

11 For example, see Fr. Bernadine B. Myers, "Life Adjustment Education—A General Statement," *Bulletin of the National Catholic Educational Association* 45 (August 1948) and Sister Mary Janet, "Life Adjustment: Opens New Door to Youth," *Educational Leadership* 7 (December 1954).

12 U.S. Office of Education, pp. 35–36.

13 Douglass, pp. 12–13.

14 Adolph Unruh, "Life Adjustment Education—A Definition," *Progressive Education* 29 (February 1952), p. 138.

15 J. Dan Hull, "Second Commission on Life Adjustment Education Appointed," *School Life* 33 (April 1951), pp. 361–62.

16 For some of the leading criticism of progressive education, see James D. Koerner, ed., *The Case for Basic Education* (Boston: Little, Brown, and Co., 1959); Mortimer Smith, *And Madly Teach: A Layman Looks at Public School Education* (Chicago: Henry Regnery, 1949); Bernard I. Bell, *Crisis in Education* (New York: McGraw-Hill Book Co., 1949); Albert Lynd, *Quakery in the Public Schools* (Boston: Little, Brown, and Co., 1953); Robert M. Hutchins, *The Conflict in Education in a Democratic Society* (New York: Harper and Brothers, 1953).

17 Arthur E. Bestor Jr., *Educational Wastelands: The Retreat from Learning in Our Public Schools* (Urbana: University of Illinois Press, 1953) and *The Restoration of Learning: A Program for Redeeming the Unfulfilled Promise of American Education* (New York: Alfred A. Knopf, 1955).

18 Bestor, *The Restoration of Learning*, pp. 3–4.

19 Ibid., p. 7.

20 Ibid., pp. 35–36.

21 Harold C. Hand, "A Scholar's Documentation," *Educational Theory* 4 (January 1954), pp. 22–23.

22 Max Rafferty, *What They Are Doing to Your Children* (New York: Signet Book Co., 1962).

23 Clay Blair Jr., *The Atomic Submarine and Admiral Rickover* (New York: Henry Holt and Co., 1954).

24 Hyman G. Rickover, *Education and Freedom* (New York: E. P. Dutton and Co., 1959), p. 131.

25 *Report on Russia by Vice Admiral Hyman G. Rickover, USN: Hearings Before the House Committee on Appropriations, 86th Congress* (Washington, DC: U.S. Government Printing Office, 1959).

26 Hyman G. Rickover, *American Education—A National Failure* (New York: E. P. Dutton and Co., 1963).

27 Hyman G. Rickover, *Swiss Schools and Ours: Why Theirs Are Better* (Boston: Little, Brown, and Co., 1962), pp. 30–31.

28 Rickover, *Education and Freedom*, p. 32.

Further Reading

Bagley, William C. *Education and Emergent Man: A Theory of Education with Particular Application to Public Education in the United States*. New York: Thomas Nelson, 1934.

Bell, Bernard I. *Crisis in Education*. New York: McGraw-Hill Book Co., 1949.

Bestor, Arthur E. *Educational Wastelands: The Retreat from Learning in Our Public Schools.* Urbana: University of Illinois Press, 1953.

Bestor, Arthur E. *The Restoration of Learning: A Program for Redeeming the Unfulfilled Promise of American Education.* New York: Alfred A. Knopf, 1956.

Brodinsky, Ben. *Defining the Basics of American Education.* Bloomington, IN: Phi Delta Kappa Educational Foundation, 1977.

Conant, James B. *The American High School Today.* New York: McGraw-Hill Book, Co., 1959.

Counts, George S. *Dare the School Build a New Social Order?* New York: John Day Co., 1930.

Cremin, Lawrence A. *The Transformation of the School: Progressivism in American Education.* New York: Alfred A. Knopf, 1961.

Dewey, John. *Experience and Education: The 60th Anniversary Edition.* West Lafayette, IN: Kappa Delta Pi, 1998.

Gilbert, James. *A Cycle of Outrage: America's Reaction to the Juvenile Delinquent in the 1950s.* New York: Oxford University Press, 1986.

Gutek, Gerald L. *Basic Education: A Historical Perspective.* Bloomington, IN: Phi Delta Kappa Educational Foundation, 1981.

Gutek, Gerald L. *The Educational Theory of George S. Counts.* Columbus: Ohio State University Press, 1970.

Gutek, Gerald L. *George S. Counts and American Civilization.* Macon, GA: Mercer University Press, 1984.

Hutchins, Robert M. *The Conflict in Education in a Democratic Society.* New York: Harper and Bros., 1953.

Kandel, Isaac L. *The Cult of Uncertainty.* New York: Macmillan, 1934.

Kandel, Isaac L. *William Chandler Bagley: Stalwart Educator.* New York: Teachers College Press, 1961.

Keats, John. *Schools without Scholars.* Boston: Houghton-Mifflin Co., 1958.

Koerner, James D. *The Case for Basic Education.* Boston: Little, Brown, and Co., 1959.

Lynd, Albert. *Quackery in the Public Schools.* Boston: Little, Brown and Co., 1953.

Perkinson, Henry J. *The Imperfect Panacea: American Faith in Education, 1865–1965.* New York: Random House, 1968.

Prosser, Charles A. *Secondary Education and Life.* Cambridge: Harvard University Press, 1939.

Rafferty, Max. *Suffer Little Children.* New York: Signet Book Co., 1962.

Rickover, H. G. *American Education—A National Failure.* New York: E.P. Dutton and Co., 1963.

Rickover, H. G. *Education and Freedom.* New York: E.P. Dutton and Co., 1959.

Rickover, H. G. *Swiss Schools and Ours: Why Theirs Are Better.* Boston: Atlantic-Little, Brown and Co., 1962.

Smith, Mortimer. *And Madly Teach: A Layman Looks at Public School Education.* Chicago: Henry Regnery, 1949.

Woodring, Paul. *Let's Talk Sense about Our Schools.* New York: McGraw-Hill, 1953.

5

The Cold War, Anti-Communism, McCarthyism, and Education

The decade from 1945 to 1955 marked one of the most intense periods of antisubversive, anti-Communist investigations and activities in the United States. This ten-year span, however, was not the only time when such a sociopolitical and educational phenomenon occurred.[1] Some historians cite the Salem witchcraft trials of 1692 as the earliest example of many "witch-hunting" activities on American soil.[2] (The playwright Arthur Miller wrote a thinly veiled drama about the Salem happenings, *The Crucible*, which was in fact a criticism of the 1950s' anti-Communist investigations.) In the 1840s, the intense nativist "Know Nothing" movement directed against Catholics and the foreign-born generated wholesale xenophobia and anti-Catholic hysteria. Later, as a result of fears of a world revolution due to the Bolshevik seizure of power in Russia in 1917, U.S. Attorney General A. Mitchell Palmer, in 1919, ordered the Federal Bureau of Investigation (FBI) to compile files on radical groups and individuals. The FBI compiled a list of 200,000 suspects. The post–World War I "red scare" was conducted with raids on suspect organizations and persons and with the deportation of many individuals identified as subversives.

World War II saw the enactment of antisubversive legislation which, though directed against German and Japanese espionage, set precedents for the anti-Communist investigations of the late 1940s and 1950s. In 1939, Congress enacted the Hatch Act, which prohibited federal employees from membership in any political party or organization advocating the overthrow of the U.S. constitutional form of government. This was followed by the Smith Act in 1940, directed against seditious activities.

The anti-Communist period and its origins and aftermath are especially significant in American educational history. This stressful period of questioned loyalty reveals the fragility of academic freedom, even in a democratic society, when that society faces threats to its existence, both real and imagined. The decade of the 1950s also shows the susceptibility of educational institutions and educators to the prevailing popular climate. Much of the antisubversive investigations focused on higher education. However, elementary and secondary schools, too, felt the impact of antisubversive investigators. Public school personnel were subjected to loyalty oaths and to intense criticism regarding their loyalty. In a few districts, administrators and teachers were dismissed for what was loosely defined as un-American activities, which, in addition to former membership in the Communist Party or its "front organizations," took the form of ambiguous charges such as being "soft on Communism" or associating with "fellow travelers," people who were sympathetic with the doctrines of Communism but were not members of the Communist Party. Zealous anti-Communists scrutinized textbooks and other curriculum materials, looking for hints of Communism.

We begin with some definitions that are useful in viewing the series of events that began in the late 1940s and continued until the collapse of the Soviet Union in 1990. These definitions provide lenses by which to view the events of the 1950s in particular, as well as those that would persist for the following three and one-half decades.

As discussed previously, the term "cold war" refers to the high state of international tension that existed as the United States and the Union of Soviet Socialist Republics became the world's two military super powers, each of which had the capacity to unleash a nuclear war. An important element in the cold war, not present at other times of international tension, was the atomic and then the hydrogen bomb. (See chapter 3 for a discussion of civil defense education related to atomic attack.) The United States, for a short time from 1945 to 1949, held a monopoly on atomic weapons. This monopoly was lost, however, when the USSR successfully detonated an atomic bomb. Part of the scenario in the Soviets' atomic program was that they received secret information about the bomb from Claude Fuchs, a scientist who had worked on the U.S. atomic project at Los Alamos. The fear of Communist spies, aiding the Soviet Union, then became part of the cold war series of events. Spying for the Soviet Union, in the minds of many Americans and especially anti-Communist investigators, became synonymous with either past or present membership in the U.S. Communist Party or in organizations identified as pro-Communist.

Many of the international events of the years from 1947 through 1990 can be interpreted through the lenses of "bipolarity," which means the world was divided into alignments based on two poles: one pole was located in the United States, the leader of the parliamentary democracies, and the other was in the Soviet Union, the leader of the Communist nations. "Anti-Communism" refers to the dominant ideological phenomenon that drove America politically, economically, and to a large extent educationally, during the cold war era, particularly from 1947 through the early 1960s. Although not unique to that period, the anti-Communist temperament meant that many policies, both international and domestic in the United States, originated in the general context of opposition to Communism, seen as the regnant ideology in the Soviet Union and as the rival to American democracy and capitalism in the world.

Although Senator Joseph McCarthy, the junior U.S. senator from Wisconsin, was but one of a number of leading investigators of what was alleged to be the "Communist Conspiracy" in the United States, the term "McCarthyism" is used generically to explain the virulent anti-Communist mood and movement of the 1950s. For hunters of subversives, education, in general, and institutions of higher education, in particular, were targets for anti-Communist investigations. The anti-subversive investigations, however, began before McCarthy took a role and continued after his censure by the U.S. Senate.

The cold war with its bipolar rivalry between the United States and the Soviet Union and the prevailing mood of anti-Communism had serious implications for education. These implications ranged from urging schools to take civil defense measures to protect teachers and students from atomic attack, to the development of units and lessons illustrating the menace of Communism to the American way of life, to investigations of teachers and professors accused of Communist Party membership or sympathy.

To develop our discussion of the period we shall: (1) examine the situation among professional educators regarding the Soviet Union and Communism prior to the cold war, particularly during the 1920s, 1930s, and 1940s; (2) discuss the relevance of certain characteristics of the cold war for education; (3) present the outlines of the anti-Communism of the McCarthy period of the 1950s; (4) discuss antisubversive activities in the states; and (5) look at the response of educational organizations to these investigations.

Professional Educators, the Soviet Union, and Communism in the 1920s, 1930s, and 1940s

While the general perception of the Bolshevik Revolution and the coming of Lenin's Communists to power in the Soviet Union in 1917 was one of general suspicion, there were Americans, especially leftist liberals, socialists, and others, who viewed the Soviet experiment with Marxism with keen and often supportive interest.

After sustaining itself through a cruel civil war, the new Soviet regime, first under Vladimir Lenin and then under his successor, Joseph Stalin, embarked on a pervasive campaign of five-year plans, designed to transform the USSR from Europe's slumbering agricultural backwater into a modern industrial nation. Stalin's five-year plans emphasized the theme of centralized national planning in which the efforts of all sectors of Soviet society and economy, including education, schools, and teachers, were mobilized to achieve modernization. In turn, during the 1920s, the Soviets showed interest in some aspects of American progressive education, especially Dewey's emphasis on socialized learning and Kilpatrick's group-centered project method which seemed suited to the Soviet emphasis on collectivism.

During the earlier years of the Great Depression of the 1930s, especially from 1930 to 1937, some of the leaders of the social reconstructionist-wing of progressive education showed a keen interest in events in the Soviet Union. The case of George S. Counts, professor of education at Columbia University's Teachers College and author of *Dare the School Build a New Social Order*, editor of *The Social Frontier*, and director of research of the American Historical Society's Commission on the Social Studies in the Schools is particularly revealing. Counts, who was labeled a dangerous radical by the Hearst Press, argued, during the depression years, that teachers in the United States should join with other progressive forces in building a new social order and that schools no longer should reflect the status quo but should become originative agencies of deliberate social change. While Counts did not spell out precisely the nature of this projected social change, he argued that the age of individualism was obsolete and that the social patterns of the future would be collectivist and corporativist. American educators should work to ensure that the coming new social order would be one of "democratic collectivism." Further, the school curriculum should stress the need for comprehensive planning so that the scientific, technological, and economic features of the new era would be framed within a democratic social and political context.

A further dimension of Counts's career as a professional educator was his interest in comparative education, especially Soviet education. Counts made a series of investigative research trips to the Soviet Union and recorded his impressions in a series of books that began with the early years of the Communist experiment and went through the years of the cold war until his death in 1974. After his first visit, Counts was highly impressed with the Soviet efforts at centralized planning and the mobilization of all segments of the society, including education, to advance modernization. He compared the Soviets' concerted planning with the persistence of an obsolete individualism in the United States and the country's inability to climb out of the economic morass of the depression with its massive unemployment.

Upon subsequent research trips to the USSR, Counts seriously began to revise his interpretation of the Communist experiment in the Soviet Union. As a result of Stalin's purges, many of the Soviet educators whom he met on his earlier travels in the USSR had become nonpersons or had completely disappeared. He lost his optimism about the Soviet experiment. Gone were the possibilities for positive social change. He came to see Soviet Communism, as shaped by Lenin and Stalin, as a tyrannical species of revolutionary Machiavellianism in which the doctrine that the end justified the means was brutally applied in purges and gulags.[3]

Not only did Counts reinterpret his original views of the Soviet Union, but he also came to see the American Communist Party as playing a sinister role in demoralizing American liberalism, socialism, and trade unionism. Rather than seeing the Communist Party like another typical political party, Counts came to see it as a domestic tool of the Soviet Union. He found that the Communist Party, through its cells in the New York City teachers unions, had gained control of the American Federation of Teachers. As the candidate of the anti-Communist forces in the union, he stood up to and defeated the Communist faction and then purged the Communists from key positions in the union. As early as 1943, Counts and his progressive Teachers College colleague, John Childs, warned that the American Communist Party would pose a serious threat to a genuine understanding between the United States and the USSR in the post–World War II era.[4]

While Counts is an especially interesting case study in how an American progressive educator turned from being sympathetic to becoming adversarial to the Soviet Union and to Communism, his case is not unique. Many American liberals, including progressive educators, underwent the same kind of experience. John Dewey, the leading voice of experimentalism, presided over a mock trial of Leon Trotsky, the former associate of Lenin, who had been purged and exiled from the Soviet Union as a "capitalist agent." Dewey's tribunal exonerated the former old Bolshevik from the charges.[5] Sidney Hook, originally a Marxist philosopher who sought to reconcile Marxism and pragmatism, experienced a kind of intellectual conversion experience that turned him into one of the nation's committed anti-Communists. While these liberal progressives became "convinced" anti-Communists, the conservatives in the United States had been opposed to Marxism, Communism, and the Soviet Union all along.

The liberal antagonism to Stalinism was acerbated in the summer of 1939 when the two archrivals, Nazi Germany and the Communist USSR, signed the Molotov-Ribbentrop agreement, a nonagression pact. The Nazi-Soviet agreement suddenly reversed the antagonism that had existed between Nazi Germany and the USSR, when, for example, Hitler's speeches had excoriated the Bolshevik USSR and Nazi Germany had outlawed that country's Communist Party. From 1936 to 1939, during the Spanish civil war between Francisco Franco's fascist Nationalists and the Republicans, both Hitler and Stalin had dispatched military units to support the conflicting combatants. Hitler and Benito Mussolini, the dictator of fascist Italy, had sent military units to aid Franco. The USSR, in turn, aided the Republic, which was supported by a Spanish coalition of liberals, socialists, communists, and anarchists. Thus, from the mid-1930s until 1939, Stalin had encouraged Popular Front movements in which Communists were instructed to cooperate with liberals and socialists against fascism and Nazism. In the United States, the defense of the Spanish Republic against fascism drew strong support from progressives, liberals, and socialists, who often found themselves, cooperating with members of the American Communist Party in a common cause. Liberals and socialists, however, in a state of profound shock when in 1939 the USSR suddenly changed its policy toward Nazi Germany, felt betrayed by Stalin's duplicity. Immediately, with the signing of the German-Soviet nonaggression pact, the American Communist Party altered its position in conformity to the Party line emanating from Moscow. When Germany invaded Poland on September 1, 1939, the Soviet Union invaded the hapless country two weeks later. The Molotov-Ribbentrop Pact contained secret provisions that divided Poland between the two bordering totalitarian giants. Any remnants of liberal friendship toward the Soviet Union were further eroded when the Soviet Union invaded Finland later in 1939.

The German invasion of Poland marked the beginning of World War II. France and the United Kingdom, allied with Poland, entered the war against Germany. After the German conquest of France, Belgium, the Netherlands, Denmark, and Norway in 1940, Britain, against great odds, struggled alone. Then on June 22, 1941, the Germans struck east, attacking the USSR. The German invasion brought the USSR into the war as one of the Allied powers.

While World War II was waging in Europe, Americans, deeply divided, debated the role to be played by the United States. Isolationists, organized as the American First Committee, opposed American assistance to the Allies. Countering them was the Committee to Defend America by Aiding the Allies, which supported stopping Hitler's agression by providing assistance to the Allies, especially the United Kingdom. The debate was suddenly ended by the Japanese attack on Pearl Harbor on December 7, 1941, which brought the United States into the conflict. In 1941, the United States and the USSR, along with the United Kingdom and other nations, were allied against Nazi Germany in Europe. (The USSR did not declare war on Japan until 1945.) Now that the Soviet Union was allied with the United States in mortal combat against Hitler's Germany, old fears were temporarily put aside.

For the war's duration, domestic debates about the USSR and Communism were stilled. Official U.S. policy and wartime propaganda cast the USSR in a friendly light. The Hollywood film, *Mission to Moscow*, depicted an American diplomat's travels through the USSR. The film showed the Soviets as an energetic and determined people who were using all of their resources to resist the Nazi invasion of their homeland. Even the Soviet dictator Joseph Stalin was depicted as a benign leader, "Uncle Joe," who was saving his country from Hitler's tyranny. John Dewey, however, running against the tide of public opinion, was openly critical of the film and the book upon which it was based.[6]

Early Developments in the Cold War

When World War II ended and rivalries mounted between the former allies, the United States and the USSR, fears of a militarily powerful Soviet Union and a Communist conspiracy resurfaced as the cold war began. Americans heard and responded to Winston Churchill's warning that an "iron curtain" from Stettin in the Baltic to Trieste in Adriatic had fallen across a divided Europe.

Revisionist historians contend that President Harry S. Truman, though a vigorous anti-McCarthyite, contributed to the antisubversive mood of the late 1940s and 1950s by issuing in 1947 Executive Order 9835, which established a loyalty program for federal employees. Truman most likely was trying to set in place internal security measures to forestall irresponsible witch-hunts.[7] His critics contend, however, that Truman's actions had the opposite effect in that they could be interpreted as conceding the existence of a serious security problem.

Conflicting Ideologies

Along with its military security and great power rivalry aspects, the cold war was heavily ideological. Indeed, its national security and ideological characteristics were so interpenetrating that they often blurred needed distinctions in policy making. After World War II, the United States and the Union of Soviet Socialist Republics were the world's two great military powers, each of which possessed a nuclear arsenal of mass destruction. U.S. efforts to contain Soviet expansion through diplomacy and military alliances was not a new feature in world affairs. However, the threat of nuclear war was a new, greatly

feared, and little understood feature. This threat was so anxiety pro-
ducing that it could be referred to as generating a worldwide *angst*.

The Soviet Union's revolutionary origins and development were
guided not only by military considerations but also by its official and
pervasive Marxist-Leninist ideology, known worldwide as Communism. According to Lenin's interpretation of Marxist dialectic, Communism, represented by the Soviet Union as the world's foremost Communist country, would inevitably, irresistibly, and eventually triumph
over capitalism, represented by the United States. The United States,
in turn, portrayed itself as defending democracy and freedom against
Soviet totalitarianism. The struggle between the United States and the
USSR was portrayed as a struggle for the hearts and minds of men and
women. In this struggle, education was proclaimed to be a weapon in
each nation's ideological arsenal. Each nation used persuasive information and propaganda techniques to win adherents to its cause
throughout the world. In the psychology of the cold war, the term
"mind control" and "brainwashing" emerged as key terms. Education
was regarded as the key tool in the ideological struggle.

Establishment of the PRC and the Korean Conflict

While the U.S. was developing a successful containment policy for
the Soviet Union in Europe, two major events in Asia produced unsettling reverberations at home: the establishment of the People's Republic of China (PRC) in 1949 and the Korean War, 1950–52. The United
States supported the Kuomintang, or Nationalist, government of its
wartime ally, Chiang Kai-shek, in the Chinese civil war against the
Communist forces led by Mao Tse-tung. The Communist victory and
proclamation of the PRC in 1949 sent shock waves through the United
States. For years, a group, identified as the "China Lobby," composed
of Christian missionaries, businesspeople, and some West Coast politicians, steadfastly supporting Chiang Kai-shek's government, created
a favorable image of the Nationalist Party in China. Other commentators on China, however, had indicated that Chiang's government, growing increasingly ineffective and corrupt, would likely fall to Mao's
forces unless significant reforms were undertaken. In the political
repercussions that followed Chiang's flight from China's mainland and
refuge on Taiwan (Formosa), charges were made by critics of the Truman administration that Chiang had been sold out by traitors, or at
least pro-Communist sympathizers, in the U.S. State Department.
These charges would become an important part of the antisubversive
investigations of the 1950s.

The Korean War, 1950–1952, had important effects on the American psyche regarding the power of psychological persuasion. Familiar
with the unconditional surrender terms of World War II, the American

public had great difficulty in understanding and accepting the limited goals and operations of the Korean conflict. A dramatic event would be President Truman's firing of the popular General MacArthur as Commander of UN troops, principally U.S. and South Korean forces, over the scope of military objectives in Korea. (See chapter 1 for MacArthur's role in the occupation of Japan.) The protracted military conflict in Korea caused political recriminations domestically. A small group of American military prisoners of war had made propaganda speeches for their North Korean and Chinese Communist captors. It was charged by some critics that American schools had not prepared these defectors to withstand Communist brainwashing. Too much progressive education had not prepared them to stand up for their country nor given them the kind of patriotic education needed to best the Communists in debate. An argument was mounted that, though simple on the surface, had subtle interpretive underpinnings. American schools needed to be proactive in the ideological battle against Communism. They had to educate students about the evils of Communism without conveying sympathy for its theories and doctrines.

Anti-Communist Educational Critics

As indicated in chapter 4, the 1950s was a period of intense educational criticism. Note the sharp debates between the proponents of life adjustment education and academic critics such as Robert Hutchins and Arthur E. Bestor. There were also critics of the schools who felt that too many professors, administrators, and teachers were "soft on Communism." However, academic critics like Hutchins and Bestor were decidedly different from the antisubversive critics and had nothing in common with them. As noted later in this chapter, Hutchins successfully defended the University of Chicago faculty against charges of Communist subversion. Bestor, too, a long-time member of the American Civil Liberties Union (ACLU) and a noted historian of the U.S. Constitution, staunchly defended civil rights and processes. We turn here, to those critics who were part of the antisubversive milieu rather than to the academic critics discussed in chapter 4. It might be noted that Max Rafferty had taken an anti-Communist stance that was similar in some ways to the antisubversive critics. Although Admiral Rickover was not part of the antisubversive group of educational critics, he did relate education to national security issues. (See chapter 4 for this discussion.)

There were three groups of critics of American education that surfaced as part of the antisubversive milieu of the late 1940s and 1950s: (1) historically patriotic organizations, (2) organizations formed specifically to counter the perceived Communist threat, and (3) politicians who called for antisubversive investigations. Historically patriotic groups and organizations such as the American Legion and the Daughters of the American Revolution wanted schools to teach more "Americanism" and sponsor more patriotic activities. At times, these organizations expressed concern about and called for investigations of Communism in the schools. They also recommended courses on patriotism to counteract the Communist threat. However, their zeal for patriotic Americanism was ongoing, really not born in but rather intensified by the cold war.

Some new organizations formed in specific reaction to what their members saw as a Communist conspiracy in the schools. Such organizations were the National Council for American Education and the Committee for Constitutional Government, which distributed literature throughout the country. Allen Zoll's National Council produced pamphlets and materials that warned Americans that the Communists' chief objective was to infiltrate and control American education. Zoll, who had long been associated with right-wing causes and organizations such as the American Patriots, alleged that John Dewey and other progressive educators, by stressing cooperative group learning and relativist values, had prepared the way for Communist infiltration of the schools. Antisubversive critics such as Zoll claimed that progressives either unwittingly or consciously had undermined the learning of basic skills and patriotic values in the public schools.[8]

There were national, state, and local politicians who accused the educational profession of harboring Communists and Communist sympathizers. Although the most infamous of these politicians was Senator Joseph McCarthy (Republican from Wisconsin), there were others such as Senator Pat McCarran (Democrat from Nevada), William Jenner (Republican from Indiana), and Congressman Harold Velde (Republican from Illinois). Richard Nixon, gaining national prominence as a member of the House Committee investigating Alger Hiss, a State Department employee accused of being a Soviet spy, was elected senator from California and then elected vice president of the United States in 1952. Illinois state Senator Paul Broyles, Republican, led antisubversive investigations in his state. These politicians used their positions to introduce legislation for investigations of subversives in universities, colleges, and schools and then were often named to well-publicized investigating commissions and committees.

Because of the interrelated nature of the cold war, international and domestic issues were often linked. Investigations of educators had both an international and a local-domestic frame of reference. Events like the fall of China or defections in the Korean War, occurring thousand of miles away, could be linked with what was allegedly happening in the state university or the local school district. In turn, what was regarded as too much progressive education, not enough attention to the basics, or reading materials that did not stress old-fashioned patriotism in the local school, could be criticized as having dire implications for America's global security.

The House Committee on Un-American Activities

Although McCarthy was but one of many players in the anti-Communist and antisubversive activities of the 1950s, it was his recklessness, ruthlessness, and disregard for individual rights and due process that made him the caricature for the period. However, antisubversive investigations at the national level predated McCarthy. In this section, we review the stage-setting investigations of the U.S. House of Representatives Un-American Activities Committee (HUAC).

In the late 1930s, the U.S. House of Representatives created a special Committee on Un-American Activities, chaired by Congressman Martin Dies, a conservative Texas Democrat. HUAC was charged with investigating subversive organizations and individuals. Like other committees of the U.S. Senate and House of Representatives, its mission was to conduct investigations to gather information for use in drafting legislation. Juridically, committees such as HUAC were not courts, nor were they legally empowered to conduct trials. However, HUAC's inquiry techniques tended to be like those in a court trial rather than those used in mere information gathering. Its methods established the style for subsequent anti-Communist subversive hearings.

Important among these precedents was the right of witnesses to invoke the Constitution's Fifth Amendment protection against self-incrimination. The sole way in which a witness legally could refuse to answer questions about his or her political associations and associates was to invoke the Fifth Amendment. However, a witness could not choose to answer questions selectively. If he or she answered one question, the witness had to answer all that were asked; refusal to do so would lead to a citation for contempt of Congress. Even if some witnesses would have been willing to answer questions about their own political activities, several did not want to implicate others by naming associates.[9] Witnesses' refusal to testify seemed to rest on two motives: (1) they believed the committee was making an unwarranted and illegal invasion of their rights to engage in political activity; (2) they believed that by identifying their associates they were contributing to the "guilt by association" technique, insidious to the period. Committee investigators condemned "taking the Fifth Amendment," saying that any good American would testify willingly about the Communist Party, which was a threat to U.S. security. Some, like Senator McCarthy, would characterize witnesses who refused to testify as "Fifth Amendment Communists."

Another feature of anti-Communist investigations was the investigators' reliance on the testimony of former Communists, people who had defected from the Party, as expert witnesses.[10] Investigators claimed that these expert witnesses, with their thorough knowledge of the Communist Party apparatus, were performing an invaluable national service. Their critics either saw them as opportunists or as political zealots who traded one kind of Machiavellianism for another.

HUAC Hollywood Hearings

One of HUAC's dramatic investigations focused on the Hollywood film industry.[11] Generally, the film industry was regarded as being more liberal than conservative. Further, a number of well-known actors were also known as supporters of liberal and left-wing causes. Anticipating the coming HUAC investigations, key producers, the heads of major motion picture studios, claiming to have nothing to hide, invited the committee to come to Hollywood to conduct its investigation. The film studio owners and producers tended to be more conservative politically than the more liberal screenwriters, actors, and actresses, who would be subject to investigation.

Already briefed by the Federal Bureau of Investigation, in 1947 the HUAC investigators held hearings in Hollywood, determined to concentrate their investigation on a group of "leftist" screenwriters, first called the Hollywood Nineteen and then when its ranks thinned by defection the Hollywood Eleven and Hollywood Ten. First, experts on Communism were called by the committee to establish that the American Communist Party was part of the international Communist conspiracy orchestrated by Moscow. Some of these expert witnesses were former Communists, who left the Party and then became professional anti-Communist experts, frequently testifying before investigating committees. Next, conservative right-wing actors were called to testify about their own patriotism and antagonism to Communists in the film industry. Among the witnesses was Ronald Reagan, the future conservative Republican president, then leader of the Screen Actors Guild, the actors' union. Interestingly, Reagan, then a liberal, testified that while he opposed Communism he did not believe that any political party should be outlawed. Then the interrogators called the screenwriters, their principal targets, to the stand to testify.

The HUAC investigation of Hollywood was significant in that it set the tenor for other investigations. The screenwriters, the Hollywood Ten, decided not to cooperate with HUAC, which they believed was an unconstitutional body exceeding its legislated scope and violating their civil rights, especially freedoms of expression and association. The leading question put to the witnesses was, "Are you now or have you ever been a member of the Communist Party?" If the witness responded yes, then he or she would be required to name others who had been associated with him or her in Party membership. The screenwriters refused to answer questions and unsuccessfully attempted to read statements challenging the committee's constitutionality and right to question them. Their only way out was to take the Fifth Amendment and refuse to answer on the grounds that it would tend to incriminate them. Committee Chairman J. Parnell Thomas, calling them unpatriotic, would gavel them down. Then, they would be charged with contempt of Congress.

The Hollywood Ten appealed their case to the U.S. Supreme Court. Believing that the HUAC proceedings were unconstitutional and that they violated their First Amendment rights, the screenwriters raised a legal challenge that they hoped would overturn the contempt charges. The Court, by refusing to hear the case, upheld HUAC's authority. Eight of the Hollywood Ten were given one-year prison sentences. Two, Herbert Bibermen and Edward Dmytryk, received six-month sentences. Under intense pressure, Dmytryk reversed himself and provided names of other suspected Communists.

The consequences of HUAC's Hollywood hearings were significant for establishing the pattern for anti-Communist investigations throughout the 1950s: (1) leading anti-Communist authorities, including former Communists who had quit the Party, were called to give "expert" testimony about the Communist conspiracy; (2) suspected or former members of the Communist Party, who were under investigation, would be called to testify about their membership in or association with the Party; they usually took the Fifth Amendment and refused to cooperate with the investigating committees; (3) uncooperative witnesses were held in contempt of Congress, lost their jobs, and were unable to find employment in their professions; (4) vocal members of investigating committees gained a national political prominence that often took them to a higher office. This strategy would be played out over and over again, especially in institutions of higher education. Finally, as indicated, Hollywood had been a pace-setting and style-making environment for the nation culturally. Now a chill fell over the film industry, which avoided making motion pictures of serious social significance, turning to light entertainment or films about the Communist menace to national security, such as *The Red Menace* and *I Was a Communist for the FBI.*

The Hiss-Chambers Case

Just as the film industry had been put on trial, the anti-Communist investigations fell heavily on leading intellectuals, particularly on those employed or once employed by the federal government. In 1946, HUAC heard testimony from Elizabeth Bentley, a former Communist who was now an expert witness on the Communist conspiracy, that a pro-Communist group had attempted to infiltrate the federal government. Among those identified as being part of the group were some prominent individuals who had served as administrators in the federal government, such as Alger Hiss and Harry Dexter White, an assistant secretary of the Treasury. Bentley's testimony had important political implications in that it suggested that the New Deal had been infiltrated by Communists.

J. David Whittaker Chambers was called by the Committee, claiming that he could corroborate Bentley's testimony, especially about Alger Hiss, a prominent New Deal appointee. Chambers was a graduate of Columbia University and a senior editor of *Time* magazine. In his testimony, Chambers admitted that he had been a member of the Communist Party from 1924 to 1938, when he left the Party. Chambers further identified Alger Hiss as an associate and member of the Party. Hiss had served in the upper echelons of the State Department until 1946. Hiss quickly denied the allegations and volunteered to testify before the committee. Appearing before the committee, Hiss, refuting Chambers's allegations, denied that he had ever been a Communist or had ever known Whittaker Chambers. At first, Hiss appeared to be a highly creditable witness. However, it became apparent that either Chambers or Hiss was lying. Hiss, in his second appearance before the committee, seemed less sure of himself.

As the Hiss-Chambers controversy unfolded, Richard M. Nixon, future president of the United States, then a Republican congressman from California and a member of HUAC, began to take a leading role in the investigation, particularly in what came to be called the "pumpkin papers" episode. Found on Chambers's farm, in a hollowed-out pumpkin, was a cache of microfilmed State Department documents on the Far East, which appeared to have been typed on a typewriter once owned by Hiss. Although Hiss continued to proclaim his innocence, he had two trials for perjury. The first resulted in a hung jury, but he was convicted of perjury at the retrial and sentenced to a five-year prison term.

The Hiss-Chambers episode had important political and psychological fallout that contributed to the mood of the period. In many respects, Hiss personified the kind of person most despised by political conservatives.[12] Educated in prestigious Eastern institutions and then serving in government during the New Deal, he appeared to be a liberal intellectual who was "soft on Communism," if not a "fellow traveler."

Chambers became associated with William F. Buckley and served as an editor of *The National Review*. Nixon's role in the investigation gave him national prominence. He was elected to the U.S. Senate in

1950, defeating Helen Gahagen Douglas, the wife of actor Melvyn Douglas. In 1952, Nixon, the running mate of Dwight Eisenhower, was elected vice president of the United States and in 1968 would win the office of president.

The Hiss-Chambers episode occurred against a backdrop of momentous international affairs that contributed to a mounting anxiety about the Communist threat to U.S. national security. In 1949, the Soviet Union successfully exploded an atomic bomb, ending the United States's nuclear monopoly. In the same year, Chiang Kai-shek's Nationalist regime fell in China. The defeated Chiang, supported by the United States, took refuge on the island of Taiwan. Mao Tse Tung proclaimed the Communist People's Republic of China. In 1950, the United States was embroiled in a limited war defending the Republic of South Korea against Communist North Korea.

In 1953, Representative Harold B. Velde (Republican from Illinois), upon becoming chairman of HUAC, announced that he was commencing an anti-Communist investigation of public education, especially state colleges and universities. Although his investigations produced no substantive results, they placed the investigation of higher education at center stage, encouraging state and local investigations and causing sharp divisions in the higher education community.[13]

McCarthy and McCarthyism

Senator Joseph R. McCarthy (1908–57), Republican from Wisconsin, was elected to the U.S. Senate in 1946, gained prominence as the country's leading and most publicized anti-Communist investigator, and was censured by the Senate in 1954. The high-tide of McCarthyism was from 1950 to 1954. McCarthy, on February 9, 1950, in a speech in Wheeling, West Virginia, grabbed headlines by claiming to have a list of 205 State Department employees who were members of the Communist Party.[14] A special subcommittee of the Senate Foreign Relations Committee, chaired by the respected Senator Millard Tydings (Democrat from Maryland), was established to investigate McCarthy's startling allegations. The Democrats on the committee believed that McCarthy's charges were unfounded and that they could disprove them quickly and send McCarthy into political oblivion. However, they severely underestimated McCarthy and his techniques. On March 21, 1950, McCarthy announced that he had evidence to "unmask the top Russian agent, the boss of Alger Hiss."[15]

McCarthy's target, Owen Lattimore, who was once affiliated with the Institute of Pacific Relations, was director of the Walter Hines Page School of International Relations at Johns Hopkins University. An aca-

Senator Joseph McCarthy, who conducted anti-Communist investigations during the 1950s. Today, the style of these types of investigations bears his name, McCarthyism. (Reproduction from the Collections of the Library of Congress.)

demic expert on China, Lattimore, in 1941–42, had been an American adviser to Chiang Kai-shek. In his reports, Lattimore had warned the U.S. government that Chiang's politically corrupt and increasingly inept regime was unlikely to survive against Mao Tse-tung's Communists. Lattimore, like Hiss, was an Eastern intellectual, the kind of figure that conservatives like McCarthy intensely disliked. McCarthy claimed that he had a star witness, a former Communist, Louis Budenz, who would substantiate the case against Lattimore.

On July 17, the Tydings Committee ended its five-month investigation of Lattimore and what was called the "Amerasia Case."[16] The Committee, controlled by a Democratic majority, rejected McCarthy's allegations, charging that McCarthy had perpetrated "a fraud and hoax on the Senate of the United States and the American people."[17] However, the Senate voted to accept the Tydings report on a straight party-line vote, with Democrats accepting and Republicans rejecting it. McCarthy showed his political muscle by campaigning against Tydings, in Maryland, who was defeated for reelection.

Although McCarthy could not prove his allegations against Lattimore, his accusations had won him newspaper headlines and national prominence. A Gallup Poll showed that 40 percent of those polled believed McCarthy was doing a commendable service for the nation. McCarthy was now being described as the country's leading anti-Communist investigator by supportive journalists such as Walter Winchell, Westbook Pegler, and H. V. Kaltenborn.[18]

Lattimore was also ordered to testify by the Permanent Internal Security Committee of the Senate Judiciary Committee, chaired by Senator Patrick McCarran (Democrat from Nevada) during the 82nd Congress. McCarran's successor as chair in the next Congress, Senator William Jenner (Republican from Indiana), continued the hearings and also conducted investigations of alleged subversive activities in education. McCarran, like McCarthy, was a determined anti-Communist investigator. But unlike the Wisconsin Senator, McCarran was more effective. Under interrogation, Lattimore's testimony appeared inconsistent, and he was charged with perjury. These charges were later dismissed by a federal district court as being without foundation. During his ordeal, Lattimore was suspended from his duties, with pay, by Johns Hopkins University. He later regained his position as professor of history, but the School of International Studies, which he once directed, was closed. McCarthy continued to attack Lattimore and sought to connect other professors and diplomats with him. Lattimore would leave Johns Hopkins to become a scholar-in-residence at the University of Leeds, in the United Kingdom.[19]

In 1952 Dwight Eisenhower, a Republican, won the presidential election, defeating Adlai Stevenson, his Democratic opponent. (For the Eisenhower administration, see chapter 3.) Now, the political circumstances had changed in that if McCarthy were to continue his activities he would be investigating his own party, the Republicans. In the new Congress, McCarthy was named chairman of the Permanent Investigating Subcommittee on the Government Operations Committee, a position he used for mounting further anti-Communist investigations.

In September 1953, McCarthy and his new chief counsel, Roy Cohn, a tough and determined investigator, began an investigation of alleged subversive activities at the Army Signal Corps at Fort Monmouth, New Jersey, a probe that would bring unsuspecting people under attack and put McCarthy on a collision course with the U.S. Army.[20] During one of the hearings that resulted from the McCarthy-Cohn probe, McCarthy berated General Ralph Zwicker, commander at Fort Monmouth, for his negligence in the investigation process.

Then, a singular event that took but a few minutes showed McCarthy's ruthlessness. Despite an agreement arranged between Cohn and Joseph Welch, the Army's chief attorney, McCarthy began an attack on a young member of Welch's law firm, Frederick Fisher, who as a young student was briefly a member of the National Lawyers Guild, an organization listed as subversive by HUAC. McCarthy's attack was so vicious that Welch, an articulate and highly respected attorney, responded to McCarthy, saying, "You have done enough. Have you no sense of decency, sir, at long last? Have you left no sense of decency?" The audience, momentarily stunned, burst into sustained applause. McCarthy seemed not to comprehend the turn of events, but his aide, Cohn, showed embarrassment. McCarthy had met his match in Welch.[21] On June 17, 1954, the hearings ended, after twenty-two sessions and 3,000 pages of testimony. A member of the committee, Senator McClellan (Democrat from Arkansas), who had often challenged McCarthy, called the hearings "one of the most disgraceful episodes in the history of our government."[22]

The Army-McCarthy hearings set in motion the last events in Joe McCarthy's career. In October 1954, a special Senate committee, formed to consider a resolution of censure, recommended that McCarthy be censured on two counts: his abuse of General Zwicker and his contempt of a Senate committee. On December 2, the Senate, in a sixty-seven to twenty-two vote, voted to censure McCarthy. Although he remained in the Senate, McCarthy was clearly a broken man. His health, aggravated by heavy drinking, deteriorated. He died on May 2, 1957.

Former President Truman, often the recipient of attacks by McCarthy, perhaps best summed up McCarthy, the man, and McCarthyism, the movement, as "descendants of the ancient order of witch-hunters" who had "no more respect for the due process of law and order than the communists they say they hate but whose methods they copy." Truman warned that their wild charges damaged the "faith of Americans in their country's institutions" and "undermined the respect and confidence Americans must have in one another."[23]

The States, Anti-Communism, and Educational Targets

The HUAC and McCarthy investigations provided a national backdrop for the anti-Communist inquiries of the 1950s. While the dramatic, headline-capturing allegations were made nationally, the substantive actions in education came at the state, local, and institutional level.

Many states passed legislation that public employees, including teachers and professors, sign loyalty oaths, affirming they were not members of subversive organizations seeking to overthrow the federal and state governments. Taking these oaths was usually a condition for being employed or for continuing employment in public agencies and educational institutions. Along with loyalty oaths, state legislators established investigating committees to identify alleged subversives, especially Communist Party members, engaged in labor union or educational activities. These investigating committees often broadened their interpretation of "subversive" to include former Communist Party members, associates of Communists who were not Party members, and even those suspected of having left-wing sympathies.

In 1951, twenty-six states required public school teachers to take loyalty oaths. Twenty-two states also enacted statutes to disqualify "disloyal" teachers for reasons other than for refusing to take or for violating loyalty oaths. Fourteen states prohibited teachers from being members of what they labeled "subversive organizations." Nineteen states had laws restraining teachers from advocating or teaching subversive doctrines. Six states prohibited Communist Party members from teaching in public schools.[24] States throughout the country enacted antisubversive legislation and conducted antisubversive investigations that had a definite, and often demoralizing, impact on educators and educational institutions. The following sections contain examples of these tactics in Washington, New York, Maryland, California, and Illinois.

Washington

In 1948, an Un-American Activities Committee, established by the Washington state legislature and chaired by Albert Canwell, investigated alleged Communist infiltration of the University of Washington.[25] Unlike the stand Robert Hutchins would take to protect academic freedom at the University of Chicago, the University of Washington's president, Raymond J. Allen, cooperated with the committee. (It should be noted, however, that the University of Chicago was a private institution and the University of Washington was a public one.) Allen himself believed that the American Communist Party was part of an international subversive conspiracy directed by the Soviet Union and that Party members had a deleterious effect on academe.[26] Thirty-three faculty members were subpoenaed to testify before the committee, which publicly questioned ten of them. Following the typical pattern of such investigations developed by HUAC, former Communists were used as expert witnesses.

Three professors, believing that the committee was violating their civil rights, refused to discuss their political activities. Three other professors acknowledged that they had once been Communist Party members; two others admitted that they were still Party members but, like the Hollywood Ten, refused to name others who had been members. As a consequence of the investigation, the university then brought charges against six tenured professors, who either refused to testify or admitted Communist Party membership, before the Faculty Committee on Tenure and Academic Freedom. The faculty committee recommended that the university drop all charges against the three former Communists. Although the majority of the committee believed that Communist Party members should not teach at the University of Washington, it reluctantly recommended that the two Communist Party members should not be dismissed because the institutional bylaws did not provide for such terminations. The committee did recommend dismissal, however, for one professor, who refused either to deny or confirm membership in the Communist Party. Although the faculty committee advised against their dismissal, the University of Washington's Board of Trustees, upon President Allen's recommendation, dismissed three professors, the two Party members and the uncooperative one. The other three were placed on a two-year probation and warned not to participate in any type of subversive activity.[27]

The action taken against the professors at the University of Washington set important precedents that some other institutions followed. Being called before an investigating committee and refusing to testify or name other possible suspects brought institutional retaliation against the suspect. It was somewhat like the practice used during the Inquisition—those convicted of heresy by church courts were turned over to the state for punishment. In the case of the anti-Communist investigations, those identified as suspect by state investigating committees were then punished by their own institution's administration.

New York

Antisubversive investigations had taken place in New York State even before the cold war period. In the early 1940s, the state legislature had established the Rapp-Coudert Committee to examine New York City schools' financial problems, but the committee broadened its scope to include the investigation of subversives. While the investigation included Nazis and Fascists, the committee concentrated primarily on alleged Communists in the City College of New York (CCNY) system and the New York City Teachers Union. The committee questioned more than five hundred persons, eighty-eight of them publicly. The committee's style of conducting its probe was precedent setting for future investigations. Typically, a witness was questioned, at a private session, by the committee. Witnesses at these private hearings were not allowed representation by legal counsel, nor were they permitted to have a transcript of their testimony. The American Civil Liberties Union and the New York Teachers Union protested this "secret," Star Chamber, technique but to no avail. If the committee deemed that there was sufficient evidence of subversive activity, then the witness was ordered to testify at a public hearing. Based on the Rapp-Coudert Committee investigations, the New York Board of Higher Education adopted a policy not to retain members of "any Communist, Fascist or Nazi group" or individuals advocating or teaching "subversive doctrines."[28] The result was the dismissal of more than thirty faculty members from the CCNY system for "conduct unbecoming a member of the staff."[29]

The New York legislature, in 1949, enacted the Feinberg Law, related to alleged subversive activities by public employees, including school personnel. The law declared that, despite the existence of preventative statutes, members of subversive groups, especially the Communist Party and its affiliated organizations, had infiltrated and were employed in public schools. Because of this danger, the New York State Board of Regents, which exercised supervisory power over the state's public elementary and secondary schools and institutions of higher education, was ordered to enforce the Education Law (1917) and the Civil Service Law (1940) to remove public school employees who advocated or taught the violent overthrow of the government. The Education Law, passed during World War I, provided for the removal of school personnel who uttered "any treasonable or seditious word or words" or committed "any treasonable or seditious act or acts." The Civil Service Act prohibited public employment of those who advocated or taught or were members of groups advocating or teaching the violent overthrow of the government.[30]

The Feinberg Law required the New York State Board of Regents to compile a list of allegedly subversive organizations. Membership in any of these organizations would constitute grounds for dismissal. The regents were further required to submit annual reports to the legislature regarding their enforcement of the law. School principals were required to provide their superintendents with annual reports on each teacher or employee under their supervision. In turn, the superintendents were required either to file formal charges against suspect teachers or to reject the principal's findings. School districts were compelled to file annual reports to the board of regents documenting their compliance with the law.

The Feinberg Law was twice declared unconstitutional by the New York State Supreme Court, a finding that in turn was overruled by the state court of appeals. In 1953, the U.S. Supreme Court upheld the constitutionality of the Feinberg Law in a six-to-three decision. Justice Sherman Minton, in the majority opinion, stated that "persons (employed or seeking employment in New York's schools) have the right under law to assemble, speak, think and believe as they will. It is equally clear that they have no right to work for the state in the school system on their own terms." In a dissenting opinion, Justice William O. Douglas countered that the Feinberg law "inevitably turns the school system into a spying project" in which "principals become detectives" and "students, the parents, the community become informers." Affirming academic freedom, Douglas argued that as long as teachers were "law-abiding" citizens, whose performance met "professional standards," their "private life," "political philosophy," or "social creed" should not cause reprisals against them.[31]

Maryland

Maryland's legislature, in 1949, enacted the Ober Law, one of the most sweeping state antisubversive acts. The act made it a felony for public employees to become or remain a member of a subversive group. Each public agency, including public schools, was responsible for barring subversive persons from employment. Subversive persons were broadly defined as anyone

> who commits or aids in the commission, or advocates, abets, advises or teaches by any means any person to commit, attempt to commit, or aid in the commission of any act intended to overthrow, destroy, or alter, or to assist in the overthrow, destruction, or alteration of, the constitutional form of the government of the United States, or the State of Maryland, . . . by revolution, force, or violence; or who is a member of subversive organization.[32]

The act was declared unconstitutional by lower but upheld by higher courts in 1950. In a referendum in 1950, Maryland's voters, by a two-to-one margin, voted to retain the Ober Law.

California

In the late 1940s, California established a Senate Fact-Finding Committee on Un-American Activities, which probed alleged Communist activity in labor unions and higher education. In July 1950, the Senate, voting unanimously to continue the committee, named Senator Hugh Burns its chairperson. The committee, continuing a line of investigation that had begun in 1947, conducted hearings about alleged Communist activity at the University of California's Berkeley campus, especially its radiation laboratory. Following what had become a standard practice in anti-Communist investigations, the committee called upon former, now repentant Communist Party members to be "expert" witnesses about subversive activities. A former Communist, Mrs. Paul Crouch, claimed to have attended a Communist Party meeting in 1941 at the house of Dr. J. Robert Oppenheimer, who was then at Berkeley. At the time of the allegation, Oppenheimer, a well-known atomic scientist, was director of the Institute for Advanced Studies at Princeton.[33] Oppenheimer quickly issued a denial of the allegation to the press. Although allegations were directed against him, Oppenheimer was neither provided with advance notice of the proceedings nor invited to appear before the committee. The Oppenheimer case is an example of how some legislative investigating committees conducted themselves during the 1950s.[34]

California also had a serious conflict between its board of regents, who required faculty and staff to sign a loyalty oath stating that the signatory was not a member of certain subversive organizations, primarily the Communist Party, and faculty members who contended the oath violated academic freedom. The faculty argued that the oath placed the criteria for employment outside of the control of the profession and interfered with its right to self-governance. The issue was ultimately resolved by a compromise engineered by California Governor Earl Warren, an ex officio member of the board of regents.[35]

Illinois

In Illinois, the legislature established the Seditious Activities Investigating Commission in 1947. The commission, chaired by state Senator Paul Broyles, was composed of fifteen members appointed by the governor, five from the Illinois Senate, five from the House, and five from the general public. Known as the Broyles Commission, it conducted lengthy investigations of alleged subversion throughout the state. Broyles focused attention on two private universities, the University of Chicago and Roosevelt College. At a preliminary hearing, a number of students and faculty from the two institutions protested the projected investigation. The legislature responded by approving funding for the Broyles Commission to conduct a thorough investigation of alleged subversion at the two institutions. Governor Adlai Stevenson, the Democratic governor, in April 1949, refused to sign the bill funding the commission's investigations but allowed the bill legalizing the investigations to become law. Expressing his disapproval of the investigations, Stevenson, a liberal Democrat and future presidential candidate, declaring that there was no need for the investigation, stated:

> Because some one hundred students from institutions numbering 15,000 exercise their right as citizens to oppose antisubversive legislation, it hardly follows that they are being indoctrinated with Communism as this resolution seems to imply . . . I think the University of Chicago, one of the great centers of learning in the world, and Roosevelt College, a new institution dedicated to education of those of limited means . . . [should have] an opportunity to be heard.[36]

The anticipated investigation encountered a strongly mixed reaction in Illinois. The state, divided between big-city Chicago and small-town and rural downstate, was almost equally divided between Democrats and Republicans and between liberals and conservatives. Three of the four major Chicago newspapers opposed the coming investigations. Even the usually pro-Republican, conservative, isolationist *Chicago Tribune* was against the investigation. Only the Hearst *Chicago Herald American* endorsed the Broyles investigation. Among the organizations challenging the investigation were the American Civil Liberties Union, the Chicago Methodist Ministers Association, the Chicago Federation of Labor, the Illinois Congress of Parents and Teachers, the Illinois Conference of the American Association of University Professors, and the Citizens' Schools Committee. The American Legion, however, gave strong support to Broyles.[37]

Prior to the commission's hearings, Laird Bell, chairman of the board of trustees of the University of Chicago, in a public letter to Broyles, called for the observance of due process, in open hearings, in which the two institutions would have the right to: (1) reasonable prior notice of the hearings; (2) representation by counsel; (3) the opportunity to cross-examine witnesses; (4) a full transcript of the proceedings. While Broyles accepted most of the procedures urged by Bell, he refused to grant the institutions the right to cross-examine witnesses. The Chicago press severely criticized Broyles's denial of the institutions' right of cross-examination. With the issue generating controversy, several commission members, opposing the chairman's decision, urged that the right to cross-examine be made part of the investigation process. Reluctantly, Broyles yielded and accorded to the institutions the right to cross-examine witnesses.

Robert Hutchins, the University of Chicago's eminent and erudite chancellor, the commission's first witness, eloquently defended his institution. Referring to the subpoena summoning him to testify about "subversive activities at the University of Chicago," Hutchins stated, "This is a leading question: the answer is assumed in the question. I cannot testify concerning subversive activities at the University of Chicago, because there are none." Defending academic freedom, Hutchins asserted that the university had such a "distinguished faculty" because it "guarantees its professors absolute and complete academic freedom." He went on to attack the allegations that professors belonged to Communist-front organizations as an "un-American doctrine of guilt by association." He pointed out that the federal government had entrusted the university to conduct the creation of the first atomic chain reactor. Not only did Hutchins defend his University, but he also attacked the Broyles investigation and proposed antisubversive legislation as aiming at "thought control," which was contrary to the American way to "encourage thought and discussion as a path to peaceful change and improvement."[38] Throughout the hearings, Hutchins remained steadfast that there were no subversive activities at the University of Chicago and that the university would not limit academic freedom by monitoring faculty or student associations.

Following Hutchins, the student-chairman of the Communist Club at the University of Chicago was called to testify. After he had answered questions about the club's membership, J. B. Matthews, the commission's chief investigator, asked him if he was member of the

Communist Party, if he would fight for the United States in a war against the Soviet Union, and if he thought the Communist Party was an illegal organization. The student refused to respond to Matthews's questions on the grounds that his answers might tend to incriminate him or that the questions were an inquiry into his political beliefs, which were protected by the Constitution. Matthews then questioned Edward Sperling, President of Roosevelt College, who essentially reiterated the points scored by Hutchins.

Having been bested by Hutchins and Sperling, Matthews called a surprise witness, Howard Rushmore, a journalist who claimed to have expert knowledge of Communist-front organizations. Rushmore identified twenty faculty members of the University of Chicago who had Communist-front affiliations. He focused his allegations on eight professors: Wayne McMillen, professor of social service administration; Harold C. Urey, professor of chemistry; Robert J. Havighurst, professor of education; Ernest W. Burgess, professor of sociology; Malcolm P. Sharp, professor of law; Rexford G. Tugwell, professor of political science, Maude Slye, associate professor emeritus of pathology; and James Luther Adams, professor of religious ethics. Rushmore did not distinguish between past and current affiliations, with some charges of affiliation dating back to the early 1930s. One of the professors on Rushmore's list, Urey, had worked on the atomic bomb. Rushmore stated his opinion that professors who failed to discern the Communist-front nature of the organizations of which they were members should be prohibited from teaching.[39]

When called to testify, Urey maintained that Rushmore's testimony against him was a "partial story and the partiality makes it wholly false." Stating that he supported the Loyalists against the Fascists in Spain and that he was a member of the Committee to Defend America by Aiding the Allies prior to the German attack on Russia, Urey contended, "I cannot help it if the Communists fellow-traveled with me on the Spanish situation. I didn't fellow-travel with them. It was the reverse. Since then, they have seen fit not to fellow-travel with me."[40]

After concluding its hearings, the Broyles Commission, on May 10, 1949, reported on its investigation of the University of Chicago and Roosevelt College to the Illinois General Assembly by merely sending the transcript of hearings, which the commission declared "speaks for itself." The majority of the commission, with two dissents, made the following recommendations to the General Assembly: (1) any student, attending a tax-exempt or tax-supported institution, who refuses to answer the questions of whether or not he or she is a Communist and whether or not he or she or would defend the United States in the event of a war with the Soviet Union, should be expelled by the institution; (2) any professor who refuses to resign from Communist-front organizations should be dismissed; (3) schools should stop the sale of Communist propaganda, books and magazines and deny the use of facilities to those advocating Communist principles; (4) a survey should be made of textbooks and other materials for the purpose of identifying and removing those advocating Communist theories and doctrines; (5) any school or university that continues to employ teachers or professors affiliated with Communist or Communist-front organizations should be denied tax-exempt status; (6) if the board of trustees of tax-exempt institutions fails to comply with these recommendations, they should be removed from office.[41]

The commission's sweeping recommendations to eliminate alleged antisubversive activities died in the Illinois House of Representatives, which adjourned on June 30, 1949, without acting on them. The Senate defeated a bill to extend the commission for another two years, thus ending the episode. Although the commission's recommendations did not pass, they provide evidence of the kind of sweeping legislation to combat alleged subversive activities among professors and teachers that was proposed during the late 1940s and early 1950s in several states. While the Broyles Commission's recommendations died in Illinois, a variety of antisubversive legislation was enacted throughout the country.

Educators' Responses to Anti-Communist Charges

In 1949, the Board of Regents of the University of California prescribed that all faculty members in the system be required to take a loyalty oath as a condition of continued employment. A majority of faculty officially protested the requirement. In what amounted to a "sign or leave" confrontation, however, only thirty-two professors refused to sign and were subsequently dismissed. They were restored to their positions three years later by a state supreme court decision.

A usual scenario of an antisubversive investigation was that those suspected of subversive activities, such as membership in the Communist Party or in a Communist-front organization, would be summoned to testify before an investigating committee. Following the pattern set in the HUAC Hollywood hearing, those who refused to testify were often cited for contempt. If they testified, they were expected to inform on others, thus, broadening the number of suspects. Witnesses who refused to testify or were judged uncooperative were frequently dismissed by their colleges. Not only were the witnesses subjected to personal harassment, but they also lost their income.

The educational response to the antisubversive investigations of the period was at best a mixed one. Like some of the actors in Hollywood, some educators sought to prove their loyalty by becoming vocal antisubversives themselves. Others turned to an intense, often highly complicated, discussion of the meaning of academic freedom. The educational organizations, too, had a mixed response—sometimes they zealously defended their colleagues and at other times they looked the other way.

The Debate among Educators

Educators during the McCarthy period did not speak with a single mind but differed on the strategy to take in response to subversive allegations. In some respects, their divisions mirrored earlier differences of the 1930s about appropriate responses to Communism. Professional responses to the anti-Communist investigations inevitably led to the definition of academic freedom. Simply stated, *academic freedom* meant the freedom of teachers to teach and of students to learn. Most educators believed academic freedom should be defined by the teaching profession itself and that the profession should ensure that it was being protected. Typically, the matter of academic freedom was most debated in higher education, by the professoriate.[42] However, like most matters academic, stipulating the definition of academic freedom, a broad concept, became very complicated and subject to frequent emendations and qualifications.

The issue of defining academic freedom was further complicated by how one viewed the nature of the American Communist Party. Was the Communist Party like any other political party? Or, was it a domestic agency of the Soviet Union bent on destroying American democracy? Some professors argued that a person's political activities and memberships had no bearing on the right to teach. Others, who saw the American Communist Party as inextricably linked to the Soviet Union, argued that membership in the Communist Party was different from membership in other political parties. Further, they claimed that the American Communist Party's blind allegiance to the Soviet Communist Party line made its members incapable of the intellectual objectivity needed to sustain academic freedom. Then, there were those who took a third compromise position. While a Communist could teach science or mathematics, subjects that were nonpolitical, they could not teach subjects, such as history or political science, that could be used for political indoctrination. In other words, some educators believed that evidence of Communist Party membership was sufficient, by itself, to prove unfitness to teach. However, they often disagreed as to what constituted evidence. Others held that membership in the Communist Party alone was insufficient cause for dismissal and that a teacher's competency should be determined only by an examination of the individual's educational competency.

Sidney Hook, professor and chairperson of the Philosophy Department at New York University, was a well-published and highly articulate proponent of the view that Communist Party members should not be employed as teachers. Hook, in his early career, had been a Marxist and had attempted to develop a synthesis of Marx's and Dewey's philosophies. Like other leftist-leaning socialists and liberals in the United States, he grew increasingly critical of Stalin's totalitarianism in the Soviet Union, particularly the purge trials of the 1930s. Like Counts and others, Hook, viewing the American Communist Party as a domestic arm of the Soviet Party, saw it as a Machiavellian organization that worked against genuine liberalism.

Hook argued that it was not because of holding divergent ideas that a Communist Party member was unfit to teach but rather because of his or her professional misconduct in joining a conspiratorial organization that used the teaching process for political indoctrination. He believed such teachers were educationally incompetent because they subordinated themselves to the Party line in their teaching, institutional and professional activities, and research.[43] He did not believe that dismissal of Communist Party members from teaching positions violated their civil rights. Any action against proven Party members should begin with the teaching profession—the community of teachers or professors—as an internal professional matter and not with state agencies. However, he warned, if the teaching profession failed to act, then state intervention was likely.[44]

Professional Educational Organizations' Reactions

The response of educational organizations, such as the American Association of University Professors (AAUP), when subversive allegations were made against their members was affected by time and cost. The cost of mounting a defense against antisubversive charges was expensive, especially for individuals. It was quick, easy, and newsworthy to charge a person with being subversive, but the charge required a self-defense that was often protracted and costly. The most successful defense against antisubversive charges was mounted when the educational institution used its legal resources on behalf of its faculty rather than aiding the accusers. A case in point was the successful defense of the University of Chicago and Roosevelt College against the Broyles Commission investigations of these institutions in Illinois. When an institution offered no support or took an adversarial stand against the alleged subversives on its faculty, mounting a defense was difficult. The funds and the willingness of organizations to underwrite the defense of its members, while initially there, often was not sustained. Further, those who needed to defend themselves also needed a quick legal response. Organizations, depending on organizational consensus and procedures, were slow, often too late, in defending their members.

The National Education Association (NEA). The nation's largest professional organization of educators, the NEA is an umbrella-like association with divisions and subdivisions for administrators, curriculum specialists, teachers, early childhood educators, librarians, and other educational personnel. It also serves as a collective bargaining agent for teachers in many school districts.

During the period of antisubversive investigations, the NEA responded to charges against educators through its National Commission for the Defense of Democracy Through Education. Organized in 1941, the commission's initial efforts were directed largely against totalitarianism, namely, Nazism and Fascism. Generally, the commission sought to educate Americans about the relationships between American democracy and education and to defend education and teachers against infringements on their rights as teachers in a democratic society. The commission performed an educational mission that informed the profession and public about the role of the schools in a democratic society and also assisted in defending educators it regarded as unjustly accused by antisubversive investigators.

American Association of Universities (AAU). Under the auspices of the AAU, the presidents of thirty-seven major universities issued a statement, "The Rights and Responsibilities of Universities and Their Faculties," on March 24, 1953. The statement sought to reassure the public that the universities were aware of and would take the necessary actions against Communism and Communists. It also urged professors to behave responsibly by cooperating with antisubversive investigating committees. The statement warned that taking the Fifth Amendment "places upon a professor a heavy burden of proof of his fitness to hold a teaching position and lays upon his university an obligation to reexamine his qualifications for membership in its society."[45]

The AAU statement, in many respects, summed up the position taken by colleges and universities during the anti-Communist investigations of the 1950s. It indicated that there were limits and qualifications on academic freedom that did not extend to certain political activities, such as membership in the Communist Party. The general stance was to make a statement decrying the Communist menace and membership in the Communist Party and then proceed to a kind of "we can take care of cleaning our own house" stance. Some institutions adopted bylaws and procedures and established committees for dealing with and dismissing Party members and others suspected of belonging to organizations seeking to overthrow the government. Despite these reactive measures, the universities and especially their professors made easy targets for anti-Communist investigators. Suspects confronted a kind of double jeopardy, facing both federal and state investigators and their own institution's committees.

American Association of University Professors (AAUP). Founded in 1915 to represent college and university faculty, the AAUP had the most consistent record of the various professional organizations in defending academic freedom against antisubversive investigators. Its key defense committee was Committee A on Academic Freedom and Tenure, which primarily was concerned with ensuring faculty participation in the institutions' faculty appointments and tenure policies and in protecting professors' freedom to teach.[46]

Throughout the period of antisubversive investigative intensity, the AAUP steadfastly opposed the view that membership in the Communist Party was sufficient grounds to warrant dismissal or to refuse employment in a college or university. The AAUP insisted that professional performance was the key criterion in assessing a teacher. The Report for Committee A on Academic Freedom and Tenure, in 1947, stated:

> If a teacher as an individual should advocate the forcible overthrow of the government or should incite others to do so; if he should use his classes as a forum for communism or otherwise abuse his relationship with his students for that purpose; if his thinking should show more than normal bias or be so uncritical as to evidence professional unfitness, these are the charges that should brought against him. If these charges should be established by evidence adduced at a hearing, the teacher should be dismissed because of his acts of disloyalty or because of professional unfitness, and not because he is a Communist. As long as the Communist party in the United States is a legal political party, affiliation with that party in and of itself should not be regarded as a justifiable reason for exclusion from the academic profession.[47]

Despite its strong stand, the AAUP operated under serious handicaps in its efforts on behalf of its members' accused of subversive activities. It, like other organizations operating largely by consensus, was slow to respond. Further, it had a small staff, maintained by its members' professional dues. For example, AAUP did not censure the University of Washington for its dismissal of professors, which had occurred in 1949 until 1956, a period of seven years.

Conclusion

The 1950s was a decade that gave the deceptive appearance of social and political conformity, with a mixture of anxiety about the future. Though the United States was enjoying economic growth and prosperity, the cold war and the fear of impending conflict with the Soviet Union was part of the national context. This uneasiness generated a climate of suspicion that subversives, primarily Communists, were undermining American democracy and national security. The term "McCarthyism," used by historians to depict the climate of fear, was coined as a result of Senator McCarthy's ruthless investigating methods.

While American elementary and secondary schools and colleges and universities were enjoying a decade of growing enrollments and expanding facilities, McCarthy-like antisubversive investigations brought apprehension to the educational community. In the climate of political anxiety, loyalty oaths and other measures were used against those suspected of being a subversive or of being a member of a politically suspect organization. McCarthyism generated an era of conformism, when holding and expressing divergent ideas, especially political ones, was suspect. In the 1960s, this conformism would be shattered by political divergence and the emergence of the counterculture.

Notes

[1] A historical perspective on American anti-Communism is provided in M. J. Heale, *American Anti-Communism: Combating the Enemy Within, 1830–1970.* (Baltimore: Johns Hopkins University Press, 1990).

[2] For the symbolic implications of the witch-hunts, see Bernard Rosenthal, *Salem Story: Reading the Witch Trials of 1692* (New York: Cambridge University Press, 1995).

[3] For example, see George S. Counts, *The Soviet Challenge to America* (New York: John Day Co., 1931). Twenty-six years later, Counts was highly critical of the USSR in his *The Challenge of Soviet Education* (New York: McGraw-Hill Book Co., 1957).

[4] John L. Childs and George S. Counts, *America, Russia, and the Communist Party in the Postwar World* (New York: John Day Co., 1943).

[5] Alan Ryan, *John Dewey and the High Tide of American Liberalism* (New York: W.W. Norton & Co., 1995), pp. 247–48.

[6] Ibid., pp. 334–5.

[7] For an account of Truman and national security, see Michael J. Hogan, *A Cross of Iron: Harry S. Truman and the Origins of the National Security State* (New York: Cambridge University Press, 1998).

[8] Robert C. Morris, "Era of Anxiety: An Historical Account of the Effects and Reactions to Right-Wing Forces Affecting Education During the Years 1949–54," doctoral dissertation, Indiana State University, 1976, pp. 150–51.

[9] Ellen Schrecker, "Academic Freedom and the Cold War," *Antioch Review*, 38 (1980), p. 319.

[10] For a discussion of communist techniques by a former Communist Party turned expert witness, see Louis F. Budenz, *Techniques of Communism* (Chicago: Henry Regnery Co., 1954).

[11] For an account of the investigations, see Eric Bentley, *Are You Now or Have You Ever Been: The Investigation of Show Business by the Un-American Activities Committee 1947–1958* (New York: Harper Colophone Books, 1972).

[12] Richard M. Fried, *Men Against McCarthy* (New York: Columbia University Press, 1976), p. 147.

[13] Walter Goodman, *The Committee* (New York: Farrar, Straus and Giroux, 1968), pp. 326–32.

[14] Richard Rovere, *Senator Joseph McCarthy* (New York: Harcourt Brace, 1959), p. 143.

[15] Fried, p. 190.

[16] For an account of the Amerasia Case, see Harvey Klehr and Ronald Radosh, *The Amerasia Spy Case: Prelude to McCarthyism* (Chapel Hill: University of North Carolina Press, 1996).

[17] David M. Oshinsky, *A Conspiracy So Immense* (New York: The Free Press, 1983), p. 276.

[18] Ibid., p. 204.

[19] For Lattimore's account, see Owen Lattimore, *Ordeal by Slander* (Boston: Little, Brown, and Co., 1950).

[20] For Cohn's pro-McCarthy account, see Roy Cohn, *McCarthy* (New York: The New American Library, 1968).

[21] Lately Thomas, *When Even Angels Wept* (New York: William Morrow and Co., 1973), p. 197.

[22] Fried, p. 248.

[23] Harry S. Truman, *Freedom and Equality*, David S. Horton, ed. (Columbia: University of Missouri Press, 1960), p. 74.

[24] E. Edmund Reutter, Jr., *The School Administrator and Subversive Activities: A Study of the Administration of Restraints on Alleged Subversive Activities of Public School Personnel* (New York: Bureau of Publications, Teachers College, Columbia University, 1951), p. 1.

[25] Robert W. Iversen, *The Communists and the Schools* (New York: Harcourt, Brace and Co., 1959), pp. 269–76.

[26] Schrecker, "Academic Freedom and the Cold War," pp. 317–18.

[27] Ibid., pp. 316–17.

[28] Ibid., p. 314.

[29] Walter Gellhorn, ed., *The States and Subversion* (Ithaca, NY: Cornell University Press, 1952), pp. 257–58.

[30] Reutter, p. 26.

[31] Iversen, pp. 66–67.

[32] Reutter, p. 27.

[33] Gellhorn, pp. 40–45.

[34] Ibid., p. 47.

[35] For the controversy, see David P. Garner, *The California Oath Controversy* (Berkeley: University of California Press, 1967).

[36] *Chicago Daily Tribune* (April 11, 1949, Part 2), p. 4; *Chicago Daily News* (April 11, 1949), p. 16, as quoted in Gellhorn, pp. 49–90.

[37] Gellhorn, pp. 91–93.

[38] Transcript of hearings prepared for the University of Chicago, pp. 15–18, as quoted in Gellhorn, pp. 95–99.

[39] Gellhorn, pp. 112–13.

[40] University of Chicago transcript of hearings, pp. 575–78, in Gellhorn, p. 118.

[41] Gellhorn, pp. 128–31.

42 The definitive work on anti-Communist investigations in higher education during the 1950s is Ellen W. Schrecker, *No Ivory Tower: McCarthyism and the Universities.* New York: Oxford University Press, 1986).

43 Sidney Hook, "What Shall We Do About Communist Teachers?" *Saturday Evening Post* (September 10, 1949), pp. 33, 164–66.

44 Sidney Hook, "Academic Integrity and Academic Freedom," *Commentary* (October 1949), pp. 329–39.

45 Schrecker, "Academic Freedom and the Cold War," p. 324.

46 Schrecker, *No Ivory Tower: McCarthyism and the Universities*, p. 18.

47"Academic Freedom and Tenure: Report of Committee A for 1947," *American Association of University Professors Bulletin*, 34 (1948), p. 126.

Further Reading

Adams, John G. *Without Precedent.* New York: W.W. Norton and Co., 1983.

Anderson, Jack, and Ronald W. May. *McCarthy, the Man, the Senator, the Ism.* Boston: Beacon Press, 1952.

Bentley, Eric. *Are You Now Or Have You Ever Been?: The Investigation of Show Business by the Un-American Activities Committee 1947–1958.* New York: Harper Colophone Books, 1972.

Bernstein, Walter. *Inside Out: A Memoir of the Blacklist.* New York: Alfred A. Knopf, 1996.

Buckley, William F. Jr., and L. Brent Bozell. *McCarthy and His Enemies.* Chicago: Henry Regnery Co., 1954.

Budenz, Louis F. *Techniques of Communism.* Chicago: Henry Regnery Co., 1954.

Cohn, Roy. *McCarthy.* New York: New American Library, 1968.

Conant, James B. *Education in a Divided World.* Cambridge: Harvard University Press, 1948.

Counts, George S. *The Challenge of Soviet Education.* New York: McGraw-Hill Book Co., 1957.

Counts, George S. *The Soviet Challenge to America.* New York: John Day Co., 1931.

Dick, Bernard F. *Radical Innocence: A Critical Study of the Hollywood Ten.* Lexington: University Press of Kentucky, 1989.

Feurerlicht, Roberta Strauss. *Joe McCarthy and McCarthyism: The Hate that Haunts America.* New York: McGraw-Hill Book Co., 1972.

Fried, Richard M. *Men Against McCarthy.* New York: Columbia University Press, 1976.

Garner, David P. *The California Oath Controversy.* Berkeley: University of California Press, 1967.

Gellhorn, Walter, ed. *The States and Subversion.* Ithaca, NY: Cornell University Press, 1952.

Goodman, Walter. *The Committee.* New York: Harcourt, Brace and Co., 1959.

Heale, M. J. *American Anti-Communism: Combating the Enemy Within, 1830–1970.* Baltimore: Johns Hopkins University Press, 1990.

Hogan, Michael J. *A Cross of Iron: Harry S. Truman and the Origins of the National Security State.* New York: Cambridge University Press, 1998.

Iversen, Robert W. *The Communists and the Schools*. New York: Harcourt Brace, and Co., 1959.

Klehr, Harvey, and Ronald Radosh. *The Amerasia Spy Case: Prelude to McCarthyism*. Chapel Hill: University of North Carolina Press, 1996.

Kransdorf, Martha. *A Matter of Loyalty: The Los Angeles School Board vs. Frances Eisenberg*. San Francisco: Caddo Gap Press, 1994.

Latham, Earl. *The Communist Controversy in Washington*. Cambridge: Harvard University Press, 1966.

Lattimore, Owen. *Ordeal by Slander*. Boston: Little, Brown, and Co., 1950.

Lewy, Guenter. *The Cause That Failed: Communism in American Political Life*. New York: Oxford University Press, 1990.

McIver, Robert M. *Academic Freedom in Our Time*. New York: Columbia University Press, 1955.

Navansky, Victor S. *Naming Names*. New York: Viking Press, 1980.

O'Neill, William L. *A Better World: The Great Schism: Stalinism and the American Intellectuals*. New York: Simon and Schuster, 1982.

Oshinsky, David M. *A Conspiracy So Immense: The World of Joe McCarthy*. New York: The Free Press, 1983.

Ravitch, Diane. *The Troubled Crusade: American Education, 1945–1980*. New York: Basic Books, 1983.

Reeves, Thomas C. *The Life and Times of Joe McCarthy*. New York: Stein and Day, 1982.

Reutter, E. Edmund Jr. *The School Administrator and Subversive Activities: A Study of the Administration of Restraints on Alleged Subversive Activities of Public School Personnel*. New York: Bureau of Publications, Teachers College, Columbia University, 1951.

Rogin, Michael P. *The Intellectuals and McCarthy: the Radical Specter*. Cambridge, MA: M.I.T. Press, 1967.

Rovere, Richard H. *Senator Joseph McCarthy*. New York: Harcourt Brace and Co., 1959.

Ryan, Alan. *John Dewey and the High Tide of American Liberalism*. New York: W.W. Norton & Co., 1995.

Schrecker, Ellen. *The Age of McCarthyism*. Boston: St. Martin's Press, 1994.

Schrecker, Ellen. *No Ivory Tower: McCarthyism and the Universities*. New York: Oxford University Press, 1986.

Stouffer, Samuel A. *Communism, Conformity and Civil Liberties*. Garden City, NY: Doubleday, 1955.

Thomas, Lately. *When Even Angels Wept*. New York: William Morrow & Co., 1973.

Vaughn, Robert. *Only Victims: A Study of Show Business Blacklisting*. New York: G.P. Putnam's Sons, 1972.

Whitfield, Stephen J. *The Culture of the Cold War*. Baltimore: Johns Hopkins University Press, 1991.

6

Racial Desegregation and Education

Though the crucial event in the desegregation process was the U.S. Supreme Court's ruling in the *Brown v. Board of Education of Topeka* decision in 1954 that racial segregation in public schools was unconstitutional, the movement to racial integration was part of a larger and more complex history of race relations in the United States. The effort to desegregate and then integrate public schools began in the mid-1950s and continued through the next decades of the twentieth century. The sections of chapter 6 provide the historical context and describe the integration process. The chapter also examines how the movement for racial desegregation generated important changes in educational theory and practices.

Historical Context

With the end of Reconstruction in the South and a change in the national mood regarding race relations, Congress and the Supreme Court turned away from earlier efforts to bring African Americans into the civil rights of full citizenship. The national mood of the late-nineteenth and early-twentieth centuries, unlike the period of abolitionism before and Reconstruction after the Civil War, reverted to the view that the role and status of the black population was once again the South's peculiar problem.

The national climate of a "hands-off" stance with regard to race relations, as expressed by the country's political and economic elites, can be interpreted in several ways. First, the national political leadership as well as many voters had grown weary of the Civil War and its aftermath. Although the "bloody shirt" would be waved in election campaigns in both the North and the South, the conflict between the two regions had grown increasingly symbolic and was being fought in memory—in books and articles—rather than in political reality. Second, the nation's industrial growth, spurred by the war, had continued as "captains of industry" built economic empires and fortunes in both the North and South. In this time of industrial development, the idea of a "New South" was current in economic thinking. No longer an economically backward agricultural region, the New South would be one of coal, iron, and steel production. Third, the sociological rationale for political and economic policy had shifted from dedicated abolitionist-driven civil rights to social Darwinism, which stressed "survival of the fittest" and the "white man's burden." According to social Darwinism, nature's inexorable law of biological evolution also applied to human society. Nature was not subject to human legislation; rather, human legislation was in the long run subject to nature's law. According to social Darwinist interpretations of history, Nature, through the laws of competition for survival, had brought the white race forward to lead the rest of humanity, especially the people of color. This climate of opinion contributed to racial segregation, by law in the South as well as unlegislated segregation, in fact, in much of the North.

Since the end of Reconstruction, the U.S. Supreme Court, too, reflected the national mood that Southern race relations could best be dealt with by the South in the South. With the Southern states, after Reconstruction, controlled by whites bent on the legal separation of the races, the Supreme Court, the Congress, and the presidency stood as either observers or accomplices in the segregation process. The Supreme Court had invalidated much of the civil rights legislation by interpreting it to benefit the industrial corporations and the white establishment rather than to protect the rights of African Americans.

In 1896, in the *Plessy v. Ferguson* case, the U.S. Supreme Court's crucial eight-to-one vote upheld the constitutionality of a Louisiana law segregating railway passengers by race, provided that the separate facilities were equal. The impact of the Court's ruling for policy and practice was that as long as the facilities were equal, there was nothing unconstitutional about racial segregation. The lone dissent came from Justice John Marshall Harlan who, arguing that the Constitution was color blind, denied that the states had the power to regulate citizens according to race.[1] As indicated, the *Plessy v. Ferguson* decision had significant and far-reaching consequences for American education. Giving legal sanction to segregation, it inaugurated and fortified what would be the long-standing doctrine of "separate but equal."[2]

Developing a Legal Strategy to Overturn Segregation

Since the *Plessy v. Ferguson* decision established a legal precedent for segregation, those who sought to overturn the Court's 1896
ruling had to build a body of counterprecedents that might lead to the
decision's reversal. In the American common law tradition, based on
English antecedents, law was argued on basis of *stare decisis*, building
arguments in a case on precedents from earlier decisions. What followed from 1896 when the Supreme Court gave "separate but equal"
legal sanction to the *Brown* case of 1954 was a painstaking and slow
effort to develop a strategy to overturn segregation.

Although the legal fiction was that segregated schools were to be
"separate but equal," in reality, they were separate but unequal. What
had developed in the South and in many border states was a dual educational system based on race—separate schools for whites and
blacks. These schools were unequal in terms of expenditures per
child, facilities, teacher qualifications, and physical plants. White
schools enjoyed a higher expenditure of public funds, longer school
terms, and better qualified and compensated teachers. For example, in
1945, South Carolina spent three times more per pupil for whites than
for blacks. Further, the value of white school facilities in the state were
six times those of black schools. Mississippi, in the same year, spent
four and a half times as much on white than on black students.[3]

The National Association for the Advancement of Colored People
(NAACP) became the leading organization seeking to reverse the separate but equal doctrine that gave legal sanction to racial segregation. In
the 1930s, the NAACP received funds from the American Fund for Public Service to support litigation against the unequal apportionment of
public funds for education and against discrimination in public transportation. Charles H. Houston, the highly respected associate dean of
Howard University's School of Law, was engaged to begin the legal
assault on racial segregation.[4]

Houston and the attorneys working under his direction faced the
challenge of creating precedents that could constitute a counterargu-
ment against the separate but equal doctrine. The NAACP developed a
carefully planned legal strategy to create precedents in cases dealing
with higher education, especially in graduate and professional programs, rather than dealing directly with public elementary and secondary schooling. There were several reasons for developing this strategy.
First, it would deal with a much smaller number of adult students
rather than children. Since the numbers were smaller and involved
adults, the setting for the cases would be less emotionally charged than
if it involved public elementary and secondary school students. Second, many Southern states were most vulnerable in higher education,
especially in graduate and professional education, where no pretense

was made of providing separate but equal facilities. They either existed or did not. In contrast, there was a dual system of white and black elementary and secondary schools. If the initial attack on segregation came at the lower level, it was likely to bog down in an interminable inventorying of facilities, an accounting of revenues, and comparisons of taxation rates.

While the NAACP was evolving its strategy, some Southern and border states were designing a counterplan to maintain segregation in their universities' professional and graduate schools. Some states enacted standby statutes that authorized creating separate but equal facilities, if and when African Americans applied for admission to existing institutions. Other states created scholarship funds to be awarded to blacks for tuition in other states that had racially integrated facilities.[5]

Between 1935 and 1950, the U.S. Supreme Court and lower courts heard several cases relating to segregation in higher education from the border states of Maryland, Missouri, Oklahoma, and Texas. All the cases were decided in favor of the African American plaintiffs. While the decisions were still based on the "separate but equal" precedent established in *Plessy v. Ferguson* in 1896, these legal victories were important in the NAACP's legal strategy that eventually would overturn racial segregation in public schools.

Murray v. The University of Maryland

In 1935, Donald Murray, an African American, applied to but was refused admission to the University of Maryland's Law School. Murray then filed a suit against the university, alleging it had violated his rights as a citizen of Maryland. At that time, Maryland had not enacted standby legislation to create an alternative law school and had only a meager scholarship fund of $200 to subsidize out-of-state tuition. When Murray's case reached the Maryland Circuit Court of Appeals, the court ruled in his favor. The court reasoned that since Maryland had enacted no authorization for a separate law school for blacks, it could not provide equal treatment for the plaintiff. The University was ordered to admit Murray to its law school.[6]

Missouri v. Gaines

Using the precedent established in the Murray decision, the NAACP undertook a similar case, *Missouri ex. rel. Gaines* (1938). Lloyd Lionel Gaines, an African-American resident of St. Louis, applied for admission to the University of Missouri Law School.[7] Gaines was a graduate of Lincoln University, a state black college in Missouri. Rejecting Gaines's application for admission, the University of Missouri Law School advised him to apply to Lincoln University, which, however, had no law school, or to apply to an out-of-state institution in which case Missouri would provide financial aid.

The case reached the U.S. Supreme Court and the NAACP attorneys, led by Charles Houston, argued that Missouri, under the separate but equal doctrine, would have to provide facilities equal to those provided for white law students. Further, they contended that constructing a new law school for blacks or providing out-of-state tuition would not constitute equal treatment. In a six-to-two decision, the Supreme Court upheld Gaines, accepting the NAACP attorneys' arguments. The Court ruled that the validity of the separate but equal doctrine rested "upon the equality of the privileges" that the state's laws give to its separated groups. In providing a law school exclusively for white students, Missouri had created a privilege for whites that it denied to blacks. While the white resident was provided legal education by the state, it denied the same right to the African-American resident, who with the same qualifications, is advised to go outside of the state. The Court ruled that Gaines, the plaintiff, was entitled to admission to the University of Missouri Law School. Gaines, however, did not enroll and did not test implementation of the decision.[8] However, the *Gaines* case along with the *Murray* case were important legal building blocks in the NAACP strategy to overturn *Plessy v. Ferguson.*

Sipuel v. Oklahoma Board of Regents

Sipuel v. Oklahoma Board of Regents (1948), a case similar to that of *Gaines*, provided a further precedent in the NAACP's legal strategy.[9] Ada Lois Sipuel, an African American, had applied for admission to the University of Oklahoma's Law School. A graduate of the Oklahoma State College for Negroes, Sipuel was denied admission to the all-white University of Oklahoma Law School. The Law School advised that she delay her application until Oklahoma had established a law school for African Americans. In its decision, the U.S. Supreme Court ruled that Oklahoma, obligated to conform to the equal protection clause of the Fourteenth Amendment, was required to provide Sipuel with a legal education in the same time frame that it did for applicants from any other group.[10] Oklahoma, in response, quickly established a "makeshift" law school for African Americans. Again, as in the *Gaines* case, implementation was untested as the Supreme Court did not hear the case to determine if Oklahoma's action met the standards required by the doctrine of equality of separated groups.

Sweatt v. Painter

The *Sweatt v. Painter* case was highly significant in virtually ending litigation over racial segregation in professional and graduate education. It moved the NAACP closer to realizing a coming victory in the

Brown school desegregation decision.[11] Heman M. Sweatt, the plaintiff, had been denied admission to the all-white University of Texas Law School, the only state law school in Texas. On May 16, 1946, NAACP attorneys, representing Sweatt, filed a suit in the Travis County District Court to compel the university's Board of Regents to admit him to the university's law school. A district court, which heard the case, agreed that Sweatt had been denied equal protection of the laws guaranteed by the Fourteenth Amendment. However, it stayed implementation of its order for six month so that Texas could establish a separate but equal law school for blacks. The state had announced that a law school for blacks would be operating in Houston by February 1947. Unlike the well-funded University of Texas Law School, the new law school for blacks had only a part-time faculty, three classrooms, and one student. In a new trial, NAACP attorneys argued that the law school for blacks was patently unequal to the one at the University of Texas. A lower court, hearing the case, ruled against Sweatt and the Texas Supreme Court refused to hear his appeal.[12] In June 1950, the case reached the U.S. Supreme Court, ruling that Texas had failed to provide "substantial equality" to white and black law school students and ordering the University of Texas Law School to admit Sweatt.[13]

The Supreme Court's decision in *Sweatt v. Painter* had portentous, but mixed, implications for future racial segregation cases. The Court's specific identification of "equality" requirements needed to sustain separate schools suggested that segregated schools and equality of educational opportunity could not coexist. Concurrently, however, the Court refused to rule on the legality of segregation and to consider evidence to assess the effects of segregation on students.

McLaurin v. Oklahoma Board of Regents

Moving ever closer to the *Brown* decision, the U.S. Supreme Court, in 1950, heard the case of *McLaurin v. Oklahoma Board of Regents*.[14] In this case, George W. McLaurin had applied for admission to the doctoral program in the University of Oklahoma's Graduate School of Education. The University, complying with a lower federal court's order to admit McLaurin, admitted him but on a segregated basis. He was segregated from other students in roped-off sections of classrooms, at a segregated desk in the library, and a separate table in the cafeteria. Thurgood Marshall, the counsel for the NAACP and a future Supreme Court Justice, argued that these segregating conditions "created a badge of inferiority" that negatively affected McLaurin's relationships with professors and other students. With the *McLaurin* case, the Supreme Court had embarked on a line of reasoning that related to pursuit of an effective graduate education as well as to previous equity issues. Importantly, Marshall had succeeded in adding less-

Thurgood Marshall, who developed the NAACP's anti-segregation arguments in the *Brown* case in 1950; later an associate justice of the U.S. Supreme Court. (Reproduction from the Collections of the Library of Congress.)

tangible psychological and social issues to the usual consideration of a descriptive access to institutions and facilities.[15] This use of psychological and sociological evidence would become an important part of the evidence in the *Brown* case. Finding that McLaurin's segregation impeded his acquiring an effective graduate education, the Court ordered Oklahoma to remove all state-imposed restrictions that limited his pursuit of an effective graduate education.

Brown v. Board of Education

The legal strategy developed by the NAACP reached its decisive moment in *Brown et al. v. Board of Education of Topeka et al.*, which challenged state-enforced racial segregation in elementary and secondary schools. In 1952–53, the U.S. Supreme Court heard a number of cases that challenged segregation laws in Kansas, South Carolina, Delaware, and Virginia. Collectively, the cases were known as *Brown v. the Board of Education of Topeka.*

Heading the defense of the states was the highly skilled constitutional lawyer, John W. Davis. Davis and the team of attorneys defending the state's segregation laws contended that the states constitutionally had the power to control education and that the "separate but equal" precedent had definitively settled the matter of racial segregation.

The NAACP legal team, headed by Thurgood Marshall, was determined to challenge racial segregation itself, rather than focus on the question of the equity of separate facilities. Consideration of concrete equity issues of school facilities and staff might win them a limited victory. It might require states with segregation laws to move to equalize their facilities but would leave segregated schools basically intact. Marshall and his co-counsels mounted a multifaceted argument that centered on the states' violation of the Fourteenth Amendment and used psychological and sociological evidence to establish the negative impact of segregation on children's psychological and educational development. They contended that the use of racial classification was forbidden by the Fourteenth Amendment. Citing precedents against racial classifications in jury service, property occupancy, voting, employment, and graduate education, they argued that the Fourteenth Amendment precluded "a state from imposing distinctions or classifications based upon race or color alone." The power of the earlier precedents involving professional and graduate education were now marshalled against the *Plessy v. Ferguson* "separate but equal" precedent.

Marshall and the other NAACP attorneys scored a victory when the Court permitted them to call expert witnesses in sociology and psychology to testify. Kenneth B. Clark, a noted psychologist at the City College of New York, testified that segregation potentially damaged all children, both black and white. The effects of segregation, Clark stated, were most powerful on the minority group, however; separated from the larger society, they were assigned to an inferior status. Sociologist Ira De A. Reid, concurring with Clark, testified that the segregated world imposed on blacks produced a distorted sense of reality.[16] The testimony of the expert witnesses built the argument that state-imposed racial segregation, causing low self-esteem and a sense of inferiority, adversely affected the development of African-American children and their right to an effective education.[17]

On May 17, 1954, the U.S. Supreme Court reached its decision, ruling unanimously for the plaintiffs that state-imposed racial segregation in the public schools was unconstitutional. Its decision dealt a death blow to the "separate but equal doctrine" that had governed public education since *Plessy v. Ferguson*. Speaking for the Court, Chief Justice Earl Warren, who had worked diligently for a unanimous decision, stated:

> Segregation of white and colored children in public schools has a detrimental effect upon the colored children. The impact is greater when it has the sanction of the law; for the policy of separating the races is usually interpreted as denoting the inferiority of the negro group. A sense of inferiority affects the motivation of a child to learn.

U.S. Supreme Court
Chief Justice Earl Warren,
who delivered the deseg-
regation decision in the
Brown Case in 1954.
(Reproduction from the
Collections of the Library
of Congress.)

Segregation with the sanction of law, therefore, has a tendency to
retard the education and mental development of negro children and
to deprive them of some of the benefits they would receive in a
racially integrated school system. . . . It is doubtful that any child
may reasonably be expected to succeed in life if he is denied the
opportunity, where the state had undertaken to provide it as a right
which must be made available to all on equal terms . . . in the field
of public education the doctrine of separate but equal has no place.
Separate educational facilities are inherently unequal.[18]

The Supreme Court's decision in the *Brown* case gave legal sanction to two fundamental principles that would guide court-sanctioned
desegregation in the future. One, racial separation, enforced by law,
establishes schools that are inherently unequal. Two, the promise of
equality before the law, guaranteed in the Fourteenth Amendment, is
incompatible with the use of law to establish two separate classes of
people. While the fundamental principles were clearly asserted, their
implementation in practice set a major part of the national agenda in
the ensuing decades.

Reactions to *Brown*

The Supreme Court delayed implementation of its decision in the
Brown case for one year, until 1955. In the second *Brown* decree in

May 1995, the Court, addressing the process and timing of desegregation, ruled: (1) since school conditions vary, local officials, acting in
good faith, have the primary responsibility to solve desegregation problems; (2) the courts should be guided by the principles of equity, characterized by a practical flexibility in shaping remedies; (3) compliance
must be achieved "with all deliberate speed," including "a prompt and
reasonable start" toward achieving full compliance "at the earliest
practicable date."[19] Using the "all deliberate speed" doctrine, the
Supreme Court remanded cases that related to implementation to federal district courts.

States most affected by the *Brown* decision were Southern and
border ones. The initial reaction in these states was mixed. Desegregation proceeded more smoothly and rapidly in the border states but met
strong resistance in the Southern states. As their designation implies,
border states, located between North and South, with less rigidly
defined attitudes on race, were more flexible in their response. In the
year following the *Brown* decision, desegregation began in Delaware,
Maryland, Missouri, West Virginia, and the District of Columbia. In
most of the border states, the governors expressed their intentions of
complying with the law of the land. For example, Delaware Governor J.
Caleb Boggs instructed the State Board of Education to work to implement the Court's decision. Two school districts in Arkansas and two in
Texas also began to implement desegregation.[20]

The process of desegregation in the border states can be illustrated by a case in St. Louis, Missouri. St. Louis represents an interesting example because it illustrates the problems of ending de jure segregation, based on law, and also de facto segregation, based on
residential patterns. For St. Louis as well as other large urban areas,
especially in large Northern cities, de facto segregation proved the most
difficult challenge.

Even before the *Brown* decision, St. Louis had been taking steps
toward desegregation. Its two universities, the Catholic school system,
and municipal facilities were already desegregated at the time of the
1954 decision. To bring its schools into compliance with the Court's
decision in *Brown*, the St. Louis Board of Education, in June 1954,
adopted a process to phase in school desegregation. In phase one,
beginning in September 1954, all schools and agencies, such as junior
and teacher colleges and special schools that provided educational services on a city-wide basis, were to be desegregated. Phase two would
commence in January 1955 with the desegregation of all high schools,
excluding technical schools, and all adult education programs. In
phase three, beginning in September 1955, all elementary schools and
technical high schools would begin desegregation. Tenure rights were
to be preserved in the integration of professional staff. New school
attendance boundaries were to be redrawn on a nonsegregated basis

by November 1954. Students were to attend the school within their designated attendance area. An exception was that school officials could transfer students to alleviate overcrowding. These step-by-step procedures succeeded in integrating both elementary and secondary schools.[21]

While St. Louis had success in ending de jure racial segregation, de facto segregation, reflecting residential patterns, proved to be a much more difficult challenge. In fact, the demographic patterns that developed in St. Louis and other large cities in the 1950s and 1960s brought about what was called "resegregation." The demographic pattern was that the white population moved out from the central city to the city's periphery or to outlying suburbs while the black population concentrated in the city's center. With the traditional neighborhood school policy in force, schools, reflecting the attendance areas they served, would again become racially segregated.

Governors in the South, where racial attitudes were deeply ingrained and the affected populations larger, believed they could develop strategies to avoid desegregation. Governors and officials in Mississippi, Georgia, Alabama, Virginia, and South Carolina were convinced that their states could invent means to maintain racially segregated dual school systems. Mississippi's Governor Hugh L. White summed up the deep South's white establishment's reaction, "We're not going to pay any attention to the Supreme Court's decision. We don't think it will have any effect on us down here at all."[22] An exception was Florida's Governor LeRoy Collins, who sought to develop strategies of peaceful accommodation to the Supreme Court's racial desegregation ruling.

President Eisenhower, opposed to federal interference in local affairs, particularly in schools, gave few signs of enforcing the Court's school desegregation ruling. Philosophically, Eisenhower cautioned that laws alone could not change people's hearts and minds. (For a discussion of the Eisenhower administration, see chapter 3.) Further, the Justice Department, under Attorney General Herbert Brownell, did not pursue litigation to seek compliance with the ruling. The inactivity of the Eisenhower administration did little to encourage those political and educational officials in the South who might have been willing to begin desegregation efforts. Indeed, the opponents of desegregation were emboldened. There was a revival of the Ku Klux Klan and the organization of White Citizens' Councils. In the mid-1950s, many African Americans were still disqualified, unregistered, or effectively discouraged by threats from voting. The result was that in many Southern states, moderates on the desegregation issue were defeated. Candidates running on segregationist platforms were elected.

The legislatures of Virginia, Alabama, Mississippi, and Georgia, calling for massive resistance to desegregation, passed resolutions claiming a state's right to interpose itself between the federal government and the people of the state. The interposition argument reiterated John C. Calhoun's discredited contention, in 1828, that states could nullify federal laws. Some Southern white politicians, opposing desegregation, resurrected the states' rights argument. In 1956, 101 of 128 congressmen from Southern states signed the "Southern Manifesto," pledging determined resistance to school desegregation.

Several Southern states passed legislation that transferred more educational authority from the state to the local school district, especially in determining pupil placement. By 1956, Alabama, Georgia, Florida, Louisiana, Mississippi, North Carolina, South Carolina, Tennessee, and Virginia had enacted some type of pupil placement legislation. An example was the Florida law which gave local school superintendents authority to assign pupils to schools for which they were "best fitted." South Carolina authorized local boards to transfer pupils "to promote the best interest of education."[23] Although local authorities could no longer overtly use race in pupil assignment, the pupil placement laws permitted use of a variety of other factors, such as psychological, moral, health and other considerations. The result was that boards typically assigned black and white pupils to different schools, maintaining segregation, but using stated criteria other than race.[24] Further, if segregation was challenged in the courts, cases would have to be argued against many separate districts rather than on a statewide basis.[25]

Attempts of Southern states to thwart desegregation through state laws ultimately failed. The courts ruled pupil placement laws, voluntary segregation, and attempts to end compulsory and state-supported public education invalid in a series of cases between 1954 and 1958. However, desegregation's progress in the South was slow. Desegregation moved more rapidly in the border states where, by 1964, nearly 55 percent of African-American students were attending school with white students. In the deep South, however, only 1.18 percent of the 2.9 million African-American students were attending school with white students.[26]

The Little Rock Crisis

The situation that developed in Little Rock, Arkansas, in the Fall of 1957 illustrated a Southern governor's attempt to thwart desegregation and the federal role in securing compliance with the Supreme Court's 1954 decision. In the following section, the scenario, events, and roles played by the principal actors in the crisis are examined.

On May 24, 1955, the School Board of the Little Rock School District developed a policy and plan to desegregate its public schools. The board's plan would desegregate schools gradually in three phases: (1) beginning with the senior high school in 1957; (2) followed by the junior high school in 1959–1960; (3) and concluding with elementary schools in 1962–63.[27]

A suit was filed on behalf of African-American plaintiffs who complained that the desegregation process was too slow. Judge Miller, hearing the case in the U.S. District Court in May 1957, upheld the adequacy of the desegregation plan, ruling the board was acting in good faith.[28] Then, on August 29, 1957, the Pulaski Chancery Court, an Arkansas state court, hearing Governor Orval E. Faubus's testimony that the desegregation of Central High School might lead to violence, issued a restraining order to prevent the board from beginning its desegregation plan. On August 30, 1957, the school board petitioned the U.S. District Court, Eastern District of Arkansas, to enjoin the plaintiffs in the state court action from "preventing or interfering with the opening of the integrated schools in Little Rock School District."

In petitioning the U.S. district court, the board, seeking to comply with the desegation law, was appealing to federal authority to provide a way out of the impasse with Governor Faubus. Faubus, however, decided to block the school board's effort to implement the desegregation plan before the district court could rule. On September 2, 1957, Governor Faubus issued a public statement that put him on a direct collision course with the federal government:

> It will not be possible to restore or to maintain order and protect the lives and property of the citizens if forcible integration is carried out tomorrow in the schools of this community. The inevitable conclusion therefore must be that the schools in Pulaski County, for the time being, must be operated on the same basis as they have been operated in the past.[29]

Faubus ordered Arkansas National Guard units to be stationed at Little Rock's Central High School to "preserve the peace and good order." He also mobilized the Arkansas State Police to "act as an arm of the State Militia in maintaining or restoring the peace and order of the community." At this point, no public disorders had taken place. Faubus directed the National Guard to turn black students away from entering the school. He ordered General Sherman T. Clinger, the National Guard Adjutant General: "You are directed to place off limits to white students these schools for colored students and to place off limits to colored students those schools heretofore operated and recently set up for white students."[30]

Faubus's action encouraged segregationist organizations and activities. Crowds of demonstrators who converged on Central High School, chanting anti-integration slogans, sought to prevent any attempt of nine black students to enter the building.

President Eisenhower after meeting with Governor Orval Faubus in an attempt to avert the Little Rock school desegregation crisis. (Courtesy Dwight D. Eisenhower Library.)

The school board then requested that "no negro students attempt to attend Central or any white high school until this dilemma is legally resolved." It then requested the federal district court to exempt it and the superintendent from any charge of contempt and provide instructions on what action was to follow. Quickly responding, Judge Davies, presiding in the federal district court, ruled on September 3 that the Little Rock School Board and superintendent of public schools was to proceed to integrate the schools according to the court approved plan.

Although President Eisenhower had tried to avoid entanglement in local school affairs and in the desegregation process, he found himself locked in a rapidly unfolding dramatic and televised overt confrontation with Faubus, now a highly visible Southern governor. (For the educational policies of the Eisenhower administration, see chapter 3.) On September 14, Faubus met with Eisenhower at the Newport Naval

Station. Assuming that he had reached an agreement with Faubus, Eisenhower recorded in his diary:

> I suggested to him that he go home and not necessarily withdraw his National Guard troops, but just change their orders to say that having been assured that there was no attempt to do anything except to obey the Courts and that the Federal government was not trying to do anything that had not been already agreed to by the School Board and directed by the courts; that he should tell the Guard to continue to preserve order but to allow the Negro children to attend Central High School. . . . I further said that I did not believe it was beneficial to anybody to have a trial of strength between the President and a Governor because in any area where the Federal government had assumed jurisdiction and this was upheld by the Supreme Court, there could be only one outcome—that is, the State would lose, and I did not want to see any Governor humiliated.[31]

On September 20, the Eighth Federal Circuit Court issued an injunction restraining Governor Faubus and the National Guard commanders from further interference in the court-ordered integration process. Faubus responded by removing the National Guard on September 21, an action that sparked more anti-integration demonstrations by the crowd gathered at the school.

When school opened on the following Monday, September 23, approximately one thousand people were milling about the school. Nevertheless, the nine black students entered the school. After three hours of demonstrations outside the school, local officials, fearing for the black students' safety, had them removed from the school.

As the situation grew more threatening, Mayor Mann of Little Rock wired an urgent appeal to President Eisenhower:

> THE IMMEDIATE NEED FOR FEDERAL TROOPS IS URGENT. THE MOB IS MUCH LARGER IN NUMBERS AT 8AM THAN AT ANY TIME YESTERDAY. PEOPLE ARE CONVERGING ON THE SCENE FROM ALL DIRECTIONS. MOB IS ARMED AND ENGAGING IN FISTICUFFS AND OTHER ACTS OF VIOLENCE. SITUATION IS OUT OF CONTROL AND POLICE CANNOT DISPERSE THE MOB. I AM PLEADING TO YOU AS PRESIDENT OF THE UNITED STATES IN THE INTEREST OF HUMANITY LAW AND ORDER AND THE CAUSE OF DEMOCRACY WORLD WIDE TO PROVIDE THE NECESSARY FEDERAL TROOPS WITHIN SEVERAL HOURS. ACTION BY YOU WILL RESTORE PEACE AND ORDER AND COMPLIANCE WITH YOUR PROCLAMATION.[32]

Frustrated by Faubus's action and preparing to act, Eisenhower secured legal opinions from his Attorney General Herbert Brownell. Brownell reported that, "Mob force h..d successfully frustrated the carrying out of the orders of the court and had demonstrably overpowered such police forces as could be mustered by the local officials." Advising the president, the attorney general stated that the governor was not using his powers to support the local authorities and that "the mere existence of a threat of domestic violence would be insufficient to justify the governor in taking action to nullify the order of the court by the use of force." Citing precedents, Brownell assured Eisenhower that federal courts had jurisdiction to determine the legality of a state governor's action when it contravenes a federal court order.[33] Also, a governor's use of force should be to uphold rather than thwart the implementation of federal law. According to Brownell:

> The action of a State Governor in using troops to invade rights protected by the Federal Constitution, and, in particular, to frustrate by direct action the order of a federal court, is reviewable by the Federal judicial process. The mere existence or threat of domestic violence, disorder or riot cannot serve as justification for such invasion of rights or frustration of a court order; where domestic violence arises, it is the overriding duty of the State authorities to use its forces to protect such rights against invasion and such court orders against obstruction.[34]

Brownell further advised that state officers have a duty to suppress disorders in a manner that will not "nullify and . . . permit the effectuation of state and federal law. . . . When State officers refuse or

Soldiers on patrol at Central High School in Little Rock, Arkansas. (Reproduction from the Collections of the Library of Congress.)

fail to discharge their duty in this respect, it becomes the responsibility of the national government, through the Chief Executive, to dispel any such forcible resistance to Federal law."[35] The president had the

> undoubted power, under the Constitution and laws of the United States, to call the National Guard into service and to use those forces, together with such of the armed forces as you consider necessary, to suppress the domestic violence, obstruction and resistance of law then and there existing.[36]

Eisenhower, on September 24, issued Executive Order No. 10730 federalizing the Arkansas National Guard and sending the 101st Airborne Division to Little Rock to assure that the federal court's orders were carried out. He then addressed the nation about his action at Little Rock. For the rest of that year, troops from the 101st Airborne Division patrolled the school, escorting the African-American students to classes.

The events at Little Rock showed a somewhat reluctant but eventually firm Eisenhower determined to enforce the law. It also made Faubus into a model for other recalcitrant Southern governors. It is interesting to note that Faubus was re-elected governor in 1958.

The Kennedy Justice Department and Civil Rights

The Kennedy administration, succeeding Eisenhower in 1961, faced a series of civil rights and school integration crises. (See chapter 7 for the Kennedy administration's general educational policies.) The Justice Department, headed by President Kennedy's brother, Robert Kennedy, tended to act in a determined way to secure civil rights and school integration. Again, like the events at Little Rock, civil rights and school integration efforts and the segregationist attempts to block them were covered dramatically by nationwide television. An interesting contrast in presidential styles is revealed by Eisenhower's more cautious approach, but one that used overwhelming federal force at Little Rock, with the Kennedy style of managing a crisis.

The first dramatic crisis for the Kennedy administration occurred in September 1962 at the University of Mississippi in Oxford, where James Meredith, an African American, sought to enroll. The Kennedy administration was soon locked in conflict with Mississippi's segregationist governor, Ross Barnett. The U.S. Court of Appeals had, in 1961, found Barnett guilty of contempt for blocking Meredith's admission. The court then directed the Justice Department to enforce its order that the university admit Meredith as a student.

Negotiations between the Kennedy administration and Barnett reached an impasse with the president seeking to uphold the law and the governor determined to maintain segregation and states' rights. Facing mounting mob demonstrations in Oxford, the president, in a dramatic speech on the night of Sunday, September 30, ordered federal troops to the campus to ensure Meredith's enrollment at the university. A night of rioting followed, causing several deaths. The next morning, however, Meredith, protected by federal marshals, enrolled at the University of Mississippi.

In June 1963, a situation similar to the episode with Ross Barnett occurred, this time with Governor George Wallace of Alabama. Wallace stated that he would "stand at the school-house door" to keep Alabama's schools segregated.[37] Wallace, pledging to keep the University of Alabama segregated, sought to block the enrollment of two African Americans, Vivian Malone and James Hood. Again, the unfolding events were televised nationally. Wallace, standing at the doorway entry of the administration building to block the students' entrance, confronted Nicholas Katzenbach who sought to register Malone and Hood. After his symbolic posture, the students went through a side entrance and proceeded to register.

Promoting Racial Desegregation and Integration

The racial desegregation of the public schools, ordered in the *Brown* case in 1954, moved slowly, painfully, and unevenly in the next decades. While de jure racial segregation was struck down, it survived through various machinations, especially in the deep South. However, even more difficult to end was de facto segregation where school attendance areas were segregated, not by law, but by the residential areas the schools served. In many cases, de facto segregation was deeply entrenched in large Northern cities. Then, there was the seemingly simple but highly complex question: Could schools be desegregated, if they were not racially integrated?

An attempt to evade desegregation occurred in Prince Edward County, Virginia, which closed its public schools in 1959 and then made $2 million in tuition payments to a private school established for white children. The consequence was that sixteen hundred African-American students had no access to public schools. The Supreme Court, in *Griffin v. Prince Edward County School Board* in 1964, ruling such an evasion of desegregation illegal, ordered the board to stop its payment to the private school and reopen its public schools.[38]

In the Southern and border states where racial segregation had been in force legally before the Supreme Court's decision in *Brown* in 1954, the task was to desegregate schools that were rigidly segregated. In some of these states, a strong anti-desegregation movement had developed among whites, which had political, economic, and educational implications. Rejecting various state-erected subterfuges to circumvent desegregation, federal courts were insisting on compliance. Further, U.S. Office of Education guidelines were set in place in 1965–66, which required districts receiving federal aid to move the desegregation process forward. (For the Civil Rights Act, see chapter 7.) In the Southern situation, the educational challenge was complex but somewhat more direct than in the North. In the South, it was necessary to dismantle the segregated school system, bring about desegregation, and achieve racial balance for pupils and teachers. In the North, where racial segregation was de facto, the integration process ran into segregated residential areas and neighborhood schools that served these areas.

In 1954, racial segregation had appeared to be a Southern problem. By the 1960s, however, it was clear that it was a national issue. Demographic changes had resulted from the migration of Southern African Americans to large Northern cities, such as Chicago, New York, Cleveland, Philadelphia, and Boston. Between 1940 and 1966, four million African Americans had migrated from the South to the North's big industrial cities. In these large cities, residential patterns typically reflected ethnic and racial patterns in which neighborhoods were largely homogeneous. The African-American migration, beginning and continuing since World War I, had been to inner-city central core areas. Between 1950 and 1966, the African-American population of central cities almost doubled, increasing from 6,500,000 to 12,100,000. In 1966, 56 percent of African Americans were living in central city areas, compared to 27 percent of the white population.[39] Whites were moving to the peripheries of cities or to the growing suburbs that surrounded them in concentric circles.

The Northern pattern of school segregation was based on the neighborhood school pattern in which attendance areas served geographical localities. Since neighborhoods tended to be ethnically or racially homogenous, so were the schools' student population. The result in Northern big cities was de facto residential segregation rather than the de jure, or legal, segregation found in Southern states. Thus, racial desegregation and integration were national issues, not limited to the South. Northern big-city racial integration was part of a complex of serious political, economic, social, and educational issues. While Southern racial segregation was overt, the Northern situation was shaped by subtle but pervasive forms of segregation and discrimination.

By the mid-1960s, several important issues had developed relating to desegregation. Did desegregation also require racial integration? That is, if legal requirements that required segregation were removed, did school districts also need to take positive steps to bring about racial integration? The legal opinion, based on federal court rulings and actions of the U.S. Justice Department, was that school districts, to comply with the law, had to develop strategies to bring about racial integration.

Given the diversity of school districts, the challenge of determining what processes should be used to implement integration was highly complex. The issues varied from the very large urban districts such as Boston or Chicago to the smaller suburban and rural districts. To bring about integration in large urban districts, several strategies were developed. Attendance areas within a district might be redrawn to eliminate all-white or all-black schools. Reconfigured districts could then include students from both white and black neighborhoods. Still, another approach was to bus students to achieve racially integrated schools. This approach, especially when it involved neighborhood elementary schools, often became emotionally charged. If the district was large enough, magnet schools, with special academic programs, might attract students from throughout the district.

The issue of racial integration was even more complex when it was considered in terms of large cities and the surrounding suburbs, each with its own school district or districts and school boards. As indicated, demographic patterns had developed in which large cities had the largest African-American population and suburbs had the largest white population. Would the court require interdistrict procedures to bring about integration?

By the late 1960s, a body of court rulings emerged to provide some further general legal guidelines for the ongoing desegregation process. Among these principles were:

1. The assignment of teachers, as well as pupils, is an important element in eliminating racial discrimination.

2. School boards must develop meaningful plans that promised "immediate progress toward disestablishing state-imposed segregation," that have "real prospects for dismantling" state-imposed dual systems "at the earliest possible date."

3. The key test in determining if a local school board is complying is the extent to which racial separation persists under its plan.

4. The argument of avoiding "white flight" cannot be used to perpetuate a dual school system.[40]

In 1968, the Supreme Court, in *Green v. New Kent County School Board*, ruled that local boards were required to develop workable school desegregation plans. In 1969, the Court in *United States v. Montgomery County (Alabama) Board of Education* ruled that a federal judge can order integration of school staffs.[41]

In 1971, in *Swann v. Charlotte-Mecklenburg Board of Education,* the U.S. Supreme Court affirmed the constitutionality of mandatory racial integration in school districts.[42] In this case, the Court specified the legal obligations of local districts in implementing the earlier *Brown* decision. The Court suggested several procedures that districts might use to comply with integration requirements such as redrawing district boundaries and attendance areas, clustering schools, or deliberately transferring and transporting students to achieve desegregation.[43] A highly significant part of the Court's ruling was its sanctioning of busing to achieve public school racial integration. In upholding the use of busing to bring about court-ordered desegregation, the Court authorized federal judges to determine the standards required of local districts.[44]

Among African Americans, there were some changes in attitude and strategy between the 1950s and the 1960s. The strong, nationally visible, and older mainstream civil rights organizations, such as the NAACP and the Urban League, continued to work for racial integration in education as in other areas. For these organizations, the strategy continued to be primarily legal and through the courts. The Southern Christian Leadership Conference, in which Dr. Martin Luther King, Jr. was the major leader, pursued an integrationist strategy, rooted in the

Dr. Martin Luther King, Jr., a leading civil rights crusader, addressing supporters at a rally. (Reproduction from the Collections of the Library of Congress.)

black churches, which used massive nonviolent passive resistance to segregation. By the mid-1960s, a few African-American organizations had moved from an integrationist to a separatist position. For example, some members of the Student Nonviolent Coordinating Committee (SNCC), which initially were integrationist, were now stressing black power, black nationalism, and separatism.

Developments in Educational Theory

The legal and political actions related to racial desegregation and integration generated a refocusing of many educational theorists and researchers on race relations and the issues facing minority children in schools. This refocusing of educational theory and research was stimulated, in part, by legislation such as the Civil Rights Act of 1964 and the Elementary and Secondary Education Act in 1965 as part of President Lyndon Johnson's Great Society and War on Poverty Programs. (For a discussion of the Johnson administration policies, see chapter 7.)

Throughout the 1960s and 1970s, attention focused on what politicians, sociologists, educators, and commentators called the "urban crisis." In educational theory and practice, the urban crisis, school integration, and President Johnson's War on Poverty contributed to a significant redirection. It also contributed to what became known as educational policy making. Educational policy studies attempted to examine and resolve issues from political, economic, and sociological perspectives as well as from a pedagogical one. However, the results of educational theorizing were often ill-defined, highly complex, and frequently divergent.

A number of significant questions debated in educational policy circles emerged. Among them were: (1) To what extent did school facilities, staff, and resources influence students' academic achievement? Would equalization of such resources equalize academic opportunities, especially for minority students? (2) Was students' school success, especially academic achievement, largely a product of social factors such as family, community, and peers? If the school was the key factor, then school facilities could be improved. Though costly, school improvement, especially in facilities, was something that could be focused on and dealt with in terms of a direct quantitative input of resources into schools. However, if the key factors were sociological, then more massive socioeconomic strategies of both a quantitative and qualitative nature were necessary to improve urban environments.

Beginning in the mid-1960s, attention focused on what was called the urban crisis and the pathology of poverty. Although there had long been economically disadvantaged rural areas, the greatest attention focused on the urban ghettos, the big-city slums. Slum neighborhoods had high crime rates, youth gangs, high illiteracy, disease, drug addiction, and alcoholism. Just as suburban schools reflected the more affluent neighborhoods they served, schools in slum areas reflected their disadvantaged surroundings. They were characterized by low teacher expectations, low student academic achievement, poor discipline, truancy, high dropout rates, and high teacher turnover.[45]

As indicated earlier in chapters 1 and 3, the United States experienced a monumental demographic transformation during the 1950s as a great migration took place from large city to suburb. The social, economic, and educational implications of this change would occupy policymakers in the 1960s and subsequent decades.

Conant's *Slums and Suburbs*

As early as 1961 in his book *Slums and Suburbs*, James B. Conant, a generally moderate liberal educator, pointed out the discrepancy in the quality of education between inner-city schools, often extremely impoverished, and affluent suburban schools. While the United States did not develop a structural dual system that sorted students according to occupational destination on a socioeconomic class basis as in Europe, the American principle of local control and neighborhood schools in effect created an informal dual system. Anticipating James S. Coleman's 1966 report (discussed on pp. 146–47), Conant found that the schools' programs and academic effectiveness were directly related to the surrounding community they served. Further, he noted marked quantitative differences in the resources available in inner-city and suburban school districts. Per capita expenditure was more than twice as high in the suburban schools than in the big-city high schools. Suburban schools, tending to be newer and employing more professional staff, emphasized a college preparatory function. Schools located in inner-city areas were often housed in deteriorating overaged facilities, had fewer professional staff, and faced a highly mobile population of both students and teachers. While 80 percent of the graduating classes in suburban high schools entered college, nearly 50 percent dropped out of high school in slum schools.[46]

Conant warned that "social dynamite" was building up in the big cities with large populations of frustrated unemployed or underemployed African-American and Hispanic youth. The result was a "climate of despair," characterized by persistent failure and growing social alienation. While championing the American comprehensive high school ideology, Conant recommended that inner-city schools develop extensive vocational education programs based on marketable skills. He was also an early advocate of the decentralization of large school districts to allow local schools greater autonomy in devising their educational strategies.[47]

Sociocultural Effects on Educational Strategies

The general research and policy making of the 1960s was to relate educational issues, especially with regard to race and poverty, to the socioeconomic environment and family and other social structures found in disadvantaged urban areas. Officially, the Johnson administration's War on Poverty and Great Society assumed that the school was part of the larger society and that schooling and society were interrelated. The schools could improve society, but society in turn either advanced or retarded schooling. Working from the same premise, social scientists, educators, and policymakers focused on the culture of poverty to identify the impediments that interfered with learning.

Some theorists emphasized the interrelationships between the culture of poverty and racial segregation and individual psychological development. An important factor reinforcing and giving impetus to this reasoning was the Supreme Court's acceptance of psychological evidence in the 1954 *Brown* case, in which the plaintiffs argued that racial segregation impeded healthy self-esteem and psychological development.

From this frame of reference, several general working assumptions were current during the late 1950s and 1960s. Children's ability to learn in school, their academic achievement, was either enhanced or impaired by the specific sociocultural environment in which they lived. The specific sociocultural environment meant the immediate family, the peer group, and various adults who came in contact with the children, as well as more general economic, social, religious and cultural agencies and conditions. The possibilities for academic achievement in schools were impaired by conditions of economic poverty in the sociocultural environment and by the prejudice children experienced. With these assumptions, several generalizations were developed regarding the society, the school, and children.

American society, with its long history of slavery and racial segregation, had a deeply ingrained racism that caused discrimination in employment, education, housing, and other areas. American society needed to identify and eliminate racism and the discrimination it produced. The schools, regardless of who taught in them or attended them, were basically white middle-class institutions that stressed the knowledge and values of that class. The critical theorist educators of the 1980s and 1990s would reiterate these themes but talk about the hegemony of one class over another and the use of schooling to reproduce class status and orientation. Further, children who were not from the middle class were essentially forced to attend an institution that stressed knowledge and values alien to their own culture. Thus, the educational agenda was becoming highly ambitious to change society and schooling. How to bring about this change became the subject of research, discussion, disagreement, and intense debate among policy-makers and educators.

Several generalizations guided educational policymaking, curric-ulum, and instruction in the 1960s. One current that surfaced early in the period was that children's home and neighborhood environments in the culture of poverty lacked the "cultural advantages" found in mid-dle-class families. The middle-class family stressed activities and behaviors that fostered predispositions in children that were condu-cive to schooling. The middle-class homes had books and games. Mid-dle-class parents stimulated reading readiness by reading stories to their children. By taking their children to zoos and museums, middle-class parents were moving children to broader vistas upon which teachers could build in school. In contrast, according to the theory reg-nant in the early 1960s, children living in poverty often lacked the experiences that generated a readiness for subsequent learning, espe-cially in schools. A related corollary generalization saw public schools as sociocultural agencies that reinforced middle-class aspirations and values. These basically middle-class institutions had not adjusted their purposes, curriculum, and instruction to the needs of children from other socioeconomic classes, especially minorities and the poor. As a result, children from the lower socioeconomic groups dropped out as soon as it was legally possible. One educational strategy that was developed as a result of these findings was that schools would provide compensatory activities and experiences that would substitute for the perceived deficiencies of the urban sociocultural environment. Com-pensatory education gave children from low-income families the extra resources and activities to reproduce the middle-class environment with its favorable predispositions to schooling.

Compensatory Education and the Urban Child

During the 1960s and 1970s, social scientists, especially sociolo-gists, developed a new educational terminology that reflected the issues of racism, poverty, and the urban crisis. In particular, the atten-tion of researchers and policymakers fixed on the relationships between race, socioeconomic class, and academic achievement. The term "compensatory education" took on a generally agreed-upon meaning—to provide special kinds of learning assistance to aid identi-fied deprived groups. However, it proved more difficult to agree upon a term that identified the target group.

Among the various terms used were "culturally disadvantaged," "culturally deprived," "underprivileged," "culturally different," and "the urban child."[48] While all generally agreed that most of the children needing compensatory education were likely to be minority children, particularly African Americans in inner cities, educators experienced considerable difficulty in formulating the appropriate terminology. "Culturally disadvantaged" and "culturally deprived" rested on comparative assumptions that black urban culture was deficient compared to white middle-class culture. It was further assumed, as in the Head Start program, that white middle-class culture provided the experiences that led to learning readiness in schools while black urban culture did not. The terms popular in the mid-1960s were obviously biased, attacked, and eventually discarded. The term "underprivileged" was too vague in that everyone is underprivileged in relationship to someone else. The term "urban child" was in vogue for a time but, it too, was very nonspecific in that any child living in an urban area was an urban child. Finally, the term "culturally different," foreshadowing the multiculturalism of the 1980s and 1990s, proved most acceptable.

Frank Riessman's *The Culturally Deprived Child*, published in 1962, was an early book that signaled a shift in educational focus from the academic emphasis on mathematics, science, and foreign languages of the late 1950s to the problems of poverty-impacted children living in inner cities. Riessman argued that economically disadvantaged children as well as minority group children had culturally different values from those typically imposed by schools. For these children and their families, their own cultural values were of intrinsic importance, even if they deviated from the middle-class value orientation found in public schools. Rather than seen as something to be imposed on minority children for their own good, the middle-class value schema was viewed as an impediment for economically disadvantaged children to overcome.

A voice for cultural pluralism that anticipated multicultural education, Riessman urged teachers to seek to understand and appreciate the cultures of economically disadvantaged minority children and to use these children's cultural strengths as an authentic path to learning. Riessman recommended a change in teaching style and strategy. Inner-city and other minority-group children, he recommended, should be taught through techniques that emphasized visual and physical learning, often nonverbal activities, rather than the verbalism and passive learning used in many public schools.[49] The arguments of Riessman and his like-minded colleagues suggested not merely infusions of compensatory education into the public school curriculum but a remaking of the school and its curriculum in urban areas. Not only would urban schools need to be reconfigured but teacher education programs, too, needed to be different than those which followed the traditional middle-class value orientation.

Compensatory Education and Cultural Deprivation

A significant meeting, sponsored by the U.S. Office of Education, took place in June 1964 at the University of Chicago. Prominent social scientists and educators convened to recommend solutions to the problems of cultural deprivation and urban crisis. The result was a report, *Compensatory Education for Cultural Deprivation*, authored by Benjamin Bloom, Allison Davis, and Robert Hess. The authors used the terms "culturally disadvantaged" or "culturally deprived" to refer to children whose home environments did "not transmit the educational patterns necessary for the types of learning characteristic of the schools and the larger society."[50] Among the report's recommendations were:

1. The school and community should provide children with breakfast, lunch, and appropriate medical care and clothing if parents are unable to do so.

2. Nursery schools and kindergartens with a curriculum and activities that stimulate mental, emotional, and motor development—the learning readiness—found in more favorable settings, should be provided for culturally deprived children.

3. Every child should have an individualized learning prescription, prepared and followed during her or his first three years of elementary school, that focuses on the development of fundamental language, reading, and arithmetic skills as well as on the general skill in learning.[51]

The *Compensatory Education* report's terminology and recommendations were highly significant in shaping educational research and policies, as well as curriculum and instruction during the 1960s and early 1970s. The recommendation that schools provide food, clothing, and medical services moved schools into a more multipurpose direction. The suggestion that schools should be multipurpose community agencies was not new but echoed themes raised earlier in the century by progressive educators. The multipurpose ideology reversed the *Sputnik*-generated, subject-matter, academic emphasis of the late 1950s and early 1960s. While generally accepted by educators in the 1960s and 1970s, the multipurpose role would be challenged again by the basic education and neoconservative revival of the 1980s and 1990s.

The recommendation for early childhood education to cultivate learning readiness found an eager acceptance as a strong working assumption in the Head Start program. Like other successful proposals designed initially for the education of disadvantaged children, the early childhood emphasis became popular with middle-class families as well. The accentuation on developing learning readiness influenced not only preschools and kindergartens but also the media, where the popular television show *Sesame Street*, with Big Bird and Ernie, built readiness in a dramatic, fast-paced style. The report's recommendation that economically disadvantaged pupils have learning prescriptions for their first three years of elementary school was, indeed, prophetic. It foreshadowed the Individualized Education Program (IEP) that was later required as part of the education of children with special needs.

There were critics of what became the educationally regnant theory of cultural deprivation. More essentialist educators contended as they had against the earlier progressivism that the many social multifunctional prescriptions being placed on schools would weaken their academic role. Others, such as Kenneth Clark, attacked the "cult of cultural deprivation" for creating educational stereotypes that created low academic achievement expectations for black and other economically disadvantaged pupils.[52] Some educators argued that black children failed in middle-class schools because of broader social ills, especially racism and discrimination.

Historian Diane Ravitch identified several models of schooling contending for support among policymakers and educators. The "deficit" model of schooling featured compensatory programs with intensive remedial skill-building lessons for disadvantaged children. In the deficit model school, disadvantaged children were to be taught needed skills and values that narrowed the gap between them and middle-class children. A second, more ambitious, model required restructuring urban public schools away from their middle-class knowledge and value orientation. Here, the assumption was that urban children would enjoy and perform better in schools that affirmed their own culture and values. Related to both of these models was the general orientation, fostered both by funding from Johnson's Great Society programs and supported by many educators, that the school should become a multifunctional community agency that provided food, clothing, health care, and other social services along with academics.[53]

The Coleman Report

James S. Coleman's *Equality of Educational Opportunity* (1966), a study commissioned by the U.S. Office of Education to fulfill the mandate of section 402 of the Civil Rights Act of 1964, examined racial desegregation and integration and the relationship of school resources and facilities to students' academic achievement.[54] The educational community generally anticipated that Coleman's report would empirically validate the conventional wisdom that differences in a school's staff, facilities, and resources had a significant impact on pupil achievement. However, Coleman, finding a limited relationship between academic achievement and school facilities, identified family, neighborhood, and social class as the important determinants of school success. According to *Equality of Educational Opportunity*:

> Schools bring little influence to bear on a child's achievement that is independent of his background and general social context; . . . this very lack of an independent effect means that the inequalities imposed on children by their home, neighborhood, and peer environment are carried along to become the inequalities with which they confront adult life. . . .[55]

Among the Coleman report's conclusions were: (1) the academic achievement of minority pupils was generally below that of the white majority; (2) there was not a significant difference in the quality of school facilities attended by either group; (3) the environment in the family, community, and peer group, as well the school, played a significant role in a child's academic achievement; (4) pupil motivation was significant in academic achievement; (5) when they exhibited some degree of racial balance, racially integrated schools produced the most positive results in school achievement.

The Coleman report had important implications for questions of equity, especially equality of educational opportunity. Apparently, equalization of a school's physical facilities and staff would not necessarily provide equality of educational opportunity. It was a child's total life context, his or her environment, that had the greatest influence on academic achievement.

Moynihan and *The Negro Family*

Daniel Patrick Moynihan, in *The Negro Family: The Case for National Action*, raised several issues that would prove controversial in urban and minority education. Moynihan decided that the factors of motivation and the total social environment were highly significant in affecting academic achievement, especially of minority students. Children's education, Moynihan argued, was a product of the total environment in which they lived. Schools were only one of several factors influencing a child's development and education.[56] One of these significant factors was the instability of the black lower-socioeconomic-class household, which was often a family headed by a single woman. Moynihan recommended that there was a general need to create family stability and that federal programs should be established to improve employment, housing, and health care.[57] Critics of Moynihan's book contended that his emphasis on the structural instability of the black family minimized the existence of a national pathology of racism and discrimination. Racism, they countered, was the key problem that needed to be addressed if black family life was to improve.

Daniel Patrick Moynihan, author of *The Negro Family: The Case for National Action* and later U.S. senator from New York. (Reproduction from the Collections of the Library of Congress.)

Jencks on Inequality

Christopher Jencks, a professor at Harvard University, in a massive study on inequality, found that schooling had little effect on a person's potential earning power.[58] While finding an uneven distribution of educational access and resources, he argued that even if these differences were equalized, disparities in educational attainment would still persist. Rather than eradicating inequalities, he contended that schools tended to legitimize them. Further, neither educational opportunity nor achievement caused economic and social success. He attributed economic success largely to certain job-related behaviors and skills.[59] Rather than concentrating on school facilities, Jencks found the problem to be a much larger one that related to the control and functioning of economic institutions.

Conclusion

The Civil Rights movement gathered momentum following the Supreme Court's 1954 decision in the *Brown* case, which ruled that racial segregation in public schools is unconstitutional. The *Brown* decision, however, proved to be just the beginning rather than the climax of the movement for racial desegregation. There was strong resistance against desegregation in the South. However, determined and persistent efforts finally brought change to the schools in that region. While de jure segregation was struck down by the 1954 decision, the de facto residential segregation, especially in large urban areas, proved more difficult to change. Throughout the century's remaining decades, the effort to achieve racial integration in the country's public schools continued. The movement for civil rights and racial integration will be discussed in later chapters.

Notes

1 Diane Ravitch, *The Troubled Crusade* (New York: Basic Books, 1983), p. 119.

2 For the federal government's role in sustaining racial discrimination before the 1960s, see Desmond King, *Separate and Unequal: Black Americans and the U.S. Federal Government* (New York: Oxford University Press, 1995).

3 Ravitch, p. 121.

4 Henry A. Bullock, *A History of Negro Education in the South: From 1619 to the Present* (Cambridge: Harvard University Press, 1967), p. 226.

5 Ibid., p. 227.

6 *Donald G. Murray v. The University of Maryland*, 169 Maryland 478, 488 (1936).

7 *Missouri ex. rel. Gaines v. Canada*, 305 U.S. 337 (1938).

8 Ravitch, p. 122.

9 *Sipuel v. Board of Education*, 332 U.S. 631; 68 Sup. Ct. 299 L. Ed. 604 (1948).

10 Bullock, pp. 228–29.

11 *Sweatt v. Painter*, 339 U.S. 629 (1950).

12 Bullock, 229–30.

13 Ravitch, pp. 123–24.

14 Ibid., p. 124.

15 William H. Chafe, *The Unfinished Journey: America Since World War II* (New York: Oxford University Press, 1995), p. 150.

16 Bullock, pp. 233–34.

17 Chafe, p. 151.

18 *Brown v. Board of Education of Topeka*, 347 U.S. 483 (1954).

19 Richard Nixon, "Statement by the President on Elementary and Secondary School Desegregation," (March 24, 1970), p. 3.

20 Bullock, p. 235.

21 Ibid., pp. 237–38.

22 As quoted in Reed Sarratt, *The Ordeal of Desegregation: The First Decade* (New York: Harper & Row, Publishers, 1966), p. 1.

23 Bullock, pp. 257–58.

24 Harvard Sitoff, *The Struggle for Black Equality 1954–1980* (New York: Hill and Wang, 1981), p. 28.

25 Chafe, pp. 157–58.

26 Bullock, pp. 260–61.

27 Special Collections Eisenhower Library, Attorney General Brownell to President Eisenhower, p. 1.

[28] *Aaron v. Cooper*, 143 F. Suppl. 855, 866 (August 28, 1956).

[29] Attorney General Brownell to President Eisenhower, Special collections, Eisenhower Library. (n.d), p. 4.

[30] Ibid., p. 6.

[31] Diary: Notes dictated by the President on October 8, 1957 concerning visit of Governor Orval Faubus of Arkansas on September 14, 1957. Archives Eisenhower Library.

[32] Brownell to Eisenhower, p. 24.

[33] Specifically, Brownell cited the precedent in *Sterling v. Constantin*, 287 U.S. 378 (1932).

[34] Brownell to Eisenhower, pp. 7–20.

[35] Ibid., p. 17.

[36] Ibid., p. 20.

[37] Sarratt, p. 7.

[38] *Griffin v. Prince Edward County School Board*, 377 U.S. 218 (1964).

[39] Ravitch, p. 147.

[40] Richard Nixon, pp. 3–4.

[41] *Green v. New Kent County School Board*, 391 U.S. 430 (1968) and *United States v. Montgomery County (Alabama) Board of Education*, 395 U.S. 225 (1969).

[42] *Swann v. Charlotte-Mecklenburg Board of Education*, 402 U.S. 1 (1971).

[43] S. Alexander Rippa, *Education in a Free Society: An American History* (New York: David McKay Co., 1976), pp. 277–78.

[44] For a detailed analysis of the impact of *Swann v. Charlotte-Mecklenburg Board of Education*, see Davison M. Douglas, *Reading, Writing, and Race: The Desegregation of the Charlotte Schools* (Chapel Hill: University of North Carolina Press, 1995).

[45] Ravitch, p. 149.

[46] James B. Conant, *Slums and Suburbs* (New York: McGraw-Hill Book Co., 1961).

[47] Ibid., pp. 33–53.

[48] Ravitch, p. 150.

[49] Frank Riessman, *The Culturally Deprived Child* (New York: Harper & Row, 1962).

[50] Ravitch, p. 152.

[51] Ibid., p. 152.

[52] Ibid., p. 157.

[53] Ibid., p. 158.

[54] James S. Coleman, et al., *Equality of Educational Opportunity* (Washington, DC: U.S. Government Printing Office, 1966).

[55] Ibid., p. 325.

[56] Daniel P. Moynihan, *Maximum Feasible Misunderstanding* (New York: The Free Press, 1970), p. 184.

[57] Ravitch, p. 161.

[58] Christopher Jencks, et al., *Inequality: A Reassessment of the Effect of Family and Schooling in America* (New York: Basic Books, 1972).

[59] Rippa, pp. 376–77.

Further Reading

Adams, Julianne Lewis, and Thomas A. DeBlack. *Civil Disobedience: An Oral History of School Desegregation in Fayetteville, Arkansas, 1954–1965*. Fayetteville: University of Arkansas Press, 1994.

Anyon, Jean. *Ghetto Schooling: A Political Economy of Urban Educational Reform*. New York: Teachers College Press, 1997.

Baker, Liva. *The Second Battle of New Orleans: The Hundred-Year Struggle to Integrate the Schools*. New York: Harper Collins, 1996.

Bickel, Alexander. *Politics and the Warren Court*. New York: Harper and Row, 1962.

Bullock, Henry A. *A History of Negro Education in the South: From 1619 to the Present*. Cambridge: Harvard University Press, 1967.

Conant, James B. *Slums and Suburbs*. New York: McGraw-Hill Book Co., 1961.

Cremin, Lawrence A. *American Education: The Metropolitan Experience 1876–1980*. New York: Harper and Row, 1988.

Douglas, Davison M. *Reading, Writing, and Race: The Desegregation of the Charlotte Schools*. Chapel Hill: University of North Carolina Press, 1995.

Fass, Paula S. *Outside In: Minorities and the Transformation of American Education*. New York: Oxford University Press, 1989.

Gossett, Thomas F. *Race: The History of an Idea in America*. New York: Oxford University Press, 1997.

Higham, John, ed. *Civil Rights and Social Wrongs: Black-White Relations since World War II*. University Park: Pennsylvania State University Press, 1997.

Jencks, Christopher, Marshall Smith, Henry Acland, Mary Jo Bane, David Cohen, Herbert Gintis, Barbara Heyn, and Stephen Michelson. *Inequality: A Reassessment of the Effect of Family and Schooling in America*. New York: Basic Books, 1972.

Katz, Michael B., ed. *School Reform: Past and Present*. Boston: Little, Brown and Co., 1971.

King, Desmond. *Separate and Unequal: Black Americans and the U.S. Federal Government*. New York: Oxford University Press, 1995.

Linden, Glenn M. *Desegregating Schools in Dallas: Four Decades in the Federal Courts*. Dallas, TX: Three Forks Press, 1995.

Marable, Manning. *Black Leadership*. New York: Columbia University Press, 1998.

Martin, Waldo E., Jr. *Brown v. Board of Education: A Brief History with Documents*. New York: Bedford/St. Martins, 1998.

Mills, Nicholaus, ed. *The Great School Bus Controversy*. New York: Teachers College Press, Columbia University, 1973.

Mostern, Kenneth. *Autobiography and Black Identity Politics: Racialization in Twentieth-Century America*. New York: Cambridge University Press, 1999.

Ravitch, Diane. *The Troubled Crusade: American Education, 1945–1980*. New York: Basic Books, 1983.

Riches, William T. Martin. *The Civil Rights Movement: Struggle and Resistance*. New York: St. Martin's Press, 1997.

Robnett, Belinda. *How Long? How Long? African American Women in the Struggle for Civil Rights*. New York: Oxford University Press, 1997.

Wellman, David T. *Portraits of White Racism*. New York: Cambridge University Press, 1993.

Williamson, Joel. *From Brown to Bakke: The Supreme Court and School Integration: 1945–1978*. New York: Oxford University Press, 1979.

Wilson, Paul E. *A Time to Lose: Representing Kansas in Brown v. Board of Education*. Lawrence: University Press of Kansas, 1995.

7

Educational Policies in the 1960s: The Kennedy and Johnson Administrations

Earlier chapters examined education in the immediate post–World War II era and during the 1950s. Chapter 6, which discussed racial desegregation, spanned the 1950s and 1960s. The 1960s were the era of President John Kennedy's New Frontier and President Lyndon Johnson's Great Society, a time when racial integration and civil rights ranked high on the nation's agenda. Unlike President Eisenhower, who believed the federal government should play a limited role in education, both Kennedy and Johnson took initiatives for a larger federal presence in educational development and reform. During the 1960s, the cold war continued unabated, nearly reaching a nuclear confrontation between the United States and the Soviet Union over the latter's placement of missiles in Cuba. American initiatives during the cold war that had significant educational dimensions were international development and the Peace Corps.

The Kennedy Administration

John F. Kennedy, president from 1961 to 1963, was concerned about foreign policy but took a general but moderately cautious interest in education. Personally, Kennedy was most interested in preparing the academically gifted, the prospective talented scientists, which he, in Jeffersonian terms, called an "aristocracy of intellect." Kennedy, who

had a sister with special needs, also took a strong interest in the problems of mental retardation and the education of children with special
needs. In 1961, he appointed the Presidential Panel on Mental Retardation, which made recommendations for improving services. These
recommendations contributed to the enactment of PL 88-164, The
Mental Retardation Facilities and Metal Health Construction Centers
Act of 1963.

President Kennedy and his advisers were well aware of the controversies that an increased federal role, especially regarding funding,
had generated for his predecessors, particularly President Truman.
Although he had been embroiled in controversies regarding school
desegregation at Little Rock, Eisenhower, Kennedy's predecessor, had
attempted to avoid the time-consuming and energy-sapping morass
resulting from most of the previous proposals for federal aid. Except
for some support for school construction, President Eisenhower basically adhered to the traditional Republican view of the 1950s that education was best left to states and local school districts. An exception,
however, was the enactment of the *Sputnik*-induced National Defense
Education Act in 1958. Differing ideologically from the moderate
Republican Eisenhower, Kennedy, a moderate liberal Democrat, was
attuned to his party's orientation that the federal government should
aid education to promote the welfare of the country. While generally
committed to federal aid for education, Kennedy was wary of becoming
embroiled in the issue of aid to nonpublic schools. As the country's
first Roman Catholic president, he was careful to avoid allegations that
he was jeopardizing separation of church and state. The Kennedy proposals on education suffered from the administration's inability to
guide them through Congress and from the absence of the high priority
to education exhibited by his successor, Lyndon Johnson.

Kennedy's Background

Scion of politically powerful and well-connected Irish Catholic
Massachusetts families, the Kennedys and Fitzgeralds, John Kennedy
attended elite private Eastern schools.[1] He attended the Choate
School, a highly selective private preparatory school in Wallingsford,
Connecticut, graduating in 1935, sixty-fourth in a class of 112.[2] In
reflecting on his schooling at Choate, Kennedy reminisced that the
school had instilled in him a strong sense of public service. In the summer of 1935, Kennedy was at the London School of Economics, where
he encountered Harold Laski, a leading Fabian socialist theorist,
whose penchant for government socioeconomic planning influenced
some New Deal strategists. Kennedy's stay in London was cut short,
however, by illness which caused him to return to the United States. He
enrolled at Princeton University in fall 1935 but was enrolled for only

one year. In 1936, back in his hometown, Boston, he attended Harvard University. During his first two years, he maintained a "gentleman's B" average. Unlike his successor Lyndon Johnson, Kennedy's forays into campus politics proved unsuccessful, being defeated for freshman class president and student council representative.[3] Kennedy spent part of 1938 in London, where his father, Joseph Kennedy, was ambassador at the Court of St. James. This foreign experience heightened his interest in world affairs and diplomacy. Becoming a more serious student, he majored in government, reading extensively in history and politics, a practice that would become a life-long pursuit.[4] Kennedy, in the honors program, wrote a thesis on the British Prime Minister Neville Chamberlain's appeasement of Hitler at Munich. He graduated from Harvard in 1940, receiving the Bachelor of Science degree, with honors. Kennedy's thesis was later published as *Why England Slept*.[5] Though his father was an isolationist, Kennedy, like many of his generation, became an internationalist who opposed appeasement of would-be aggressors. He later wrote *A Nation of Immigrants*, an early statement on multiculturalism, in which he argued that immigrant groups could become American without losing their ethnic heritage.[6]

During World War II, Kennedy served as a naval officer in the Pacific. After the war, he entered Massachusetts's Democratic politics, winning election to the U.S. House of Representatives in 1946. In Congress, Kennedy proved to be a moderate liberal. He was a member of the House Education and Labor subcommittee. During the heated controversies over federal aid during the late 1940s and 1950s, Kennedy, representing a largely Catholic district, took a moderate position on federal aid to nonpublic schools. He opposed direct aid to nonpublic schools, which he felt was unconstitutional, but favored indirect assistance for the children who attended them, for transportation, health services, and lunches. He introduced a bill in 1949 that would have provided federal funds for busing, health services, and textbooks for pupils attending private and parochial schools. His bill died in committee, however, when federal aid legislation was largely incorporated into the Taft bill, which passed the Senate but died in the House of Representatives.[7] (See chapter 2 for a discussion of the federal aid controversies of the late 1940s and early 1950s.

Kennedy, defeating his Republican opponent, the incumbent, Henry Cabot Lodge, was elected U.S. Senator from Massachusetts in 1952, the year Eisenhower won the Presidency. Reelected in 1958, Kennedy served on the Senate Committee on Government Operations and the Senate Committee on Labor and Public Welfare, which was also responsible for education legislation. He supported the National Defense Education Act, which passed in 1958. Kennedy's own bill for school construction loans and grants to alleviate the classroom shortage died in committee, however. While in the Senate, he wrote a book,

John F. Kennedy when
he was a U.S senator;
(Reproduction from the
Collections of the Library
of Congress.)

Profiles in Courage, published in 1957, about U.S. Senators who
exhibited courage by taking unpopular stands that often cost them
their political careers.[8]

Campaign of 1960

Kennedy, who was the first Roman Catholic to be elected President, was cautious about church-state issues related to education during his campaign for president in 1960 and during his administration.
During the campaign, church-state issues held center stage. Kennedy
wanted to demonstrate that his Roman Catholic religion would not
interfere with his duties as president. He and his advisers were well
aware of how the issue of aid to private schools had jettisoned federal
aid initiatives during the Truman administration. At the same time,
Kennedy followed the general Democratic policy of favoring federal aid
to education.

Kennedy, the Democratic presidential nominee in the 1960 election faced his Republican opponent, Richard Nixon, Eisenhower's vice

president, from 1953–1961. Although education was not the major issue in the campaign of 1960, the positions of the contenders outlined the differences between the major parties. Kennedy, using the phrase, "the missile gap," alleged that the Soviet Union was outdistancing the United States in the technology needed for nuclear deterrence and the space race. He promised to recapture the American lead in science and education. Careful to avoid the aid to religious schools controversy, Kennedy supported federal aid for public schools only and supplemental assistance for public schools in poorer states. Addressing education in the campaign, he advanced three main aid-to-education proposals: (1) a program for school construction and improved teachers' salaries; (2) a program for college and university construction; (3) continuation of the NDEA.

Nixon's educational platform promised federal programs that would match state grants for school construction and some supplemental assistance for teachers' salaries. In higher education, the Republican candidate endorsed matching grants for construction of classrooms, libraries, and laboratories and for tuition tax credits.[9]

An unprecedented high point in the 1960 election was the series of televised Kennedy-Nixon debates. Viewed by millions, the debates made clear that television would be a crucial dynamic in American politics. In an extremely close election, Kennedy defeated Nixon.

The Task Force Approach

Kennedy's inauguration in 1961 launched the "New Frontier" in American politics.[10] Like President Franklin Roosevelt's New Deal, the New Frontier used experts from the professions, universities, and foundations who, organized into task forces, were to design the Kennedy administration's legislative proposals. For education, the task force was chaired by Frederick L. Hovde, president of Purdue University. Among the distinguished task force members were Alvin Eurich, vice president of the Ford Foundation, Francis Keppel, dean of the Harvard School of Business, John Gardner, president of the Carnegie Corporation, Russell Thackery, executive secretary of the Land Grant Colleges Association, and Benjamin Willis, the superintendent of the Chicago Public Schools and the president of the American Association of School Administrators. The task force report urged a massive federal aid program that included large grants to the states for public schools, an equalization bonus for the poorer states, support for higher education construction, and extension of the NDEA. Although the administration could use the report's broad outlines urging large-scale federal aid, the recommendations lacked a specificity tied to fiscal realities. Further, the report, which did not include aid to private schools, came under the attack of Cardinal Spellman and others in the Catholic hierarchy.[11]

Kennedy's educational policy was largely developed within the parameters established by the Bureau of the Budget, particularly its labor and welfare staff. Using the budget as a planning instrument, the approach departed from the usual federal aid strategy. The Hovde task force had developed a federal aid package along the lines favored by the leading educational organizations, namely, aid to the states which, in turn, would distribute funds to public schools. The working assumptions of the Bureau of the Budget, which shaped federal initiatives for the next decade, were: (1) federal aid should stimulate a greater local and state contribution rather than substitute for it; (2) the federal role should be defined clearly; (3) the federal role should be planned within the larger context of administration policies.[12] While the Kennedy administration would be less than successful in many of its educational initiatives, these three principles would also be used to shape the more ambitious and successful policies pursued by the Johnson administration's War on Poverty. Educational policies would be related to the larger socioeconomic context and would give the federal government a larger role in schools.

Leadership for education in the Kennedy administration came from Abraham Ribicoff, secretary of Health, Education and Welfare, and then from Anthony Celebrezze, a former mayor of Cleveland, who later replaced Ribicoff. Heading the Office of Education was U.S. Commissioner of Education Sterling McMurrin, who had been a professor of philosophy and an administrator at the University of Utah. McMurrin's successor would be Francis Keppel, dean of the Harvard School of Education, who became U.S. commissioner of education in 1962. Another key figure who passed judgment on any matter dealing with education was Edith Green, a Democratic congresswoman from Oregon. Those in the administration who were in charge of educational initiatives had to reckon with Representative Green's support or opposition.

Kennedy's Education Proposals

On February 20, 1961, President Kennedy presented his special message on education, which recommended federal assistance for: (1) public elementary and secondary school construction and improving teachers' salaries; (2) loans to state colleges and universities for construction; (3) state scholarships for talented students in financial need; (4) creation of an advisory board to evaluate and improve vocational education programs.[13] No aid was recommended for private schools, and nonpublic schoolchildren were excluded in the funding formula. As had occurred with federal aid proposals in the past, Kennedy's generated controversy.[14] The National Catholic Welfare Conference opposed aid to elementary and secondary education that excluded private schools. After negotiations, an amendment to the NDEA was proposed that included loans to private schools for construction of classrooms in science, mathematics, foreign languages, English, and physical education and provided a school lunch program. Nevertheless, the Kennedy education proposals for aid to elementary and secondary education floundered on the same shoals that earlier attempts at such legislation had encountered.[15] Public school organizations favored aid that excluded private schools; private school organizations, especially Roman Catholic ones, opposed legislation that excluded their institutions. (Again, refer to chapter 2 for shifting coalitions in support of federal aid.) The administration retreated from its proposals to avoid religious controversy, which would have proved exceedingly difficult for the country's first Catholic president. Although the Senate passed a comprehensive bill, The School Assistance Act of 1961, it died in the House, where the Rules Committee withheld action.[16] Legislation for the Juvenile Delinquency and Youth Offenses Control Act and the extension of the NDEA were enacted, however. Whereas Kennedy had difficulty in securing passage of the administration's domestic education program, he was more successful in the international area. His proposal for establishing a Peace Corps passed in 1961. (For a discussion of the Peace Corps, see the following section on international education and the Peace Corps.)

Kennedy's State of the Union Message on January 11, 1962, announced his administration's intention to renew its efforts for federal aid for public school construction and support for teachers' salaries. In his second Special Message on Education, delivered on February 6, 1962, Kennedy, relating education to the national interest, called it a national investment in the future, necessary in order for the country to keep pace with a rapidly changing technological world. Reiterating his proposals of 1961, Kennedy called for: (1) a comprehensive school aid program for classroom construction and improving teachers' salaries; (2) assistance to higher education; (3) aid for programs in special education, medical and dental education, science and engineering, adult education, migrant workers education, educational television, children with handicaps, and the arts.[17] Again, the administration's proposals excluded private schools. For many of the same reasons that had killed educational legislation in 1961, most of Kennedy's 1962 proposals died in congressional committees. Small victories were won, however, in the enactment of the Educational Television Act and a funding increase for the National Science Foundation. With Kennedy's approval, the non-Communist disclaimer affidavit was eliminated from the National Science Foundation Act of 1950 and the National Defense Education Act of 1958.[18]

In higher education, the Kennedy proposals were directed to the construction of facilities, federal scholarships, and federally subsidized loans. The proposals became mired in controversy over the issue of loans, which at that time were prohibited by several states. Kennedy also proposed forgiveness on the repayment of student loans for those entering fields related to national security. The Kennedy proposal failed. If it had passed, it would have turned a loan into a grant.

In 1962, Kennedy appointed Francis Keppel, a former dean of the Harvard Graduate School of Education, as commissioner of education. Keppel played an important role in redesigning the Kennedy education proposals for the 1963 sessions of Congress.

By 1963, the Kennedy administration, responding to advice from the Bureau of the Budget (BOB), modified its strategy on educational legislation. The new approach sought to avoid the obstacles that had defeated aid to education in 1961 and 1962 when the administration's bills failed. In this strategy, the administration divided its proposals into separate initiatives rather than a general omnibus bill. However, the new tactic did not succeed. Each separate bill generated the activities of specific special interest education lobbies, either for or against the bill.[19] Consequently, the administration's energies were dissipated and the support of the educational community splintered. The BOB then recommended a general omnibus strategy in which aid for education would be tied to the country's broad social welfare and economic productivity. While not as dramatic as Johnson's Great Society programs would be two years later, Kennedy's revised strategy marked a move in that direction.

The proposed new strategy, linking education to the society's well-being, inclined federal policymakers toward educational theory. Seen as more than simple aid to schools, the broadened strategy suggested that education, defined as more than schooling, was related to the nation's general social and economic well-being. This new social direction also was moving the federal government out of the national defense syndrome that limited educational aid to science and mathematics into more general directions. Rather than parceling out federal aid as supplemental funds to the states to be redistributed to their local school districts, the new approach would target special innovative programs which would move education in a new rather than in the same direction. While it would take the Johnson emphasis on the Great Society and the War on Poverty to complete the theoretical and strategic realignment regarding education, the beginnings of the new framework were being put into place.

Kennedy's State of the Union Address on January 14, 1963, called for an investment in American youth by expanding education and manpower training and by creating a domestic version of the Peace Corps. Following the new strategy to put forth a single omnibus bill rather than separate pieces of legislation, Kennedy's Special Message on Education delivered on January 29, 1963, was accompanied by the administration's National Education Improvement Act of 1963. Kennedy, stressing broad national goals, sought to unite the profederal aid constituencies, especially those in Congress. Arguing that the quality and availability of education was vital to national security and domestic well-being, Kennedy set forth the goals of the Education Improvement Act:

> First, we must improve the quality of instruction provided in all of our schools and colleges. We must stimulate interest in learning in order to reduce the alarming number of students who now drop out of school or who do not continue into higher levels of education.
>
> Second, our education system faces a problem of quantity—of coping with the needs of our expanding population and of the rising educational expectations for our children which all of us share as parents.
>
> Third, we must give special attention to increasing the opportunities and incentives for all Americans to develop their talents to the utmost—to complete their education and to continue their self-development throughout life.[20]

The Education Improvement Act sought to integrate the categorical approach directed to specific programs with a general thrust to educational innovation. It would provide assistance to specific areas, such as increasing teachers' salaries, classroom construction, and aid to higher education, with special selected programs designed to improve educational quality. This approach would put the federal government behind innovative programs rather than merely adding funds to existing ones. The funds for these categories would be channeled through the states which could use them only within the specified categories. Again, following Kennedy's desire to escape embroilment in church-state issues, the aid was only for public and not for private schools.

Despite a more streamlined strategy, Kennedy's proposed education legislation soon was bogged down in Congress. The House Committee on Education, headed by the often unpredictable Adam Clayton Powell (Democrat from New York) and including Oregon's Edith Green, who regarded education as her area of special expertise, went the traditional route of dividing the Education Improvement Act into separate bills dealing with aid to elementary and secondary education, higher education, vocational and adult education, extension of NDEA programs, and aid to federally impacted areas. Like the House, the Senate Labor and Public Welfare Committee also decided to report separate bills rather than an omnibus bill. Though a new approach, the omnibus bill approach did not work in Congress. Only smaller pieces of the proposed Education Improvement Act survived, enacted as a college aid bill, an NDEA extension, and aid to federally impacted areas.

While Kennedy's federal aid initiatives generally met with failure, the administration's actions against racial segregation experienced greater success. In 1961, the Office of Education began requiring a nondiscrimination clause in contracts with colleges and universities that were selected for the sponsorship of NDEA institutes. Effective as of 1963, funds would be withheld from segregated school districts that were receiving federal aid under the impacted areas funding. In 1963, the Justice Department filed its first suit to withhold federal funds from the impacted area in Prince George County, Virginia. The administration also stood firm against attempts by Governor Ross Barnett of Mississippi and Governor George Wallace of Alabama to block integration of higher education in their states. (For the civil rights and integration efforts of the Kennedy administration, see chapter 6.) While the nation was moving forward with its agenda of racial integration, the cold war which had preoccupied the earlier Truman and Eisenhower administrations continued to engage the energies of Kennedy and his successor, Lyndon Johnson.

International Relations and the Peace Corps

Although his administration's efforts to maneuver federal aid to education legislation through Congress were less than successful, Kennedy did enjoy success in international relations. In particular, his concept of the Peace Corps marked an important development that related to international aid and development programs. While it originated as an American initiative in the cold war, the Peace Corps's significance extends beyond both the Kennedy and Johnson eras.[21]

During the cold war, American strategy was multifaceted. Key elements involved using military force and deployment, economic assistance and development, diplomacy, and the power of persuasion.[22] The organization of the North Atlantic Treaty Organization, NATO, was an example of using military force to counter the perceived Soviet threat in Europe. Beginning with the Marshall Plan of aid to reconstruct war-torn Europe, U.S. foreign policy involved an economic dimension. The rationale for foreign assistance programs was: Weak economies produce destabilizing political situations that lead to internal weakness conducive to Communist intrigues. Strong economies, in contrast, produce stable political systems, which can withstand the Communist-Soviet threat. Since the cold war involved a struggle of two ideologies—communism and democracy—a large part of the conflict involved each proponent's use of persuasion through propaganda and education to strengthen the commitment of believers in one or the other and to convert the unaligned to either the American or the Soviet persuasion.

While all of the elements in the containment policy held educational implications, the economic and the persuasive, or propaganda, dimensions were highly significant. The economic emphasis, born with the successful Marshall Plan, contributed to the concept that the United States could build underdeveloped economies into developed ones by importing American technologies and training to such countries. It would be possible to develop nations, particularly those in postcolonial Asia and Africa, creating friendly allies. The persuasive aspect took the form of propaganda (not used negatively here but referring to persuasive messages delivered via such organizations as Radio Free Europe, the Voice of America, the U.S. Information Service, and private agencies as well) to present the cause of democracy and expose Soviet deceitfulness and totalitarianism.[23]

During the 1960s, the newly independent, postcolonial nations faced a highly difficult policy decision. In order to build their infrastructures, they often needed assistance from at least one of the two competing superpowers, the United States or the USSR. While some attempted to remain nonaligned in the cold war, others took aid from either the United States or the Soviet Union. The decision to accept economic assistance, however, carried with it advantages and disadvantages for the newly independent "third world" countries.[24] On the one hand, the United States appeared as the defender of democracy, but on the other hand, it also was tied in its European alliances to the former colonial powers—the United Kingdom, France, Belgium, and the Netherlands—which had subjugated them. Critics of U.S. policy in the newly independent, former colonies condemned the American efforts as a new species of neocolonialism. A popular novel and motion picture, *The Ugly American*, portrayed the ineptness of American diplomats in dealing with people in what was called the "third world." The USSR had the apparent advantage of being a revolutionary power that was challenging the old colonial order. However, its repressive actions in Eastern Europe, particularly in Hungary and Czechoslovakia, also made some of the unaligned nations suspicious of Soviet intentions.

Economic Assistance

The post–World War II origins of economic assistance as a component of American foreign policy go back to 1947 when President Truman, responding to Communist insurgency in Greece, announced the Truman Doctrine, which provided military and economic aid to Greece and Turkey. In 1948, Secretary of State George Marshall proposed massive U.S. assistance to aid in European recovery. The motivation was partly humanitarian and partly political. The humanitarian phase was an evident need to prevent suffering in a war-devastated Europe. The political phase rested on what would become a long-standing and determining U.S. policy position. Political instability was caused by economic instability. Countries with economic stability would be more likely to follow democratic political structures and free enterprise economics than those plagued by an unstable economy. In 1948, Congress accepted The Marshall Plan and passed a massive assistance program, The Economic Cooperation Act for a European Recovery.

The Marshall Plan was a great success in rebuilding the economic structures of Western Europe. Here, such major recipients of aid as the United Kingdom, France, Belgium, and the Netherlands already had well-established infrastructures. Damaged in the war, these infrastructures were reconstructed. The success of the Marshall Plan contributed to a dominating postwar strategy of economic development. It was believed that the success in Western Europe could be replicated throughout the world, including in the newly independent former colonies of Africa and Asia. Congress enacted the International Development Act in 1950 to extend U.S. technical, agricultural, scientific, and engineering assistance to the underdeveloped nations of the world. In 1953, the training of teachers and other forms of educational assistance were added to the act. In 1956, during the Eisenhower administration, the International Cooperation Administration was created as a semiautonomous agency within the U.S. Department of State. A highly important U.S. international agency, the Agency for International Development (AID) was established in 1961 during the Kennedy administration.[25]

International Development

By midpoint in the cold war, many American educators had embraced the strategies of international development and development education. Essays in *The United States and International Education* provided a clear statement of the reigning educational opinion of the 1960s and 1970s.[26]

Spurred by foreign aid programs of AID, many American educators believed that education could be a force for deliberate social and economic engineering. The development rationale held that modern institutions and processes could be transferred from the United States to underdeveloped nations abroad. According to the rationale: (1) the United States and American education had an international role; (2) some nations were developed and modern and others were less developed and more traditional; (3) American educators could play a leading role in international development by providing the expertise to assist underdeveloped nations to become developed and modern; (4) as educational, health care, and economic infrastructures were developed, emergent postcolonial newly independent countries could be transformed into modern countries by "nation building."

Like other terms in education, those related to development experienced change. In the 1960s, the terms "developed" and "underdeveloped" as well as "third world" were commonly used. By the 1980s, "underdeveloped" had been discarded for the phrase, "less technologically developed." During the cold war, the designations "first world" referred to the West, to Western Europe and North America, especially the United States, which were developed nations, with democratic governments and stable free market economies; the "second world" were the Communist nations—the USSR and the Soviet bloc; the "third world" referred to the postcolonial independent nations of Africa, Asia, and parts of South America, also called "emerging nations."[27]

The American development educators argued that the transfer of modern (often defined in American terms) institutions and processes could aid developing countries in institution building—creating educational, medical, agricultural, commercial, governmental, and transportation infrastructures—that would enable traditional societies to become modern nations. An abbreviated way of referring to the complex process was "nation building." While there was general allegiance to nation building, educators, like Cole Brembeck, pointed out the differences between Western and non-Western conceptions of the role of institutions and how they developed.[28]

U.S. development education, exported abroad, also carried with it the American pragmatic emphasis on the practical, the vocational, and the applied. It challenged the inherited postcolonial systems of education that existed in many developing nations, which stressed literary and humanistic classics on the British or French model. A redirection in educational thought from a literary emphasis to more applied scientific and engineering forms would be an important element in the modernizing process. Thus, nation building and applied knowledge were key ingredients in the American development educators' frame of reference.

The typical strategy used in implementing assistance in the 1960s and 1970s was top down, usually starting at the government level. Representatives of the U.S. government—State Department and AID officials—would develop a program of assistance that might involve military, economic, agricultural, health care and educational components. Contracts would then be issued to U.S. institutions and agencies to implement components of the assistance program. The major actors in the aid scenario were U.S. universities, which provided technical expertise in areas such as health care and sanitation, agriculture, public and business administration, engineering, science, marketing and education.[29] In the field of education, U.S. development educators emphasized the establishment of vocational training programs, creat-

A village primary school in India. Peace Corps and other international development programs often included aid to schools in less technologically developed countries. (Reproduction from the National Archives, photo #306-PS-60-19178.)

ing comprehensive secondary schools on the American model, and adult literacy programs. American foreign assistance personnel, often university professors and researchers, would then work with host country counterparts to implement the particular project.[30]

During the late 1960s and into the 1970s, development projects were lauded as bringing about important changes in the developing nations. Since many developing nations were agricultural, agricultural science was given a key role. Following the U.S. pattern in which large state universities operated agricultural extension services and model experimental farms, American agricultural educators sought to implement similar approaches in developing countries. Important components in agricultural development were irrigation projects, crop rotation, and the use of fertilizers and pesticides. For example, hybrid wheat was introduced in India, and hybrid, high yielding rice was brought to the Philippines. It was proclaimed that a "green revolution" of improved production was taking place, which in turn improved the economic condition of the people.

A class in a primary school in India, where a development worker is assisting a teacher. (Reproduction from the National Archives, photo #306-PS-50-10589.)

The Peace Corps

In his 1960 presidential campaign, Kennedy, echoing the theme of a New Frontier, proposed sending "young men and women" to work as "teachers and nurses" in different countries for the "cause of freedom."[31] On November 2, 1960, Kennedy proposed the establishment of "a peace corps of talented young men and women" who would volunteer to serve the United States for a period of three years. Kennedy stated that the Peace Corps volunteers were to be

> well qualified through rigorous standards, well trained in the language, skills and customs they will need to know. . . . We cannot discontinue training our young men as soldiers of war, but we also want them to be ambassadors of peace. . . .[32]

Kennedy's proposal was not unique. Congressman Henry Reuss and Senator Hubert Humphrey had proposed legislation to support young Americans to work as volunteers in developing nations. Reuss, in particular, had collaborated with Professor Samuel Hayes, an expert in international economic programs at the University of Michigan, in developing the concept of government-supported international volunteers.[33]

Kennedy reiterated in his inaugural address that a "new generation of Americans" had an international responsibility to dedicate themselves to advancing freedom throughout the world. Dedicated persons could volunteer to represent the United States abroad by working in worthy development projects such as health care, sanitation, and education.[34]

Kennedy's suggestion of a volunteer corps of Americans working in the developing world gained considerable popular support, with 30,000 letters received in support of the idea.[35] Newspaper editorials, too, generally endorsed the idea of a force of international volunteers. For example, *The New York Times*, supporting the Peace Corps concept and emphasizing the urgency of the proposed volunteer corps, stated that half of the world's people were ill-fed. In developing countries, education was an imperative in the war against illiteracy. Further, health care was either poor or nonexistent. Garnering public support, Kennedy, in his first State of the Union Address, urged "formation of a National Peace Corps."[36]

On March 1, 1961, President Kennedy created the Peace Corps by executive order on a "temporary pilot basis" as an agency within the Department of State and named R. Sargent Shriver, his brother-in-law, as its director. Congress subsequently passed PL 87-293 authorizing the Peace Corps on September 22, 1961. President Kennedy appointed Vice President Lyndon Johnson to chair the Peace Corps National Advisory Committee.

The committee included distinguished individuals from government, higher education, business, and organized labor. Among the members were Harris Wofford, professor of law from the University of Notre Dame; Gilbert White, from the University of Chicago; Walter Reuther, president of the United Auto Workers; as well as members from the federal Bureau of the Budget. The task force identified the major objectives of the Peace Corps as: (1) contributing to the development of critical countries and regions; (2) promoting international goodwill toward the United States; (3) contributing to the international education of the American public and to "more intelligent American participation in the world."[37] The committee, enthusiastic about the prospects of the Peace Corps, supported Sargent Shriver's idea of a "bold, large, fast-moving trained cadre of volunteers that would become a truly significant force in the world arena."[38]

Peace Corps training programs were designed cooperatively by colleges and universities, international agencies, and private organizations. Universities, however, were the key agencies in preparing volunteers for their work overseas. The first training program was at Rutgers University, where volunteers were prepared by doing community development fieldwork in Colombia. By 1962 nearly fifty universities were training volunteers.[39] The role played by universities in Peace Corps training programs was but one example of higher education's involvement in international aid and development programs.

The Peace Corps volunteers were interested in living in another culture and assisting people in developing nations to improve their condition. At first, volunteers came from those whose interest had been sparked by Kennedy's call to work abroad for peace. When the pool of applicants proved too small to meet the demand for volunteers, the Peace Corps turned to active recruiting. For example, in 1962, 20,000 applications were received, up from the 13,000 of the previous year. Typically, one out of five applicants was accepted and sent to training.[40] The volunteers were often college-educated young people with an altruistic global orientation.

Applicants had to sustain a six-hour comprehensive examination, assessing their general knowledge and aptitude in a foreign language. This was followed by a medical examination to determine if the applicant's health was adequate to meet the challenges of a demanding overseas assignment.

After acceptance, volunteers completed a rigorous training program at a college or university. The training curriculum consisted of: (1) a survey of world political problems, including the dangers of Communist subversion; (2) a review of American history; (3) a survey of medical problems volunteers would likely encounter; (4) recreational activities; (5) a study of the customs, culture, and histories of the countries that would host Peace Corps volunteers; (6) intensive language instruction in the host country's language; (7) a field experience that simulated what life would be like in the host country.[41]

A discussion of the Peace Corps training program illustrates U.S. thinking of what was needed to mount a successful international effort and to counter the "Ugly American" image. While the program contained much that was altruistic, it was, in its origin, also part of the U.S. global anti-Communist strategy. Peace Corps volunteers were to be sophisticated emissaries of the United States who were able to recognize Communist intrigues. That the volunteers should know their own country's history and political structure was an important phase of the program. Another key part of the training program was immersion in the culture and language of the host country. Americans abroad, including some in the diplomatic corps and the military, had long been accused of being ignorant of the culture of the host country. The stereotype of the "tongue-tied" American often accompanied the unflattering image of the "Ugly American," whose lack of cultural sensitivity insulted those in the host country. Language teaching was no easy task. While instructors and materials were plentiful in the familiar

European languages such as French, German, and Spanish, it was a different case with many of the languages of the developing countries such as Hindi, Urdu, Tamil, Malay, Thai, Ebo, and Hausa.

An important culminating phase of the training program prior to actual overseas assignment was a field experience in which volunteers encountered simulated situations similar to those they would face in the host country. For example, volunteers going to Latin American assignments had field experience in Puerto Rico; those going to the Himalayan region had experience in the Rocky Mountains to accustom them to work in high altitudes.[42]

Volunteers received a living allowance, based on the cost-of-living index in the host country, which would permit a style of life comparable to host country co-workers. This averaged about $300 per month. Travel, medical, and housing expenses were provided. A readjustment allowance of $75 for each month of satisfactory service was paid at the completion of service to assist volunteers to return to life in the United States.

The major overseas projects of volunteers were in education, community development, health care, and agriculture. Volunteers taught in elementary and secondary schools, technical institutes, teacher training institutions and universities. Those involved in community development projects helped to build schools and health care clinics, roads, and sanitation facilities. Agricultural projects included basic farming, establishment of demonstration centers, and creation of rural cooperatives.

Since its founding, the Peace Corps has continued to the present. The degree to which it has been funded has depended on presidential and congressional priorities. Nevertheless, its sustained record makes it an important part of the history of American international education.

In the third year of his presidency, Kennedy had scored some successes in the international area. However, the larger concept of assistance to elementary and secondary education was delayed, albeit temporarily, during the Kennedy administration. President Kennedy was assassinated in Dallas, Texas, on November 22, 1963, and the fate of his educational as well as other legislation would be in the hands of the new President, Lyndon Baines Johnson.

Lyndon Johnson and Education for the Great Society

Lyndon Baines Johnson came to the presidency after a long career in local, state, and national politics and government. His term as president, beginning with Kennedy's tragic assassination in 1963, was marked by great legislative triumphs, especially for education, but also by the political pathos of entrapment in the war in Vietnam. If there truly was an "education president" in the twentieth century's second half, it was Lyndon Johnson.

Johnson's Background

Johnson's own early life and education is highly instructive for revealing the strengths and weaknesses that would mark his presidency.[43] His father, Sam Johnson, a local politician and steadfast Democrat, served in the state legislature. His mother, Rebekah Baines Johnson, a well-educated woman, exercised a strong, often controlling influence on her son.

Born in New Stonewall on the Pedernales River in Texas, Johnson's elementary education was in a one-room school near his home. His secondary education was at the Johnson City high school, from which he graduated in 1924. He was admitted to Southwest Texas State Teachers College at San Marcos. Always quick to size up the politics of a situation, Johnson had the uncanny ability to develop a mental flow chart of the operations and personnel of an institution. Drawn to the college's higher administration, Johnson made himself known in the president's office and became an unofficial "appointments secretary" to Dr. Cecil Evans, the college's president. He was also adept at building his own political network on the campus and served as editor of the College newspaper, *The College Star*, from 1927 to 1930.[44]

Johnson's editorials in the *Star* provide early indications of the importance he gave to education, schooling, and teaching. Believing that education enabled individuals to develop their best and highest talents, he would work for greater access to and participation in schools and colleges, for all, and especially for underrepresented groups. Praising teaching as a vocation worthy of praise and respect, he saw the teacher as imparting knowledge, serving humanity, and leading the young.[45]

Needing funds to complete his college education, Johnson took a one-year assignment as principal and teacher at the Welhausen School in Cotulla, Texas, a largely Mexican-American elementary school. In addition to teaching and administrative responsibilities, he coached the boys' baseball team and was the debate coach, playground supervisor, and when needed, janitor. These tasks gave him firsthand experience with the educational effects of socioeconomic deprivation, a theme emphasized in his War on Poverty programs. To motivate his students and build their self-esteem, he inaugurated a number of competitive activities. Recognizing the importance of community and parental involvement, he organized a school volunteer program—a precursory feature of Head Start and other educational programs of his Great Society and War on Poverty. Johnson, however, did not break

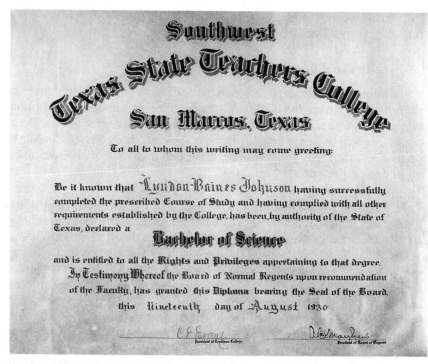

Lyndon B. Johnson's diploma from Southwest Texas State Teachers College, San Marcos, Texas. (Courtesy LBJ Library Collection.)

the mold that governed public schools in Texas at the time. Not allowing the use of Spanish, he ran an English-language-only school. After a year at Cotulla, Johnson returned to Southwest Texas State Teachers College to complete his degree requirements. After graduation, he took a teaching position at Sam Houston High School in Houston, Texas.[46]

Though attracted to education as a career, politics was the all-consuming force in Johnson's personality. He left teaching to serve as secretary to Congressman Richard Kleberg, a Texas Democrat. Just as he "sized up" who ran Southwest Texas State, he constructed a similar mental flow chart of how the U.S. House of Representative functioned and began to make the right connections. His political acumen led to his appointment as Texas director of the National Youth Administration (NYA) during the depression. The NYA included myriad projects designed to put young people to work. Several of these, such as the Freshman College Centers and the College Aid Program, were directed specifically to education.

Johnson's position with the NYA during President Roosevelt's New Deal shaped his perspective on how government should work. Like Roosevelt, whom he greatly admired, Johnson came to believe that the federal government had an indispensable role to play in promoting social welfare. As a young man coming to professional maturity in the pre-World War II era, he also learned from Roosevelt that democracies should never again appease dictatorships. While he successfully applied the lesson that government had a social role in his Great Society programs, he misapplied the nonappeasement lesson to Vietnam, which would negate many of his successes as president.

From 1937 until 1948, Johnson served in the U.S. House of Representatives. He then was elected to the U.S. Senate, serving for twelve years from 1949 to 1961. In the Senate, Johnson became the leader of the Democratic caucus, serving as majority leader when his party held control. As a senator, Johnson continued to support federal aid to education. He supported legislation for school construction, facilities improvement, raising teachers' salaries, college student loans, and international education. He also supported the National Defense Education Act passed in 1959.

In the election of 1960, Johnson ran as Kennedy's vice presidential running mate. Kennedy's assassination in November 1963 brought Johnson to the presidency. Johnson, the liberal Democratic nominee, won a landslide victory over his conservative Republican opponent, Barry Goldwater, in the election of 1964. The Democrats also won large majorities in Congress: sixty-eight Democrats to thirty-two Republicans in the Senate and 295 Democrats to 140 Republicans in the House of Representatives. Johnson, an astute politician who knew that you had to have the votes to pass legislation, believed that he could now secure the enactment of federal aid to education legislation.

Johnson's Educational Strategy

With years of legislative experience as a congressman and senator, Johnson was well attuned to the nuances of lawmaking. His tactical strategy was to be well prepared, knowledgeable, and then to use all the pressures and niceties that could be applied to convince members of Congress to support his programs. Further, Johnson, whose early formative Washington experiences had occurred during Roosevelt's New Deal, had a broad view of the socioeconomic and educational role of the federal government. A former teacher and school principal, he was earnestly committed to a larger federal role in education, and like others to follow him in the presidency, wanted to be known and remembered as the "education president."

Drawing on the experiences of the Roosevelt "brain trusts" of the New Deal, Johnson, like Kennedy, used task forces to provide the needed background for formulating his legislative program. Johnson's task force on education was chaired by John W. Gardner, president of the Carnegie Corporation, and included William Cannon of the Bureau of the Budget. What came from the task force and the BOB was a further refinement in the strategy that was emerging in the last year of the Kennedy administration. The Johnson educational strategy, which incorporated ideas already present during the Kennedy administration, included the following: (1) education, considered in larger context than schooling, should be related to national socioeconomic well-being; (2) educational legislation should be framed more as a total package of related programs, rather than as separate items that appeared disconnected; (3) educational programs, supported by federal aid, should move education in new, innovative directions rather than reinforce and subsidize the status quo. Additionally, school districts receiving federal aid should be actively moving toward racial desegregation. The prospects for success in federal aid for education brightened under Johnson's aegis. Unlike the Roman Catholic Kennedy, he did not have to be as wary of the church-state issue that had plagued federal aid proposals in the past. Importantly, Johnson's interest in education was a stronger one than that of Kennedy who, though he supported federal aid, was more personally drawn to other issues, particularly those in foreign policy.

As the Johnson advisers prepared their strategy for enacting federal legislation for education, they examined why this area had been so perilously difficult in the past and how it might be approached success-

President Lyndon Baines Johnson. (Photograph by Yoichi R. Okamoto, courtesy LBJ Library Collection.)

fully by the new administration. Since World War II, the most successful federal programs in education had been the GI Bill, signed by President Roosevelt in 1944, and the NDEA, signed by President
Eisenhower in 1958. Otherwise, proposed federal programs, especially those designed to aid elementary and secondary programs, had
floundered after they had first generated intense competition among
the special-interest groups in education and stirred considerable sec-
tarian conflict on the church-state issue of aid to nonpublic institutions.

In the post–World War II era, federal education legislation had
been based on needs specified by the special lobbies representing the
educational establishment, such as vocational education and agricultural education, local school board associations, state officers of education, and school administrator organizations. The typical congressional bills, based on this input, were designed to aid selected parts of
the American educational system. For example, proposed legislation
sought to provide funds to supplement teachers' salaries, expand vocational education, aid school facilities construction, and provide loans
or grants to college students. In the course of the legislative process,
the bills would become entangled in the agendas of various lobbies that
pressured for more aid for constituent organizations, usually at the
sacrifice of others. What had proved most perilous was that federal aid
proposals would be wrecked by the church-state controversies that
surfaced when nonpublic, particularly parochial, schools were either
included or excluded. (For a discussion of such entanglements, see
chapter 2.) Johnson's advisers, in their review of recently failed federal
aid proposals, sought to avoid the failures of Truman and Kennedy,
their Democratic predecessors, in providing federal aid to schools.
Taking a larger socioeconomic perspective, they reasoned that these
piecemeal, more or less traditional approaches, if enacted, would not
have led to real educational change but merely would have reinforced
an inadequate status quo.

The Johnson strategy for enacting federal aid to education rested
on several working assumptions. Federal aid proposals would be key
elements in a comprehensive program that was part of a context of
broad socioeconomic change. In this way, programs to aid schools
would not be isolated but would be part of the larger Great Society and
War on Poverty agenda. Education, they argued, was needed as part of
a comprehensive federal policy for eliminating poverty and promoting
social welfare and economic growth. Rather than relying on how the
lobbies representing the educational establishment defined its needs,
the administration, in consultation with educators, would define educational goals and propose programs to achieve them. Rather than
supplementing existing efforts by states and local districts, federal programs would be used to stimulate and diffuse innovations throughout

the nation's schools. Finally, and most importantly, such an ambitious federal program would require massive assistance.[47] The new strategy, based on the New Deal experience and the Kennedy efforts at omnibus educational legislation, became part of the Johnson administration's strategy to enact legislation for a massive program of federal aid to education.

Based on the new strategy, the Gardner Task Force began to shape general principles into more specific programmatic proposals that the administration would present to Congress. To build a large supportive consensus that related education to the larger War on Poverty, concerted efforts were directed at improving education in the poverty-impacted urban areas. (See chapter 6 for education and the urban crisis.) To avoid the vexing church-state issue, aid would be directed to poverty-impacted children, rather than directly to schools, in both public and private institutions. State departments of education would be strengthened to make them into change agents capable of diffusing educational innovations. Educational centers for research and development would be created. A network of regional demonstration and dissemination laboratories would be established.[48] In higher education, there was to be a massive expansion of student loans.

As the administration's proposals for federal aid were being honed, Johnson's landslide victory in 1964 over Senator Barry Goldwater, the Republican nominee for president, carried with it large Democratic majorities in both the Senate and the House of Representatives. Johnson, a clever legislative leader with a politically supportive Congress, had bright possibilities to achieve his programmatic goals. Further, the enactment of the Civil Rights Act of 1964, which empowered the federal government to bring suit and to withdraw funds to enforce desegregation, helped to take the race issue out of the federal aid to education debate.

The War on Poverty and Education

Johnson's essential strategy was to relate education to the larger context of Great Society social, political, and economic issues, especially the War on Poverty. His approach, employing strategies emerging at the end of the Kennedy administration, would relate aid to education to broad social and economic change rather than merely to adding funds to existing programs. Federal aid to education would be innovatively transformative rather than a series of add-ons. An ideological heir of Roosevelt's New Deal, he saw the federal government taking a leading role in alleviating and ending poverty in the United States.[49] The War on Poverty, however, was not just a 1960s' rendition of the New Deal's antidepression measures of the 1930s. In general, the country was enjoying prosperity. However, serious areas of poverty in

America's big-city, urban ghettoes and in some rural areas, especially Appalachia, were festering economic ulcers. Not only was the War on Poverty a long-standing Johnson agenda, but it reflected current social theory. John Galbraith, the liberal economist, in his *Affluent Society*, had called attention to the existence of pockets of poverty, a residual problem in a seemingly prosperous economy. Liberal economic theory linked poverty to two conditions: the residual factor identified by Galbraith; and structural adjustment, unemployment due to low or inappropriate skills in a technological economy. The War on Poverty sought to correct both of these deficiencies by eliminating poverty in its residual pockets and by establishing training and educational programs to readjust the workforce. (Again, refer to chapter 6 for educational programs designed to alleviate the urban crisis.)

Another important feature of Johnson's War on Poverty was that the programs, requiring community participation, would be community-building strategies for the Great Society. This feature, too, was congruent with social theory that saw the poor as victims of a pathology of poverty, which was epidemic in the country's urban ghettoes. War on Poverty programs would require community support and action that, by changing the environment, would work to bring about positive change. A key element in the Johnson approach was that he would be the architect of a great American consensus for guided social change. Events in the later 1960s, however, would replace his ideas of consensus with conflicts as angry students demonstrated on campuses and the inner cities exploded in urban disorders. (See chapter 10 for the student activism of the 1960s.)

Educational Provisions of the Civil Rights Act of 1964

Earlier efforts to pass federal aid to education legislation, especially during the Truman administration, generally had been wrecked by racial issues relating to segregation as well as by religious ones relating to separation of church and state. The enactment of the Civil Rights Act of 1964 removed many racial issues from the consideration of federal aid legislation. Johnson's use of the child benefit theory rather than aid to religious schools helped to defuse the religious issues upon which previous efforts had floundered. Here, we turn to the Civil Rights Act of 1964. The act forbade racial discrimination in federally funded programs and authorized that federal funds were to be cut off from agencies where illegal discrimination was found. No person was to "be excluded from participation in, be denied the benefits of, or be subjected to discrimination under any program" receiving federal aid because of "race, color or national origin."

Title VI of the act gave new and highly important powers to the U.S. Office of Education, then part of the Department of Health, Education and Welfare (HEW). The office was empowered to disburse federal funds and to assure that districts were complying with the act's provisions prohibiting discrimination. Department guidelines for qualifying for federal funds specified: (1) districts were to file an assurance of compliance that segregation had been eliminated in pupil and faculty assignment; (2) districts in the process of desegregation were to report on their progress, especially in the assignment of pupils and faculty; (3) districts could file a voluntary plan indicating how they would fully desegregate their schools by 1967.[50] These guidelines were revised in 1966, with the addition of "performance criteria" that increased the percentages of black students who were integrated in a particular district's schools. The Civil Rights Act, together with the Elementary and Secondary Education Act of 1965 (ESEA), had the effect of stimulating school districts to desegregate and begin working toward racial integration. (For a fuller discussion of racial desegregation and integration see chapter 6.)

The Elementary and Secondary Education Act of 1965

Johnson sent his education message to Congress on January 12, 1965. Based on it, Carl Perkins introduced the administration bill H.R. 2362 in the House of Representatives and Wayne Morse introduced S. 370 in the Senate. Despite some maneuvering by Adam Clayton Powell, chairman of the House Education Committee, and serious questioning by Edith Green, both houses passed the administration's education package. President Johnson signed the ESEA on April 11, 1965, outside of the one-room schoolhouse where he began his education. At his side at the signing ceremony was his first teacher, Katherine Deadrich Loney.

Running throughout the ESEA as well as other educational legislation of the Johnson administration was an overt connection between federal aid to education and the larger War on Poverty. Title I programs, which received most of the funding, were allocated to meet the educational needs of educationally deprived children, in both public and nonpublic schools. Educational deprivation, at this time, typically meant children who had learning deficits due to growing up in an environment of poverty. The ESEA provided funds for impoverished children, model schools, pilot programs, community centers, books and educational materials, guidance, remedial compensatory instruction, libraries, special services, and health. It provided for improvement of educational research, dissemination of information about educational practices, educational laboratories, and teacher education.

The ESEA provided federal grants to the states, which in turn redistributed the funds to local school districts. The districts would use the funds according to guidelines approved by state and federal

President Lyndon B. Johnson and Katherine Deadrich Loney, his first teacher, at the signing of the Elementary and Secondary Education Act on April 11, 1965. (Courtesy LBJ Library Collection.)

educational agencies. An important provision in the ESEA was the requirement that programs were to be evaluated. Districts were to submit annual objective evaluations of the effectiveness of programs implemented with ESEA funding. This provision would have important consequences that eventually would lead to the Coleman Report. (The Coleman Report, discussed in chapter 6, grew out of this requirement.) Another key provision was that districts were to disseminate information about promising educational practices.[51]

Preschool Head Start Programs

An important weapon in Johnson's educational arsenal in the War on Poverty was Operation Head Start, a preschool program for poverty-impacted children. Key assumptions in the Head Start program were: (1) the environment of poverty created cultural deficits that had a negative impact on children's learning; (2) it was possible to compensate for deficits and remediate them by an early intervention in the child's life; (3) such an early intervention would create a learning readiness that would give poverty-impacted children a needed head start at school.[52]

The experts in early childhood education who crafted the Head Start programs generally subscribed to the whole child concept developed by earlier progressive educators. An appropriate education, according to the whole child theory, was one that encompassed all the needs and interests of children—emotionally, physically, and culturally as well as academically. For them, it was more important to nurture children in a secure environment and to develop learning readiness than to emphasize an early introduction to the academic basics. Thus, Head Start programs incorporated a range of objectives: the children's all-round social, psychological, cultural, and motor skill development; the development of a family's parenting skills; and general health and nutrition.[53]

In addition to its child-centered progressivism, Head Start programs incorporated elements of the older progressive New Deal com-

Children in a Head Start Class in Washington, D.C., an example of Johnson's War on Poverty Programs. (Reproduction from the Collections of the Library of Congress.)

munity building along with newer sociological theory. Head Start programs were to be based in the economically disadvantaged community and were to have advisory boards of parents. The aim was to make the Head Start early childhood program a part of the larger community. Further, an idea behind Head Start was that community involvement would enhance the program and, hopefully, secure positive results. Such concepts of community involvement are also present in more current efforts at decentralization and site-based management. Although there were problems, Head Start was launched with enthusiasm as 500,000 children were enrolled during the first summer of the program.

The Higher Education Act of 1965

This act upgraded college and research university libraries, aided black colleges, provided guaranteed student college loans, and established a National Teacher Corps. It was signed by Johnson at Southwest Texas State University at San Marcos, on November 8, 1965.

Enactment of Sixty Education Laws

Johnson's administration was marked by prodigious success in securing the enactment of federal aid to education legislation, a process that had vexed his Democrat predecessors Harry S. Truman and John F. Kennedy, both of whom were sympathetic to such programs. During Johnson's administration, a total of sixty laws aiding education were passed. In 1963, they included: the Higher Education Facilities Act, the Vocational Education Act, and the Manpower Development and Training Act. The year 1964 saw passage of the Library Services and Construction Act, the Civil Rights Act, the Juvenile Delinquency and Youth Offenses Control Act, the Economic Opportunity Act, the National Arts and Cultural Development Act, the Nurses Training Act, Loans to Students of Optometry Act, the NDEA and Federally Affected Areas Act. In 1965, Johnson's success record soared with enactment of the Appalachian Regional Development Act, the Elementary and Secondary Education Act, the Manpower Act, the National Technical Institute for the Deaf Act, the Juvenile Delinquency Control Act, the Training Teachers of the Handicapped Act, the National Foundation of the Arts and Humanities Act, the National Vocational Student Loan Insurance Act, the Health Professional Education Assistance amendments, the Medical Library Assistance Act, and the Higher Education Act. In 1966, legislation included: the Veterans Readjustment Benefits Act (called the cold war G.I. Bill), the Child Nutrition Act, the Model Secondary School for the Deaf Act, the International Education Act, and the Allied Health Professional Personnel Training Act. For 1967, major educational laws passed were the Education Professions Development Act and a series of amendments continuing major educational programs such as college work study, library construction, and economic opportunity. In 1968, amendments continuing programs were passed for vocational rehabilitation, the National Science Foundation, higher education, and vocational education.

Problems of Implementation

Johnson's Great Society and War on Poverty was marked by a multifaceted approach to engineer social change. Among the initiatives were the Job Corps, VISTA, work training programs, Head Start, community action programs, education for migrant workers, and work-study programs for college students.

The Johnson educational aid programs were rapidly passed. Indeed, never before in U.S. history had so many programs been enacted. The Department of Health, Education and Welfare and the Office of Education, within it, had problems in administering the myriad of new programs. The Office of Education traditionally had been a statistics-generating and an information-disseminating office. Its officials were not used to the new roles in which they were cast by the Great Society. Several times, the office was reorganized in efforts to adapt to the new role.

Further confusion was caused by the lodging of antipoverty and related educational programs in various federal agencies in addition to the Department of Education. While the antipoverty programs had the strength of being a concerted effort that was interdepartmental, the Washington bureaucracy was more attuned to working departmentally. The implementation stage of the Great Society's War on Poverty encountered a maze of interagency and intergovernmental procedures, delays, and jurisdictional disputes.[54]

While the Johnson administration was highly successful in passing educational legislation, implementation of new programs at the state and local levels did not always proceed quickly or smoothly. Serious strains occurred at the state and local district levels, where school administrators had to cope with a bewildering growth of red tape, regulations, and forms. Later Republican administrations—the Nixon, Ford, Reagan, and Bush administrations—would argue that the growth of federal bureaucracy was hampering educational reform. They would campaign on pledges to reduce federal bureaucracy and return educational prerogatives to the states and local school districts.

Conclusion

Kennedy's election in 1960 had appeared to mark the beginning of change on the American political and cultural scene. What appeared to be change, however, was in some respects a shift in the national mood rather than a substantial departure from the earlier patterns of the postwar era. Cold war tensions remained unabated and, at times, intensified. Eschewing the hesitancy of his predecessor, Kennedy was determined to move the cause of civil rights forward. Though supporting federal aid to education, Kennedy proved unable to persuade Congress to pass the necessary legislation. It remained for his successor, Lyndon Johnson, to succeed in enacting the country's most ambitious federal aid to education agenda.

Although Johnson's victory for federal aid was the most impressive of any up to that time, it did not mean that federal aid to education was now an unquestioned part of the fabric of American education. While the amount of federal assistance to schools was continually debated, there were still many who contended that the federal government should stay out of the schools. For them, education was still a state and local matter, not a federal one. Munger and Fenno, in their analysis of the history of federal aid, pointed out its cyclical rather than linear character. They wrote, "in each phase of the struggle support has been mobilized only to be lost again. Then, after a delay, the effort has been renewed again."[55] Rather than being an established principle with funding increasing each decade, federal aid seemed to be debated anew in ensuing years.

If his success in securing federal aid to education was cyclical rather than permanent, Johnson's belief that poverty could be eradicated by government policy and intervention was even less secure in the American future. Johnson's optimistic social and educational programs largely fell victim to the political and ideological polarization that occurred in the wake of dissatisfaction with his interventionist policies in Vietnam and of a growing neoconservative revival in American politics. Some critics contended that the social and educational policies of the War on Poverty and the Great Society, though well intentioned if not noble, were unrealistic. Critics on both the right and left challenged the liberal middle ground that Johnson attempted to occupy. Assessments of the War on Poverty ushered in a major ideological chasm in how Americans viewed social welfare programs.[56]

Neoconservatives, who would gather strength in the next decades and come to power with Reagan's victory over Carter in 1980s, saw the Johnson programs as a massive expansion of the federal role that caused unnecessary intrusions of a growing bureaucracy into the lives of individuals and subverted historical state and local prerogatives. According to neoconservative politicians and economists, the Johnson policy, like liberal social welfare and educational policies in general, rested on a denial of the real strengths of the market-driven free enterprise economy. Rather than eliminating poverty, these social welfare policies resulted in and reproduced a socially isolated permanent underclass. The social programs of the Great Society helped to create a culture of poverty and, in effect, eroded the sense of personal accountability and self-improvement.[57]

Liberal defenders of the Johnson programs countered these attacks by pointing to successes such as the Head Start programs and by arguing that continued funding, rather than abandonment, was needed. For example, defenders of the War on Poverty programs pointed out that the number of Americans living below the poverty line had decreased from 20 percent in 1960 to 8 percent in 1980.[58] Johnson's programs, for liberal defenders of social welfare programs, rested on the assumption that the situation of poverty was temporary for individuals. With the appropriate social and educational measures, the federal government could assist persons and groups to move from poverty to economic self-sufficiency.

Notes

[1] Cheryl M. Nuzbach, "Presidential Leadership in Education; 1961–1963," M.A. Thesis, Loyola University, Chicago, 1976, pp. 8–29.

[2] Victor Lasky, *J.F.K.: The Man and the Myth* (New York: Macmillan Co., 1963), p. 71.

[3] *Ibid.*, pp. 69–72.

[4] James MacGregor Burns, *John Kennedy: A Political Profile* (New York: Macmillan Co., 1963), p. 33.

[5] John F. Kennedy, *Why England Slept* (New York: W. Funk, Inc., 1961).

[6] John F. Kennedy, *A Nation of Immigrants* (New York: Harper and Row, 1964), p. 67.

[7] Hugh Davis Graham, *The Uncertain Triumph: Federal Education Policy in the Kennedy and Johnson Years* (Chapel Hill: University of North Carolina Press, 1984), p. 3.

[8] John F. Kennedy, *Profiles in Courage* (New York: Harper and Co., 1961).

[9] Graham, p. 7.

[10] For commentaries on Kennedy as President, see Arthur Schlesinger, Jr., *A Thousand Days: John F. Kennedy in the White House* (Boston: Houghton Mifflin Co., 1965); Theodore Sorensen, *Kennedy* (New York: Harper and Row, 1965); Henry Fairlee, *The Kennedy Promise: The Politics of Expectation* (New York: Double Day and Co., 1973); Herbert Parmet, *JFK: The Presidency of John F. Kennedy* (New York: Dial Press, 1983).

[11] Graham, pp. 12–13.

[12] Ibid., pp. 14–15.

[13] U.S. President, *Public Papers on the Presidents of the United States* (John F. Kennedy, 1961) (Washington, DC: Office of the Federal Register, National Archives and Records Service, 1961–63), pp. 107–11.

[14] For Kennedy's efforts on aid to education, see Robert Bendiner, *Obstacle Course on Capitol Hill* (New York: McGraw-Hill, 1964).

[15] Tom Wicker, *JFK and LBJ: The Influence of Personality upon Politics* (New York: William Morrow and Co., 1968), p. 131.

16 For commentaries on the legislation's defeat, see John F. O'Hara, ed., *John F. Kennedy on Education* (New York: Teachers College Press, Columbia University, 1966), p. 20, and Malcolm E. Smith, *Kennedy's Thirteen Great Mistakes in the White House* (New York: National Forum of American, Inc., 1968), p. 181.

17 U.S. President, p. 116.

18 Nuzbach, pp. 59–61.

19 Ibid., pp. 70–74.

20 U.S. President, pp. 105–16.

21 For a recent history of the Peace Corps, see Elizabeth Cobbs Hoffman, *All You Need is Love: The Peace Corps and the Spirit of the 1960s* (Cambridge: Harvard University Press, 1998).

22 For American foreign policy, see Thomas J. McCormick, *America's Half-Century: United States Foreign Policy in the Cold War and After* (Baltimore: Johns Hopkins University Press, 1995).

23 Conventional and revisionist interpretations of the cold war are discussed in J. Joseph Huthmacher, *The Truman Years* (Hinsdale, IL: Dryden Press, 1972), pp. 17–40.

24 For competition for unaligned nations, see Bernard A. Wisberger, *Cold War, Cold Peace: The United States and Russia Since 1945* (Boston: Houghton-Mifflin, 1984), p. 212, and Gordon A. Craig and Alexander L. George, *Force and Statecraft Diplomatic Problems of Our Times* (New York: Oxford University Press, 1983), p. 117.

25 R. Freeman Butts, "America's Role in International Education: A Perspective of Thirty Years," in Harold Shane, ed., *The United States and International Education*, 68th Yearbook of the NSSE (Chicago: University of Chicago Press, 1969), pp. 24–27.

26 Harold Shane, ed., *The United States and International Education*, 68th Yearbook of the NSSE (Chicago: University of Chicago Press), 1969.

27 My narrative uses the terms in current use at a particular time.

28 Cole Brembeck, "United States' Educational Designs Woven into the Fabric of International Education," in Shane, pp. 187–219.

29 Ibid., pp. 189–92.

30 John Lunstrum, "The U.S. and Other Great Powers in International Interaction," in Shane, pp. 223–24.

31 Gerard T. Rice, *The Bold Experiment* (South Bend, IN: University of Notre Dame Press, 1985), p. 18.

32 As quoted in Robert G. Carey, *The Peace Corps* (New York: Praeger Publishers, 1970), p. 5.

33 Rice, p. 19.

34 For Kennedy's emerging plan for the Peace Corps, see Coates Redmon, *Come As You Are* (New York: Harcourt Brace Jovanovich, Publishers, 1986), p. 29 and Morris I. Stein, *Volunteers for Peace* (New York: John Wiley and Sons, Inc., 1966), p. 238.

35 R. Sargent Shriver, *Point of the Lance* (New York: Harper and Row, 1964), p. 11.

36 Rice, p. 39.

37 Shriver, p. 14.

38 Rice, p. 41.

39 Ibid., p. 144.

40 Ibid., p. 144–45.

41 Ibid., pp. 150–56.

[42] For training programs, see Roy Hoopes, *The Complete Peace Corps Guide* (New York: Dell Publishing Co., 1965) and Carey.

[43] Biographies of Johnson include: Alfred Steinberg, *Sam Johnson's Boy: A Close-Up of the President from Texas* (New York: Macmillan Co., 1968); Doris Kearns Goodwin, *Lyndon Johnson and the American Dream* (New York: Harper and Row, 1976).

[44] Janet Fredericks, "Lyndon Baines Johnson: An Educator and His Library," *Vitae Scholasticae*, 2 (Spring 1983), pp. 203–5.

[45] Ibid., pp. 205–6.

[46] Ibid., p. 206.

[47] Graham, pp. 60–61.

[48] Ibid., pp. 62–68.

[49] For Johnson's programs, see James MacGregor Burns, *To Heal and to Build: The Programs of President Lyndon B. Johnson* (New York: McGraw-Hill Book Co., 1968).

[50] Diane Ravitch, *The Troubled Crusade: American Education, 1945–1980* (New York: Basic Books, 1983), pp. 163–64.

[51] Ibid., pp. 159–60.

[52] Ibid., p. 158.

[53] Edward Zigler and Susan Muenchow, *Head Start: The Inside Story of America's Most Successful Educational Experiment* (New York: Basic Books, 1992), pp. 17–21.

[54] Graham, pp. 106–10.

[55] Frank J. Munger and Richard F. Fenno, Jr. *National Politics and Federal Aid to Education* (New York: Syracuse University Press, 1962), pp. 17–18.

[56] Edward J. Harpham and Richard K. Scoth, "Rethinking the War on Poverty: The Ideology of Social Welfare Reform," *Western Political Quarterly*, 41 (March 1988), p. 194.

[57] Charles Murray, *Losing Ground: American Social Policy 1950–1980* (New York: Basic Books, 1984), p. 146.

[58] John E. Schwarz, *America's Hidden Success: A Reassessment of Twenty Years of Public Policy* (New York: Norton, 1983), p. 57.

Further Reading

Adams, Don, and Robert M. Bjork. *Education in Developing Areas.* New York: David McKay Co., 1969.

Auletta, Kenneth. *The Underclass.* New York: Random House, 1982.

Babbidge, Homer D., and Robert M. Rosenzweig. *The Federal Interest in High Education.* New York: Columbia University Press, 1962.

Burner, David. *John F. Kennedy and a New Generation.* Boston: Scott, Foresman, and Co., 1988.

Burns, James MacGregor. *To Heal and to Build: The Programs of President Lyndon B. Johnson.* New York: McGraw-Hill Book Co., 1968.

Carey, Robert G. *The Peace Corps.* New York: Praeger Publishers, 1970.

Danziger, Sheldon, and Daniel P. Weinberg. *Fighting Poverty: What Works and What Doesn't.* Cambridge: Harvard University Press, 1986.

Dendiner, Robert. *Obstacle Course on Capital Hill.* New York: McGraw-Hill, 1964.

Fairlie, Henry. *The Kennedy Promise: The Politics of Expectation*. New York: Doubleday, 1973.

Goodwin, Doris Kearns. *Lyndon Johnson and the American Dream*. New York: Harper and Row, 1976.

Graham, Hugh D. *The Uncertain Triumph: Federal Educational Policy in the Kennedy and Johnson Years*. Chapel Hill: University of North Carolina Press, 1984.

Gutek, Gerald L. *American Education in a Global Society: Internationalizing Teacher Education*. Prospect Heights, IL: Waveland Press, 1997.

Hanson, John W., and Cole S. Brembeck, eds. *Education and the Development of Nations*. New York: Holt, Rinehart and Winston, 1966.

Hoffman, Elizabeth Cobbs. *All You Need Is Love: The Peace Corps and the Spirit of the 1960s*. Cambridge: Harvard University Press, 1998.

Hoopes, Roy. *The Complete Peace Corps Guide*. New York: Dell Publishing Co., 1965.

Jordan, Barbara C. and Elspeth D. Rostow, eds. *The Great Society: A Twenty-Year Critique*. Austin, TX: Lyndon Baines Johnson Library and Lyndon B. Johnson School of Public Affairs, 1986.

Keppel, Francis. *The Necessary Revolution in American Education*. New York: Harper and Row, 1966.

Levy, David W. *The Debate Over Vietnam*. Baltimore: Johns Hopkins University Press, 1995.

McCormick, Thomas J. *America's Half-Century: United States Foreign Policy in the Cold War and After*. Baltimore: Johns Hopkins University Press, 1995.

Meranto, Philip. *The Politics of Federal Aid to Education in 1965*. Syracuse: Syracuse University Press, 1967.

Miroff, Bruce. *Pragmatic Illusions: The Presidential Politics of John F. Kennedy*. New York: David McKay, 1976.

Munger, Frank J., and Richard F. Fenno, Jr. *National Politics and Federal Aid to Education*. New York: Syracuse University Press, 1962.

Murray, Charles. *Losing Ground: American Social Policy 1950–1980*. New York: Basic Books, 1984.

O'Hara, John P., ed. *John F. Kennedy on Education*. New York: Teachers College Press, Columbia University, 1966.

Paper, Lewis. *The Promise and the Performance: The Leadership of John F. Kennedy*. New York: Crown, 1976.

Parmet, Herbert. *JFK: The Presidency of John F. Kennedy*. New York: Dial Press, 1983.

Ravitch, Diane. *The Troubled Crusade: American Education, 1945–1980*. New York: Basic Books, 1983.

Rice, Gerard T. *The Bold Experiment*. South Bend, IN: University of Notre Dame Press, 1985.

Schlesinger, Arthur M., Jr. *A Thousand Days: John F. Kennedy in the White House*. Boston: Houghton Mifflin Book Co., 1965.

Schwarz, John E. *America's Hidden Success: A Reassessment of Twenty Years of Public Policy*. New York: Norton, 1983.

Shriver, Sargent. *Point of the Lance*. New York: Harper and Row, 1964.

Sorensen, Theodore. *Kennedy*. New York: Harper and Row, 1965.

Stein, Morris I. *Volunteers for Peace.* New York: John Wiley & Sons, 1966.

Stenberg, Alfred. *Sam Johnson's Boy: A Close-Up of the President from Texas.* New York: Macmillan Co., 1968.

Sunderquist, James. *Politics and Policy: The Eisenhower, Kennedy, and Johnson Years.* Washington: Brookings Institution, 1968.

Textor, Robert B. *Cultural Frontiers of the Peace Corps.* Boston: M.I.T. Press, 1966.

Tiedt, Sidney W. *The Role of the Federal Government in Education.* New York: Oxford University Press, 1966.

Todaro, Michael. *Economic Development of the Third World.* New York: Longman, 1985.

Weisberger, Bernard A. *Cold War, Cold Peace: The United States and Russia Since 1945.* New York: Houghton Mifflin, 1984.

Whitfield, Stephen J. *The Culture of the Cold War.* Baltimore: Johns Hopkins University Press, 1996.

Wicker, Tom. *JFK and LBJ: The Influence of Personality Upon Politics.* New York: William Morrow and Co., 1968.

Zigler, Edward and Susan Muenchow. *Head Start: The Inside Story of America's Most Successful Educational Experiments* New York: Basic Books, 1992.

8

Reforms and Critiques of Schooling, Curriculum, and Instruction: The 1960s and 1970s

Some major shifts in educational theory and practice took place in the 1960s and 1970s, particularly as relating to curriculum and instruction in the schools. Some of these shifts were associated with the large issues of economic readjustment, racial integration, demographic change, and the cold war. Others were centered more directly on the culture of schooling. After reviewing the historical background, we will consider the efforts to introduce new modes of curriculum and school organization in the early 1960s and 1970s. Then, we examine the critique of humanist, open, and other educators during this period.

Historical Context

As suggested in chapter 4, the history of curriculum and instruction in the United States can be visualized as a pendulum swinging back and forth between the forces of stasis and those of change. In the course of its action, the pendulum always returns to center. In much the same way, patterns of curriculum and instruction also swing to and fro. Changes that often seem important, hailed as reforms in new directions, tend to encounter educational tradition and generally return to schooling's institutional center.

Still another way of viewing the history of curriculum and instruction is to see it as a push-pull tug of war between two sets of educators.

Recall that on the one hand there are those who construe the primary purpose of education to be transmission of basic academic skills and subject matter in a teacher-directed sequential manner to students. On the other hand, others, often labeled as progressives, see education as a process in which pupils are engaged with direct experiences and problem solving. At certain periods in the United States, the subject-matter forces appear to be dominant in the schools. Then, there will be a counterreaction in which process-oriented educators take center stage and bring about curricular change. Then, a reaction occurs as the subject-matter educators seek to regain their dominance. The result is that the curriculum is pushed in both directions and becomes a composite of subject matter and process learning. In this chapter, we examine the swinging curricular pendulum and the push and pull of these seemingly opposing educational forces. An important qualification is to be cautious as we approach the use of the words "reform" and "reformers." Advocates of both positions will use these words. A useful consideration, however, is to carefully identify who is doing the reform, what is being reformed, and why the reform is occurring.

The Soviet success in orbiting *Sputnik* in 1957 and the enactment of the National Defense Education Act in 1958 stilled and changed the character of the educational debates that had taken place earlier in the 1950s between proponents of life adjustment education and their academic critics. (For these debates and the enactment of the NDEA, see chapters 3 and 4.) The ending of the debates gave an apparent, but not complete, victory to academic critics such as Bestor and Rickover. However, large remnants of life adjustment, particularly the emphasis on counseling and guidance and a process-oriented, experience-based curriculum, had taken root in many public schools. These characteristics of life adjustment would be manifested in the middle school movement of the 1960s.

James Conant, former president of Harvard University and U.S. high commissioner to Germany, took a moderate, middle-of-the-road course regarding educational reform in a series of reports funded by the Carnegie Corporation. In *The American High School Today* (1959), he strongly endorsed the ideal of the comprehensive high school. His endorsement was designed to offset critics of comprehensive secondary education, who believed U.S. schools should be reorganized into specialized academic and vocational schools on the European model. While Conant opposed tracking students into separate schools, he recognized the need for ability grouping. But he believed that the viability of comprehensive schools could be maintained by providing a core of common courses for all students with elective options for college preparatory and other students. He reasoned that the historically evolved comprehensive high school best served the educational needs of a community's youth. High schools should be sufficiently large to embrace a range of programs and draw a student population from an attendance area that was large enough to contain a variety of social, ethnic, and racial groups. He also outlined the curricular core that comprehensive high schools should offer:

1. There should be a general core for all students in English, American literature and composition, and the social studies.

2. For students not enrolled in the college preparatory program, there should be elective vocational, commercial, and work-study courses.

3. For academically talented students, there would be advanced courses in mathematics, science, and foreign languages.[1]

New Approaches to Curriculum, Organization, and Staffing

In the late 1950s and 1960s, school reform movements tended to develop in two directions: one emphasized improving subject matter and instruction in mathematics, science, and foreign languages, spurred by the NDEA; the other concentrated on innovations in organization and scheduling. The subject area reforms came mainly from academic projects that were led by university professors in the arts and sciences. The innovations in school organization and scheduling came primarily from professional educators and professors of education, namely school administrators. At times, the two sets of reforms converged, and at other times they were introduced independently. Due to the state and local governance of public schools, the reforms, while having a national stimulus, were implemented differentially in the country's myriad school districts.

Curricular Innovations

The National Science Foundation (NSF), established by Congress in 1950, worked to promote basic research and improve curriculum and instruction in mathematics and the sciences. The foundation funded committees, usually of professors and educators, to revise the secondary curriculum in mathematics, physics, biology, chemistry, and occasionally social studies. A result was a series of "new" curricula—the "new physics," the "new chemistry," the "new math," and the "new social science." To implement the new curricula in the schools, the foundation sponsored institutes and other special in-service programs that brought university scientists together with classroom teachers. Those teachers who were selected to participate in these in-service experiences were expected to introduce the new curricula in their schools, where they would be catalysts for change.[2]

The curricular innovations in mathematics, science, social studies, and history tended to follow a common frame of reference. The innovators in these fields criticized what they regarded to be the weaknesses of conventional classroom teaching, namely textbooks and teacher-led lectures and discussions. Textbooks, they argued, contained predigested information that was heavy on facts, dates, and lists of definitions and principles. Much classroom instruction featured assignments from textbooks, with teachers asking questions about the material and leading fact-centered discussions. The subject area innovators recommended that the conventional style of teaching be replaced by a new approach that replicated the methodologies used by scientists in laboratories, by historians using primary sources, and by social scientists using field studies. Students replicating these research methods would reason or discover the key concepts in an academic field through inquiry processes. For example, in history instruction, students would use primary sources to learn about selected topics, such as the secession of a particular state during the Civil War, rather than a general narrative textbook.

Examples of efforts to revitalize mathematics and science curricula occurred at the University of Illinois and the Massachusetts Institute of Technology. Mathematicians at the University of Illinois in Urbana had inaugurated a project in 1952 to develop new materials for high school teachers. (Recall that the Urbana campus had been the locale of some of the major debates between Bestor and his opponents in the university's College of Education.) The University of Illinois project aimed to introduce students to the way in which mathematicians think and work. In mathematics education, the School Mathematics Study Group (SMSG) developed new programs for both elementary and secondary schools. The program was adopted by many school districts. In 1956, scientists at MIT formed the Physical Science Committee under the leadership of Jerrold Zacharias, a physicist. The committee sought to revise the content and methods of physics teaching and to attract more students to careers in science.[3]

A highly controversial curricular innovation in social studies was "Man: A Course of Study" (MACOS), which was funded by the NSF for use in the upper elementary grades. Highly innovative in content and methodology, MACOS, featuring the discovery method, raised a series of questions about human nature such as; What is human about human beings? How did human beings get the way they are? The course linked history, social science, and biology by comparatively examining the life cycles of salmon, herring gulls, baboons, and Netsilik Eskimos. By making comparisons between fish, birds, animals, and human beings students were to reach some conclusions about human nature. The course included a number of highly controversial topics dealing with infanticide, wife swapping, and abandoning of the elderly as once practiced by the Netsilik Eskimos that, generating opposition, led to a congressional investigation in 1976.[4]

A prominent approach influenced by James Bruner's *Process of Education* was called the "structure of disciplines." Through the discovery method, students were to gain an understanding of the structure of a discipline, its essential key concepts and methodology, rather than trying to cover all the factual content in an area. In structuring knowledge for children's learning, Bruner argued that there should be but a minimal set of propositions to guide the process. From these propositions, learners could explore alternatives in the environment and generate their own new propositions.[5]

The strategy for implementing the new curricula followed a common pattern. First, pilot projects, usually conducted by university professors in academic fields, would be funded either by the federal government through NDEA or NSF or by private foundations. Professors in the sciences took the dominant lead role. If involved at all, professors of education had a minor role. Curriculum packages and programs featuring the new math, new chemistry, new physics, and so on were developed and introduced to selected teachers at summer institutes or special workshops at various universities. The selected teachers, upon returning to their schools, were to be curricular change agents as they introduced the new curricula. At the same time, some textbook publishers revised their book lists and introduced the new discovery-centered approach. Between 1956 and 1975, the NSF funded fifty-three projects; forty-three in mathematics and science and ten in social studies.

The New Math. A clear illustration of the curricular innovations of the late 1950s and 1960s is provided by what was called the new math, intended to bring about fundamental changes in the understanding and teaching of mathematics. Like other curricular reforms of the period, the new math was both a reaction to larger issues of social change and an initiative of scholars in the field. In the post-*Sputnik* climate, improvements in the teaching of mathematics were seen as imperative to national defense and security in the cold war. Along with these cold war imperatives was the chronic complaint that many teachers, especially in elementary schools, lacked sufficient academic preparation in mathematics. During the 1940s and 1950s, mathematicians in universities and institutes had developed new ways of thinking in the field.

The foundations for the new math were created by the University of Illinois Committee on School Mathematics Project, which had been established in 1952. The Illinois Committee included professors from the Colleges of Education, Engineering, and Liberal Arts, who cooperatively sought ways to improve mathematics content and instruction. Emphasizing the discovery approach, the committee encouraged the reorganization of mathematics content in terms of sets, structure, logical deduction, and axiomatic proofs.[6] The Illinois Committee's curricular innovations were included in several of the new series of textbooks featuring the new math.

The College Entrance Examination Board was also a force for change in mathematics education. Its Commission on Mathematics, appointed in 1955 and funded by the Carnegie Corporation, like the Illinois project, involved the cooperative work of mathematicians and educators. In urging a new program for mathematics education at the secondary level, the commission recommended greater emphasis on: (1) concept formation in calculus and analytical geometry; (2) deductive reasoning in algebra and geometry; (3) unifying ideas such as sets, variables, functions, and relations.[7] So that the new developments in mathematics would enter high schools, the commission further recommended extensive changes in mathematics courses that were part of teacher education programs. Similar to the Illinois Committee and the Commission on Mathematics, the University of Maryland Mathematics Project, the Madison Project, and the Cambridge Conference on School Mathematics worked to redesign mathematics curriculum and instruction.

A concerted national effort for the new math came from the School Mathematics Study Group (SMSG), established in 1959 and funded by the National Science Foundation. The study group created a wide range of publications and materials designed to reinvigorate mathematics instruction in elementary and secondary schools by incorporating an emphasis on mathematical structure, precise use of language, deductive proof, and the discovery method.[8]

Proponents of the new math sought to replace the traditional, often rote learning of mathematics by introducing "real life" mathematics into classrooms in such a way that students would be excited to learn and would think like mathematicians. In some ways, the emphasis on stimulating students' interests returned to themes found in progressive education. However, in other ways it was a reemphasis on subject matter. It was an emphasis on learning the structure of the field, its fundamental modes of reasoning, and how to think as mathematicians thought as they worked through problems in their discipline. The new math could be seen as both a revival of progressivism as well as a victory for the advocates of subject-matter discipline, such as Bestor and Rickover.

Foundational to the new math, as well as to other innovations in instruction during the 1960s, was Jerome Bruner's spiral curriculum theory, expressed in *The Process of Education*. Arguing that subjects could "be taught effectively" in an "intellectually honest form to any child at any stage of development," Bruner advocated organizing curricula on the structure of disciplines but in a way that recognized students' readiness and interests.[9] The Conference Board of the Mathematical Sciences National Advisory Committee on Mathematical Education found Bruner's arguments a "persuasive justification . . . to emphasize conceptual understanding of mathematical methods—understanding to be conveyed by stress on unifying structures of the discipline." Equally compelling to the board was Bruner's emphasis on psychological issues such as "readiness, intuitive versus analytical thinking, and concrete versus formal experience."[10]

To bring new math into the schools, the National Science Foundation, beginning in 1953, sponsored a series of summer institutes to train teachers. Such teachers were to become agents of change in curriculum and instruction in their school districts. Textbook publishers developed series based on the new mathematics as schools revised their curriculum in light of the new thinking on how to teach mathematics.

As is frequently the case with innovations in education, the new math, which had been so eagerly adopted by publishers and school districts, began to encounter criticisms from teachers, parents, and "unconvinced" educators. Stressing "sets," numeration in bases, and mathematical reasoning, critics found it overly abstract and neglectful of fundamental applications. Some critics alleged that the new math's proponents were operating from an inadequate research base in education and, in their enthusiasm, had failed to develop proper strategies for teacher implementation. Some critics contended that it was a feasible approach only for the academic upper one-third of students and that it was too abstract and formal for use at primary and intermediate levels in elementary schools.[11] Some teachers, prepared in pre–new math methods, had difficulty in making the transition to the new program. Basic education critics contended that it neglected fundamental computation skills.

Morris Kline's popular book, *Why Johnny Can't Add: The Failure of the New Math*, suggested several reasons why the new math did not succeed in bringing about the highly proclaimed revolution in mathematics education. Kline believed that the various committees and commissions promoting the new math had not done enough research on its effectiveness with divergent groups of students. While the logical presentation of mathematics might intrigue mathematicians, Kline argued that: its stress on deduction did not always stimulate students; its emphasis on precise language resulted in an expanded terminology that, though precise, was often unclear to students; it frequently took students into remote levels of abstraction, rather than into the real world.[12]

Although features of the new math stayed in mathematics education programs, more conventional modes of instruction reappeared in the 1970s and blunted the thrust of the new math. Despite the resurgence of more traditional curriculum and teaching, the new math had an impact on mathematics instruction, especially in secondary schools and in the development of textbooks and teaching materials.[13]

Varied Acceptance. The actual results of curricular innovations were mixed, however, as they usually are in cases of educational reform. There is often a general scenario that accompanies attempts to introduce innovations. The central sources of the innovation are often places of high enthusiasm as those who developed the particular innovation share it with others who often become its disciples. As the innovation is carried from both the time and place of origin, it tends to lose some of its initial excitement but still carries a great hope for change. As the innovation moves still further from its center in time and space, the core elements in the innovation tend to run into the existing curriculum and teachers and others who are invested in it. Then, the innovation begins to take on features of the existing curriculum. What results, at best, is a synthesis of the old and new, but more commonly a hybrid in which the new element, like a limb, is grafted on to the older curricular trunk.

In the case of the innovations of the early 1960s, a new subject curriculum was often launched with great enthusiasm by its proponents, who saw it as signaling an educational revolution. When the new curriculum was introduced in some schools, it took hold, especially if there was a cadre of teachers committed to it and an administration that understood it and provided preparatory in-service training. In other cases, new curricula took on a bandwagon effect that dissipated after the initial wave of enthusiasm. In these cases, the teachers who were supposed to be change agents for their schools worked in isolation amidst colleagues who resisted the change. Sometimes, the only real change was in jargon and terminology rather than in substance as the old curriculum remained but with a new name.

Innovations in Organization and Staffing

From the late 1950s through the 1970s, several concerted efforts to restructure the organization and staffing of schools occurred. The initial impetus for school restructuring was generated by teacher and classroom shortages of the 1950s, which motivated educators to develop new ways of using staff and facilities more efficiently and effectively. Although the impetus dealt with a highly urgent need to provide trained teachers for a growing pupil population, it moved from this specific need into the larger dimension of a major restructuring and reorganization of schools. Importantly, the movement, which involved leading educational administrators, did not seek to transform schools in a revolutionary way but rather sought, as reorganization implies, to modify and improve existing patterns. Further, much of the impetus for reorganizing staff and facilities came from within rather than from without the educational establishment. As an insiders' kind of reform, it tended to sponsor incremental rather than transformative change.

The efforts to restructure schools received support from the Ford Foundation's Fund for the Advancement of Education, especially its School Improvement Program and other foundation sources. These efforts were eagerly endorsed by professional organizations, especially those of school administrators, which sought and gained Ford Foundation support. A key role in school reorganization was exercised by the Commission on the Experimental Study of the Utilization of the Staff in the Secondary School (Staff Utilization Study), of the National Association of Secondary School Principals (NASSP), which had attracted Ford Foundation support. J. Lloyd Trump, a former school superintendent and professor of educational administration at the University of Illinois, directed the study and the subsequent reorganizations that it sponsored.[14]

The initial charge of the NASSP's Commission on Staff Utilization was to devise ways of solving the secondary school teacher shortage through improved utilization of professional staff. When the commission began its work in 1955, the shortage was estimated at 45,000 teachers.[15] As insiders in the educational establishment, Trump and his associates began their work directly in the schools rather than being concerned with the larger social and economic changes occurring outside of but impacting schools. Unlike the larger reform agendas of later critics of the 1960s and 1970s, administrative reformers like Trump worked from the inside of the school. They began with what they knew best—scheduling, instruction, and staff utilization. What they sought to reform by incremental changes was the traditional secondary school with its lockstep organization of classes of thirty students to one teacher, meeting five days a week, in fifty-minute periods, for one school year. The changes they introduced sought to modify this organizational framework rather than change the purpose of secondary education.

During its first four years from 1956 to 1960, the commission sponsored, encouraged, and analyzed experimentation with staff utilization in one hundred selected secondary schools across the country. During this time, the commission identified the following ways of better utilizing professional staff: (1) some tasks related to classroom management could be performed by subprofessionals to give teachers more time to devote to educational responsibilities; (2) educational technologies, such as closed-circuit television, overhead projectors, FM radio, recording devices, and programmed learning, could be used more effectively in classrooms to enhance instruction; (3) learning activities where students worked independently in libraries, laboratories, and resource and materials centers could be encouraged and used more frequently.[16]

Like other similar groups, the Commission on Staff Utilization enlarged its mission from the original charge of finding ways to resolve the shortage of secondary teachers into the much larger and grander mission of creating the school of the future. Using the large and influential NASSP constituency, the commission disseminated its findings and recommendations in publications and presentations. Trump, the commission's director, in the much-circulated and well-publicized *Images of the Future—A New Approach to the Secondary School*, portrayed his vision of effective schools to a national audience of school administrators.[17] To visualize the secondary school of the future for large audiences, the commission adeptly produced a combined television and motion picture presentation, *And No Bell Rings*. The title suggested that in the new school, unlike the school of the past, no bells, signaling the end and beginning of classes, would ring to interrupt instruction. Narrated by Hugh Downs, *And No Bells Ring* portrayed actual schools and teachers in a variety of new organiza-

Students in an electronics laboratory at Nova High School, an example of the educational developments of the 1960s. (Reproduction from the Collections of the Library of Congress.)

tional patterns—large- and small-group instruction, team teaching, independent study in learning centers, use of paraprofessionals, and use of educational technology. Encouraged by its success, the NASSP continued its effort to improve secondary schools into the early 1960s, with Trump named as director of a second commission.

By 1960, the NASSP's projected secondary school of the future was being covered in the popular media and professional literature as the "Trump Plan" and the "Trump School.[18] By 1961, at least one thousand secondary schools were implementing Trump's ideas on staff utilization and curricular and facilities reorganization. Among these ideas, frequently pointed to as major innovations, were team teaching, independent study, large- and small-group classes, flexible scheduling, use of teacher assistants and subprofessionals, and introduction of new instructional technologies. These efforts to reorganize secondary schools were significant in-house developments that marked further educational change in the late 1960s and early 1970s (see the section on open education later in this chapter). These innovations were not limited to secondary schools but also had an impact on elementary, junior high, and middle schools. Since the Trump innovations were organizational rather than ideological, they found their way into Catholic and other private as well public schools.[19]

Trump and other administrative reformers sought to change the focus of instruction from the traditional classroom where instruction took place for fifty-minute class periods by providing more options. Rather than meeting as a class of thirty students with one teacher, instructional blocs were organized into large groups, small groups, and independent study. With this greater organizational flexibility, time and effort could be used more efficiently and effectively. In large groups, 100 to 150 students might hear a lecture, view a movie, or witness a demonstration; small groups of fifteen students were suited for discussions; and independent study allowed students to pursue their own learning in laboratories, libraries, or learning centers. Instead of the traditional one teacher per classroom, teachers could be organized into teams, where they collaboratively planned instruction and based it on team members' strengths. Since the organization of instruction required greater flexibility, the design of schools, too, needed greater architectural flexibility as well. Rather than consisting of corridors of identical classrooms, existing schools were remodeled and new ones constructed to include a variety of learning spaces—large rooms, smaller discussion rooms, and learning centers. Some instructional programs were not graded.

While the efforts at restructuring were myriad, the major thrust of the programs was to introduce new technology such as teaching machines, programmed instruction and educational television, including closed-circuit programming, into the schools. In addition, they

Nova High School, an example of the new school architecture of the 1960s. (Reproduction from the Collections of the Library of Congress.)

emphasized collaborative curricular and instructional efforts that organized teachers into teams.

Change: A Blunted Impact

The vaunted educational transformation was a blunted one. It produced some change of an academic and organizational nature that became an important feature of the schools. However, it probably was so much of a "four walls," school-based reform that it neglected the larger socioeconomic and political events taking place outside of schools. During the 1960s, the United States was experiencing a major era of social change. It was the era of racial desegregation and integration, Johnson's Great Society and War on Poverty, and protests over the war in Vietnam. It was a period of discontent and demands for change from feminists, multiculturalists, and environmentalists. While the structure of disciplines approach and team teaching had their impact, it was limited by large issues that were having an impact on society and schools. In defense of educational reform by educational insiders, they believed that genuine reform had to begin with teachers and students in the schools. For them, change that had a chance of persisting was incremental. Some of the larger visions of reform, for them, would have been utopian and ephemeral.

Humanistic and Romantic Critics

While curricular and organizational reformers were working to restructure schools incrementally, a group of angry critics, appearing in the mid-1960s and early 1970s, mounted a multifront assault on

Students in a language laboratory at Nova High School, an example of the use of instructional technology during the 1960s. (Reproduction from the Collections of the Library of Congress.)

what they regarded to be an entrenched political and educational establishment. It is difficult to identify precisely one particular niche that fits the new critics who broadly challenged a wide array of targets—the military-industrial complex, bureaucratic school administrators, and insensitive teachers. Some critics, like John Holt, appeared to suggest a new rendition of Rousseau's romantic educational novel, *Émile*, in which Rousseau tells about the education of a boy, from the time he was a baby until he became a man. Instead of being educated by society, Émile develops naturally—stimulated by his own inclinations and not influenced by a corruptive society.

Holt, in particular, is representative of education's new critics. Like other critics, he personally was positioned outside of the educational establishment. Holt's interest in education derived from his experience as a teacher. Dissatisfied with traditional schooling's bureaucratic restraints, he urged classroom freedom and liberation in his books, *How Children Fail* (1964), *How Children Learn* (1964), *The Underachieving School* (1967), and *What Do I Do Monday?* (1970). His *Freedom and Beyond* (1972) exposited his idea of educational reform through liberated learning in open classrooms. Like Rousseau, Holt proclaimed that by their very nature children are "smart, energetic, curious," and eager learners.[20] Teachers, following the rules and regulations of conventional schools, imposed too many prescriptions, proscriptions, and interventions that restrict children's natural eagerness to experiment and learn about their environment. Truly liberating education, Holt argued, occurs when children initiate and carry on their own self-directed rather than other-directed learning. This kind of freedom enables children to create and act upon their own reality. Although not as grounded in social and educational psychology, Holt's argument that children should be permitted to construct their own knowledge base anticipated the constructivist movement of the 1990s.

In some ways, there were similarities between the new "romantic" critics such as Holt and some child-centered progressives of earlier decades. Like earlier child-centered progressives, the more recent critics looked to the child's nature and children's creative powers as the keys to learning. They found that informal and nonformal experiences held greater educational power than the formal school's structured and sequenced lessons. If the new romantic critics of the 1960s were progressive, their progressivism, lacking Dewey's instrumental pragmatism, was Rousseauean and child-centered. More socially-oriented progressives such as George Counts would have likely labeled them "romantics" because of their beliefs that children created their own reality rather than learning about the space, time, and structure of the larger world and society.

Other critics, operating from a more socially-oriented perspective, saw schools as agencies of the dominant classes' machinations to exert social control over minorities and those at society's lower economic rungs. These critics drew their inspiration from the Frankfort School of social analysis, especially from Juergen Habermas, or from neo-Marxists, such as Antonio Gramsci. Still others, like Paulo Freire, took a stance for "liberation pedagogy," which like "liberation theology," would empower the dispossessed. Then, there were those, like Ivan Illich, who contended that schools provided the initial environment for institutionalizing society by indoctrinating the young with the false promises of a consumer-based lifestyle. Urging deschooling as the first step in liberating society from institutionalization, Illich called for replacing formal schools with nonformal modes of learning. (Illich's ideas are discussed later in the chapter.)

Just as a variety of subject-matter enthusiasts had challenged public schools as being anti-intellectual in the 1950s, the mid- and late 1960s saw the rise of a new group of critics. Rather than challenging public schools' lack of academic rigor as did Bestor and Rickover, these new critics challenged schools as being overly bureaucratic and insensitive to the needs of children and youth, especially those from economically disadvantaged backgrounds. The new critics called on schools to create a humanistic milieu in which feelings would receive as much emphasis as academic subjects.

An early critic was A. S. Neill, a British educator, who emphasized that students should have the greatest possible freedom of choice. Working with "problem children" who often had a strong aversion to schooling, Neill determined that children would learn when they are ready and interested in learning. His book, *Summerhill* (1960), named after his residential institution, stressed the widest possible child latitude and freedom.[21]

Paul Goodman, an advocate of alternative education, anticipated Illich in his criticism of compulsory schooling. He argued that the state-enforced prolongation of schooling for adolescents was "psychologically, politically, and professionally damaging." Attacking large bureaucratic school systems, he argued that the entire city, rather than the school's four walls, was the place for real learning. The huge urban schools should be decentralized into small learning units of twenty to fifty students whose education could be guided by dedicated adults, rather than by certificated teachers.[22]

Publications by a number of critics challenged conventional schooling and teaching. Among them were: Jonathan Kozol's, *Death at an Early Age* (1967); George Dennison's, *The Lives of Children* (1969); Joseph Featherstone's, *Schools Where Children Learn* (1971); Herbert Kohl's *36 Children* (1967) and *The Open Classroom* (1970); Nat Hentoff's *Our Children are Dying*; James Herndon's *The Way It Spozed to Be* (1968) and *How to Survive in Your Native Land (1971)*; George Leonard's *Education and Ecstasy* (1968); Terry Borton's *Reach, Touch and Teach: Student Concerns and Process Education* (1970).[23]

Although they came from widely differing ideological and educational perspectives, the anti-institutional critics of the mid- and late 1960s raised serious issues and, in some ways, paved the way for two educational movements of the late 1960s and the 1970s: open education and deschooling. The open educators sought to reform public schools by changing their goals, organization, structures, and methods. The open educators wanted to free schools from unnecessary bureaucracy rather than making them more efficient through team teaching and modular scheduling, as did the reformers of the late 1950s and early 1960s. They also contributed to the argument that there needed to be alternative schools, which like the charter schools of the 1990s were to be free to create their own educational environments and learning styles. Proponents of alternative schools saw them as ways to reduce student alienation and retain students who might drop out. Still others, who saw schools as the first agencies in the process of human institutionalization, argued that schools could not be reformed but rather that society should be deschooled; that is, informal educational settings should replace formal ones.

The Open Education Movement

The open education movement of the late 1960s and early 1970s was shaped by three major elements: (1) ideas and practices emanating from the British Primary School in the United Kingdom; (2) reformers, within U.S. schools, who sought to reduce institutional formalism by injecting more informal and nonformal modes of instruction and behavior; (3) those, inside and outside of schools, who advocated a more humanistic educational milieu.

The British Primary School

A significant stimulus for the open education movement came from comparative education sources, namely, American educators' interest in the British primary school. Joseph Featherstone's articles in the *New Republic* in 1967 lauded the British "infant school." Reporting his observations in "Schools for Children," Featherstone noted that classroom discipline was a "less paramount" problem among the independently motivated children in the British schools than in the United States.[24] Beatrice and Ron Gross, in the *Saturday Review*, reiterated Featherstone's theme that "children want to learn and will through firsthand experience."[25] Of great appeal to American teachers, who continually are searching for ways to solve discipline problems and motivate children, was the promise that children, through their own self-motivated and self-initiated learning, would be virtually self-managed.

It should be noted that what is called the infant stage in British education does not actually correspond to infancy as defined in the United States but rather refers to the first three grades or forms of primary schooling attended by children from five to seven years of age. The British infant stage corresponds to the primary grades in U.S. schools. British children then proceed to the junior forms. While many British primary schools remained quite conventional, some featured more relaxed and informal processes of early childhood learning and new concepts of classroom organization that emphasized learning centers. These informal approaches, which were then current in the United Kingdom, had resulted in a reconceptualization of the role of primary teachers.[26]

The British primary school philosophy rested on the pedagogical rationale that: (1) children's learning, residing in play and activities, was experience based; (2) experienced-based teaching, in response to children's interests and needs, should be relaxed and informal; (3) children's chief motivation to learn came from their choosing to engage in activities and projects in which they had an interest.[27] The premises upon which the British primary school rested should not have been new to American educators since they were also core beliefs of such American progressive educators as Francis Parker, Marietta Johnson, John Dewey, Harold Rugg and others. Teachers in British primary schools determined school routines but allowed children to have their own learning options. These learning choices were enhanced by a classroom environment that was rich in stimulating learning activities.

In the United Kingdom, the Plowden Commission, after a study of the new informal approaches to early childhood education, endorsed the activity-centered primary school.[28] The crux of the British primary school method was that more formal school structures should yield to an informal environment, with larger blocs of unstructured time, where children were free to work individually or in small groups on a wide variety of activities. Quietly guided by nonintrusive teachers, children learned by pursuing their own curiosity and interests. In addition to the Plowden report, books by British authors on the new approach to early childhood education gained a wide readership among American educators. Among them were Sybil Marshall's *An Experiment in Education* (1966), Mary Brown and Norman Precious's *The Integrated Day in the Primary School* (1970), and John Blackie's *Inside the Primary School* (1971).

Many American educators, eager to learn about what seemed to be a successful innovation, traveled to the United Kingdom to visit primary schools and to talk with educators who were leading the new movement. These American educational travelers encountered a new terminology, including the "free day," "integrated curriculum," and "integrated day," which they imported with enthusiasm to the United States. These terms referred to a school day and curriculum in which children were free to explore a learning environment that contained learning centers, which featured various objects designed to stimulate children's interests. Children were free to choose to work at activities that drew on their interests. This style of learning, guided by teachers, was designed to develop skills in an integrated, or undifferentiated, manner that related to the chosen activity rather than by completing specific drills or lessons. For example, Charles Silberman, an influential American commentator on education, enthusiastically endorsed the British primary schools as places in which children, learning from their environment, came "to enjoy the present" and "get ready for the future" by having the opportunity to be "human beings."[29]

British experts on the new method of primary education came to the United States to speak and offer workshops. Progressive private schools were among the early American institutions to incorporate the British primary school philosophy into their programs. Between 1968 and 1973, the National Association of Independent Schools sponsored workshops throughout the country that featured the British primary school philosophy. The movement then reached the public schools where it was reshaped into open education.

Open Education in the United States

Influenced by the attention given to innovations in British primary schools, an open education movement developed in the United States. Its advocates could be found in the U.S. Office of Education, state departments of education, among school administrators, and in schools of education such as the Bank Street College of Education and the New School of Behavioral Studies in Education at the University of North Dakota. Lillian Weber, a professor at the City College of New York, who had observed primary schools in England, endorsed and popularized open education. The Education Development Center, which disseminated information about open education, emphasized informal teaching methods, use of manipulative materials, process learning, and the physical restructuring of classrooms.[30]

Open education was a widely lauded innovation among some educators who believed it would revolutionize American schools. Many educators, including district superintendents, were eager converts who proceeded to recast open education into a variety of formats, especially making instruction more informal and restructuring the physical layout of classrooms and schools.

The teaching method associated with open education derived heavily from its origins in primary schools. Although similar to the academic subject reforms of the late 1950s and early 1960s, the open education movement did not occur downward from universities and colleges into high schools and then into junior high and elementary schools; instead it rose upward from primary to secondary levels. Open education rested on several assumptions about children and how they learn, such as: (1) children are naturally curious and eager to learn; (2) their curiosity leads them to explore and investigate their environment; (3) the classroom environment, if structured with materials that stimulate this curiosity, can be a rich place of learning; (4) since they are free to choose their own learning activity, this freedom helps them to become independent and self-sustained learners; (5) conventional schools, by their formality and rigidity, have constrained children's inclination to learn by exploratory activities; (6) teachers, if informal and relaxed, can guide children's learning; (7) hands-on, process-oriented activities are the most effective learning activities.

These assumptions, forming open education's methodological base, had a highly significant impact on classroom and school layout and architecture. School administrators and others related pedagogical openness and informality to the actual design of classrooms. They reasoned that the more formal style of teaching took place in the conventional self-contained classroom where a teacher, at the center of the room, taught pupils by a structured and highly verbal method. The small, self-contained classroom with a teacher isolated from her or his colleagues and pupils pursuing constraining standardized lessons from textbooks was to be replaced by large open spaces, without restricting interior walls, in which pupils would be free to move from learning center to learning center, guided by teams of teachers working in collaboration. Many existing schools went through a remodeling process in which the walls that separated self-contained classrooms were removed to create larger learning spaces. School architects created bold designs for new schools, which featured open spaces and learning centers. The open education movement occurred during a time when more middle schools were being designed and built. Many of these middle schools reflected open education designs.

Silberman's Crisis in the Classroom

An important impetus for open education came from Charles Silberman, author of *Crisis in the Classroom*.[31] A lecturer on economics at Columbia University and an editor at *Fortune Magazine*, Silberman was director of the influential Carnegie Commission's Study of the Education of Educators. Silberman went beyond the scope of his assignment on teacher preparation and developed an in-depth analysis of schooling within its large social contexts. Silberman's interpretive framework reflected the general revisionist climate of the late 1960s and early 1970s. His major working premise was that education, while it encompassed schooling, was a much larger and broader concept. Further, much learning occurred informally in agencies other than schools. To study American education, Silberman reasoned that it was necessary to examine American culture and society, the context in which schooling occurred.[32]

Silberman essentially argued that American public schools had become overly formal, neglecting students' personal and humanistic development. Employing qualitative rather than quantitative research methods, Silberman found many public schools to be "grim," "joyless," "oppressive," and intellectually sterile. In them, docile teachers and passive students were locked into mindless bureaucratic routines.[33] Praising the British primary school's relaxed informality, Silberman argued that it, along with Dewey's experimentalism and Piaget's developmental psychology, could help liberate American public schools from their oppressive climate. Elementary schools should be transformed into informal learning centers in which instruction followed children's interests, guided by humane and caring teachers. High schools, liberated from unnecessary rules and regulations, should encourage more student input into their own learning and substantially revise their curriculum to incorporate the best features of the new mathematics and science. Teacher education programs, reflecting these needed reforms in elementary and secondary schools, could then be part of a national educational transformation. Silberman attracted a large and enthusiastic national audience as he addressed the major educational organizations.

What Happened to Open Education?

The scenario that followed the open education movement was similar to the events that accompanied earlier movements such as life adjustment in the late 1950s and the new math and science in the early 1960s. There was a burst of initial enthusiasm as a veritable educational bandwagon began to roll through the leading foundations, schools of education, and professional educational organizations. Open education moved through the American educational system like a snowball; as it rolled along it picked up materials that enlarged but also reshaped it. American educators were now adding team teaching, programmed instruction, and instructional technology to what had once been informal learning.[34] Open education seemed to be heralding a new transformation of public schooling, an educational revolution. As indicated earlier in the chapter, open education, like earlier reform movements, encountered the conventional school and curriculum. The result was that open education altered conventional schooling, but conventional schooling also altered open education.

Some teachers, parents, and pupils resisted the changes that they felt were being imposed upon them in panacea-like fashion. Large, open classrooms were noisy and appeared to be disorderly. While the defenders of open education claimed that the apparent noise and disorder were outward signs of freedom and creativity, critics contended that the method and its architecture interfered with orderly, sequential learning. Some critics alleged that the open educators, in the name of classroom freedom, had become doctrinaire in that they believed they could impose their version of freedom on others. Some teachers and parents, objecting to what they felt was permissiveness for its own sake, contended that some children wanted and needed order and structure. Teachers who resisted open education and open space slowly changed the large open-space rooms into what resembled their former self-contained classrooms as they erected bookcases, room dividers, and other devices to create separate spaces once again.

Open education, like the earlier life adjustment and new math and science, was not a total loss, however. Though its cutting edge was surely blunted, it nevertheless left its impact on teacher education, teaching methods, and school design and architecture. Many teachers adopted more relaxed, informal teaching methods. A greater repertoire of teaching styles and methods could be found in the same school, often in classes in the same subject and grade. More adaptable to different children and different situations even within their own self-contained classroom, teachers came to value a repertoire of styles and methods over one exclusive method. School architecture, too, became open to more variations as schools became an architectural synthesis of structure and openness. While there were self-contained classrooms, there were also large learning centers for group activities and instruction. Further, some of the concepts associated with the British primary school and American open education could be found in the constructivism of the 1990s.

Illustrative of the open education movements were the many middle schools established during the 1960s and 1970s. The older junior high school, typically a two-year school incorporating the upper elementary grades seven and eight, gave way to the middle school concept. Middle schools, depending on the state and district, varied in age range and grade levels. They might incorporate some combination of grades six, seven, eight, and nine. Whatever their particular grade levels, they were based on a philosophy that they were institutions devoted to the transitional years as students moved from childhood to adolescence. Though still influenced by the power of the high school on their curriculum, middle schools became places of greater exploration of life issues and careers, as the life adjusters of the 1950s had once suggested. Middle schools often incorporated the process-learning, informality and the spaces associated with open education. Then, too, their curricula exemplified many features of the new mathematics and science.

Alternative Education and Schools

The free and alternative school movement represented still another effort to break out of the conventional organization of public schooling. Free schools typically were small independent schools, designed to serve a particular category of students who were likely to drop out of the public schools. Some free schools also were created by those who wanted to use a particular curricular or methodological approach which was not generally found in public schools. Alternative schools were educational arrangements, often within public schools, that served a particular group of students or were based on a particular curricular or methodological design. The alternative schools of the 1960s and 1970s, like the charter schools of the 1990s, typically were educational arrangements within the public school system.

During the late 1960s and early 1970s, alternative schools became popular as an educational arrangement that would retain those likely to drop out by providing them with different and more relevant approaches to education. They were also used by those who wanted to attempt more experimental and humanistic modes of learning without the bureaucratic and set-curriculum restraints found in conventional schools.

By 1972, an estimated five hundred free schools, enrolling about twenty thousand students, were functioning. These schools typically were small, with average enrollments of thirty-three pupils. They tended to have a short life span of about eighteen months.[35] Their sponsors wanted to keep them free and avoid institutionalizing them. However, after an initial burst of enthusiasm, which usually included substantial volunteerism, their long-term support waned.

Alternative schools generally were optional, nonconventional arrangements, which tended to be mini-schools, small in size and enrollments, within the public system. They attempted to deregulate and free themselves from some of the bureaucratic regulations. Students had more freedom in selecting courses. There was a close, permissive, and informal relationship between students, teachers, and counselors. Academic requirements, too, were satisfied by courses, work-study programs, community service, and specially designed projects.[36]

While the alternative school movement had some impact on school systems generally, it became somewhat deflected from a general reform to more specific innovations, largely determined by the socioeconomic composition of local school districts. Most districts in the country were largely untouched by the alternative school approach. What resulted were special-interest schools, or schools within schools, that served particular groups of students, such as the academically gifted who had special interests in fine arts, drama, science, and mathematics. There were also those that took a decidedly conservative approach to schooling, stressing basic education and discipline.

Somewhat related to the alternative schools movement was the trend since the 1970s for local districts, especially those serving large urban or suburban areas, to create special-interest or magnet schools. While offering a general secondary curriculum, special-interest schools tended to feature a particular area such as foreign languages, or mathematics and science, or the fine arts. The central curricular theme, then, tended to be diffused throughout the entire curriculum. Magnet schools, serving academically gifted or highly motivated students, also emphasized particular curricular areas. Often located in large urban districts, the students who attended them were free to cross attendance-area boundaries within the district. In this way, they were used to promote racial and social integration as students from different backgrounds attended them.

Deschooling Society

Ivan Illich's theory of deschooling launched a movement, which, in the United States, enlisted some theoreticians but few practitioners. Founder of the Center for Intercultural Documentation in Mexico, Illich was concerned about the effects that the transference of Western institutions and technology had on developing countries. His concerns led to his writing of several books calling for the deinstitutionalization of society. In his *Celebration of Awareness* (1970) and *Tools for Conviviality* (1973), Illich questioned the supposed benefits of modern technology and its importation, often by multinational corporations, to less technologically developed countries.[37] He argued that indigenous wealthy elites and foreign investors profited from this Western-inspired technological importation that left indigenous masses exploited and dispossessed. Further, expensive Western-style institutions, such as international airports, large hospitals, and elaborate schools, were built as an infrastructure that served the elite but neglected the needs of the masses. Illich argued that the working people of less technologically developed nations were better served by more readily available, more informal or nonformal health care, such as village clinics and midwives and by grassroots nonformal education rather than by elaborate, expensive, and inaccessible Western institutional models.

In developing his educational theory, Illich attacked what he called the myth of "unending consumption." The myth, ignoring the particular environments in which people live, falsely promised the advance of human progress if more products and commodities are produced and consumed. The myth of consumption created a continuous cycle of higher, but unfulfilled, expectations. Schooling played a key role in perpetuating the myth by: (1) indoctrinating students to accept the consumption theory; (2) training and certifying specialists who staff institutions and schools and carry on the indoctrination process that is masked as education; (3) contributing to the desire for more products, which is mislabeled as "rising expectations." If the myth is to be made inoperative, Illich argued that society needs to be deschooled as the first step in deinstitutionalization.

Illich's *Deschooling Society* (1971), which urged eliminating formal schools and replacing them with informal and nonformal educational alternatives, was such a bold proposal that it attracted attention from some educators and the media.[38] Articles about Illich and deschooling appeared in *Time*, *The New York Times*, the *New Yorker*, and other influential and widely read publications.

Unlike the open and humanistic educators who proposed reforming schools, Illich had abandoned hope that schools could be transformed into liberating institutions. He defined schooling as an "age specific, teacher-related process requiring full-time attendance at an obligatory curriculum."[39] Schools were coercive institutions in that those in control, administrators and teachers, specified, set, and evaluated the goals of others, the students.

The schools' monopoly over education led to the erroneous but widely held belief that education must be expensive, complicated and controlled by specialists. For Illich, schools, by conditioning people to live in an institutionalized society, were the first step in the institutionalizing dependency mechanism. Closely tied to schooling was the process of certification, the creation of educational bureaucracies in that only those possessing appropriate certificates could hold administrative and teaching positions. Rather than certificated personnel, Illich found the most effective educators to be peers, experienced adults, and the environment itself.

Once education is freed from schooling, Illich argued, then learning, too, can be liberated. Instead of formal and coercive schools, people can learn by sharing their skills with each other and can have access to the situations and resources, the things (objects and products), that contribute to learning. For learning specific kinds of skills—such as reading, speaking and reading a foreign language, or computer programming, for example—the student would study with a competent practitioner. Competent practitioners, identified in a skill bank or exchange, would simply agree to instruct those seeking to learn the skill, often by drilling and modeling. Instead of being monopolized by schools, there would be wide access to learning environments—machine shops, libraries, laboratories, offices, photography and art studios, and so forth. Liberal education would take place through the discussions of interested peers. These discussions would be facilitated through peer-matching, the voluntary association of individuals, who would meet in learning circles to discuss the issues that concerned them.

Deinstitutionalizing and deschooling society, Illich asserted, would generate a veritable social revolution. In contrast to Western consuming societies, Illich claimed that a new model, "the convivial society," would emerge in the less technologically developed countries. The convivial society would encourage persons to be creative, autonomous, and direct in their interaction with the environment. While modern mass society allocated power to specialists in health care, education, and other areas, a convivial society empowered the people who used these services.[40]

Although deschooling generated interesting debates in the media and at professional educational meetings, its real influence was more on international development education than on schools. Development education, which emerged in the 1960s, was based on the premise that American educators could aid in the development of less technologically developed third world countries. Illich's arguments for deschooling, as well as Paulo Freire's arguments for liberation pedagogy, challenged the then-prevalent theory that development should be directed to modernizing traditional societies and economies. Illich argued that nonformal, project-specific education, which ensures sustainable development, is more appropriate than modernization through Western-imported institutions and technologies. Arising from grassroots needs, the peoples of third world nations can empower themselves rather than allow others to disempower and exploit them in the name of modernization.

Open educators, for example Silberman, while agreeing with Illich that institutions, such as schools, had grown overly coercive, disagreed that learning could be entirely casual. In contrast, Silberman contended that education, in schools, needed to be the "deliberate . . . purposeful . . . creation" and "transmission of knowledge, abilities, skills, and values."[41]

The ideas of Illich had a continuing appeal to a significant group of educational theorists in the late 1980s and 1990s. Illich's questioning of the power of institutionalized education and its control by politically powerful socioeconomic elites appealed to these critical theorists, who gained influence in educational studies and in teacher education. Like Illich, critical theorists would call for the empowering of those who were exploited and dispossessed. However, unlike Illich, who felt that schools were so intertwined with the status quo, critical theorists believed a transforming revolution could occur within schools, if teachers could be educated to be consciousness-raising agents of change. Like Illich, the critical theorists' impact remained largely in articles and books about educational philosophy and theory rather than in actual practice. More powerful than either Illich or the critical theorists were neoconservatives, who urged that schools return to basic education.

The Revival of Basic Education

By the late 1970s, a neoconservative countertrend began to shape education, especially in secondary schools. The new neoconservative movement, coalescing around basic education, of course was not really new. Like other reforms—liberal or conservative, progressive or essentialist—it incorporated strong elements of the educational past. This new movement, which reiterated old themes, began as a return to basic education, to an essentialist framework of skills and subjects for all students. Opposing the permissive and unstructured style of humanistic and open education, it stressed the primacy of skills, subject matter, and sequence. Much like Bestor, Rickover, and the critics of the 1950s, the emphasis among advocates of basic education was on history, mathematics, science, English, and foreign language, with the addition of basic computer literacy and competency. The subject matters were to be taught in effective schools, with strong principals as instructional leaders and highly motivated teachers with high expectations of their students. The school's goals were to be clearly stated, its regulations known in advance and consistently applied in specific cases. To counteract rising violence in or near schools, the effective school, its principal and teachers, were to maintain order and discipline in a no-nonsense style. Further, competency testing, administered to students at particular grade levels, was to ensure teacher accountability. (For the impact of basic education in the 1980s, see chapter 12.)

The basic education movement grew into a larger national movement for educational reform. It led to the educational policies of the Reagan and Bush administrations. In 1983, *A Nation at Risk* signaled a national thrust that incorporated many themes of the basic education movement.

Conclusion

Like a pendulum, educational movements moved back and forth in the 1960s and 1970s, from an academic subject orientation toward the new math and science, to humanistic and open education, and then back to basic education. While each of these movements had its own impact on the schools, they did not succeed in transforming them into completely different kinds of educational institutions. Rather, the changes introduced with the new math, the new science, the structure of disciplines, humanistic education, open education, and basic education resulted in what turned out to be incremental changes, often additions, to the curriculum and instruction. Whether this failure to effect transformative change should be judged as good or bad, positive or negative, is difficult to determine historically. However, it can be stated that the school remains a mighty fortress that, while not completely impermeable to change, certainly shows the power of continuity.

Notes

[1] Diane Ravitch, *The Troubled Crusade: American Education 1945–1980* (New York: Basic Books, 1983), p. 230.

[2] Ibid., p. 231.

[3] Ibid., p. 229.

[4] Ibid., pp. 263–64.

[5] Jerome Bruner, "Needed: A Theory of Instruction," *Educational Leadership*, 20, No. 8 (May 1963), pp. 523–32.

6 Mary Margaret Grady Nee, "The Development of Secondary School Mathematics Education in the United States," Ph.D. dissertation, Loyola University, Chicago, pp. 112–50, and Stephen S. Willoughby, *Contemporary Teaching of Secondary School Mathematics* (New York: John Wiley and Sons, 1967), p. 44.

7 College Entrance Examination Board, *Report of the Commission on Mathematics: Program for College Preparatory Mathematics* (Princeton: Educational Testing Service, 1959), pp. 1–34.

8 Warren C. Seyfert, *The Continuing Revolution in Mathematics* (Washington, DC: National Council of Teachers of Mathematics, 1968), pp. 23–25.

9 Jerome Bruner, *The Process of Education* (New York: Vintage Books, 1960), p. 33.

10 National Advisory Committee on Mathematics Education, *Overview and Analysis of School Mathematics Grades K–12* (Washington, DC: Conference Board of the Mathematical Sciences, 1975), pp. 3–4.

11 Leroy G. Callahan and Vincent J. Glennon, *Elementary School Mathematics: A Guide to Current Research* (Washington, DC: Association of Supervision and Curriculum Development, 1975), pp. 10–11.

12 Morris Kline, *Why Johnny Can't Add: The Failure of the New Math* (New York: St. Martin's Press, 1973), pp. 24–103.

13 Nee, "The Development of Secondary School Mathematics Education in the United States, 1950-1965, pp. 261–64.

14 For a thorough study of J. Lloyd Trump and the "Trump Plan," see William R. Shields, "J. Lloyd Trump: An Historical Perspective of an Innovator in American Education," doctoral dissertation, Loyola University, Chicago, 1998.

15 J. Lloyd Trump and Dorsey Baynham, *Guide to Better Schools: Focus on Change* (Chicago: Rand McNally and Co., 1970), p. 1.

16 Lloyd S. Michael, "What Are We Trying to Accomplish in the Staff Utilization Studies?" *The Bulletin of the National Association of Secondary School Principals*, 43 (January 1959), pp. 5–8.

17 J. Lloyd Trump, *Images of the Future—A New Approach to the Secondary School* (Reston, VA: NASSP Publication, 1959).

18 *Time Magazine* (October 20, 1961), p. 42 as cited in Smith, chapter 3.

19 For example, see C. Albert Koob and J. Lloyd Trump, eds. *Shaping the Future* (Washington, DC: National Catholic Educational Association, 1966).

20 John Holt, *How Children Fail* (New York: Pitman, 1964) and Holt, *Freedom and Beyond* (New York: E.P. Dutton and Co., 1972).

21 A. S. Neill, *Summerhill: A Radical Approach to Child Rearing* (New York: Hart, 1960).

22 Ravitch, p. 236.

23 For a discussion of the radical and romantic critics, see Ravitch, *The Troubled Crusade*, pp. 235–38.

24 Joseph Featherstone, "Schools for Children," *The New Republic* 158 (August 10, 1967).

25 Beatrice and Ronald Gross, "Little Bit of Chaos," *Saturday Review*, 55 (May 16, 1970), pp. 71–73.

26 Ravitch, p. 239.

27 Ibid., pp. 239–40.

28 Central Advisory Council for Education, *Children and Their Primary Schools* (London: Her Majesty's Stationery Office, 1967).

29 Charles Silberman, *Crisis in the Classroom* (New York: Random House, 1970), p. 207.

30 Ravitch, pp. 241–42.

31 Charles Silberman, *Crisis in the Classroom*; Silberman's earlier books were *Crisis in Black and White* (New York: Random House, 1964) and *The Myths of Automation* (New York: Harper and Row, 1966).

32 Silberman, *Crisis in the Classroom*, pp. 4–5.

33 Ibid., pp. 3-11.

34 Marylin Hapgood, "The Open Classroom—Protect it from its Friends," *Saturday Review*, 55 (September 18, 1971), pp. 66–69.

35 Ravitch, p. 252.

36 Ibid., pp. 253–254.

37 Ivan Illich, *Celebration of Awareness: A Call for Institutional Revolution* (Garden City, NY: Doubleday and Co., 1970).

38 Ivan Illich, *Deschooling Society* (New York: Harper and Row, 1970).

39 Ibid., pp. 113–14.

40 Ivan Illich, *Tools for Conviviality* (New York: Harper and Row, 1973), p. 11.

41 Silberman, *Crisis in the Classroom*, p. 2.

Further Reading

Barker, Charles M., Helen Curran, and Mary Metcalf. *The "New" Math: For Teachers and Parents of Elementary School Children*. San Francisco: Fearon Publishers, 1964.

Blackie, John. *Inside the Primary School*. London: Her Majesty's Stationery Office, 1967.

Brown, Mary, and Norman Precious. *The Integrated Day in the Primary School*. New York: Agathon Press, 1970.

Bruner, Jerome. *The Process of Education*. New York: Vintage Books, 1960.

College Entrance Examination Board. *Report of the Commission on Mathematics: Program for College Preparatory Mathematics*. Princeton, NJ: Educational Testing Service, 1959.

Davis, Robert B. *The Changing Curriculum: Mathematics*. Washington, DC: Association for Supervision and Curriculum Development, NEA, 1967.

Dennison, George. *The Lives of Children*. New York: Random House, 1969.

Featherstone, Joseph. *Schools Where Children Learn*. New York: Liveright, 1971.

Freire, Paulo. *Pedagogy of the Oppressed*. New York: Herder and Herder, 1971.

Herndon, James. *The Way It Spozed to Be*. New York: Simon and Schuster, 1968.

Holt, John. *How Children Fail*. New York: Pitman Publishing Corp., 1964.

Holt, John. *How Children Learn*. New York: Pitman Publishing Corp., 1967.

Holt, John. *The Underachieving School*. New York: Pitman Publishing Corp., 1967.

Holt, John. *What Do I Do Monday?* New York: E.P. Dutton and Co., 1970.

Illich, Ivan. *Celebration of Awareness: A Call for Institutional Revolution*. Garden City, NY: Doubleday and Co., 1970.

Illich, Ivan. *Deschooling Society*. New York: Harper and Row, 1971.

Kline, Morris. *Why Johnny Can't Add: The Failure of the New Math*. New York: St. Martin's Press, 1973.

Kohl, Herbert R. *36 Children*. New York: New American Library, 1967.

Kohl, Herbert R. *The Open Classroom*. New York: Random House, 1970.

Kozol, Jonathan. *Death at an Early Age*. Boston: Houghton Mifflin Co., 1967.

Marshall, Sybil. *An Experiment in Education*. New York: Cambridge University Press, 1966.

Plowden, Lady Bridget, et al. *Children and Their Primary Schools: A Report of the Central Advisory Council in Education*. London: Her Majesty's Stationery Office, 1966.

Ravitch, Diane. *The Troubled Crusade: American Education 1945–1980*. New York: Basic Books, 1983.

Seyfert, Warren C. *The Continuing Revolution in Mathematics*. Washington, DC: National Council of Teachers of Mathematics, 1968.

Silberman, Charles. *Crisis in the Classroom*. New York: Random House, 1970.

Trump, J. Lloyd. *Images of the Future—A New Approach to the Secondary School*. Reston, VA: NASSP Publications, 1959.

Trump, J. Lloyd, and Dorsey Baynham. *Guide to Better Schools: Focus on Change*. Chicago: Rand McNally and Co., 1970.

9

Student Activism in the 1960s: Campus Unrest, Vietnam, and the Counterculture

The dramatic unrest and activism among young adults, especially college and university students, from the mid-to-late 1960s and early 1970s, was both a domestic phenomenon related to social change in American society and higher education and also an international phenomenon in which young people challenged the socioeconomic and political establishment.[1] Kirkpatrick Sale, in his history of the Students for a Democratic Society (SDS), wrote that "the growing international consciousness of the young American left helped to turn it in a deliberately revolutionary direction." While French students greeted student demonstrations at Columbia University "with great enthusiasm," American students were inspired by their French counterparts' revolt against de Gaulle's government.[2]

In the United States, student protests challenged what was called the military-industrial complex and the unpopular war in Vietnam. In Eastern Europe, the challenge was directed against the Soviet satellite regimes in Czechoslovakia, East Germany, and Poland. In Western Europe, in addition to the French students who protested against the Gaullist government, students protested against their system of government and against the U.S. government's role in Vietnam. Rather than copying earlier youth movements, the German movement of the 1960s borrowed strategies from their American counterparts.

Interpreting the 1960s

The activism, protests, and social discontent, which reached its intensity from 1965 to 1972, does not appear to have a single cause. In the United States, it was an amorphous multidirectional phenomenon rather than an organized movement. In retrospect, several interpretations can be used to explain the causes of the phenomenon that gripped the nation, especially its institutions of higher education, during this era of discontent. Among these interpretations are: (1) cyclical generational conflict; (2) continuation of radical politics; (3) educational reaction and reform.

Cyclical Generational Conflict

The young people's activism of the 1960s might have been a cyclical generational reaction against the conformism of the so-called silent generation of the 1950s. The 1950s, the era of McCarthyism, was a quiet time on the campuses when colleges of engineering and business attracted large enrollments and students were reluctant to become involved, or were disinterested, in social and political issues and change. Despite the general conformist attitudes that led students to good-paying jobs and a home in the suburbs, there existed an undercurrent of alienation at the margins of youth society, the "beat generation" of the 1950s. These peripheries of alienation might have been sources that stimulated the larger mobilization of protesting youth of the 1960s. As the protests of the 1960s gained momentum, they became a countercultural reaction that manifested itself in generational conflict against the values of the previous decade.

The counterculture generated a style of cultural radicalism with its sexual freedom and experimentation with drugs that directly challenged the 1950s' staid conformism. In this light, the occurrences of the 1960s were part of a more pervasive social change that had important educational consequences. Among these consequences were a greater permissiveness toward social behavior and a greater acceptance of life alternatives than was known previously. The counterculture's political and educational ideology, rejecting hierarchical institutions and thinking, urged politics by participation and freedom through uninhibited self-expression.

A Continuation of Radical Politics

A second line of interpretation that is less social and more political regards the 1960s' activism as a continuation of the unfinished radical political agenda of the 1930s. The radical politics, the programs of the various alignments of Popular Fronts such as the Marxists, Trotskyites, Socialists, and even the progressives who had been artic-

Student Activism in the 1960s **221**

ulate during the economic depression of the 1930s, had been ignored during World War II in the fight against Nazism and Fascism. Rather than resurfacing, radical politics in the United States had been submerged by the anti-Communism of the cold war and by the liberal consensus in American politics and education.

During the McCarthy era, radicalism was suspect and dangerous. While liberals opposed McCarthyism, they had developed a consensus that enlarged the middle classes and the moderate-centrist point of view. The liberal consensus, which politicians such as Lyndon Johnson and Hubert Humphrey epitomized, was that the New Deal had done its work in saving, humanizing, and regulating American capitalism so that representative institutions were now securely in place in a modest social welfare state. The establishment perspective in history, the social sciences, and education was that future change could be moderate and incremental, along the lines of a quiet New Deal, without the necessity of radical transformation.

When the activists of the 1960s became political, their movement took the shape of the "New Left," represented by the SDS and like-minded organizations. It appeared to be a revived neo-Marxist or activist, socialist movement rather than a liberal one. Indeed, the liberals, in politics, government, and education, were seen as the enemy. The New Left of the 1960s, rekindling the Popular Front politics of the 1930s, doing battle against the corporate capitalism of the military-industrial complex, sought to lodge itself in higher education.

A focal target of radical politics and counterculture ideology was the industrial-military complex. The moderate Republican President Dwight Eisenhower, once overall commander of allied forces in World War II, had warned of the growth of a military-industrial complex, which, in the cold war, was growing into a source of political and economic power that covertly manipulated decision making in the United States. The sociologist C. Wright Mills, in *The Power Elite* (1956), wrote about a cadre of top business executives, high-ranking military officers, and key politicians and government bureaucrats—the power elite. This interlocking directorate of people in powerful positions directed national policy to serve its own needs. Those who challenged official American policy during the cold war era believed this military-industrial complex was determining U.S. policy, at home and abroad. When the student activism of the 1960s gained momentum, activists would attack the universities' research and development role for the military-industrial complex.

Also part of the background context for the student activism of the later 1960s was the Civil Rights movement of the 1950s and early 1960s. The movement for civil rights for African Americans in the South had enlisted the efforts of both black and white college students. For example, in the summer of 1964, the Student Nonviolent Coordinating Committee (SNCC) had enlisted one thousand white volunteers to work along with African Americans at freedom schools and on voter registration drives.[3] Through massive protests, sit-ins, and nonviolent resistance, young people joined the ranks of the Civil Rights movement to overturn racial segregation and secure employment and voter rights for blacks. The spirit of the Civil Rights movement and its strategy inspired young people to apply these same tactics against the universities, which they construed to be similar to the South's white power structure. Student activists would come to use the tactics of provoking a confrontation with university authorities by insisting on the acceptance of "non-negotiable" demands.

The 1960s activism could be viewed as a rebirth of ideology as a force in U.S. politics and education. Despite Daniel Bell's argument in the *End of Ideology* that ideology had been buried by the pervasive moderate liberal consensus of the 1950s, events were to prove that ideology's demise and burial had been premature. In the late 1960s, ideologies resurfaced as the "New Left" radicalism and a revived neoconservatism challenged liberalism. The reassuring, complacent "New Dealish" liberalism that characterized much historical and social science writing and teaching at many universities was now attacked by the Left and Right. Consensus-style politicians, such as Lyndon Johnson and Hubert Humphrey, would find themselves virtually immobilized when the decade of the 1960s reached its tumultuous climax.

Educational Reaction and Reform

While the above commentary offers social and political interpretations for the student protests and activism of the 1960s, a third line of explanation sees the period's turbulent events as an educational response to developments that had taken place in U.S. higher education during the post–World War II era. Stimulated by the GI Bill and the population increase of the postwar baby boom, U.S. colleges and universities continued their expansive cycle of growth throughout the 1950s and the 1960s. An important consequence of this growth was the creation of what Clark Kerr called the multiversity, large multipurpose universities, enrolling thousands of students. For example, student enrollments increased from 2,000,000 in 1946 to 8,000,000 in 1970.[4] This growth was the most dramatic at large state universities, whose rapid development eclipsed the slower pace of private institutions. As student enrollments grew, faculty ranks also increased from 165,000 in 1946 to 500,000 in 1970. College and university attendance was less selective than in the prewar years. With one out of three persons in the age cohort enrolled in institutions of higher education, college education was becoming part of an upward extension of the high school, especially for the white middle class. The process of growth brought consequences, some anticipated and others not.

The purpose of university education, particularly at the large state institutions, was becoming multifaceted and less clear. State universities were growing into huge institutions that served a large number of constituencies. Private institutions, particularly those under church auspices, too, were feeling the impact of change as their original denominational mission weakened and they moved toward a greater secularism.

The traditional teaching and research functions of universities began to be restructured and redefined, too. Faculty and institutions were seeking grants from federal and corporate sources.[5] For faculty the role of consultant to outside corporate and government agencies was becoming important enough to diminish the traditional roles of teaching and research. The growth of the undergraduate student population meant that, though there were more professors, many faculty at the higher ranks had less contact with undergraduates. Especially in large institutions, the teaching function was being relegated to graduate students, serving as teaching assistants and instructors. The large multipurpose universities, the multiversities of the 1960s, were appearing to many students as being administratively bloated, bureaucratic machines—large, impersonal educational factories. Mirroring the economic affluence and powerful consumerism of the late 1940s and 1950s, college and university programs, geared to the new economy, were less centered on general academic education and more focused on economic needs and the job market for graduates. Less concerned with humanistic and social issues, higher education had become more professionally and technologically specialized. Geared to training engineers, managers, and other kinds of technological experts, it had neglected social problems, especially the educational interests and needs of underrepresented groups, such as women, African Americans, Hispanics, and other minorities. Student activist critics contended that higher education, an agency of corporate social control, was concerned with reproducing and serving the society's economic and political power sectors. The protests of the 1960s galvanized into educational demands for change: for a more participatory governance of colleges and universities that included students, for the ending of the *in loco parentis* regulations that governed student life, and for the establishment of new curricula for black, women's, environmental, and peace studies. In addition to these demands, the more radical activists wanted colleges and universities to purge themselves of research and development grants and programs related to national security, especially to the military and intelligence functions.

While the generational conflicts, radical political ideology, and educational change formed the backdrop, the immediate flash point for the student activism of the 1960s was U.S. involvement in the war in Vietnam.

Student Activism and Protests

From 1965 to 1972, from the University of California at Berkeley to Kent State University in Ohio, there were sit-ins, teach-ins, and demonstrations by students, some of which were peaceful while others were not. Although the forms of student activism varied from institution to institution, a common framework of the various actors on the scene can be used to examine these occurrences in higher education. Among the actors were students, faculty, administration, trustees, and media persons. Before turning to specific scenarios, we examine the roles played by these actors against the backdrop of the issues.

The Issues

The issues of the 1960s still remain difficult to disentangle for historical analysis. While there were many issues throughout the country, some protests were, at least initially, sparked by a single issue. This issue might be war, peace, race, poverty, curriculum, or even visiting hours at women's residence halls. Over time, they merged into a large snowball effect. After the first wave of protests occurred, then the issues tended to multiply into demands for a black studies program, removal of ROTC, and so on. Finally, the issues merged into in a large crossgenerational, antiadministration, antiestablishment, antiwar confrontation focused against American involvement in Vietnam.

The Students

Again, the students, their organizations, and their causes were as varied as the issues that drew them into protests and demonstrations. There were some national student organizations that featured prominently in the activism of the 1960s as well as many that were located on particular college and university campuses. Further, many student protesters simply joined in and were not affiliated with any organization.

In terms of their academic identification, students in the humanities and social sciences were drawn into protests and activism more than those in business, science, engineering, and professional studies. In many instances, there would be a core group of student activists who pressed the issues against the administration. These students might be members of activist political organizations, or they might be those involved in particular on-campus agendas. The majority of students were at first watchers, observers, or largely indifferent bystanders. As the university administrations took a stronger and what appeared to be a more repressive reaction, a larger number of students would be attracted to support the core group. Some student activist core groups used the politics and strategies of confrontation. They would, through a sit-in, provoke the administration into a reaction; the reaction, if repressive, would draw more recruits to the cause. Then would come another administration reaction and the cycle would continue and escalate. In terms of campus politics, the result of the cycle was the weakening of moderate liberalism among students as more of them veered into the activist camp. Not to be ignored was the formation of small conservative student groups, such as the Young Americans for Freedom, Goldwater supporters, and others who would become part of the neoconservatism revival of the late 1970s and 1980s.

The Students for a Democratic Society. In some respects, the SDS represented a revival of 1930s radicalism. Indeed, it represented a revival of the student affiliates of the League for Industrial Democracy who restyled themselves as the SDS. Among the national student organizations, the SDS attempted to articulate a coherent ideology. The SDS was launched on June 16, 1962, at the FDR Labor Camp, near Port Huron, Michigan. Its Port Huron Statement, drafted under the leadership of Tom Hayden, attacked racism, inequitable distribution of wealth, and the cold war's militarism. It pledged to create a political existential humanism that would empower the dispossessed in a new form of community. The SDS endorsed a political process called participatory democracy, in which individuals would "share in those decisions affecting the quality and direction" of their lives.[6] However, participatory democracy, meaning different things to different people, was never really defined. SDS members were participants in long and inconclusive debates about strategies to resist the Selective Service draft, about the extent to make racism the paramount cause, and the degree to affiliate with other radical groups.

Eschewing its predecessor's older attempts to create an old style Popular Front coalition of leftist students and workers, the SDS planned on raising the consciousness of the young university-based intelligentsia. Indeed, when they attempted to enlist members of labor unions, or white ethnics of the working class, they encountered resistance from these groups, which often opposed the "spoiled" upper-middle-class kids. During the 1960s, the SDS was one of the larger and better organized radical student groups, growing from twenty-nine chapters in 1964 to 247 in 1967.[7] Among the SDS leaders were Tom Hayden, a student at the University of Michigan, Mark Rudd, a student at Columbia University, and Bernardine Dohrn, a graduate of the Uni-

versity of Chicago Law School. Hayden, in particular, was instrumental
in shaping the early SDS ideology and agenda.

The SDS approach to using universities for ideological change,
however, encountered resistance by those academics who believed that
universities should not be politicized. Unlike continental European
and Latin American universities, those in the United States traditionally were not politicized or tied to a particular ideology. Those who
defended the political neutrality of the U.S. university proclaimed that
its role was that of scholarly and objective inquiry. The SDS countered
this claim, saying that scholarly objectivity was a masquerade in which
institutions, tied to the liberal consensus politics of the 1950s and
1960s, were linked ideologically to maintaining a repressive status
quo.

Radical student organizations such as the SDS experienced the
same phenomenon that had weakened leftist socialist and Marxist
groups in the past—splitting into factions over ideological and strategic
issues. While the sit-ins and politics of confrontation brought more students into the general movement, the specific core groups, which saw
themselves as its vanguard, tended to be factionalized. Some SDS
members wanted to affiliate and organize a third-party movement. The
more radical, ideologically disciplined students, attracted to Maoism,
organized a small splinter group. The progressive labor forces, both
within and independently of the SDS, argued for a worker-student coalition in support of local strikes and community action.[8] In addition to
those who were organized into some type of political-ideological group,
there were also the "uncontrollable" who, like the old anarchists and
nihilists doing "their own thing," eschewed any discipline, be it from
the institutionalized establishment or from student radical political
organizations.

While there is a tendency to identify the SDS as the leading activist antiwar organization, it was but one of several organizations active
in protesting U.S. government policy. For some local antiwar groups,
the SDS was far too ideological and insufficiently pragmatic. Some
local activist groups took steps to distance themselves from the SDS.

The Young Americans for Freedom. While the SDS was a focal
group for student radicalism on the left, there was also activism on the
right—conservative students who opposed the disruption of campus
life and university instruction. Among the conservative organizations
was the Young Americans for Freedom (YAF). YAF and other right-wing
student organizations drew their inspiration from the conservative
intellectuals, William Buckley, a noted writer and commentator, and
Russell Kirk, a political philosopher. Ideologically, YAF featured a synthesis of traditional conservative themes of political freedom, coupled
with personal responsibility, and classical liberal doctrines of free-

market economics. Strongly anti-Communist, it opposed collectivist trends in American politics.

While YAF was a relatively small organization, it took a decided stand against campus radicalism. For some participants, YAF was a training ground for young people who would later support Ronald Reagan's neoconservative revivalism. At the various campuses where leftist students were leading demonstrations, YAF and related local organizations organized counterdemonstrations, encouraging administrators to stand firm against the radicalization of higher education. For example, the Students for a Free Campus (SFC) was organized at Columbia University; the Student Committee for a Responsible University was organized at Pennsylvania State University.

Black Student Activism. The role that African-American students would take in the student activism of the 1960s depended on several factors: (1) what was happening nationally in the Civil Rights movement; (2) the location and type of institution attended; (3) the degree of identification with African-American culture and education; and (4) often, as with white students, their academic majors. As with other students, these factors varied with individuals and their situations.

By the mid-1960s some significant changes had taken place in the Civil Rights movement. While young African Americans during the 1950s and early 1960s had worked for integrationist mainstream civil rights organizations, such as the NAACP and Martin Luther King's Southern Christian Leadership Conference (SCLC), by the late 1960s some turned to more directly activist, sometimes separatist organizations. Even before King's assassination in 1968, some young black activists had moved outside of the more mainstream organizations such as the NACCP and the SCLC. Stokely Carmichael, who had been active in the Civil Rights movement in the South, helped organize the Student Nonviolent Coordinating Committee (SNCC), which moved from its nonviolent origins with the SCLC to a more activist stance.[9]

The Black Panthers, influenced by Frantz Fanon's justification of revolutionary violence in *The Wretched of the Earth* (1966), took a more radical stance. Fanon, who had attacked colonialism in Asia, Latin America, and Africa, was an especially appealing ideologist for the Black Panthers, who saw African Americans as being victims of a similar internal colonialism. Led by Huey Newton and Bobby Seale, they endorsed revolutionary black nationalism. Photographed with weapons, they carried Chairman Mao's *Red Book of Revolutionary Sayings*.

The Nation of Islam, or Black Muslims, led by Elijah Mohammed, was a more conservative but strongly separatist black power organization. Urging its members to practice personal discipline, the Islamic group called for black-owned and black-patronized businesses, schools, and institutions. Malcolm X, a dynamic leader and forceful speaker, attracted a large following in the Nation of Islam and then left it to form his own association, the Organization of Afro-American Unity (OAAU). Malcolm X, who was assassinated on February 21, 1965, while addressing the OAAU, became a heroic model for the new style of black activism.

In addition to the developments related to the national Civil Rights movement, there were also changes in the location and situation of African-American students in higher education. African-American enrollments, still underrepresented, were growing. They tripled from 1960 to 1969, growing from 174,000 to 522,000, and reached over a million in 1976. Colleges and universities throughout the country were trying to increase their African-American student enrollments. Because of the attempts of these institutions to attract African Americans, the historically all-black colleges and universities faced competition that they had not known before. In 1950, 80 percent of African-American students were enrolled in historically black institutions; twenty years later, in 1970, 75 percent were attending predominantly white institutions.[10] While some protests occurred at historically black institutions, their incidence was lower than at other institutions. As with white students, the academic field with which black students identified played a role.

Still another feature was the growing interest of young African Americans in their history and culture. These cultural interests were sparked by political issues and, in turn, the cultural interests sparked political and educational interests, leading to demands for the inclusion of African-American educational programs and courses in the curriculum. Among the demands that surfaced from African-American students were: (1) establishment of black studies programs; (2) hiring more African-American faculty and administrators; and (3) increased efforts at recruiting and retaining more African-American students. Generally, the students succeeded in winning concessions from administrators and faculty. However, two other demands generated more controversy. Particularly at issue was that black students should have a role in hiring and firing faculty for the new programs. This demand challenged the traditional practice that faculty should play the key role in faculty selection, appointment, promotion, and termination. A second demand was that there should be separate dormitories for African-American students. College and university administrators, who were trying to integrate their institutions racially, opposed what they considered to be a restoration of segregation, even if the demand came from previously segregated persons. The development of Afrocentric programs, courses, and scholarships led to a legacy of black cultural consciousness on campuses and to the multicultural controversies of the 1980s and 1990s.

The Administration

Many college and university administrators were conceptually unready and strategically unprepared for the student protests of the 1960s. Because administrators were used to dealing with boards of trustees, alumni/ae, and faculty committees, their administrative style was slow and reactive. At large universities, it took time for university officials to consolidate their approaches into a unified policy and strategy. Relying on experiences of the quiet campus atmosphere of the 1950s, when major student affairs pertained to issues like fraternity parties, few administrators were prepared for the tumultuous events of the 1960s. At first, administrators, relying on familiar procedures, sought to use meetings, discussions, and task force reports to deal with the student protests. As student activism took a more direct and confrontational approach—sit-ins and occupations of university buildings—many administrators used force, campus or municipal police, to eject the demonstrators. Others pursued a more cautious policy of waiting out the demonstrators. Administrators in state institutions faced pressures from boards of trustees and state legislators who called for speedy and more direct measures against students who were disrupting educational activities. Further, they often faced divided faculties.

The Faculty

Just as college and university administrators were unprepared to deal with the student protests, so were faculty. Faculty, however, did not face the direct challenge that administrators did, but they, too, experienced the disruption of regular academic routines. Faculty members were divided on their responses to student activists.

Some faculty members identified with and promoted such student causes as ending the war in Vietnam, creating new black and women's studies programs, and aiding poverty-impacted minority groups. These faculty members defined the purpose of higher education as transforming U.S. society and economy into a more participatory democracy. Generally sympathetic to student activism, these faculty members supported students' demands, spoke at sit-ins, and took an antiadministration stance. While some faculty supported the student movement from a general identification with social reform, others were determined to become change agents themselves. Among these were members of the New University Conference, who sought to mobilize campus radicals to create a network of mutual support and centers of radical initiatives at institutions and in professional academic organizations. They sought to forge alliances with student activists to "expose and dislocate university collaboration in war research and social manipulation, and join with black and white radicals" to demand that universities respond to the "needs of black communities. . . ."[11]

Just as some supported student activism, other faculty were decidedly opposed to the disruption of the educational processes at their universities. Siding against the students, they supported a response by the administration against what they regarded as a leftist politization of higher education.

The majority of faculty tended to take a more ambiguous position; while supporting student activism as an expression of freedom of speech, most faculty wanted these expressions to follow more acceptable and conventional academic processes of discourse. They believed that it might be possible for differences between students and university administrators to be resolved by using peaceful, nonviolent procedures. The end result was that most faculties, veering in several directions, were aligned neither with students nor with administrators. However, their own internal divisions and generally ambiguous stand disenabled them from playing a decisive role.

The Media

Like the events of the Civil Rights movement in the South and the war in Vietnam, nightly television newscasts carried stories about student demonstrations on the nation's campuses. Names of student activist leaders such as Mario Savio, Mark Rudd, Clark Kissinger, and Tom Hayden surfaced. Distinguished news commentators such as Walter Cronkite and Eric Sevareid struggled to place the unprecedented happenings at colleges and universities into some kind of perspective. In addition to the direct coverage of television and radio, newspapers and magazines featured articles about the confrontations taking place on the campuses.

Using the above framework for interpreting the actions of key actors during the student activism of the 1960s, it is possible to examine several selected cases.

Situating Student Activism: The University of California at Berkeley

Student activism at the University of California at Berkeley was not new, but it became more intense in the 1960s. Previously, some students and faculty had protested against House Un-American Activities (HUAC) investigations of alleged Communist cells at the University. (See chapter 5 for HUAC and other anti-Communist investigations.)

By the 1960s, the Berkeley campus had grown into what its President, Clark Kerr, called a multiversity, serving multiple constituencies.

Though a usually astute educational administrator, Kerr misinterpreted the storm of protests that engulfed the University in the 1960s. Initially, he did not regard Berkeley's student activism as unusual. Kerr believed that each generation of students experienced its own periods of revolt against established authority.

In contrast to Kerr's interpretation of the demonstrations as a generational reoccurrence, Berkeley's protesting students saw themselves as participants in a dynamic flow of events of historic dimensions and as harbingers of significant socioeducational reforms. The core of dissenting students, led by Mario Savio, perceived itself to be an oppressed class like other minority groups in the United States.

The event that provoked the early student protests occurred during the academic year 1964–65 when the university administration banned tables for distributing literature on university property. In 1964, the University of California at Berkeley had a rather liberal policy that allowed any speaker to speak at the university campus; it required that the university receive a seventy-two hour prior notice of the planned event and that a tenured faculty member chair it. Recruitment for off-campus activities was confined to a strip of brick walkway, which, although on university property, was unofficially regarded as off campus. In September 1964, the university's chancellor, Edward M. Strong, announced that the walkway could no longer be used for political activities. His administrative decision was quickly challenged by the student activists, led by Savio, who led a demonstration on September 30, 1964, to protest the administration's ruling.[12]

The Berkeley administration met a forceful and eloquent opponent in the charismatic Mario Savio, a twenty-one-year-old junior majoring in philosophy. Articulate and passionate, Savio, who had been a former SNCC volunteer in the South, leading the students' Free Speech Movement (FSM), applied lessons learned in civil rights activism to Berkeley. A major confrontation between students and administrators came on October 1, 1964, when an ex-student, Jack Weinberg, was arrested while working at what the university claimed was an illegal fund-raising table. After a long demonstration in which students surrounded and immobilized a police car for thirty-two hours, President Kerr appeared to reach an agreement with the FSM, which was formed as a student umbrella organization to protest what it regarded as an unfair university prohibition on political activity.[13] The university administration conceded that advocacy of off-campus political action would be allowed on campus but would not permit on-campus planning of illegal off-campus activities. Breaking off negotiations, the FSM resumed confrontational tactics, including massive rule violations. On December 2, thousands of students staged an all-night sit-in in university buildings in which 814 students were arrested. The administration also suspended some of the offending students for these infractions.

The Board of Regents, meeting on November 20, 1964, had concurred with the administration that off-campus groups would be permitted to recruit and fund raise on the campus but would not be allowed to use campus facilities to plan illegal activities. The regents also upheld suspensions of eight students cited by university officials as engaging in disruptive activities. During the Thanksgiving recess, Savio and other FSM leaders received notifications that they were being charged with violations of university regulations. When classes resumed, 1,500 students staged a sit-in, occupying Sproule Hall. Police cleared the building and arrested 773 students. At this point, a faculty group, the Committee of 200 announcing their opposition to the presence of police on the campus, urged university administrators to drop charges against the students.[14]

When tentative agreements on the distribution of information advocating unlawful activities disintegrated, students resumed their protests, including the occupation of Sproule Hall. The core group of demonstrators grew as more students joined the protests. The issues escalated from the distribution of literature on campus to demands for restructuring the university and ending the war in Vietnam.

The faculty at Berkeley were divided on the issues. Some faculty supported the administration, others the FSM, and still others sought higher ground in a benign neutrality. The faculty response at Berkeley would be repeated later in the decade at other institutions. The Committee of 200 supported the FSM's demands for unrestricted freedom of speech and advocacy on the campus and, in turn, sought to influence the Academic Senate's Academic Freedom Committee.[15]

On December 8, 1964, the Academic Senate met to react to the situation. At this meeting, Professor Joseph Garbarino, chairperson of the Academic Freedom Committee, moved that: (1) "no university disciplinary measures" be taken "against members or organizations of the university community for activities prior to December 8," related to the "controversy over political speech and activity"; (2) the "time, place, and manner of conducting political activity . . . be subject to reasonable regulation to prevent interference with the normal functions of the university"; (3) "the content of speech or advocacy . . . should not be restricted by the university" and "off-campus student political activities . . . not be subject to university regulation"; (4) "future disciplinary measures in the area of political activity . . . be determined by a committee appointed by and responsible to the Berkeley division of the Academic Senate"; and (5) "all members of the university join . . . to restore the university to its normal functions." The motion, in effect, guaranteed amnesty to students facing disciplinary charges and supported the FSM's demands for unregulated freedom of speech and political activity. The motion was hotly debated. Professors who tried to amend it argued that students were following "uncivil" rather than civil disobedience and that undemocratic groups could use the motion to disrupt the university. Some also objected that the matter was appropriate to the board of trustees rather than to the faculty. The Academic Senate voted 824 for and 115 against the motion.[16] The senate's action won the applause of the FSM and other student protesters.

The Board of Regents responded by taking a firm proadministration stand, a typical position in the wake of campus disruption. At its meeting on December 18, 1964, the board adopted a motion that: (1) directed "the administration to preserve law and order on the campuses of the University of California, and to take the necessary steps to insure orderly pursuit of its educational functions"; (2) affirmed that "ultimate authority for student discipline . . . is constitutionally vested in the Regents," and is "not subject to negotiation"; and (3) pledged to comprehensively "review . . . University policy with the intent of providing maximum freedom on campus consistent with individual and group responsibility."[17]

The events at Berkeley continued to escalate from items related to the university campus to larger social and national issues. Since student protests and university responses were receiving national media coverage, the Berkeley campus became a place from which other social and political agendas could be mounted. The SDS, believing that they could launch a national movement that would change American history, organized human chains to stop trains carrying armed forces recruits to induction centers. Also active in the Bay Area were the Black Panthers. On October 28, 1967, Huey Newton was arrested in a situation in which a police officer was killed. In 1968, students staged demonstrations, protesting the university administration's refusal to award credit for a course taught by Eldridge Cleaver, a Black Panther leader.[18]

The Berkeley situation evoked national attention as the media—press, radio, and television—covered the events. Television, using coverage similar to that of civil rights marches in the South, gave Berkeley a national audience. Berkeley also became a kind of inspirational and motivational catalyst for dissatisfied students at other institutions. It also introduced a style of protest that featured polarization around the slogan, "Are you with us or against us?," rather than compromise or reconciliation. During the spring of 1965, student protests gained a momentum as demonstrations took place at Yale, City College of New York, Princeton, the University of Washington in Seattle, Cornell, and other universities.

Vietnam and the Escalation of Student Activism

The events at Berkeley, broadcast nightly on national television, pointed to a growing discontent among the nation's young people, especially its college and university students. The events, taking place on college campuses such as Berkeley, that at first were campus situations, became part of a larger national phenomenon—the antiwar movement.

Dr. Benjamin Spock, noted children's doctor and anti–Vietnam War leader, addressing an antiwar rally in the 1960s. (Reproduction from the collections of the Library of Congress.)

In the presidential election of 1964, Lyndon Johnson, the incumbent Democratic nominee, appeared to be more moderate on international affairs than the outright conservative Barry Goldwater, the Republican nominee. It appeared, that while a Goldwater victory might heighten cold war tensions, Johnson would take a more measured but still anti-Soviet, anti-Communist posture. Upon election, however, Johnson began to commit more American military personnel to Vietnam. This policy entrapped Johnson in a quagmire, which overshadowed his efforts to end poverty and build a Great Society. (See chapter 7 for Johnson's Great Society.) Spring 1965 brought the first drafting of students into the armed forces, especially those with a lower academic class standing. Selective service officials required colleges and universities to submit class rankings of students to be used in the draft. Students protested, and a teach-in took place in March 1965 at the University of Michigan.[19]

The University of Chicago

In 1966, a student demonstration took place at the University of Chicago, where four hundred students occupied the administration building. Unlike Berkeley, the University of Chicago administration did not react, nor did the administration use police to remove students from the building, nor did it negotiate with students. After five days without a university reaction, the sit-in dissolved as the demonstration ended and students returned to classes. Whether the University of Chicago's strategy would have worked elsewhere remains an open question for historians. The University of Chicago was a private rather than a state university. Further, it was known as a center of academic excellence and research. With no administration response, the politics of "nonnegotiable demands" and confrontation did not work.

The University of Chicago in 1969 successfully weathered another potential crisis. When a radical sociology professor was not rehired, three hundred students occupied the administration building demanding that he be rehired and that students have a voice in faculty appointments. The administration used the strategy that had been effective earlier. Rather than using force to reoccupy the building, the administration moved into temporary quarters, deciding neither to use force nor negotiate with the demonstrators. The administration appointed a committee to review the case. The result was that the professor was offered a one-year contract and again, student protests dissipated.

Summer 1968

Nineteen sixty-eight was a dramatic and critical year for the nation and for student activism. In the spring of 1968 there were some signs that a more conventional political resolution of some of the national issues, especially the war in Vietnam, might be forthcoming.

Senator Eugene McCarthy (Democrat from Minnesota) challenged incumbent President Lyndon Johnson on an antiwar platform and made a surprisingly strong showing in the New Hampshire primary on March 12. A depressed Lyndon Johnson announced that he would not seek, nor accept, the nomination of the Democratic Party for another term as president. Students going "Clean for Gene" rallied to McCarthy's campaign as a way to use the system to end the war. The McCarthy alternative posed strategic issues for some antiwar students, particularly the SDS. McCarthy was a liberal who, using Adlai Stevenson as model, emphasized reform from within rather than from outside the system. Some leaders of the SDS, fearing that McCarthy's campaign would diminish the politics of polarization, rejected electoral politics as a liberal dodge to coopt the antiwar movement. Efforts to turn to the system dismayed some radicals in the SDS who felt it detracted from the needed confrontation strategy to bring down the system. When Senator Robert Kennedy entered the Democratic presidential primaries, many student activists switched to support him while others remained committed to McCarthy. McCarthy won the Wisconsin and Oregon primaries while Kennedy won most of the delegates in Nebraska and Indiana.

On April 4, Dr. Martin Luther King Jr. was assassinated in Memphis, Tennessee. King's murder provoked disorder and rioting in over a hundred cities, causing sixty deaths, injuries to thousands of people, and millions of dollars in property damage. Federal troops were called into Wilmington, Delaware; Baltimore; Chicago; and Washington, D.C. The National Guard was activated in these and other cities to control civil disorders.[20]

Despite Johnson's and Secretary of Defense Robert McNamara's promise of "light at the end of the tunnel," the Vietnam War continued and escalated with the Tet Offensive. The international side of student activism showed itself in France where students took to the streets of Paris in what was called the "May Rebellion." The media carried nightly telecasts of these events and the student seizure of and expulsion from buildings at Columbia University. Robert Kennedy was assassinated on June 5 after defeating McCarthy in the crucial California Democratic primary. Then, the crescendo came to a fever pitch with the massive violence in Chicago at the Democratic National Convention in August. Mayor Richard J. Daley's Chicago police were charged with using excessive force against the demonstrators. These momentous events reached the scarred inner psyche of a nation deeply divided. In November, Richard Nixon, the Republican candidate, defeated Hubert Humphrey, his Democratic opponent. While the student movement was steadily growing more impatient and strident, 1968 marked a serious turning point toward great militancy and for some an endorsement of violent tactics. While the SDS was in the throes of splintering into factions, some African-American students were rejecting Dr. King's nonviolent passive resistance and moving toward black separatism.[21]

Columbia University

The SDS had organized demonstrations at Columbia University in New York City in 1965–66. Among its early protests was a demand that the university end the practice of allowing CIA recruiters on the campus. It then successfully persuaded the university to end the policy of class rankings.

A new wave of campus demonstrations began in 1968 when, in March, Mark Rudd was elected chairperson of the SDS. Rudd, who contended that Columbia University was an instrument of the national security state, was in conflict with the institution's President Grayson Kirk, who insisted that the university remain unpoliticized and value-free on social issues.[22] After Rudd had led a delegation of protestors into Low Library with a petition on March 27, he and several other SDS leaders were put on probation. The following month, on April 22, Rudd led a demonstration against Columbia University's connections with the Institute for Defense Analysis (IDA).[23] On April 23, the SDS staged further demonstrations, demanding an end to the school's ties to the institute and a rescindment of the disciplinary action against the students. Concurrently with the SDS, the Students' Afro-American Society (SAS) mounted demonstrations against the university's plan to construct a new gymnasium in Morningside Park, an area bordering Columbia and Harlem. The protests led to a joint occupation by the SDS and SAS of Hamilton Hall, a building with administrative offices and classrooms. Files were rifled and research papers were destroyed.[24] Then, the SAS forced the white students to leave and occupy their own university building. White students then occupied the office of Grayson Kirk, president of Columbia University. The events at Columbia received high media coverage. The administration refused to negotiate with the students. An ad hoc faculty group (AHFG) attempted to intervene, urging the administration to take a more flexible stance and not bring police on the campus. The administration, in turn, postponed calling police and suspended construction on the gymnasium.[25] However, the AHFG attempted but failed to work out a compromise on student amnesty.

On April 30, the situation at Columbia escalated further when the administration called in police to clear students who were occupying offices from the university buildings. Seven hundred people, 524 of whom were students, were arrested for trespassing. While the black students filed out quietly, the white students resisted and were forcibly removed. As a result, 148 police and students were injured.

The scenario was repeated on May 7, when students, led by the SDS, occupied Hamilton Hall and the police were used to remove them. Kirk resigned in the summer of 1968 to be replaced by Andrew Cordier.[26]

Under Cordier, faculty-student committees were established to develop new procedural structures. A legislative body was established that included faculty, administrators, and students. Students were given representation on university committees, including the disciplinary one. The widening of student participation brought more students, especially those who were more moderate, into the process. This narrowed the influence of the more radical students. When the SDS again attempted to occupy buildings, it failed to attract support and the confrontational strategy failed. President Cordier dropped charges and reinstated students, cancelled the plan to build the gymnasium in Morningside Park, and severed university ties to the IDA.[27]

Developing Trends

During 1969 there were more protests, some of them violent, on 150 college and university campuses. Although only 6 percent of all of the nation's colleges and universities were involved, several demonstrations occurred at highly prestigious institutions.[28] There were some cases in which radical students disrupted classes taught by professors they opposed. A faction of students became even more radicalized, leaving the SDS to form the Weathermen, a group that would use violence. At the same time, some long-term trends were emerging from the period of student activism. Many institutions broadened their governance policies to include student representatives. This would become a permanent feature of U.S. higher education. Also, more curricular alternatives were being created in areas such as black, women's, environmental, and peace studies in response to student demands for relevance. Unfortunately, some of the areas that some students found irrelevant were important, such as foreign languages. Some institutions, yielding to student demands, dropped language, mathematics, and science requirements.

Harvard University

At Harvard University, among the country's most prestigious academic institutions, student protests led by the SDS focused on the presence of the Reserve Officers Training Corps (ROTC) on the campus, on the university's failure to take a stand against the war in Vietnam, and its refusal to withdraw investments from South Africa.[29] ROTC would also be an issue at other institutions. At Harvard, the faculty voted to remove credit for ROTC and remove ROTC instructors from faculty ranks. However, the SDS was convinced that Harvard's President Nathan Pusey was circumventing the faculty recommendations. On April 9, 1969, following the pattern used at Columbia, students occupied University Hall. In responding to the student takeover of a university building, the administration followed guidelines developed by Archibald Cox: (1) the university would avoid having multiple spokespersons who gave confused and mixed messages; (2) there would be only one university spokesperson, its president; (3) the faculty should not be convened immediately; (4) if police were to be used to clear the building, they should do it quickly.[30] However, developing guidelines was easier than following them. The situation at Harvard took a course similar to that of other institutions—administration reaction to students followed by escalated student demands. As the situation polarized, the Harvard faculty, which tried to moderate the impasse, splintered.

On April 10, 1969, police entered and cleared University Hall, arresting 184 persons of whom 145 were students. The faculty was outraged in that it had not been consulted prior to the administration's decision to use police. Once police were used, the situation took a familiar turn, as campus polarization set in. More moderate and disinterested students now joined the protests and began to strike. Similar to other institutions, the Harvard Board of Overseers, its trustees, supported the administration's actions.[31]

As at other institutions, the student protests at Harvard snowballed to other issues. In February 1969, the faculty had agreed to establish a BA degree program in Afro-American studies; however, the degree was to be awarded in combination with an allied field. Black student organizations, opposing the requirement of an allied field, wanted equal control over the program with the faculty.[32]

San Francisco State College

Unlike the more residential institutions, San Francisco State College (SFS) in California, with an enrollment of 18,000 students, was a commuter school that featured a more open and flexible curriculum. The institution, having had four presidents between 1962 and 1968, had experienced the uncertainty of frequent administrative turnover.

In May 1968, African-American students began a campaign for the creation of an autonomous Black Studies Department and for the reinstatement of George Murray, an African-American professor who was a member of the Black Panther Party. Dr. Robert Smith, SFS president, agreed to establish a Black Studies Department but required that it be approved by regular academic procedures before it began operations. Activist African-American students, organized as the Third World Liberation Front and the Black Students Union (BSU), rejected Smith's proviso. The front and the union issued nonnegotiable demands for establishing an autonomous Black Studies Department. Dr. Smith resigned in the face of mounting student protests. Smith's successor, Professor S. I. Hayakawa, a professor of English, was appointed acting president on November 28, 1968. Hayakawa, known for his scholarship in semantics, assumed the troubled institution's presidency, determined to restore law and order to the campus.[33]

Taking office in the midst of a student strike that had closed the campus, Hayakawa announced that classes would resume after the Thanksgiving break. On the day classes were to resume, student pro-

Dr. S. I. Hayakawa, president of San Francisco State University, who took a strong stand against student demonstrations. Later, he became a U.S. senator from California. (Reproduction from the Collections of the Library of Congress.)

testors assembled to enforce the strike. National television carried scenes of Hayakawa challenging the strikers. In a dramatic confrontation, Hayakawa climbed on top of a truck used by strikers, ripped out the wires of the loudspeaker, and demanded that students return to classes. When police were summoned to the campus, some seven hundred protesters were arrested. Classes resumed and Hayakawa was hailed as a no-nonsense educator, unafraid to take a stand against campus protestors. Backed by Governor Ronald Reagan and the school's trustees, Hayakawa declared a state of emergency that: forbade unauthorized use of the college's speakers' platforms and equipment; required faculty to conduct classes as scheduled; and suspended any students who were interfering with the functioning of the college. Hayakawa, now a public figure, attracted national media coverage and went on to be elected as a U.S. senator from California in 1976.[34]

The Decade's Tragic Ending, 1969–1970

Richard Nixon, the Republican candidate for president, defeated Democratic nominee Hubert Humphrey in the election of 1968. Nixon and his vice presidential running mate, Spiro Agnew, claimed they had the support of a great majority of Americans, "the silent majority," who wanted a return to "law and order" and an end to disorder. As the war continued in Vietnam, protests occurred at some universities, such as Cornell and Yale. While the momentum of campus protest appeared spent, there was an uneasiness, a kind of impending uncertainty about the future. The sense of uneasiness would turn to tragedy.

On April 30, 1970, President Nixon announced that U.S. troops had invaded Cambodia to pursue the Vietcong and to halt the transport of supplies into South Vietnam on the Ho Chi Minh Trail. Nixon's action generated antiwar protests on campuses. At Kent State University in Ohio, the ROTC building had been burned during a demonstration. Governor James Rhodes ordered Ohio National Guard units to Kent State. On May 4, 1970, National Guard members moved against students, some of whom were protestors while others were merely observers. The Guard fired on the students and four were killed. At the same time, police had shot and killed two black students at Jackson State University in Mississippi. The nation was shocked and saddened to its depths.

In the midst of mourning, the overt activism of 1960s began to ebb. There were still protests such as that at the University of Minnesota, where a large march and demonstration against the war took place, and at the University of Wisconsin (Madison) where a university building was burned and the National Guard used tear gas to break up student demonstrations. However, the focus on opposing the war was moving to more diverse interests, such as opposition to racism, the development of feminism, and the environment. Each of these areas attracted supporters during the 1970s, but they failed to provide a single galvanizing cause as did opposition to the war. Although the various causes were significant, they were not as dramatic as the antiwar movement had been. As a result, they did not receive extensive media coverage. The Nixon administration would negotiate the departure of U.S. forces from Vietnam, the South Vietnamese government would collapse, and Vietnam would be united as a Marxist state.

Conclusion

Early in this chapter, there was an effort to create a framework for interpreting the student activism of the 1960s. To conclude, there is the remaining question—what is the larger meaning of the decade?

While its larger significance still is unclear and needs interpretation and reinterpretation, several limited generalizations can be made.

When placed in the large context of American history, the occurrences of the 1960s reveal a pattern that relates to how the United States deals domestically with frustrating international events. Because of its providential sense of history, the United States historically has felt a sense of mission and omnipotence. On the side of right, it must be victorious. Since the end of World War II, especially with the long cold war, unconditional victory, like that of World War II, has been neither possible nor practicable. International conflicts have been slow to be resolved and U.S. foreign policy goals have become more limited. Serious internal strains surface when conflicts are protracted and goals limited as during the Korean and Vietnamese conflicts. During the 1960s, the Vietnam War was waged mistakenly on the same premises that had been used in World War II. However, these premises did not apply to Vietnam because the geographic, political, and strategic situations were very different, and victory did not come. Serious domestic strains developed and some of these strains served as a catalyst, albeit not the only one, that generated the activism of the 1960s. Nations, like persons, have to find meaning by examining their psyches, truthfully and courageously. Vietnam, and the wounds it caused, remains unresolved in the nation's psyche and consciousness, an issue that still needs examination and resolution.

In the 1960s, the radicalization of youth did not occur only in the United States, but it was part of a worldwide phenomenon. The student unrest of the 1960s pointed to a new radicalism that affected white middle-class youth. The United States was not unique but was experiencing a youth movement comparable to those taking place in other countries, such as France, the People's Republic of China, East Germany, and Czechoslovakia.

In some respects, the student radicalization had the unanticipated consequence of moving the United States politically more to the right than to the left. Confrontational politics worked to undermine the liberal consensus. Because of their role in the Vietnam War, liberals, especially politicians like Johnson and Humphrey, rather than conservatives like Nixon, were more often the targets of protest. Whether intentional or not, the immobilization of liberals followed a tactic used by Marxists to attack liberals, who were "false friends," rather than conservatives who were out-and-out enemies. For the radicalized students, Johnson's Great Society was a sham and the liberal forces that supported it were really part of the power elite. With liberals either politically immobilized or seriously weakened, the way was paved for Richard Nixon's victory in 1967 and the rise of the Moral Majority, the New Right, the Reagan administration, and the strong neoconservative renaissance of the 1980s. (See chapters 10 and 11 for the Nixon and Reagan administrations.)

The radicalization of the student movement took it from seeking remedies for campus grievances to larger national and international issues, which after the Vietnam War, became environmentalism, multiculturalism, and feminism. While they had political consequences, these large currents of change were more pervasively social and cultural than political.

The structure of the college and university curriculum changed. Women's, feminist, black, African-American, Chicano, Hispanic, environmental, peace, and gay and lesbian studies programs were developed and implemented. A much more multicultural milieu developed, which led to the cultural wars of the 1980s and 1990s. While American culture opened and changed, the movement of the 1960s helped to stimulate a very strong neoconservatism in politics and culture and a resurgent fundamentalism in religion.

In academe, especially in the foundations of education, the events of the 1960s continued to exert an influence throughout the 1970s and 1980s, especially with the revisionist movement in history of education and with critical theory in educational philosophy. Some of the radical activists who were graduate students in the 1960s became the professors of the 1970s and 1980s and continued to examine issues of repression and social control.

There were some actual changes in the governance of higher education. Students were added as members of academic committees. Rules and regulations regarding student life were relaxed as a more permissive campus environment developed. To a large extent, the roles that students play in governing themselves now depends on their interests and energies.[35]

Notes

1 There is serious need for comparative historical studies of the student activism of the 1960s. One of the few books on the subject is George Katsiaficas, *The Imagination of the New Left: A Global Analysis of 1968* (Boston: South End, 1987). Also, see Carole Fink, Philip Gassert, and Detlef Junker, *1968: The World Transformed* (New York: Cambridge University Press, 1998).

2 Kirkpatrick Sale, *SDS* (New York: Vintage Books, Random House, 1973), p. 405.

3 Diane Ravitch, *The Troubled Crusade* (New York: Basic Books, 1983), p. 188.

4 Ibid., p. 183.

5 For the politics of federal funding of research in higher education, see James D. Savage, *Funding Science in America: Congress, Universities, and the Politics of the Academic Pork Barrel* (New York: Cambridge University Press, 1990).

6 James Miller, *"Democracy Is in the Streets": From Port Huron to the Siege of Chicago* (New York: Simon and Schuster, 1987), pp. 13–16.

7 Ravitch, pp. 188, 198.

[8] Sale, p. 409.

[9] For recent commentaries on SNCC, see Cheryl Lynn Greenberg, ed., *A Circle of Trust: Remembering SNCC* (New Brunswick: Rutgers University Press, 1998).

[10] Ravitch, p. 210.

[11] Sale, p. 413.

[12] Stacey E. Palmer, "Berkeley, Birthplace of 1960's Unrest, Tries to Preserve Its Activist Image," *The Chronicle of Higher Education* (September 26, 1984), p. 12.

[13] Ibid.

[14] Ibid., pp. 193–95.

[15] Max Heirich, *The Beginning: Berkeley 1964* (New York: Columbia University Press, 1970), p. 228.

[16] Ibid., pp. 229–43.

[17] Ibid., p. 247.

[18] Palmer, p. 12.

[19] Ravitch, pp. 197–98.

[20] Sale, p. 424.

[21] Winifred Breines, "Whose New Left?" *The Journal of American History* 75 (No. 2) (September 1988), p. 529.

[22] William H. Chafe, *The Unfinished Journey: America Since World War II* (New York: Oxford University Press, 1991), p. 405.

[23] Sale, pp. 432–33.

[24] Chafe, pp. 405–6.

[25] Ravitch, p. 202.

[26] Ibid., p. 204.

[27] Ibid.

[28] Ibid., p. 205.

[29] Chafe, p. 406.

[30] Ravitch, pp. 207–8.

[31] Ibid., p. 208.

[32] Ibid., p. 209.

[33] S. I. Hayakawa, *Language in Thought and Action* (San Francisco: Harcourt Brace Jovanovich, Inc. 1963), is representative of Hayakawa's scholarship in semantics.

[34] Ravitch, p. 212.

[35] James Miller, *"Democracy Is in the Streets": From Port Huron to the Siege of Chicago* (New York: Simon and Schuster, 1987), p. 17.

Further Reading

Altbach, Philip G. *Student Politics in America: An Historical Analysis.* New York: McGraw-Hill Book Co., 1974.

Aronowitz, Stanley. *The Death and Rebirth of American Radicalism.* New York: Routledge, 1996.

Buzzanco, Robert. *Masters of War: Military Dissent and Politics in the Vietnam Era.* New York: Cambridge University Press, 1997.

Dickstein, Morris D. *Gates of Eden: American Culture in the Sixties.* Cambridge: Harvard University Press, 1997.

Farrell, James J. *The Spirit of the Sixties: The Making of Postwar Radicalism*. New York: Routledge, 1997.

Fink Carole, Philip Gassert, and Detlef Junker. *1968: The World Transformed*. New York: Cambridge University Press, 1998.

Gitlin, Todd. *The Sixties: Years of Hope, Days of Rage*. New York: Bantam Books, 1987.

Gorman, Paul R. *Left Intellectuals and Popular Culture in Twentieth-Century America*. Chapel Hill: University of North Carolina Press, 1996.

Greenberg, Cheryl Lynn, ed. *A Circle of Trust: Remembering SNCC*. New Brunswick, NJ: Rutgers University Press, 1998.

Heirich, Max. *The Beginning: Berkeley 1964*. New York: Columbia University Press, 1970.

Isserman, Maurice. *If I Had a Hammer: The Death of the Old Left and the Birth of the New Left*. New York: Basic Books, 1987.

Katsiaficas, George. *The Imagination of the New Left: A Global Analysis of 1968*. Boston: South End, 1987.

Kennan, George F. *Democracy and the Student Left*. Boston: Little, Brown, and Co., 1968.

King, Mary. *Freedom Song: A Personal Story of the 1960s Civil Rights Movement*. New York: Morrow, 1987.

Mendel-Reyes, Meta. *Reclaiming Democracy: The Sixties in Politics and Memory*. New York: Routledge, 1995.

Miller, James. *"Democracy Is in the Streets": From Port Huron to the Siege of Chicago*. New York: Simon and Schuster, 1987.

Patterson, James T. *Grand Expectations: The United States, 1945–1974*. New York: Oxford University Press, 1996.

Sale, Kirkpatrick. *SDS*. New York: Vintage Books, Random House, 1973.

Savage, James D. *Funding Science in America: Congress, Universities, and the Politics of the Academic Pork Barrel*. New York: Cambridge University Press, 1999.

Tracy, James. *Direct Action: Radical Pacifism from the Union Eight to the Chicago Seven*. Chicago: University of Chicago Press, 1996.

10

The 1970s: The Nixon, Ford, and Carter Administrations and Education

Historical Context

The decade of the 1970s was crucial, but is still insufficiently interpreted, in American education. The Civil Rights movement, student activism, and the national polarization over the Vietnam War in the 1960s had ushered in what appeared to be a period of momentous socioeconomic and political change in the United States. In the 1970s, the tendencies initiated in the preceding decade played themselves out, but in a revised form on the national scene. The 1970s signaled a change from the general economic prosperity and growth of the 1950s and 1960s to a climate of greater uncertainty about the future. The United States as well as other Western nations were in the process of an uneasy economic transformation from heavy industrial production to becoming "high tech" information and service societies. The decade also witnessed the emergence of Japan and the Pacific Rim countries as an important economic center. The interdependent global world had become a reality that brought change to economic production and employment patterns. The economic prosperity of the 1960s had yielded to the "stagflation" of the 1970s—inflation and recession, with little real growth. Throughout the 1970s, there were arguments about the kind of education and training that America needed in order to adjust to these significantly changing economic patterns. There needed to be a shift in educational emphasis from an industrial to what some theorists were calling the postindustrial society.

The national political mood, too, was slowly changing. President Richard Nixon and his chief foreign policy advisor, Henry Kissinger, were seeking a way to disengage American military forces from the quagmire of an unpopular war in Vietnam. After protracted negotiations with the Communist leaders of North Vietnam, Nixon and Kissinger eventually were able to extricate the United States from the morass in Southeast Asia. The antiwar student protests came to a tragic climax when members of the National Guard fired into a crowd of students, killing several of them, at Kent State University in Ohio. After Kent State and the U.S. disengagement from Vietnam, student activism slowed and eventually ended.

In education, the professional mood, too, was changing. Educators had little time to reflect on and put into a larger perspective the rapidly initiated innovations of the 1960s. Racial desegregation, integration, the War on Poverty, Head Start, student activism, open education, team teaching, environmental education, and feminism were crowding the professional educators' agenda. (See chapter 6 for racial integration and chapter 8 for the educational innovations of the 1960s.) Along with myriad interests vying for a place in education, the most serious impact on elementary and secondary schools came from changing demographic patterns, particularly in the school-age cohort. The rate of growth of the school-age population had slowed throughout the country and, indeed, had declined in some states. Some school districts that had expanded facilities in the 1950s and 1960s as a result of the post–World War II "baby boom" were now overbuilt. Instead of building new schools, many districts were closing and "mothballing" schools because of declining enrollments.

For the first time since the end of World War II, school administrators had to deal with the economic reality of retrenchment, something for which their courses in educational administration had left them unprepared. Elementary and secondary schools faced rising operating costs caused by inflation but experienced decreasing revenues because of reductions in state foundation funding due to declining enrollments. As school budgets were scrutinized for ways to contain costs, districts with declining student enrollments reduced their teaching force. Employment opportunities for teachers worsened as education entered the end of its growth cycle. Following Adam Smith's "law of supply and demand," the number of jobs available for new teachers plummeted. Enrollments in teacher education programs declined drastically, not to revive until the end of the 1980s.

The national social mood, too, was changing as the activism of youth, so notable in the 1960s, yielded to apathy about social and political causes. Rather than seeking to change society, college students were now more concerned about earning a degree that would lead to a good job and the promise of economic security. The American nuclear family, once idealized in *Dick and Jane*—mom, dad, and children living in their own home—too was undergoing change, as alternative family patterns appeared, ranging from extended to single-parent households. No longer an inner-city problem, drug addiction was growing among youth throughout the country.

Not really understood but generating pervasive uneasiness was the economic change as the United States moved from the premier position of the world's leading industrial nation into what economists and sociologists were calling the postindustrial information and service society. As the 1970s ended, Americans were unsure about the direction their country should take in the new decade. The schools' administrators and teachers, too, were unclear about the overriding goals and purposes of American education.

The Nixon Administration

Richard Nixon, the Republican candidate for president, won the election in 1968, defeating his liberal Democratic opponent, Hubert H. Humphrey.[1] Capitalizing on the student unrest and urban disorders of the late 1960s, Nixon ran on a "law and order" platform. He claimed that his election was a mandate from the "silent majority" of Americans who, disgusted with the disorders of the late 1960s, wanted the restoration of a law-abiding and orderly society.

In terms of his administration's priorities, Nixon, like John Kennedy, was more interested in foreign rather than domestic policies. He and his chief foreign policy advisor, Henry Kissinger, sought to extricate American military forces from the war in Vietnam. Despite his strong anti-Communist record as a congressman and senator, Nixon, while continuing cold war policies to contain the Soviet Union, visited the People's Republic of China, seeking to normalize relations with that country.

In terms of educational policy, Nixon succeeded the liberal Democrat Lyndon B. Johnson, who engineered the Great Society and War on Poverty programs. Johnson's programs had provided massive federal aid to education, especially through the Elementary and Secondary Education Act of 1965 and training programs sponsored by the Office of Economic Opportunity. Part of the War on Poverty, the Job Corps, which provided training programs for unemployed youth and Head Start, which provided early childhood education for disadvantaged groups, were key elements in Johnson's educational agenda. (For Johnson's educational policies, see chapter 7.) Though these Johnson-inspired federal educational initiatives were in place, Nixon sought to alter and reduce the scope of federal involvement in education.

Nixon's educational policy rested on several assumptions; some were historically based ideological premises associated with the Republican Party and others rested on selected contemporary interpretations of the consequences of federal action in education and welfare. With the exception of the immediate post–Civil War period, the Republican Party traditionally emphasized education as an appropriate responsibility of the states and local districts. The federal government was to have a very limited role. For example, President Eisenhower, for whom Nixon served as vice president, saw the federal government's role in education as a very limited one. (See chapter 3 for Eisenhower on education.) Nixon held to these essential Republican premises about educational policy but had to reckon with the inherited and expansive Johnson legislation. Further, the educational situation during Nixon's first term, from 1969 to 1972, was further complicated by issues relating to the racial desegregation and integration of schools.(Racial integration is examined in chapter 6; in this chapter, we examine integration policies associated with the Nixon and Ford administrations.)

Several large school districts, especially urban ones, were involved in either locally initiated or court-mandated busing programs. These busing efforts had generated a white backlash and often well-publicized antibusing demonstrations. Nixon's policies, then, can be considered in terms of his general philosophy that the federal government's role in education should be limited, and his administration's actions to promote desegregation, the law of the land.

Block Grants and State and Local Control

Nixon's general educational policies rested on the assumption that Johnson's earlier large federal expenditure on education had not yielded the anticipated results but rather had aggravated socioeconomic problems. The plethora of programs, quickly passed by the Johnson administration, had gone in many directions rather than being coherent and comprehensive. According to Nixon administration interpretations, the federal policy in education, in the recent past, had demanded too much of schools. Nixon stated that schools "have been expected not only to educate, but also to accomplish a social transformation." The schools should focus on academic education rather than social engineering.[2] In other words, Nixon was redefining education as schooling in academic skills and subjects rather than in Johnson's broad meaning as an agency of social change.

In line with the general Republican ideology of state and local control, Nixon's reasoning was that it would be most effective to return initiative and control for education to the states and local districts. Pragmatically, this strategy was tied to Nixon's concept of revenue sharing between states and the federal government. Importantly, Nixon's educational policy turned away from large issues that related schools to socioeconomic change. Rather, it sought more limited objectives, especially innovations more specifically related to curriculum and instruction. Thus, during the early 1970s, the federal government encouraged innovative educational programs rather than general aid or compensatory programs.

In his March 1970 address to Congress, Nixon announced the Experimental Schools Program (ESP) and the creation of the National Institute of Education (NIE), designed to connect educational research to actual school practices. According to the ESP design, local districts could apply for funding, provided they developed a comprehensive school plan to bring about curricular and instructional innovations that involved students across all grade levels. Under the ESP, $50 million was provided to participating school districts between 1970 and 1975.[3]

School Desegregation and Busing

On the issue of racial desegregation, Nixon faced a complex and volatile situation regarding the federal role in enforcing desegregation and in encouraging racial integration. His actions conformed to the long-standing Republican ideological orientation that preferred local control to federal involvement. Important in the administration's strategy were very pragmatic political considerations. In several areas, especially large cities, court-imposed busing to achieve racial integration had generated resistance and protests. Opponents of busing often mounted their protests under the banner of preservation of neighborhood schools. Politically, Nixon hoped to defuse George Wallace's third party efforts and bring these opponents of court-ordered busing into his "silent majority" coalition. Nixon's policies on racial desegregation then were a carefully honed, pragmatic stance that promised to continue to eliminate official, de facto segregation, which was the law of the land, while preserving local control and neighborhood schools. He announced that his administration would enforce the *Brown* and other decisions that prohibited de jure racial segregation in public schools while opposing "compulsory busing of pupils beyond normal geographic school zones for the purpose of achieving racial balance."[4] Nixon pointed out that judicial decisions clearly prohibited de jure racial segregation but were ambiguous and contradictory on how to achieve racial integration. He stated:

> This range of differences demonstrates that lawyers and judges
> have honest disagreements about what the law requires. There have

been some rulings that would divert such huge sums of money to non-educational purposes, and would create such severe dislocations of public school systems, as to impair the primary functions of providing a good education. . . .

I am dedicated to continued progress toward a truly desegregated public school system. But, considering the always heavy demands for more school operating funds, I believe it is preferable, when we have to make the choice, to use limited financial resources for the improvement of education—for better teaching facilities, better methods, and advanced educational materials—and for the upgrading of disadvantaged areas in the community rather than buying buses, tires and gasoline to transport young children miles away from their neighborhood schools.[5]

The key to Nixon's policies was his clear distinction between de jure segregation based on law and de facto segregation caused by racially segregated housing patterns. This distinction was crucial in his administration's announcement that it would continue efforts to eliminate official segregation in public schools while preserving local neighborhood schools. Nixon stated:

De facto racial separation, resulting genuinely from housing patterns, exists in the South as well as the North; in neither area should this condition by itself be cause for Federal enforcement actions. De jure segregation brought about by deliberate school-board gerrymandering exists in the North and the South; in both areas this must be remedied. In all respects, the law should be applied equally, North and South, East and West.[6]

With the distinction made between de jure and de facto segregation, President Nixon outlined the general principles on racial segregation that would guide his administration to: (1) eliminate the unlawful "deliberate racial segregation of pupils by official action"; (2) eliminate racial segregation of teachers so that "in each school the ratio of White to Negro faculty members is substantially the same as it is throughout the system"; (3) ensure that "individual school districts do not discriminate with respect to the quality of facilities or the quality of education . . . within the district"; (4) to allow local school boards to have the "primary weight" in devising local compliance plans; (5) recognize the neighborhood school as the most appropriate educational base; (6) not require the transportation of pupils "beyond normal geographic school zones" to achieve racial balance; (7) deter federal officials from going "beyond the requirements of law in attempting to impose their own judgment on" local school districts; (8) encourage school boards to "be flexible and creative in formulating plans that are educationally sound and that result in effective desegregation"; (9) insist on a "remedy for the de jure portion, which is unlawful, without insisting on a remedy for the lawful de facto portion," because racial imbalance in schools may be "partly de jure in origin, and partly de facto."[7]

An assessment of the Nixon administration's educational policy in contrast with Johnson's depends largely on ideology and on practical politics. While Nixon, in concert with his party, saw the federal role to be limited, Johnson made education one of the cornerstones of his domestic agenda for creating a great society. Nixon moved much more cautiously than Johnson in educational matters. While Johnson was trapped in the Vietnam War, Nixon devoted more of his energies and talents to foreign policy issues such as extricating the United States from the war and opening the diplomatic door to the People's Republic of China. Johnson's educational initiatives came in rapid-fire order and were efforts at using education as an agency of social change—ending poverty and creating a Great Society. Because his initiatives and legislation were so sweeping, the consequences, both intended and untended, also were large. Nixon, in contrast, had limited goals in educational policy, seeking to focus federal action on schooling in its more traditional academic sense. Nixon's policies were directed to encouraging innovative, but limited, curricular and instructional practices in

President Richard M. Nixon and H. R. Haldeman in the Oval Office, 1974. (Courtesy Gerald R. Ford Library.)

schools themselves, rather than seeing schools as agencies of broader socioeconomic change. While Johnson's strategy, learned during the New Deal, was national in scope, Nixon used a small-scale approach, geared to and seeking to maintain rather than change the decentralized, semi-autonomous organization of American schools.

Watergate and Efforts at Civic Education

Nixon's second term was overshadowed by his efforts to cover up his involvement in the break-in at the Democratic National Committee's headquarters at the Watergate complex in Washington, D.C. Threatened with impeachment by Congress, he resigned from office in 1973. The Watergate scandal, President Nixon's role in covering up his and his associates' involvement, and his resignation were tantamount to a constitutional crisis. The presidency passed in orderly fashion to Gerald Ford, the vice president.

While the Watergate affair was a legal and constitutional issue, it was also a moral one that related to national values, especially to civic values. There was a response to what was regarded as the erosion of civic values by some educators in the American Educational Studies Association and other organizations who called for a revival of civic education in the schools. An important leader of the civic education movement of the mid-1970s was the distinguished historian of education, R. Freeman Butts.

Concerns about civic education also were expressed by President Ford, who stated:

> We cannot perpetuate our value system merely by telling our children it is good. We can only assure its future by educating our children to admire its strengths, correct its faults, and to participate effectively as citizens. Only then will they understand why our social values are worth preserving, even though much in our society has changed.[8]

The Ford Administration

Gerald Ford, a long-time Republican congressman from Michigan and Republican leader in the House of Representatives, was named vice president after Spiro Agnew's resignation from that office. Upon Nixon's resignation, Ford took the oath of office as president on August 9, 1974. Announcing that he would work to heal the nation's wounds in the aftermath of Watergate, Ford pardoned Nixon and sought national reconciliation.[9] He completed Nixon's term and was defeated, in a close election, by Jimmy Carter, his Democratic opponent, in 1976. In his three years in the presidency, Ford inherited the foreign

and domestic issues left by his predecessor, primarily economic inflation and recession and continuing cold war tensions with the Soviet
Union. Announcing his administration's agenda as the "New Realism,"
Ford, a moderate Republican, pursued an agenda of: (1) increasing
employment and reducing the rate of inflation; (2) revenue sharing
with the states: (3) an attack on crime, violence, and drugs; (4) limiting
the role of the federal government while increasing its efficiency; and
(5) increasing military defense spending.[10] While these initiatives set
the general thrusts of his administration, we turn specifically to Ford's
educational policies.

Ford clearly subscribed to the educational ideology that guided
his Republican predecessors, Eisenhower and Nixon. Strongly believing in a limited federal role in education, Ford was convinced that education was appropriately a state and local district function. This ideology shaped his general attitudes on education, especially federal
assistance to education and court-ordered busing. In assessing Ford's
policies on education, his administration's most prominent initiatives
were: (1) efforts to consolidate federal assistance from categorical pro-

President Gerald R. Ford and Father Theodore Hesburgh, president of the University
of Notre Dame, enter the university's Athletic and Convocation Center where President Ford received an honorary doctor of law degree. (South Bend, Indiana. March 17,
1975. Courtesy Gerald R. Ford Library.)

grams into block grants; (2) efforts to limit the use and extent of court-mandated busing to achieve racial desegregation; (3) an attempt to develop a strategy linking work and education; (4) signing the Education for All Handicapped Children Act of 1975, PL 94-142. (Because the enactment of PL 94-142 had such a significant effect on American education, it is treated in depth, following a discussion of the first three initiatives.)

Consolidation of Federal Programs

Ford maintained that the educational legislation of Johnson's Great Society programs had added "program on top of program" and created "a maze of complex and often confusing federal guidelines and requirements." He stated, "At federal, state, and local levels, we have unwittingly created a heavy burden of varying regulations, differing standards, and overlapping responsibilities."[11] Building on Nixon's bloc grants concept, Ford's administration sought unsuccessfully to pass legislation to consolidate categorical federal aid programs into general grants to states. Ford's motives were to reduce federal spending during an inflationary period, limit the federal role in education, and give states and local authorities greater autonomy and flexibility in

At a ceremony in the Cabinet Room, on March 1, 1976, President Ford signs a Special Message to Congress Proposing Elementary and Secondary Education Reform Legislation. (Courtesy Gerald R. Ford Library.)

using federal assistance. A key argument in advancing consolidation was that it would reduce the bureaucratic red tape that preoccupied school administrators and allow for a more efficient use of funds for educational purposes. Ford was generally unsuccessful in efforts at consolidation. He encountered the opposition of educational organizations, which saw the administration's primary motivation to be a federal reduction in educational funding. Also, the kind of educational legislation that Ford was proposing ran into the strong opposition of various special interests in education, who feared that eliminating or reducing categorical aid would reduce funding in their specific areas. Though the House Education and Labor Subcommittee on Elementary, Secondary, and Vocational Education held hearings on Ford's proposed consolidation plan, neither the House nor the Senate acted on it.

Efforts to Limit Court-Ordered Busing

During Ford's administration, court-ordered busing had become a highly emotional area of domestic controversy, particularly in the large urban centers. While Nixon had attempted to differentiate between de jure and de facto segregation in using busing as a remedy, Ford sought to limit the courts' use of this remedy. After announcing his opposition to racial segregation and his intention to execute the laws of the land, he expressed serious reservations about using court-ordered busing of pupils to achieve racial integration. Finding the issue to be of "profound importance to our domestic tranquility and the future of American education," Ford argued that the money spent on busing pupils would be better used to improve education. Also, he was concerned that the reliance of federal courts on busing to achieve desegregation would erode local community control. His message to Congress on June 24, 1976, stated his reservations about court-ordered busing:

> It is my belief that in their earnest desire to carry out the decisions of the Supreme Court, some judges of lower Federal Courts have gone too far. They have:
>
> —resorted too quickly to the remedy of massive busing of public school children;
>
> —extended busing too broadly; and
>
> —maintained control of schools for too long.
>
> It is this overextension of court control that had transformed a simple judicial tool, busing, into a cause of widespread controversy and slowed our progress toward the total elimination of segregation.[12]

To limit the extent of court-ordered busing, the Ford administration proposed the "School Desegregation and Assistance Act of 1976," which would:

> 1. Require that a court in a desegregation case determine the extent to which acts of unlawful discrimination have caused a greater degree of racial concentration in a school or school system than would have existed in the absence of such act.
>
> 2. Require that busing and other remedies in school desegregation cases be limited to eliminating the degree of student racial concentration caused by proven unlawful acts of discrimination.
>
> 3. Require that the utilization of court ordered busing as a remedy be limited to a specific period of time consistent with the legislation's intent that it be an interim and transitional remedy. In general, this period of time will be no longer than five years where there has been compliance with the court order.[13]

The administration's reservations about court-ordered busing did not change some judges' determination to use it as a remedy to eliminate racial segregation in schools. Ford's School Desegregation Standards Act of 1976 was introduced in the Senate and the House and then referred to the Judiciary and Labor and Public Welfare Committees but was not reported out of these committees for a vote. The proposed legislation was criticized by the NAACP as a retreat on race relations. However, the area of court-mandated busing remained locked in controversy and litigation without a comprehensive resolution of the issue. Ford's policy did signal, however, the administration's reluctance to support busing efforts.

The Work Education Initiative

One of Ford's statements on education that generated wide interest among educators concerned the need to link work and education more effectively. Although administration officials, especially the secretaries of Commerce; Labor; and Health, Education, and Welfare attempted to develop a concrete strategy to link work and education, no particular legislation was proposed. Nevertheless, Ford's views on the subject merit consideration in that he seemed to be addressing an unmet need in American education, especially as the United States was changing from an industrial to a "high tech" information and service economy.

In an address at The Ohio State University on August 30, 1974, Ford made extensive comments on the bleak job prospects that university students faced upon graduation. He pointed out the need to relate the education received in school, especially in higher education, to the needs of a changing economy. Although Ford's comments were general observations rather than a policy initiative, they gained a highly favorable response throughout the country, particularly from educators. In response, the administration began efforts to do something concrete about work-related education. Ford's continuing interest in advancing his "education and work initiative" led to the creation of several joint task forces that included officials of the Departments of Labor, Commerce, and HEW. In reporting on the work of the task forces, Casper Weinberger, Secretary of HEW, commented on the president's interest:

> I think one of the things he has been mainly concerned with is the isolation of the three worlds of business, labor, and education, the fact that we spend about the first 20 years of our lives as Americans in school and the next 40 years on some kind of job. But that first 20 years is not really based on or designed to get us prepared for or started in the kind of work that most people eventually start doing and that there is a delay with people getting started on various career ladders as a result.

> So, what he is most anxious to do is merge these worlds together and kind of break down the barriers that now exist between the educational specialists who run schools and the corporations and unions who are concerned with jobs in the real world.[14]

While not devising a comprehensive program on the transition from school to work, the Ford administration, however, continued to research the issue. An interdepartmental task force identified the major problems involving transition to work as: (1) students have little knowledge of the world of work; (2) they need information and help with career plans, placement, and meaningful work experience; (3) young people are initially employed in jobs that require little training or supervision and have little incentives for building up on-the-job tenure; (4) career guidance in schools is inadequate in that it typically is not related to the local job market; (5) there is little joint planning and coordination in communities among schools, industries, and employment agencies. The administration's policy that emerged was to encourage existing programs that related to the transition from school to work. It encouraged the National Institute of Education to aid in developing and improving programs for increasing work-experience programs and career-, economic-, and competency-based education.[15] It also encouraged the involvement of business in developing transitional programs that would become a basis for partnerships between schools and businesses.

Of the various educational issues faced by the Ford administration, action on legislation for the education of children with disabilities had the greatest impact on American education. The enactment of the Education for All Handicapped Children's Act would have results that changed education at all levels, including teacher preparation. In the next section, we examine the important judicial and legislation actions related to the education of children with handicaps.

The Education of Children with Handicaps

On November 29, 1975, President Gerald R. Ford, despite his reservations about the law's detailed complexity and costs, signed the Education for All Handicapped Children Act (PL 94-142). The law marked a singular departure from the general federal role in education in that it was highly directive to the states and to the schools. It ordered states to provide a free and appropriate education for all handicapped children and delineated the procedures to be followed in the schools. We shall examine the historical background and events leading to the enactment of the act and look at its provisions.

Historical Background

The establishment of public elementary and high schools in the nineteenth century provided a ladder of state institutions, which were open to virtually all children in the United States. While it was true that schools legally were racially segregated in Southern and border states until the *Brown* case in 1954, African-American children, too, theoretically had the right to a public education. The history of the education of children with handicaps, however, was both similar to and different from that of African-American children. While the enactment of compulsory education laws in the states required school attendance until a specified leaving date, such requirements were differentially applied to students with handicaps. In many states, school boards could exclude students from public schools if the students were judged unable to benefit from instruction or if they seriously disrupted the learning process.[16] Further, students with special needs had a high drop-out rate. One trend, then generally lauded by educational reformers, was to create special schools for children with specific kinds of handicaps, such as schools for the deaf and the blind.

During the early twentieth century, the prevailing attitude among educators was that the state was responsible for educating children with handicaps but that their education should take place in separate institutions or in separate programs in a school. The conventional wisdom of the period was that this kind of "exclusion" benefitted students with handicaps by providing special services for a group of students with similar needs and that this instruction could be given by teachers who were specifically trained to provide specialized instruction. Little attention was paid to the general social and educational consequences of exclusion until there became the need for vocational rehabilitation for injured World War II veterans. An example of the shift in public attitudes is the 1948 amendment to the Civil Service Act, which forbade discrimination in hiring the physically handicapped.

The enactment of the Education for All Handicapped Children Act of 1975 was stimulated by the heightened consciousness about civil rights and racial desegregation emanating from the earlier *Brown* case. This landmark case, which ruled that racial segregation in public schools was unconstitutional, stimulated a response among those who opposed separate schools and facilities for children with handicaps. Advocates of the educational rights of persons with handicaps argued that the Fourteenth Amendment applied just as much to children with handicaps as it did to African-American and indeed to all American children.[17]

Parent interest and other advocacy groups such as the National Association for Retarded Citizens and the Council for Exceptional Children, arguing for recognition of the educational needs of children with handicaps, moved their efforts to the federal level while continuing their state and local endeavors. The enactment of the Elementary and Secondary Education Act of 1965 (ESEA), which gave the federal government a larger role in education, did not escape the attention of special education advocacy groups. When ESEA legislation came up for renewal in 1966, arguments were made for the need for federal aid in the area. It was estimated that only 25 percent of the seven million school-age children with handicaps were enrolled in either public or private schools. Further, while only approximately 71,000 teachers were available to instruct this population, it was estimated that 300,000 more teachers were needed.[18] When the ESEA was renewed, Title VI, added to the act as PL 89-750, provided aid for developing model programs and instructional materials for special education and encouraged the recruitment of more teachers in the field. It also established a Bureau of Education for the Handicapped (BEH) in the Office of Education and appointment of a National Advisory Committee on Education and Training of the Handicapped.[19]

In 1970, Congress enacted PL 91-230, which consolidated existing legislation concerning children with handicaps into a single law. It provided funds for research for the creation of model programs, and for the preparation of special educators. Significantly, it also recognized learning disabilities as a new handicapping condition.[20]

Further Movement toward PL 94-142

In 1971 and 1972, courts in Pennsylvania and the District of Columbia ruled in favor of guaranteeing the educational rights of children with handicaps. The Pennsylvania Association for Retarded Children (PARC) initiated a class action suit in federal court against the state of Pennsylvania. PARC charged Pennsylvania with violating its own constitution and the equal protection clause of the U.S. Constitution's Fourteenth Amendment by denying equal educational opportunity to children with mental handicaps. In a precedent-making decision, the court ruled that Pennsylvania was required to provide a publicly supported education for all children with mental handicaps from age six to twenty-one. The court's ruling that children with mental handicaps were to be educated in a program most like that provided for nonhandicapped children was portentous for later mainstreaming and inclusion. The court also provided for due process procedures.[21] In a similar case in the District of Columbia, the court, emphasizing due process, required that every child in the District be provided with ". . . a free and suitable publicly supported education regardless of the degree of a child's mental, physical or emotional disability or impairment."[22]

Encouraged by victories in the courts, advocates of full public education for children with handicaps renewed their efforts at the federal level. They succeeded in securing passage of the Rehabilitation Act of 1973, PL 93-112. A key provision of the act made the rights of persons with handicaps equivalent to those guaranteed by the Civil Rights Act of 1964. The act required that agencies receiving federal funds were to provide full participation in their programs to persons with handicaps. Although President Nixon vetoed the act on the grounds that it would be too costly, Congress overrode his veto.[23] A further legislative victory came with the enactment of PL 93-380 in 1974, which established the framework for: (1) educating children with handicaps in the least restrictive environment; (2) following due process procedures; (3) recognizing the right of education for all children with handicaps.[24]

In 1973–74, efforts for education for children with handicaps continued in Congress. The Education for All Handicapped Children Act, PL 94-142, was introduced to provide a federal mandate for the education of children with handicaps. In congressional hearings, parent and other advocacy groups, pointing to local weaknesses in providing services, testified to the need for a greater federal role. In addition to handicapped children's advocacy groups, the American Federation of Teachers and the National Education Association supported a stronger federal role. The Nixon administration, though under pressure due to the Watergate scandal, still opposed the enactment of additional federal legislation in this area. The administration argued that such a role would be enormously expensive and bring greater federal interference into state and local school matters. In the summer of 1975, PL 94-142 passed Congress. Although President Ford, who had replaced Nixon, had some reluctance due to anticipated costs and an undue federal role, he signed the act, believing its merits required him to do so.

PL 94-142's major thrust was to guarantee a "free appropriate public education" to all children with handicaps. Among its key provisions were:

1. State and local districts were to establish procedures to identify handicapped children.

2. Each handicapped child was to have an Individualized Education Program (IEP), specifying the type and scope of special education program. In establishing IEPs, state and local districts were to guarantee due process procedures to protect each child's rights.

3. To be eligible for funds, states were to establish procedures to assure handicapped children were educated with nonhandicapped students to the maximum appropriate extent.

PL 94-142 had far-reaching effects on U.S. education, especially the requirement that children with handicaps be educated in the least restrictive environment. Programs of teacher education were redesigned to prepare teachers to work effectively in classrooms containing both handicapped and nonhandicapped students.

The Carter Administration

Jimmy Carter, a former Georgia governor and the Democratic Party nominee, defeated Gerald Ford, the Republican incumbent, in the presidential election of 1976. The contrasts between the two candidates revealed differing orientations to the federal role in education. Although Ford had made some efforts to develop an innovative approach to link education to work and careers, he essentially believed that education was a matter best reserved for the states and local districts. He sought, unsuccessfully, to reduce myriad federal aid categorical programs into bloc grants to the states. He also was cautious about using busing to bring about racial integration.

Carter, in contrast to Ford, believed, like many in the Democratic Party, that the federal government should play a larger role in education. His support for education at the federal level won him the support of the National Education Association and other educational organizations. In an address to the national NEA convention in 1976, Carter pledged to work for the creation of federal Department of Education. Such a department, at the cabinet level, would, he argued, be an efficient way of bringing the more than three hundred federal education programs under the control of a single agency. Further, Carter stated his firm conviction that education needed to be highlighted as an important national concern.[25] In response, the NEA, with its membership of 1,800,000, for the first time in its history, endorsed a presidential candidate—Jimmy Carter.

Carter's administration was plagued by rising rates of inflation, which were caused, in part, by increasing energy costs, particularly in the cost of oil. Though an extremely hardworking chief executive,

Carter appeared unable to arrest the cycle of inflation. Hoping to reduce the nation's dependency on imported oil, Carter sought to develop an integrated policy that would reduce petroleum consumption while protecting the environment. He used the argument that Americans should regard themselves as stewards of the nation's natural resources.[26]

The concerns for energy conservation and environmental protection found their way into the school curriculum. The late 1970s, in particular, were a period when environmental concerns received emphasis in the natural and social sciences. It was the time when children learned the importance of recycling and brought their environmental attitudes home with them from school.

Department of Education

Carter's decision to create a Department of Education marked still another page in the history about the federal role in education. During the 1860s, the creation and placement of an Office of Education had been discussed. In 1867, Congressman James A. Garfield introduced legislation that led to an Office of Education with Henry Barnard as the first commissioner of education. In 1868, the office became a bureau in the Department of the Interior. Although President Harding expressed some interest in a cabinet-level department in the early 1920s, no action was taken. The Reorganization Act of 1939 removed the Office of Education from the Department of the Interior, placing it under the jurisdiction of the Federal Security Administration. In 1953, during the Eisenhower administration, the Office of Education became part of the newly established Department of Health, Education, and Welfare (HEW). It was under the jurisdiction of HEW when the office was elevated as an independent department, whose secretary held cabinet rank.[27]

There had been a long history of efforts to create a federal, cabinet-level Department of Education. Between 1908 and 1951, fifty such bills had been introduced in Congress; between 1965 and 1975, another forty-eight were introduced.[28] During the Johnson Administration, a task force on reorganization of the executive branch, chaired by Donald Price, dean of Harvard's Graduate School of Public Administration, had recommended creating a Department of Education.[29] Johnson, however, preoccupied with the War on Poverty and Great Society programs, did not take the initiative to create a department. The Office of Education was so overwhelmed by the rush of new educational legislation, such as the Elementary and Secondary Education Act, that Johnson decided on an administrative reorganization of the existing office rather than attempting to create a new department.[30]

President Carter, in his messages to Congress on education on February 28, 1978, made the case for a Department of Education. Again on February 13, 1979, he continued to plead for the department, advising Congress that it would: (1) provide a federal focus on educational policy; (2) permit closer coordination of federal education programs; (3) reduce duplication of federal requirements and regulations; (4) assist school districts in making better use of local resources.[31]

Carter's pledge to create a Department of Education was not easily redeemed. It encountered the usual divisions among professional educational organizations and other interest groups, as the situation that had jettisoned educational legislation at the federal level in the past resurfaced. Among the groups supporting the creation of a department was an imposing coalition of professional education organizations, such as the National Education Association (NEA), the National School Boards Association (NSBA), the National Parent-Teachers Association (PTA), the American Association of School Administrators (AASA), the Council of Chief State School Officers (CCSSO), the National Association of State Boards of Education (NASBE), the American Council on Education (ACE), and the American Association of Community and Junior Colleges (AACJC). An interesting split over the bill developed between the two largest national organizations enrolling classroom teachers. While the NEA supported a department, its rival, the American Federation of Teachers (AFT), opposed it. In addition, some administrators in higher education and Catholic educators had reservations that the proposed department would be dominated by public school elementary and secondary interests. Further, there was generally strong Republican opposition in Congress.

Advocates of the proposed department argued that departmental status, at cabinet rank, would give education the "visibility" it needed in Washington. They argued that education was so important to the national interest that it needed to be addressed by a federal department. Opponents charged that the creation of the new department would intrude upon the historic tradition of state and local control of education. They contended that the enlarged federal educational bureaucracy would create more "red tape" and burden local school administrators with more complicated and cumbersome regulations.[32]

In 1978, the administration's bill to create the department passed the Senate but not the House of Representatives. In 1979, a second effort succeeded, after long debate, as both the Senate and the House passed the bill in very close votes. The House vote of 210 for and 206 opposed showed considerable opposition to the new department. The enactment of the bill was one of President Carter's rare legislative victories in Congress.

On October 17, 1979, President Carter signed the Department of Education Organization Act, which legally established the Department

Shirley Hufstedler, secretary of the Department of Education, 1980–81. (Courtesy U.S. Department of Education.)

of Education (ED) as the thirteenth cabinet-level agency of the federal government. At the signing, Carter said the "time had passed when the federal government can afford to give second level, part-time attention to its responsibilities in American education. . . . Educational issues will now receive the top level priority they deserve."

President Carter's nominee as the first secretary of the Department of Education was Shirley Hufstedler, a federal appeals judge. In hearings before the Senate Committee on Labor and Human Resources, Hufstedler sought to allay the fears of those who feared the new department would breach state and local prerogatives on education. She stated:

> I believe in pluralism. The strength of our educational system is rooted in the primacy of state and local governments. Where federal involvement is necessary, our goals should be maximum efficiency and cooperation, minimum disruption and domination.[33]

Hufstedler also indicated to the Senators that she would pursue equity issues:

> I believe in equal opportunity. This is the cornerstone of our educational system and, indeed, of any just society. Federal responsibility has been clearly defined in areas ranging from eradicating race and sex discrimination to meeting the needs of the disabled.[34]

Hufstedler, confirmed by the Senate, moved to the difficult challenge of creating the new Education Department. The department had the fifth largest operating budget of its federal counterparts, $14.2 billion, and a staff of 17,000. Hufstedler and her associates had to develop structures to administer 152 programs, 140 of which had been transferred from the Department of Health, Education, and Welfare (HEW), and five from other federal agencies. She was assisted by Steven Minter, as undersecretary; Albert Bowker, assistant secretary for postsecondary education; James Rutherford, assistant secretary for educational research and improvement; and Thomas Minter, assistant secretary for elementary and secondary education.

The Department of Education had only a year to function under Carter, who would lose the 1980 presidential election. The Carter administration had two major objectives for the department: (1) streamlining, coordinating, and consolidating existing programs; (2) working to make education a national priority to restore what appeared to be a growing malaise among schools and teachers.

Hufstedler commenced on a rapid but challenging transition that would move the Office of Education from HEW to its new departmental status, staff and streamline it, and proceed to consolidate educational programs into new structures. When she left office as the incoming Reagan administration took charge, the Department of Education had been created and was functioning as an independent department.[35] However, the opponents of the department continued a concerted attack on the new department, claiming that it was unneeded, unwieldy, and bureaucratic.

The department's future was an issue in the presidential campaign of 1980. In responding to a query from the educational journal, *Instructor*, Carter, the department's creator, vowing its continuation, responded that the department would be "the catalyst of a new commitment" to make educational programs "more accountable to the students and our people. And most of all, it will heighten attention to education and the challenges it and we face today." John Anderson, a Republican congressman from Illinois, running as an independent, also endorsed the department. Reagan, the Republican nominee, simply retorted, "The $15 billion Department of Education should be abolished."[36] Chapter 11 will examine Reagan's educational policies.

Conclusion

The 1970s was an unsettling period that marked a departure from the economic assurance of the earlier postwar periods. The 1970s also marked a change in American attitudes about the future. Signs of the new interdependent global economy and the information-age society were clearly present. The difficulty in making the transition from an industrial to an informational and service economy pointed to the need for new kinds of education and training.

School administrators also were caught up in the new economic realities brought about by inflation, demographic changes caused by declining enrollments, and reduced revenues. The nation still grappled with the unresolved issue of racial integration. While the 1970s was not a generally optimistic period for education, the decade was significant, however, in bringing about the highly significant trend of making schooling more inclusive of previously underserved groups, especially members of minority groups and children with handicaps.

In the next chapter, we examine American society and education during the 1980s. Here, we shall see a revival of neoconservativism in politics and neoessentialism in education.

Notes

[1] Biographies of Nixon are Fawn Brodie, *Richard Nixon* (New York: Norton Publishers, 1981) and Earl Mazo and Stephen Hess, *Nixon* (New York: Harper and Row, 1968).

[2] Richard Nixon, "Statement by the President on Elementary and Secondary School Desegregation," (March 24, 1970), p. 9.

[3] Diane Ravitch, *The Troubled Crusade: American Education 1945–1980* (New York: Basic Books, 1983), pp. 257–58.

[4] Nixon, p. 5.

[5] Ibid., p. 6.

[6] Ibid., p. 14.

[7] Ibid., pp. 13–14.

[8] Gerald R. Ford, "Remarks to the National Association of Secondary School Principals" (February 16, 1976), p. 38. Collections, Gerald R. Ford Library, Ann Arbor, Michigan.

[9] For the Ford presidency, see John R. Greene, *The Presidency of Gerald R. Ford* (Lawrence: University Press of Kansas, 1995).

[10] Stefan A. Halper, J. Michael Luttig, James B. Shuman, and George Van Cleve, eds. *The Ford Presidency: A Portrait of the First Two Years* (Washington, DC: White House Office of Communications, 1976), pp. 1–10.

[11] Ford, p. 19.

[12] Gerald Ford, "Message to the Congress of the United States," (June 14, 1976), p. 2. Collections, Gerald R. Ford Library, Ann Arbor, Michigan.

13 Office of the White House Press Secretary, "The White House Fact Sheet—The School Desegregation Standards and Assistance Act of 1975," p. 1. Collections, Gerald R. Ford Library, Ann Arbor, Michigan,

14 "The White House Press Conference of Frederick B. Dent, Secretary, Department of Commerce, Caspar W. Weinberger, Secretary, Department of Health, Education, and Welfare, and Peter J. Brennan, Secretary, Department of Housing and Urban Development" (December 3, 1974), p. 3. Collections, Gerald R. Ford Library, Ann Arbor, Michigan.

15 Memorandum for the President on "Bringing Together Education and Work—Decisions" (December 11, 1974), pp. 2–8. Collections, Gerald R. Ford Library, Ann Arbor, Michigan.

16 A representative legal precedent for such exclusion was *Watson v. City of Cambridge*, 32 N.E. 864, 157 Mass. 651 (1893).

17 H. Rutherford Turnbull and Ann P. Turnbull, *Free Appropriate Education: Law and Implementation* (Denver, CO: Love Publishing Co., 1979), p. 14.

18 Erwin L. Levine and Elizabeth M. Wexler, *PL 94-142: An Act of Congress* (New York: Macmillan Co., 1981), pp. 13–21.

19 Ibid., pp. 31–32.

20 Ibid., pp. 36–37.

21 *Pennsylvania Association for Retarded Children v. Commonwealth of Pennsylvania, 334 F. Supp. 1257 (E.D. PA 1971).*

22 *Mills v. Board of Education, 348 F. Supp. 866 (D.DC 1972).*

23 Reed Martin, *Educating Handicapped Children: The Legal Mandate* (Champaign: Research Press Co., 1979), p. 17.

24 Richard S. Podemski, *Comprehensive Administration of Special Education* (Rockville, MD: Aspen Publications, 1984), pp. 6–7.

25 R. E. Miles, "A Cabinet Department of Education: The Time is Now," *Change*, 9 (1977), pp. 37–38.

26 Gary M. Fink and Hugh Davis Graham, eds. *The Carter Presidency: Policy Choices in the Post-New Deal Era* (Lawrence: University Press of Kansas, 1998), p. 161.

27 Beryl A. Radin and Willis D. Hawley, *The Politics of Federal Reorganization: Creating the U.S. Department of Education* (New York: Pergamon Press, 1988), pp. 15–16.

28 Congressional Research Service, *Proposals to the U.S. Congress for the Creation of a Department of Education and Related Bills Offering Similar Proposals* (Washington, DC: U.S. Congress, 1971) and Beryl A. Radin and Willis D. Hawley, p. 24.

29 Rufus E. Miles, Jr. *A Cabinet Department of Education: Analysis and Proposal* (Washington, DC: American Council on Education, 1976), p. 42. Also, see Emmette S. Redford and Marlin Blisset, *Organizing the Executive Branch: The Johnson Presidency* (Chicago: University of Chicago Press, 1981).

30 Stephen K. Bailey and Edith K. Mosher, *ESEA: The Office of Education Administers a Law* (Syracuse, NY: Syracuse University Press, 1968), p. 78.

31 House of Representatives, *Establishment of a Department of Education: Message from the President of the United States Transmitting a Draft of Proposed Legislation to Establish a Department of Education and for Other Purposes,* 96th Congress, 1st Session (House Document No. 96-32) (Washington, DC: U.S. Government Printing Office, 1979), pp. 1–2.

32 David Stephens, "President Carter, the Congress, and the NEA: Creating the Department of Education," *Political Science Quarterly*, 98 (1983–84), p. 658.

[33] Senate Committee on Labor and Human Resources, *Hearings on Nomination of Shirley Hufstedler to be Secretary of Education* (November 27, 1979), p. 21.
[34] Ibid., p. 21.
[35] For her comments on the establishment of the Department of Education, see Shirley M. Hufstedler, "A World in Transition," *Change* 12 (1980), pp. 8–9.
[36] "What's Ahead for Elementary Education?" *Instructor*, 90 (October 1980), pp. 38–39.

Further Reading

Bailey, Stephen K., and Mosher, Edith K. *ESEA: The Office of Education Administers a Law*. Syracuse, NY: Syracuse University Press, 1968.

Berman, William C. *America's Right Turn: From Nixon to Clinton*. Baltimore: Johns Hopkins University Press, 1998.

Brodie, Fawn. *Richard Nixon*. New York: Norton Publishers, 1981.

Califano, Joseph A., Jr. *Governing America: An Insider's Report from the White House and the Cabinet*. New York: Simon and Schuster, 1981.

Carter, Jimmy. *Keeping Faith: Memoirs of a President*. New York: Bantam Books, 1982.

Chambers, Jay E., and William T. Hartman, eds. *Special Education Policies: Their History, Implementation, and Finance*. Philadelphia: Temple University Press, 1983.

Evans, Rowland, and Robert Novak. *Nixon in the White House*. New York: Random House, 1971.

Fink, Gary M., and Hugh David Graham, eds. *The Carter Presidency: Policy Choices in the Post-New Deal Era*. Lawrence: University Press of Kansas, 1998.

Ford, Gerald. *A Time to Heal*. New York: Harper and Row, 1979.

Goldberg, Steven S. *Special Education Law: A Guide for Parents, Advocates, and Educators*. New York: Plenum Press, 1982.

Greene, John R. *The Presidency of Gerald R. Ford*. Lawrence: University Press of Kansas, 1995.

Heinich, Robert, ed. *Educating All Handicapped Children*. Englewood Cliffs, NJ: Educational Technology Publications, 1979.

Levine, Erwin L., and Elizabeth M. Wexler. *PL 94-142: An Act of Congress*. New York: Macmillan, 1981.

Mazo, Earl, and Stephen Hess. *Nixon*. New York: Harper and Row, 1968.

Radin, Beryl A., and Willis D. Hawley. *The Politics of Federal Reorganization: Creating the U.S. Department of Education*. New York: Pergamon Press, 1988.

Ravitch, Diane. *The Troubled Crusade: American Education 1945–1980*. New York: Basic Books, 1983.

11

Education in the 1980s: Reagan, Bush, and Neoconservative Reform

While the 1970s were marked with an aura of economic insecurity and a decline in the traditional American faith in the future, the 1980s showed the ability of the nation to rebound and to regain its confidence. The leading political figure of the decade was Ronald Reagan, who was elected president in 1980. A former motion picture actor, Reagan had been governor of California. Known as the "great communicator," Reagan was adept in using television and the media to announce that the country was "back on track." Reagan's triumph signaled the victory of neoconservativism in politics, a reversal of the general liberalism that had begun with the New Deal and continued throughout most of the cold war period. Internationally, near the end of the decade, the collapse of the Soviet Union occurred and the long cold war finally ended. This chapter examines the historical context of the 1980s, the basic education movement, the educational agenda ushered in by *A Nation at Risk*, and myriad reports on education that were issued during the decade.

Historical Context

The 1980s were important in moving American education from one variety of reforms to what was heralded as a new reform agenda. In educational history, it is necessary to approach the word "reform" with judicious qualification. It is always important to ask: Who and what are being reformed? And, who are the reformers and what is their agenda?

In the late 1960s and early 1970s, reform meant to make schools less formal, more open, and more humanistic. In the 1980s, the meaning of reform changed. It now meant to make schools more structured, more effectively managed, and geared to basic skills and subjects. Following its historic patterns, the pendulum of educational reform was swinging back from a liberal-progressive orientation to neoconservatism and neoessentialism. The neoconservative ideology of education, which had been gathering momentum since the end of the turbulent 1960s and gaining strength in the 1970s, had become the basis of President Ronald Reagan's educational policy. The educational trends of the 1980s were part of a larger historical context in which the mood of the country was changing from liberal progressivism to neoconservatism.

The neoconservatives firmly asserted that they knew how to get the country moving forward again. They were definite about what the nation and its schools needed—a return to basic education, traditional values, and old fashioned discipline.

Basic Education

Against the backdrop of the significant socioeconomic changes occurring in the United States, a movement developed in some local communities and states for "a return to the basics." Groups, often composed of laypeople rather than professional educators, demanded a return to basic skills and a subject-matter curriculum. They decried the once lauded reforms of the new math, discovery learning, open education, and values clarification as the causes of America's educational decline.

The basic education movement of the late 1970s and early 1980s, like most large movements, was an unusual mixture of people, motives, and agendas. In some ways, it resembled the pedagogical complexity of the earlier progressive education movement of the 1920s in that while its adherents knew what they were against they were not always sure what they were for.

Basic education was not a new phenomenon in the United States. The essentialists, who argued for basic skills and subjects in the 1930s, included the respected and articulate educators, William C. Bagley and Isaac Kandel. In the 1950s, the charge for basic education was led by the eminent American historian, Arthur E. Bestor Jr., a founder of the Council for Basic Education. Although Bestor was a political liberal and active in the American Civil Liberties Union, basic education began to attract right-wing conservatives and anti-Communists in the 1950s, such as Max Rafferty. (See chapter 4 for the curricular controversies of the 1950s.) The basic education movement of the late 1970s and early 1980s was a loose but persuasively powerful umbrella coalition that covered a variety of educational and political positions. Some basic education advocates were of the earlier Bagley and Bestor variety. They believed that human beings, in the course of civilization, had developed necessary and disciplined educational skills—reading, writing, and computation—and bodies of knowledge—history, mathematics, language, and science—that were indispensable skills and subjects in the school curriculum. Such indispensable skills and subjects should not be crowded out by the anti-intellectual fads popular with some educationist circles.

Others in the basic education movement opposed particular school practices that they, either correctly or incorrectly, tied to progressive education. Some parents, bewildered by the new math, wanted a return to basic computation—adding, subtracting, multiplying, and dividing. Those looking at declining academic achievement scores, such as the SAT and ACT, wanted a reemphasis on basic subjects. Businesspeople, decrying incompetent and unskilled employees, wanted an end to social promotion. Concerned taxpayers, protesting against rising property taxes, wanted school budgets trimmed by eliminating what they called "unnecessary frills and fads."

In addition to those who supported basic education because of their educational philosophy or pedagogical persuasion, there were others who saw it as part of a grand design to restore American greatness by returning to an idealized and somewhat mythical version of educational history. In the days of the McGuffey Readers (popular textbooks used after the Civil War), so went this version of educational history, schools stressed clearly defined and simple values—patriotism, telling the truth, hard work, competition, and fair play. These virtues had been nurtured in schools by dedicated teachers. Neoconservatives tended to believe that liberals, progressives, and radicals, by introducing values clarification into the curriculum and cultural relativism into the schools, had weakened and eroded fundamental American values. They condemned values clarification as a neutral process in which students learned that moral decision making merely represented choosing between personal preferences. Values clarification, for many of the basic education proponents, stemmed from Dewey's cultural relativism, which held that right and wrong were based on changing times, places, and circumstances rather than on universal moral laws. Now, the country, with its rising rates of teen pregnancy, gang violence, and drug addiction, needed traditional values as never before. Going back to basics meant, for these advocates of the movement, a return to basic values, order, and discipline.

Still, there was often another component of basic education—the religious right, composed of fundamentalist Protestants but also including some members of other denominations. The religious right wanted prayer in the public schools, the teaching of Creationism, and freedom of educational choice through vouchers. Some neoconservatives, especially the religious right, wanted Creationism, a theory of the origin of life on earth that conforms to the literal interpretation of the Bible's Book of Genesis, taught in the schools as an alternative to Darwin's theory of evolution. While Roman Catholics might disagree with some of the educational assumptions of the religious right, some Catholics found vouchers a way to assist in funding increasingly hard-pressed Catholic parochial schools.

Basic education's themes had a wide appeal—containing rising educational costs; raising the standards of academic achievement; increasing American economic productivity; and curbing violence, sexual promiscuity, and drug addiction. This wide appeal made the movement a potentially powerful political force.

The Politics of Education

Although education in the United States is constitutionally a state and local prerogative, educational issues periodically have captured national attention. For example, the U.S. Supreme Court's decision ending racial segregation in public schools in the *Brown* case in 1954 focused national attention on race relations and racial integration. (See chapter 6 for a discussion of racial desegregation.) The Soviet Union's successful orbiting of the space satellite, *Sputnik*, in 1957, created a national furor about the Soviet educational challenge to the United States that culminated in enactment of the National Defense Education Act (NDEA) in 1958. The enactment of the Elementary and Secondary Education Act was a key part of President Lyndon Johnson's War on Poverty and Great Society agenda. (The War on Poverty is discussed in chapter 7.) President Jimmy Carter's role in effecting establishment of the Department of Education in 1979 was still another instance of a national focus on education. (For Carter and the Department of Education, see chapter 10.)

In the 1980s, education once again was center stage in American politics. Local and state politicians were gaining voter support as champions of basic education. These politicians attacked declining academic standards, lack of discipline in the schools, and the need to restore academic quality to public schools. Some also drew support from the religious right by urging prayer in the schools and an emphasis on teaching "sound moral values." Ronald Reagan became keenly aware of the power of education as a national issue and kept it in the forefront of his administration, from 1981 to 1989.

Reaganomics and Social and Educational Policy

Reagan's victory over Carter in 1980 signaled that an important ideological shift in social and educational policy was taking place in the United States. Reagan's rise to power, like Margaret Thatcher's in the United Kingdom, made it clear that the political door was closing on the long-reigning Keynesian-influenced economics and social policies associated with the welfare state. It appeared that many policy assumptions set in motion during Roosevelt's New Deal in the 1930s and revivified in Johnson's Great Society of the 1960s would be reversed by what was called the "Reaganomics" of the 1980s. Reaganomics was the term coined for revived free enterprise, free market, nongovernment interventionist economics that appeared to be the foundation of Reagan's social and economic policies. Championing a neoconservative, socioeconomic, and political ideology, Reagan led an attack on "big government" and bureaucratic liberal social welfare programs. Part of the Reagan strategy was to deconstruct the policy scaffolding that Lyndon Johnson had created, which linked social welfare programs and education.

The Reagan administration's early budgets in 1981 and 1982 brought the greatest reduction in antipoverty programs. The Reagan approach to social and to educational programs was to return to the earlier Nixon and Ford efforts of the 1970s to rely on block grants to the states and to consolidate and reduce federal categorical programs. Although some efforts were attempted to reduce medicare and unemployment insurance, little real change occurred in these programs, which had the greatest middle-class support.[1]

Reagan on Education

In his campaign for president, Ronald Reagan, the Republican candidate, pressed a strongly neoconservative platform against Jimmy Carter, the incumbent Democratic candidate. Reagan's campaign put forth consistently conservative goals, such as reducing the size and power of the federal government, dismantling social welfare programs by putting more people to work, and deregulating the economy to let the free market work. In education, Reagan's position re-echoed essential conservative themes that education as properly a state and local function should be free from federal interference. Federal bureaucrats, he claimed, should stay out of public schools, which were primarily the province of the localities they served. At the same time that he argued for a reduced federal role in education, Reagan decried declining academic achievement, lowered standards, the lack of discipline, and the rise of violence in the schools. If elected, he pledged to abolish the newly created Department of Education and drastically curb federal intrusion in education.

Despite his anti-Department of Education rhetoric in the presidential campaign, Reagan took no decisive move to end its existence after his inaugural as president in January 1981. Although there were rumors that Reagan planned to reduce the department to a foundation or restore it to its previous status in the Department of Health, Education, and Welfare, the Reagan administration's proposed budget provided funding for the department, but with a budget reduction of 20 percent. Generally, the Reagan administration, at this point, focused on Reagan's campaign agenda for education: pursuing the traditional Republican ideology of endorsing the sanctity of state and local control, block grants to the states, and consolidation of federal education programs—which had been favored by the earlier Republican Nixon and Ford administrations. (See Chapter 10 for a discussion of the Nixon and Ford policies.)

Reagan's administration witnessed the triumph of neoconservative political and economic policies. Reagan's campaign had emphasized deregulation of the economy, military preparedness, and the restoration of patriotic values. The Reagan administration's educational policies sought to: (1) focus the nation's attention on the need for educational reform; (2) use the federal government to encourage reform initiatives by the states and local school districts; (3) encourage specific educational initiatives such as a basic academic curriculum, merit review and pay for teachers, parental choice in school selection through vouchers, and the restoration of discipline, patriotism, and traditional values in schools; (4) reduce federal expenditures for education.[2]

Terrel Bell

An important turning point in Reagan's educational policy came with Terrel Bell's appointment as secretary of education. A moderate Republican and experienced educator, Bell had a background as a school administrator. He had worked with a variety of educational organizations and had Washington experience, serving as commissioner of education during Ford's administration.[3] Under Bell's careful and steady leadership, education would become an increasingly important component in the Reagan agenda.

Despite Reagan's pledge during the presidential campaign of 1980 to abolish the Department of Education, he continued, guided by the prudent Bell, to use the department to advance a neoconservative educational agenda hearkening back to earlier essentialist and basic education themes. According to the Reagan educational strategy, the president and secretary of education would use their federal roles to

Terrel H. Bell, secretary of
the Department of Educa-
tion, 1981–1985. (Courtesy
U.S. Department of Educa-
tion.

advance their interpretation of educational reform. While the administration encouraged its version of reform, the states, particularly the
governors, legislatures, and local districts, were encouraged to implement the neoconservative educational agenda. Essentially, the Reagan
administration sought to: (1) improve the academic quality of schools
by emphasizing a basic subject curriculum; (2) encourage effective
schools with strong principals and high teacher expectations; (3) relate
education to national economic productivity; (4) reduce indiscipline
and violence in schools by insisting on high standards of behavior and
performance; (5) encourage changes in the teaching profession such as
merit pay, career ladders, and competency testing.

A Nation at Risk

Reagan's appointee as secretary of education, Terrel H. Bell, who
served from 1981 to 1985, was a skilled, seasoned, and resourceful
educational administrator.[4] Bell succeeded in focusing national attention on the condition of American education by appointing the National
Commission on Excellence in Education in 1981, chaired by David L.
Gardner, president of the University of California. The commission's
charge was to conduct a comprehensive review of the quality of education in the country's schools and colleges, to do a comparative study of

the academic outcomes of U.S. education in comparison to that of other countries, to examine the relationships between college admission requirements and the high school curriculum, and to make recommendations to restore excellence to American education. In 1983, the Commission on Excellence issued its report, *A Nation at Risk: The Imperative for Educational Reform.* In dramatic fashion that resembled a nation at war, *A Nation at Risk,* warned:

> The educational foundations of our society are presently being eroded by a rising tide of mediocrity that threatens our very future as a nation and a people.

> If an unfriendly foreign power had attempted to impose on America the mediocre educational performance that exists today, we might well have viewed it as an act of war. As it stands, we have allowed this to happen to ourselves. We have even squandered the gains in student achievement made in the wake of the *Sputnik* challenge. Moreover, we have dismantled essential support systems which helped make those gains possible. We have, in effect, been committing an act of unthinking, unilateral disarmament.[5]

Members of the National Commission on Excellence in Education, which issued *A Nation at Risk* in 1983. (Courtesy U.S. Department of Education.)

In describing the decline of academic standards and achievement in education, the authors of the report alleged that part of the responsibility for America's declining productivity in the face of accelerating foreign competition could be traced to the schools' poor performance. The report argued that the academic achievement of American secondary school students was inferior to that of such economic competitors as Japan and West Germany. The report cited evidence of a high rate of functional illiteracy among young people and adults, declining performance on the College Board's Scholastic Aptitude Test (SAT), and poor performance in science and mathematics. To remedy the situation, the Commission on Excellence recommended curricular reform based on the reassertion of academic subjects and standards. It recommended

> that state and local high school graduation requirements be strengthened and that, at a minimum, all students seeking a diploma be required to lay the foundations in the Five New Basics by taking the following curriculum during their four years of high school: (1) 4 years of English; (2) 3 years of mathematics; (3) 3 years of science; (4) 3 years of social studies; and (5) one-half year of computer science. For the college bound, 2 years of foreign language in high school are strongly recommended in addition to those taken earlier.[6]

A Nation at Risk received wide media coverage and spawned a number of similar reports by private foundations, business groups, and state agencies. Secretary Bell astutely kept the report in the public consciousness by organizing a series of twelve regional conferences in 1983 that were attended by ten thousand educators, political and business leaders, and media commentators.[7] Numerous articles appeared in the press about the inadequate academic performance of American students. Contrasts were made between the superior Japanese and lagging American performance in mathematics and science. Suggestions were made that American schools could profit by imitating the curriculum and scheduling of Japanese and other foreign school systems. As the campaign for educational reform unfolded, several persistent themes emerged: (1) the school curriculum, especially that of the high school, needed to be restructured to focus on basic subjects, especially in English, mathematics, and science; (2) teacher education programs needed to be restructured to emphasize more academic subjects and fewer courses in education; (3) measures to assess teacher competency needed to be put in place as part of state certification requirements; (4) new alternatives to the conventional teachers' salary schedule such as career ladders and merit pay needed to be established; (5) businesses and schools (the private and educational sectors) should develop educational partnerships to improve the quality of education.

Significantly, the administration, including the president, saw its role as using its office as a "bully pulpit" for articulating the neoconservative educational agenda. Reagan, at a national conference of educators in Indianapolis in 1983 that followed issuance of *A Nation at Risk*, claimed his administration was leading "a grassroots revolution that promises to strengthen every school in the country." The president stated that:

From Maine to California, parents, teachers, school officials and
state and local officeholders have begun vigorous work to improve
the fundamentals—not fancy budget structures, not frills in the curriculum but teaching and learning.[8]

While pressing for a return to basics, discipline, and accountability, Reagan maintained that actual implementation and funding of the
proposed reforms were a state and local district responsibility. Further, the needed reforms could be effected without a large increase in
federal funding.

The National Education Association and the American Federation
of Teachers questioned many of Reagan's assumptions, especially
about funding and teacher reform. The NEA and AFT, which had
endorsed Reagan's Democratic opponents, Carter in 1980 and Mon-
dale in 1984, called for an expanded rather than reduced federal role
and for increased federal spending for education. Additionally, the AFT
urged more federal spending on programs for poor, bilingual, and
handicapped children.

A Decade of Reports

Spawned by *A Nation at Risk*, the 1980s witnessed a deluge of
educational reports by various commissions and committees that
scrutinized and generally criticized the performance of American public schools. These reports, focusing on elementary and secondary education, alleged that students in other countries had higher rates of academic achievement than American students. They contended that
many American teachers were incompetent and inadequately prepared. They suggested a variety of remedies, such as school choice
through vouchers, competency testing of students and teachers, revision of teacher tenure laws, and major changes in teacher education
programs.

Action for Excellence

An often repeated criticism of the 1980s was that American economic productivity was declining in the face of foreign competition.
The general education and skill training of American workers had not
prepared them to compete in the new interdependent world economy.
It was frequently alleged that businesses had to retrain new employees
who entered the workforce without competency in basic skills.

Action for Excellence, the report of the Education Commission of
the States National Task Force on Education for Economic Growth,
chaired by Governor James B. Hunt of North Carolina, examined
American education in relationship to economic productivity. The

commission sought to devise strategies for improving the quality of high school graduates, especially in the skills and subjects required for national economic growth and productivity. It might be recalled that in the late 1950s the criticism of public schools had been that their academic deficiencies were weakening national security in the face of the Soviet threat. In the 1980s, the criticism was that the schools were failing to prepare Americans to compete in a changing world economy.

Secondary Education Reform

As in earlier decades of educational criticism, such as the 1950s, much debate centered on American secondary education. In both the 1950s and 1980s, the major charge was that American high schools were providing an academically inadequate education to students. (For the curriculum debates of the 1950s, see chapter 4.) Frequently cited as evidence were international comparisons that showed the academic performance, especially in mathematics and science, of American secondary students as ranking below students in other countries. Also cited as an indicator of the decline of U.S. students' performance were falling SAT scores. An often-heard charge came from college educators who claimed that many high schools were doing such a poor job in preparing students for higher education that colleges had to establish remedial programs in English and mathematics.

Some critics blamed the changes in secondary education that occurred in the 1960s as causing the academic decline. During the 1960s and early 1970s, educators such as Charles Silberman had urged open and humanistic reforms in high schools to reduce regulations and give more freedom of choice to students. Some curriculum revisions of the 1960s had touted their "relevance" to students. Courses in foreign languages had been the chief casualty as students often found them irrelevant. Also, to enhance students' freedom of choice, high schools had introduced more electives and "minicourses." (For the educational reforms of the 1960s, see chapter 8.) These, so-called reforms of the 1960s, neoconservative critics contended, had weakened the academic quality of American secondary education and needed to be eliminated. In some respects, the attack on the humanistic and open education of the 1960s was similar to the attack on life adjustment education that had occurred in the 1950s.

As the 1980s began, the educational tide was turning away from student electivism and options to an emphasis on the basics. As in earlier decades, it was reasserted in the 1980s that secondary as well as undergraduate students needed a common subject-matter core. The common core concept resembled the recommendations of the Committee of Ten in the late-nineteenth century and those of James B. Conant in the 1950s. In 1983, Ernest L. Boyer's *High School: A Report on*

Secondary Education in America, issued by the Carnegie Foundation for the Advancement of Teaching, recommended a "Core of Common Learning" that consisted of: five units of language (English composition, speech, literature, foreign languages, and the arts); two and one-half units of History (American history, Western civilization, and non-Western studies); one unit of civics (classical political ideas and the structure and functions of contemporary government); one unit of science (physical and biological); two units of mathematics; two units of technology and health; and a half unit seminar on work and independent projects.[9] While two-thirds of the curriculum would be prescribed, the remaining one-third would still be elective.

Boyer's *High School* was much discussed by secondary educators during the 1980s. His report reflected the decade's emphasis on basic subjects such as English language and literature, biological and physical sciences, mathematics, history and social sciences. Reflecting technological change, it recommended, like *A Nation at Risk*, that secondary schooling train students to be computer literate. A somewhat new recommendation was a semester course in community service. Overall, Boyer's recommendations pointed to a persistent theme of the 1980s—the need for a common curricular core at the secondary school level.

In addition to Boyer's Carnegie Foundation Report, several other national commissions issued reports outlining reforms needed in secondary education. *Academic Preparation for College: What Students Need to Know and Be Able to Do*, issued by the College Board and chaired by its president, George Hanford, sought to develop consensus on what subjects and competencies were needed to prepare high school students for success in college. *Educating Americans for the 21st Century* was issued by the National Science Board Commission on PreCollege Education in Mathematics, Science, and Technology, chaired by William Coleman and Cecil Selby. The report defined a national agenda for improving mathematics and science education. It encouraged the development of an action plan by federal, state, and local governments, professional and scientific organizations, and the private sector.[10]

A Study of High Schools, conducted under the auspices of the National Association of Secondary School Principals and the National Association of Independent Schools, was chaired by Theodore Sizer. Sizer's qualitative and somewhat impressionistic study concentrated on the daily life of students in fifteen selected high schools. Among Sizer's recommendations were the need to: (1) avoid being trapped by efforts to cover every subject; (2) personalize and individualize instruction; (3) reduce the barriers of departmentalization of subjects by connecting and integrating them; (4) provide some exhibition that gave evidence of students' mastery of learning.[11] Unlike the other reports,

Sizer's study was more concerned with the general nature of change impacting high schools. Again, it differed from the other reports in its recommendation of flexible scheduling, teaching teams, and interdisciplinary courses. Sizer's report maintained greater continuity between the emphasis on curricular innovation and flexibility of the 1960s with added emphasis of the 1980s on academic subject matter.

Common Themes of the Reports

The various reports, with some notable exceptions (such as Sizer's *Study of High Schools*), found little to praise and much to criticize about the condition of American education. Their most severe indictment was leveled against the nation's high schools. Among the common themes were:

1. American education, particularly at the secondary level, was no longer based on clearly defined purposes. The absence of a central guiding philosophy had lowered academic standards and increased discipline problems.

2. In comparison with other industrialized nations, U.S. schools expected less and got the least from students in terms of academic performance.

3. The secondary school curriculum was diluted, homogenized, and diffused by popular general courses and electives that lacked academic rigor.

4. The United States had suffered a serious decline in students' achievement in mathematics and science, areas imperatively needed for the new technological era of global competition.

Competency Testing

In the 1980s, the climate of educational criticism stimulated by *A Nation at Risk* and other national reports brought a focus on the issue of teacher competency.[12] It was alleged that lower scores by American high school students on the Scholastic Aptitude Test could be attributed to the presence of some incompetent teachers as well as to a "watered-down" secondary school curriculum. In response, many of the states mandated teacher competency testing as part of teacher certification requirements, either at the entry level or at periodic intervals in a teacher's career. By 1988, forty-six states required some form of teacher competency testing.[13]

Technology and Education

While the 1980s featured a revived neoconservatism in politics and education, it also was a decade of highly important changes related to what was heralded as the transformation of the United States from an industrial economy to an information society. Some commentators, such as Donald Senese, described the information society as generating "an integrated information and communication system that transits data and permits instantaneous interaction between persons and computers."[14]

Although computers had been introduced in educational settings in the 1970s, their widespread entry into classrooms, libraries, and laboratories in schools and colleges across the country occurred in the 1980s. In higher education, in particular, computers had become an indispensable tool in research. By the end of the 1980s, computers were becoming part of an instructional repertoire called "interactive learning," which featured teacher-student interactive communications as well as instantaneous use of graphics and pictures. Colleges and universities also embarked on programs of "distance" education, in which computers linked with telecommunications provided instruction to students in off-campus sites. Computer cataloging and retrieval of information had also made significant changes in library organization and functions in educational institutions as well as in libraries throughout the country. In elementary and secondary schools, computers were found in classrooms and in computer laboratories to teach students basic computer literacy, which was being defined as a "new basic" along with English, mathematics, science and history.

Although federal funding for education tended to be limited during the Reagan years, the projects that received priority were in technology. Grants from the Fund for the Improvement of Postsecondary Education favored projects in educational technology such as microcomputer usage in education and the use of electronic technologies in research.

AIDS Education

In the 1980s, the spread of AIDS, acquired immunodeficiency syndrome, which had begun in the 1970s, reached such serious proportions that a presidential commission was established to study the problem and make recommendations. The Centers for Disease Control recommended that AIDS education be incorporated into comprehensive school health programs. Surgeon General C. Everett Koop urged that education about AIDS begin in the elementary grades so that "children can grow up knowing the behavior to avoid to protect themselves from exposure to the AIDS virus."[15] By the end of the 1980s, twenty-nine states had enacted legislation mandating some kind of HIV/AIDS education. Most frequently, the states added an HIV/AIDS component to existing health education programs.[16] AIDS education programs generally include information about the disease, the routes of virus transmission, risk factors and sexual behaviors associated with infection, and general means of prevention. The disease has been spread by transfusion of contaminated blood, use of contaminated needles in intravenous drug abuse, and sexual intercourse by those persons infected with the illness. Although there has been a general public acceptance of the need for AIDS education, there has been controversy regarding the sex education aspects. Some want the program limited to recommendations about the need for sexual abstinence by young people before marriage and on the importance of healthy, monogamous sexual relations. Critics of these limitations argue that they are unrealistic and should include information about the use of condoms. The efforts at AIDS education, begun in the 1980s, continued into the next decade.

The Bush Administration

The reaffirmation of an enhanced local and state role had been a continuing theme of the Nixon as well as the later Ford, Reagan, and Bush administrations. The general trend was that the federal government was to play a much more limited role in financing education. It should be noted that the theme of local control was also used by Margaret Thatcher to reverse the social welfare state in the United Kingdom.

In 1988, Vice President George Bush won the Republican Party nomination for president and defeated Michael Dukakis, the Democratic nominee. Bush announced that he wanted to be known as the "education president" and continued educational policies similar to that of his predecessor Ronald Reagan. The Bush administration put forth concepts for several educational initiatives. Among them were: (1) the use of federal vouchers to be available to parents so that their children could attend the public or private school of their choice; (2) a voluntary testing program in key subjects that would constitute a national curriculum; (3) encouragement of alternative patterns of teacher and school administrator certification.

In 1990, the Bush administration issued a report, *National Goals for Education*, that was to guide the improvement of education in the state and local districts. The report reiterated some of the themes of *A Nation at Risk*, especially the need to prepare future citizens who were capable of adapting to a changing global society. Among the goals prescribed were that by the year 2000:

1. All American children would enter school ready to learn.

2. The high school graduation rate would reach at least 90 percent.

3. All students will complete grades 4, 8, and 12 with demonstrated competency in English, mathematics, science, civics, government, and history.

4. U.S. students would rank first in the world in mathematics and science.

5. Every school in the United States would be free of drugs and violence.

6. Every American adult would be literate and possess the knowledge and skills needed for citizenship and competition in the global economy.[17]

These projected educational initiatives were debated but overshadowed by international and national events, however. The United States in the Persian Gulf War led a coalition of nations, under the auspices of the United Nations, that forced the retreat of Iraq from Kuwait. Between 1988 and 1990, the Communist Soviet system disintegrated. Throughout Eastern Europe, the Soviet satellite nations—Poland, Czechoslovakia, Hungary, Romania, Bulgaria, and East Germany— threw off Communist rule and established non-Communist multiparty states. After an abortive coup by Communist hardliners failed, the Soviet Union, itself, disestablished the Communist Party. The Soviet Union ceased to exist as its once constituent republics became independent nations. While these momentous events were occurring internationally, the U.S. economy experienced persistent but slow economic growth. In 1992, Bush was defeated by the Democratic nominee, William (Bill) Clinton, who was Governor of Arkansas.

Conclusion

The 1980s were a decade in which neoconservative ideology and politics were on the ascendancy. The neoconservative ascendancy noted in national reports and reform movements signaled a renewed emphasis on the primacy of subject matter in the curriculum, effective schools in administration, and competency testing to demonstrate mastery of basic skills and knowledge. The neoconservative ascendancy, marking a surfacing and promoting of basic education, was a limited rather than a complete victory over progressivism and liberalism. Liberalizing trends, for multiculturalism, environmental studies, and women's studies, which had been generated in the 1960s, continued, albeit in a somewhat muted form.

Interesting for students of the history of American education, the educational tendencies of the 1980s were repetitive of earlier themes.

The educational critics of the 1980s, much like the critics of the 1950s, alleged that an academically inadequate curriculum, especially in mathematics and science, had dulled the nation's competitive edge. In the 1950s, the critics alleged that these academic deficits were weakening the United States in the cold war with the Soviet Union. (For the curricular debates of the 1950s, see chapter 4.) In the 1980s, the allegations were that they had weakened American productivity in the face of growing competition from other nations, especially Japan and Germany, whose students were proving to be superior in mathematics and science.

When the 1980s ended, a number of educational reforms had taken place. In response to *A Nation at Risk* and myriad other similar reports of the decade, the majority of the states had passed legislation that increased the academic requirements for high school graduation in academic subjects such as English, science, mathematics, and in some cases, foreign languages. These requirements came at the expense of general, elective and vocational educational courses. Many states mandated skill proficiency testing for pupils at certain stages in their education. In addition, many states established teacher competency testing as a condition for certification. The educational profession responded to calls for reform, at first defensively and then proactively, with what was called "effective schooling." Professional literature featured numerous articles on how principals and teachers could create effective schools. Generally, the effective school was described as one in which: (1) the principal took a strong position as an academic leader; (2) the teachers formed a cooperative body of educators who worked together to deliver academic instruction efficiently; (3) the school had clearly announced goals and expectations for its pupils. The 1980s was a time of the reassertion of the basic academic curriculum along the lines of the essentialist philosophy of education and away from progressivism and humanism.

Notes

1 Edward J. Harpham and Richard K. Scotch, "Rethinking the War on Poverty: The Ideology of Social Welfare Reform," *Western Political Quarterly*, 41 (March 1988), p. 194.

2 For Reagan's views on education, see Ronald Reagan, "Excellence and Opportunity: A Program of Support for American Education," *Phi Delta Kappan*, 66, No. 1 (September 1984), pp. 13–15.

3 D. G. Savage, "Washington Report," *Phi Delta Kappan*, 62 (1981), p. 411.

4 For Bell's account, see Terrel H. Bell, *The Thirteenth Man: A Reagan Cabinet Memoir* (New York: The Free Press, A Division of Macmillan, Inc., 1988).

5 National Commission on Excellence in Education, *A Nation at Risk: The Imperative for Educational Reform* (Washington, DC: Government Printing Office, 1983), p. 5.

[6] Ibid., pp. 23–31.

[7] T. H. Bell, *Report by the Secretary on the Regional Forums on Excellence in Education* (Washington, DC: U.S. Department of Education, 1983).

[8] "Reagan's Education Policies Get Hard Sell," *Chicago Tribune* (December 11, 1983), p. 14.

[9] Ernest Boyer, *High School: A Report on Secondary Education in America* (New York: Harper and Row, 1983), pp. 66–77.

[10] For an analysis of the various reports of the 1980s, see Allan C. Ornstein and Francis P. Hunkins, *Curriculum Foundations, Principles and Issues* (Englewood Cliffs, NJ: Prentice-Hall, 1988), pp. 137–39.

[11] Theodore R. Sizer, *Horace's Compromise: The Dilemma of the American High School* (Boston: Houghton-Mifflin, 1984), pp. 5, 33–44, 109–19.

[12] Albert Benderson, "Teacher Competence," *Focus*, 10 (Princeton, NJ: Educational Testing Service, 1982).

[13] Curtis O. Baker, ed., *The Condition of Education 1989* (Washington, DC: U.S. Government Printing Office, 1989), p. 71.

[14] Donald J. Senese, "Higher Education and Technology—The Challenge We Face in the 1980s," Address delivered at Loyola University, Chicago (April 5, 1984). Senese was then assistant secretary for educational research and improvement in the U.S. Department of Education.

[15] C. Everett Koop, *Surgeon General's Report on Acquired Immunodeficiency Syndrome* (Washington, DC: U.S. Government Printing Office, 1986).

[16] "Comprehensive School Health Education," *Journal of School Health* 54 (August 1984), pp. 312–15.

[17] *National Goals for Education*. Washington, D.C.: U.S. Department of Education, 1990.

Further Reading

Bell, T. H. *Report by the Secretary on the Regional Forums on Excellence in Education*. Washington, DC: U.S. Department of Education, 1983.

Boyarsky, Bill. *Ronald Reagan*. New York: Random House, 1981.

Boyer, Ernest L. *High School: A Report on Secondary Education in America*. New York: Harper and Row, 1983.

Cannon, Lou. *Reagan*. New York: Putnam, 1982.

Evans, Rowland, and Robert Novak. *The Reagan Revolution*. New York: Dutton, 1981.

Grant, Gerald. *The World We Created at Hamilton High*. Cambridge: Harvard University Press, 1988.

Hampel, Robert. *The Last Little Citadel: American High Schools Since 1940*. Boston: Houghton Mifflin, 1986.

Joe, Tom, and Cheryl Rogers. *By the Few for the Few: The Reagan Welfare Legacy*. Lexington, MA: Lexington Books, 1985.

National Commission on Excellence in Education. *A Nation at Risk: the Imperative for Educational Reform*. Washington, DC: U.S. Government Printing Office, 1983.

Powell, Arthur G., Eleanor Farrar, and David K. Cohen. *The Shopping Mall High School*. Boston: Houghton Mifflin, 1985.

Staff of the National Commission on Excellence in Education. *Meeting the Challenge: Recent Efforts to Improve Education Across the Nation.* Washington, DC: U.S. Department of Education, 1983.

Sizer, Theodore R. *Horace's Compromise: The Dilemma of the American High School.* Boston: Houghton Mifflin, 1984.

Task Force on Education for Economic Growth. *Action for Excellence.* Denver, CO: Education Commission of the States, 1983.

Warren, Donald, ed. *American Teachers: Histories of a Profession at Work.* New York: Macmillan, 1989.

12

American Society and Education in the 1990s

In the 1990s, American education experienced gradual rather than dramatic change. George Bush, the incumbent Republican president, was defeated for reelection in 1992 by the moderate liberal Democrat Bill Clinton, the governor of Arkansas. The decade was one of marked national prosperity, characterized by low rates of inflation, declining unemployment, and steady economic growth. Further, the large federal budget deficits of the preceding decade were reduced.

International and National Events

The 1990s was a decade of economic growth in the midst of challenging tensions both at home and abroad. Due to the media's vivid presentation, international and national events took center stage in the minds and hearts of Americans, including school administrators, teachers, parents, and students, generating discussion and questions about political and social issues and causing Americans to reevaluate core beliefs, attitudes, and values. At the decade's beginning, the cold war with the Soviet Union had ended. Indeed, the former USSR had imploded. The Russian Federation remained the largest and most powerful of the successor nations but was preoccupied with its own serious internal, political, and economic problems. The decade, however, was not free from international challenges. The Clinton administration still faced a recalcitrant Iraq, led by Saddam Hussein, who repeatedly challenged the biological weapons inspections required after the Gulf War. Foreign policy issues dealt with complex ethnonational issues as certain multiethnic states disintegrated in Africa and Eastern Europe. A serious involvement occurred in 1999 when the United States, as part of NATO, took military action in Kosovo to protect ethnic Albanians from "ethnic cleansing"—murder and forced deportations by the Serbs, the dominant group in former Yugoslavia. U.S. foreign policymakers had difficulty in framing appropriate responses to the rise of ethnonationalist tensions throughout the world, especially in Eastern Europe and Africa.

As with the Gulf War during the 1980s, U.S. and NATO use of military force in Kosovo had educational implications. Most directly, television as well as print media carried daily coverage of the events in Kosovo. Students could see the real-life, dramatic plight of ethnic Albanian refugees fleeing Kosovo and seeking refuge in neighboring countries. They could see the effects of NATO's bombs on cities and military sites in Yugoslavia. These events had to be interpreted against the background of two or more decades of Holocaust studies in which students learned about the inhumanity of the Nazi genocide against Jews, Gypsies, and others during World War II.

There was also the larger educational context of multiculturalism that aimed to educate students to have understanding, appreciation, and respect for people of other races and ethnicities. As in most foreign policy issues, there were conflicting perspectives. Did the United States have a humanitarian obligation to end the ethnic violence being perpetrated against ethnic Albanians in Kosovo? Was it really of vital interest to the United States to be involved in the Balkans? Then, there was the "ends-means" moral issue—did the end of aiding the ethnic Albanians justify the use of military force against the Serbs?

At home, during President Clinton's second term, the administration weathered several scandals, including President and Mrs. Clinton's involvement in Whitewater, a resort-development venture in Arkansas, and President Clinton's improper relationship with Monica Lewinsky, a White House intern. The long-running Whitewater investigation focused on alleged banking irregularities in funding the resort. After exhaustive investigations by an independent counsel, Kenneth Starr, charges against President and Mrs. Clinton were not substantiated. In February 1998, President Clinton's improper relationship with Monica Lewinsky surfaced as a result of his earlier testimony about his involvement with Ms. Lewinsky, given in the Paula Jones case (a case that involved alleged sexual harrassment). The original Starr inquiry was then broadened to include charges that the president had lied under oath in his testimony in the Jones case. The Clinton-Lewinsky affair was doggedly pursued by Starr; in August 1998, the president admitted to an improper relationship with Lewinsky. Clinton was impeached by the House of Representatives in December, 1998, on charges of perjury and obstruction of justice. The Senate, however, acquitted President Clinton of these charges in early 1999.

While the events relating to the Monica Lewinsky affair are likely to become a footnote in future histories of the republic, the episode was not only unflattering but was disturbing in that it showed a general lack of responsibility—recklessness on the part of the president and an overzealousness on the part of the independent counsel. Further, it revealed a media that sought to titillate rather than to inform and educate the public. Though these events did not have a direct bearing on education, they raised issues about the role of the media in a democratic society, an individual's right to privacy, and the general moral state of the nation. Articles and commentary appeared on how students, especially in elementary schools, should be educated about media coverage of the events related to the scandals involving the president. Educators found themselves addressing moral issues related to responsibility, namely, the need to tell the truth, to take responsibility, and to accept the consequences for one's actions.

Educational Issues

In the 1990s, some important developments and trends from the previous decade continued to have an impact on education. Building on the national goals adopted in 1990 during the Bush administration, Congress, with the encouragement of the Clinton administration, passed the Goals 2000: Educate America Act, in 1994. (See chapter 11 for a discussion of Goals 2000.) The 1994 act reaffirmed the national goals of the 1990s, which sought to: increase children's school readiness, increase high school students' completion rate, provide evidence of demonstrated competency at specified grade levels in basic skills and subjects, improve mathematics and science education, increase adult literacy and on-the-job competency, and maintain safe schools, free of alcohol and drugs. The 1994 act added the goals of improving the professional skills of teachers and promoting parental partnerships in the education of their children.[1]

There were still concerns that U.S. students in comparison with those from other industrialized nations were deficient in mathematics and science. The issue of U.S. deficiencies surfaced at a National Educational Summit held in March 1996. Attended by business, government, and educational leaders, the summit addressed U.S. students' academic deficiencies in mathematics and science in comparison with those from other industrialized countries. Calling for improved academic achievement, the summit recommended that state and local dis-

President Clinton at a ceremony for Goals 2000 on March 31, 1994, in San Diego, California. President Clinton is seated; standing behind the president is Secretary of Education Richard Riley; to Secretary Riley's right is Mrs. Clinton and Vice President Al Gore. (Courtesy of the White House.)

tricts establish specific standards for basic academic subjects, especially in English, science, and mathematics.

President Clinton, known as an educational reformer in Arkansas, and his secretary of education, Richard Riley, sought to make education an important part of the administration's agenda. The question of national standards remained from the previous Bush administration. Clinton favored national standards but on a voluntary basis. The U.S. Department of Education developed voluntary national standards in reading (for fourth graders) and in mathematics (for eighth graders). The tests, based on content frameworks developed for the National Assessment of Educational Progress (NAEP), were projected to be ready for use in states and local school districts in 1999. While the Department of Education would develop these standards to assess students' academic progress, states and local districts, while encouraged to adopt them, were to do so on a voluntary basis.

Though the academic deficits remained an issue of concern, there appeared to be an improvement of U.S. students' academic performance in mathematics in the 1990s. Findings from the NAEP 1996 assessment of students in grades four, eight, and twelve in mathematics indicated some improvement in performance over the 1990 and 1992 assessments.

When he addressed the summit, President Clinton called for assessment of academic competency through standardized state competency testing in basic academic subjects. Critics of the summit argued that comparisons of U.S. students' academic achievement with those of other countries rested on invalid criteria. They also argued that the summit's focus was too limited and wanted consideration of broader issues, including school choice.

Though the use of vouchers to provide public support for those who wished to attend private schools remained an issue in the states, it subsided at the federal level, lacking support of the Clinton administration. There were, however, movements to provide government-supported parental choice in selecting their children's public school. (See, for example, the discussion on charter schools later in this chapter.) The Clinton administration encouraged charter schools and supported the right of parents to choose the public school of their choice. It should be noted that unlike the previous Bush administration, Clinton supported the right to choose public schools but did not extend this right to private schools.

During the 1990s, there was large-scale development of computer and electronic information.[2] Computers were found in elementary and secondary schools and colleges and universities throughout the country. Electronic data retrieval, the Internet, and computer-assisted instruction marked a technological revolution in education. While beginning teachers were being prepared to use the new computer-driven technology in their preservice training programs, states and school districts were making concerted efforts at inservicing teachers to use the new technology. In his State of the Union Message to Congress on January 23, 1996, President Clinton recommended an educational initiative to bring the new electronic technology into American schools. He proposed that every classroom be connected to the information superhighway by the year 2000.

In the 1990s there were several tragic incidents of pupils, armed with weapons, shooting and killing their classmates. These attacks focused attention on the problem of violence in the schools and how to prevent it. Many school districts inaugurated what were called "no tolerance" programs which prohibited students from bringing any kind of weapon on school property. Violence prevention programs were also established in many schools. Drug and alcohol abuse continued to be a serious problem for young people throughout the country.

Throughout the decade, higher education costs for tuition, fees, and room and board continued to increase steadily at both public and private colleges and universities. Escalating costs were placing severe financial strains on families as they sought to finance a higher education for their children. To control rising expenditures, many colleges and universities used strategic planning, which often involved program restructuring and consolidation. The high cost of higher education was growing into a national concern. President Clinton called for expanding work-study programs, which provide stipends for students who work as aides in various capacities at colleges and universities. He also proposed providing $1,000 merit scholarships for the top 5 percent of high school graduates and making $10,000 of college tuition tax deductible on a yearly basis. Clinton reiterated his consistent argument for the need to provide federal assistance in developing retraining programs for unemployed and underemployed persons through vouchers to community colleges.

While Bill Clinton, a Democrat, won two terms as president, 1992 and 1996, Congress was controlled by Republicans. The traditional party differences of earlier decades manifested themselves in education. Republicans tended to prefer a limited federal role, were critical of what they regarded as "political correctness," and wanted limitations placed on affirmative action in higher education.[3] Democrats emphasized education as a key issue. The Democrats favored tax credits, individual retirement accounts, and tax deductions for a family's expenditures for higher education. They also favored support of national-service programs.[4] The two major parties continued to differ on "school choice" and using vouchers to provide parents with public funds for their children to attend their school of choice. While Republicans tended to support vouchers for both public and private schools, Democrats generally tended to restrict their use to public schools. Although there were proposals in Congress to reduce federal spending for education, the reductions were slight in the 1990s. For example, the total allocation for education was $25,323 billion in 1996, compared with $26,800 billion in 1995, a reduction of less than 6 percent.

President Clinton, in his 1997 State of the Union Message to Congress on February 4, "A Call to Action," made education the highest priority in his second term. Clinton presented a series of educational recommendations that included: continuing the "America reads initiative" of tutorial programs to improve children's reading scores so that "every eight-year-old" is able to read; giving public schools free access to the Internet to ensure that "every 12-year-old" is able to "log on . . ."; developing and adopting national standards for elementary and junior high school students; developing national tests to ensure fourth and eighth graders' achievement in mathematics and reading; establishing standards for teachers based on the National Board for Professional Teaching Standards so that 100,000 teachers can seek certification as "master teachers"; providing continued support to establish 3,000 charter schools; providing continued support for early-childhood education programs, especially expanding Head Start to 1,000,000 children by the year 2002; emphasizing character education to improve citizenship skills and curb violence and drug abuse; allocating $5 billion for new school construction; allowing tax deduction credits for college tuition of up to $10,000 per year, to enable every eighteen-year-old to attend college; continuing the expansion of worker training programs. Seeking to avoid charges of federal intrusion into state and local educational prerogatives, Clinton argued that the proposed standards were to be adopted and implemented by states rather than by the federal governments. Presented within a balanced budget framework for 1998, President Clinton's education proposals would cost $51 billion, a 20 percent increase over the current budget and the largest education-funding package in U.S. history.

In the late 1990s, Congress essentially continued the existing education programs and slightly increased federal funding. While only certain aspects of Clinton's program passed, educational reform and improvement remained important national agenda items.

Trends in School Organization and Instruction

The twentieth century's last decade saw sustained but moderate patterns of growth for American education. A total of 66.1 million students were enrolled in schools and colleges. Four million persons were employed as elementary and secondary teachers and as college and university faculty. An additional 4.4 million persons worked as administrators and professional staff and support persons. In 1995, the decade's midpoint, the average salary for teachers was $37,846.

Between 1985 and 1996, public elementary and secondary school enrollments had increased by 16 percent. Reversing the declining enrollments of the 1970s, the greatest growth in the school population was in elementary schools where enrollment rose 21 percent over the same period, from twenty-seven million to a record high of 32.8 million in 1996. After declining by 8 percent from 1985 to 1990, secondary school enrollments increased by 15 percent as of 1996, a net increase of 5 percent. Given the higher elementary school enrollments, secondary enrollments are projected to increase in the twenty-first century's first decade. Private school enrollments also increased, but at a slower pace than those in public schools, from 5.6 million in 1985 to 5.8 million in 1996. Higher education enrollments remained relatively steady at approximately 14.5 million.[5]

In the 1990s, several trends such as the effective schools and character education movements continued from the 1980s. The effective schools approach had been stimulated by *A Nation at Risk* and other national reports of the 1980s. This approach became highly important in the field of school administration. Focusing on the building principal, an effective school was determined to be one in which: (1) the principal was an educational leader concerned with improving curriculum and instruction; (2) administrators and teachers held high academic expectations of students; (3) teachers worked collaboratively as a team to improve learning; (4) rules and regulations were clear and fairly administered.

Along with the effective schools approach, there was a tendency toward decentralization and site-based management. The assumption behind site-based management was that if administrators and teachers in a particular school were given even more control over curriculum, instruction, and budgeting, they would feel a greater sense of ownership in the educational program. It was further assumed that this greater local initiative would result in the more effective delivery of education.

In the 1990s, administrators, especially in urban districts, faced a school facilities problem. The "brick and mortar" period of school construction of the late 1950s and 1960s had resulted in new schools being built in the growing suburbs. Three decades later, schools in many districts were deteriorating and overcrowded. School renovation and construction again became a key issue as the twentieth century came to its end.

During the 1990s, educational programs were developed for character or moral education. The need for such programs came from diverse sources, however. The Christian right believed that secular humanism had eroded traditional values. Perennialist critics, such as William Bennett, former education secretary under Reagan and co-founder of Empower America, argued for a return to the Aristotelian principle of living a virtuous life and to the enduring values of Western civilization. Others, fearing the increase of violence in the schools, wanted programs that featured peaceful conflict resolution.

Charter Schools

While they are indeed public schools, charter schools provide an alternative to the public schools that have been established and maintained conventionally by local school districts. In the charter school process, states enact legislation that allowed local districts the option to authorize charters, special agreements, often to teachers, to establish a school that offers an innovative program. Charter schools exhibit the following characteristics: (1) the state authorizes organizations to establish and operate charter schools and issues a waiver freeing them from many regulations governing public schools; (2) the school is "public," that is, nonsectarian and supported by public funds; (3) the school, through its charter, is responsible for students' academic progress; (4) the school is one of choice for educators and parents; however, the choice is in the public rather than the private sector.[6]

The charter school movement experienced continued growth in 1990s as an alternative form of public school organization. The charter school concept gained its initial impetus in Minneapolis and St. Paul, Minnesota, where, in 1985, Governor Rudy Perpich proposed expanding public school choice. By the mid-1990s, twenty-eight states, the District of Columbia, and Puerto Rico had enacted charter school legislation, permitting local school districts to issue charters to establish schools with innovative programs. As of 1996, approximately 80,000 students attended 500 charter schools, most of which were elementary schools. Sixty percent of these schools were small, with enrollments of less than 200 students.

Constructivism and Portfolio Assessment

In curriculum and instruction, the 1990s saw the continued popularity of constructivism, especially in elementary schools. Constructivism, emphasizing collaborative group learning, incorporates elements of the theories of John Dewey and Jean Piaget as well as aspects of social constructionism from modern psychology. Focusing on problem solving rather than information transmission, students are to create, or construct, their own knowledge base from direct interaction with sources in the environment from which knowledge arises. Learners, through social interaction, actively create and share meaning from their individual and group constructions of reality. Along with the constructivist method, the whole language approach to reading and "hands-on" process learning remained popular teaching methods in elementary schools.

The use of portfolios, an ongoing, cumulative record of a student's progress, was an important and popular innovation in curriculum, instruction, and assessment among educators, especially elementary and middle school administrators and teachers and teacher educators. A portfolio is essentially a purposeful collection of a student's work, called "pieces," that pupils self-select as representative samples of their academic efforts, achievement, and progress in a range of areas. It is designed to be a cumulative and formative record of a student's progress, showing both the content and the process of learning. In classrooms using portfolios, the students maintain their own records, in either books or files, with the guidance of teachers. Students, with teacher guidance, collect samples of their work and self-evaluate their long-term progress. Parents, students, and teachers can refer to these collections of student work to assess a student's own learning goals and academic progress. Among the benefits derived from using portfolios are: (1) students learn how to set their own educational goals and how to self-assess their progress; (2) teachers gain a larger and more varied perspective on each student's areas of strength and needed improvement in instruction; (3) parents, the student, and teachers have a continuous record of the student's academic progress.

Indeed, there was a national movement among educators for the use of portfolios throughout the curriculum and at all levels of education. Portfolios were being used at a wide range of sites: inner-city and suburban schools, state education departments, and in higher education and professional education programs, especially in teacher education programs.[7] As with many such innovations in the recent past, such as team teaching and informal education, the use of portfolios generated a considerable, often uncritical enthusiasm among educators. Many educators called the use of portfolios an "authentic" form of continuing assessment that linked evaluation directly with classroom instruction.

The popularity of portfolios, in part, grew out of the constructivist movement in education, in which students, through collaborative learning, created their own knowledge by their interactions with the environment. Since constructivist-based curriculum and instruction used different and multiple kinds of learning, it followed that assessment, too, should reflect this educational variety. Also, part of the movement to portfolios was a reaction, on the part of some parents and teachers, against what they regarded as the excessive use and reliance on standardized, norm-referenced, tests. Some critics argued that the evaluation requirements of federal programs and state-mandated competency testing overemphasized the use of standardized, norm-referenced tests as indicators of academic achievement. Critics of standardized testing argued that such tests provided only a one-time snapshot of a student's academic achievement, usually in factual recall, rather than in a wide range of higher level critical-thinking and problem-solving skills. Further, critics contended that standardized testing resulted in student ranking in which those with low test scores often suffered from a loss of self-esteem. Portfolios and other forms of "authentic" assessment provided a means of nonranked self-assessment that gave students a sense of ownership and pride in their own work. For example, Edward White, a proponent of portfolio assessment, argues that portfolios provide a view of student learning that is "active, engaged, and dynamic," in contrast to currently used passive modes of assessment. He argues that the use of portfolios can integrate teaching, learning, and assessment.[8]

At the same time that many elementary teachers and teacher educators were enthusiastically introducing portfolios into instruction, there was a parallel and conflicting movement toward using more standardized tests to measure student academic achievement. Since the late 1980s, there was an effort by both the Bush (Republican) and the Clinton (Democrat) administrations to develop some kind of national standardized testing. Further, there was a decided trend in most of the states to require some kind of standardized testing to measure student competency in basic academic skills at given grade levels. The two movements were going on simultaneously during the 1990s.

Gene Maeroff, for example, takes a realistic and occasionally critical view of the movement to devise and implement alternative assessment strategies. Although recognizing the need for alternatives to the reliance on standardized tests, he raises some cautionary reservations about portfolios and other alternatives. He notes that the alternative assessment approach has grown into a national movement, with forty states having alternative assessment plans. The major problem, he notes, is devising alternative assessment methods that can provide useful information while avoiding the difficulties associated with standardized, norm-referenced tests. Pointing to the need to make portfolio and other forms of alternative assessment less subjective, Maeroff stated that there are "no quick and easy ways to rate large numbers of performance based tasks or portfolios. . . ."[9]

While it is too early to determine the historical significance of the constructivist and portfolio assessment movements in education, they reveal an often repeated sequence of events that occurred earlier in American education. The proponents of constructivism and portfolios are highly and enthusiastically committed to introducing these approaches in the schools. Undoubtedly these new curricular, instructional, and assessment innovations will have an effect on education.

Persistent Educational Issues

Many of the educational issues that developed in the late 1970s and 1980s continued into the 1990s. This section examines three of these persistent, and somewhat related, issues: multiculturalism, elimination of sexism, and bilingual education.[10]

Multiculturalism

Since the 1960s, there was a marked trend in American education to multiculturalism. This emphasis on celebrating and encouraging diversity and pluralism reversed the long-standing monocultural emphasis in American public education. Historically, the early public or common schools, established throughout the country in the nineteenth century, deliberately inculcated a sense of American national identity. Public schools "Americanized" immigrant children into a common monocultural mold that was generally white, Anglo-Saxon, and

Protestant in cultural orientation. Called "common schools," public schools sought to create, by educational means, a common culture. The common culture that was imposed, however, was based on that of the dominant group.[11] Some groups, such as Roman Catholics, created an alternative private school system, which inculcated Roman Catholic religious doctrines and often the cultural background of the particular ethnic composition of the congregation. It was not until the mid-1950s that the traditional assimilationist public school orientation was challenged by those wanting multiculturalism. The enactment of the Bilingual Education Act in 1968 and the Supreme Court decision in *Lau v. Nichols*, in 1974, led to the establishment of bilingual education programs. There was also a concerted effort to eliminate stereotypic generalizations about the education of African Americans. Social psychologist Claude Steele developed the concept of "stigma," which he defined as "the endemic devaluation" that African Americans experience in American society, contributing to the educational problems they faced.[12] Steele argued that the elements of "black life and culture—art, literature, political and social perspective, music"—be included in the schools' "mainstream curriculum" and "not consigned to special days, weeks, or even months of the year, or to special-topic courses and programs aimed essentially at blacks."[13]

Debates, called the "culture wars," were waged in the late 1980s and 1990s over the degree to which American education either should build a sense of cultural commonality or should emphasize racial, ethnic, and other forms of cultural pluralism. The culture wars were a highly rhetorical struggle, fought primarily by academics in higher education, who held different ideological perspectives. Those who saw education as promoting a shared culture argued that a culturally diverse nation, such as the United States, needed a common cultural core to provide a sense of national unity and identity. Proponents of a cultural core curriculum, such as E. D. Hirsch, Allan Bloom, Arthur M. Schlesinger Jr., and others, feared that America's cultural commonality was being eroded and needed restoration. They attributed the decline of cultural commonality to a declining historical and political public literacy and to a deliberate disuniting of the strands of American cultural identity by extreme forms of multiculturalism.

Those promoting multiculturalism argued that the United States was a nation of great cultural diversity in race, ethnicity, religion, and lifestyles. For them, the schools should recognize and encourage cultural diversity. They argued that the public school curriculum should not transmit a monocultural version of American cultural identity as it did in its assimilationist past but rather should encourage racial, religious, gender, and ethnic pluralism.

James D. Hunter, in *Culture Wars*, described the ideological contest as a struggle over defining America's national identity and meaning.[14] Although race and ethnicity were key points of conflict in the culture wars, the debates covered a wide range of divergent views about religion, the family, and sexuality. The culture wars, waged primarily on college and university campuses, ranged over a number of issues such as: (1) the interpretation of American history; (2) the existence of a central, consensus style of American history or the existence of diverse parallel histories, each particular to a different racial, ethnic, or religious group; (3) the interpretation of the American past and culture that schools should emphasize in the curriculum.

The debates centered on the issue of whether education should promote a common national character and consensus or encourage multicultural diversity.[15] For example, Ronald Takaki, in *A Different Mirror: A History of Multicultural America*, a multiculturalist historian, argued that American history should be comparatively interpreted from multiple cultural, racial, and ethnic perspectives so that it will be a more accurate and authentic rendition of the nation's past. Takaki contended that the dominant white group imposed its culture and values, often ruthlessly, upon dominated minority groups.[16]

In contrast, Arthur M. Schlesinger Jr., in *The Disuniting of America*, contended that certain multiculturalist interpretations were eroding a shared American national identity. Rather than stressing a common heritage that focuses on the individual as a participant in a shared culture, multiculturalism, using "ethnic and racial criteria" has fragmented a "unifying American identity."[17] The conflict, according to Schlesinger, arose from the use of ethnic and racial categories in public schools. The historic public school mission of creating a sense of American cultural identity had been jeopardized by a "cult of ethnicity" bent on promoting ethnic and racial separatism.[18] Schlesinger argued that public schools can be both assimilationist and pluralist by conveying a sense of the past, which recognizes that while the United States is culturally diverse, it shares a common cultural heritage.

Toni Massaro, in *Constitutional Literacy: A Core Curriculum for a Multicultural Nation*, proposed a moderate position on multicultural education that avoided an either/or stance. Massaro proposed constructing a national core curriculum around the theme of the U.S. Constitution and cases related to its interpretation, especially those dealing with rights and due process. Her rationale assumed: (1) the existence of an American *paideia* (intellectual excellence and validity) that brings individuals into cultural understanding and participation; (2) that schools are a powerful force of cultural transmission and formation; (3) that a curricular core that emphasizes constitutional literacy can revitalize schooling's cultural mission; (4) that such a constitutional curricular core can accommodate both political and procedural commonalities and cultural conflicts.[19]

Arguing for a national core curriculum, Massaro believes that such a curriculum can embrace both the commonality that unites Americans as well as the diversity that enriches their society. Further, the U.S. Constitution, its rights and processes, will provide the necessary framework upon which to construct the curricular core, which can be the springboard for educating a constitutionally literate populace.[20] She believes that a core curriculum featuring "constitutional literacy" will not only encourage discussion of Americans' religious, racial, ethnic, gender, class, and other differences but will cultivate a "common sense" of mutuality.[21]

The religious issues embedded in the cultural debates of the 1980s and 1990s were deep but different from those of the 1940s and 1950s when Roman Catholics sought to share in federal aid to education. (See chapter 2 for the debates about federal aid in the late 1940s.) In the 1980s and 1990s, the religious-based issues were related to core cultural values. A new coalition called the "religious right" had become increasingly active in local, state, and national politics. It was concerned with prayer, Bible reading, and prayer clubs in public schools and with the moral content of textbooks as well as "freedom of educational choice" by the public funding of private schools through vouchers. Protestant fundamentalists as well as some Catholic conservatives and Orthodox Jews alleged that public schools were encouraging secular humanism in the curriculum. Along with the traditional Catholic parochial schools, a new Christian school system, rooted in Evangelical Protestantism, became the fastest growing sector in private education. For others, home schooling became an alternative to public schools.

The rhetoric of the culture wars was most strident in higher education, where the issues came to focus on the general education core in undergraduate programs, especially in humanities courses, such as history and literature. Multiculturalists found existing core requirements to be dominated by Eurocentric works written by white males. According to the multiculturalist arguments, the dominance of Eurocentrism meant that only a very small part of human experience was studied. Further, this selected part of the heritage was contaminated by racism, sexism, classism, and imperialism. Multicultural critics argued that the core curriculum should incorporate the works of Asian and African authors, women, and hitherto unrepresented minorities.[22] Defenders of the existing core, oriented on Western civilization, argued that it introduced students to the Western cultural heritage that was at the foundation of American culture—the ideas of Plato, Aristotle, Aquinas, Erasmus, Hegel, Marx, and Freud. Defenders of the existing core curriculum claimed that they were being subject to a new criterion of "political correctness." Unless ideas met the multiculturalist test, they were to be purged from the curriculum.

Gender Issues

Along with multiculturalism, gender issues surfaced. Many facets of society, including education, made an effort to integrate the feminist perspective and respect women's desires to have the same opportunities and rewards as men. In the 1990s, there was a continued effort to identify and eliminate sexism, particularly bias and discrimination against women.[23]

Sexism has had a long history, probably even a prehistory, in which human roles were gender specific, with women being assigned those held to be inferior. The cultural pattern historically has been patriarchal (male dominated), with older males, the group elders, setting and reinforcing the rules and rituals that govern social life. The cultural and social history of sexism created a kind of antecedent role determination for women. Girls were expected to become wives and mothers, roles that included performing tasks in the nonpublic environment, which met the needs of the family—supporting and sustaining husbands, caring for and nurturing children, cooking, cleaning, and other specific, culturally determined tasks. While male roles were also assigned in prehistory and history, they came to have a greater multiplicity outside the home. Being a husband and father, for example, did not preclude being a hunter, warrior, farmer, priest, seer, poet, or public leader.

The history of education provides many examples of the exclusion of women from formal schooling. There were, of course, exceptions, such as the convent schools during the Middle Ages. It was the Protestant Reformation, particularly in Calvinist and Lutheran religions in Europe, that encouraged the admission of girls to primary schools. However, women's education was restricted to the lower grades of primary schooling. They generally were excluded from secondary and higher schools until the mid-nineteenth century.

Historically determined sex- or gender-based roles operated to create a kind of social-cultural dualism or rigid bifurcation in male-female socialization patterns. Based on gender-determined dualism, males were to be active, independent, and aggressive; females were to be passive, dependent, and nonassertively receptive. Expressed in the cliché, "men don't cry," boys were taught to control, hide, or suppress their emotions and feelings, while the expression of emotions or feelings by girls was regarded as appropriate behavior. Conformity to the culturally inherited sex roles has impacted both males and females psychologically and socially. Deviations from predetermined roles have been punished throughout history. Despite erosion of gender-based roles, even the more technologically developed, modern societies still have large cultural residues that sanction gender-biased roles.

The industrial revolution and resulting technological society that followed in its wake generated specialization that transferred male roles from the more traditional hunter, warrior, farmer, and priest to technician, scientist, engineer, and other career specialties. While industrialization brought about some slight modification in women's role possibilities, women's roles remained those of wife and mother. By mid-nineteenth century, for example, women could become elementary school teachers, as occurred in the feminization of the common school in the United States, or they could become nurses—two roles based on caring and nurturing. It was not until the very late nineteenth and twentieth centuries that more career options became open to women.

Based on historically determined antecedent role definitions, sexism is perpetuated by the socialization patterns that ascribe male-female roles. Important in these patterns are education and schooling and the alternatives they provide for women. Educational institutions have perpetuated and transmitted "cultural stereotyped images of male and female in academic, career, and family roles." Throughout the world, women are "educated less seriously, less expensively, and to a more limited extent than men." Through their schooling, children "learn that boys are worth more and that the characteristics associated with masculinity are more valuable and more socially desirable than those associated with femininity."[24]

In the United States and in other Western countries, sexual discrimination and harassment violate the law. For example, Title IX of the Education Amendments of 1972, enacted by the U.S. Congress, states that "No person shall, on the basis of sex, be excluded from participation in, be denied the benefits of, or be subjected to discrimination, under any education program or activity, receiving federal financial assistance. . . ."[25] Title IX prohibits discrimination on the basis of sex in admissions to public vocational schools and discrimination on the basis of sex in all school programs and activities. This includes the prohibition of sex bias in course offerings, appraisal and counseling materials, and extracurricular and athletic programs.

In addition to curricular and programmatic discrimination based on sex is the issue of sexual harassment, which refers to the "action of an individual, in a position to control or influence another's job, career, or grade, who uses his or her power to gain sexual favors or punish the refusal of such favors. Sexual harassment on the job or in the classroom varies from inappropriate sexual innuendo to coerced sexual relations."[26] While legal protection against sexual discrimination and harassment is a positive action to combat sexism in employment and education, it does not ensure that such actions have ceased.

In other countries, girls and women suffer what can be called human rights violations. There are numerous examples of these violations: rape is often used as an instrument of military subjugation and ethnic cleansing, such as against Muslim women in Bosnia and ethnic Albanian women in Kosovo; in Southeast Asia, girls from economically disadvantaged families are sold for prostitution; female circumcision is practiced among certain tribes in Africa; in India, there are cases of brides being killed over infractions of dowry disputes; throughout the world, especially in less technologically developed third world countries, girls have severely limited opportunities to attend school, especially if they live in rural areas.

Changes in curriculum reflect the trend to eliminate gender bias in education. The recent history of American education, especially the last decades of the twentieth century, shows determined efforts to eliminate sexual bias and stereotyping from the curriculum.[27] Contemporary curriculum revision has worked to eliminate sexist language in education. Historically, in the United States as well as in other Western countries, the majority of girls completed secondary schooling with fewer courses in mathematics than boys. This lack of preparation in mathematics acted as a kind of curricular sorting or screening, which limited women's access to careers that required a mathematical foundation, such as science, technology, and engineering. Now, many states, however, require high school students to take at least three years of mathematics and science, especially if they want to attend college. These changes in curriculum requirements for high school graduation have evened the academic playing field.

Historically, the contents of school textbooks, especially primers used in reading, have contained gender biased language and have contributed to sexual stereotyping by portraying men and women in stereotypic roles. Content analyses of textbooks used in American elementary, secondary, and higher education, including preservice teacher education, showed that with the exception of textbooks written for home economics and domestic science courses, women were largely absent from textbook pages. When textbooks did include women, they tended to convey and reinforce socially generated images of male and female roles—"men work and women mother; boys climb and girls cry."[28] In recent years, many leading publishing companies have responded to the problem of biased language and sexual stereotyping by issuing guidelines to authors and editors to help them avoid using sexist language and biased character and role portrayals.

Like curricular reform and textbook revision, teacher education programs, in recent decades, have included standards that promote a multicultural approach and that eliminate sexism. Historically, teachers' attitudes, expectations, and interactions with students unconsciously promoted gender bias. Generally, boys received more classroom attention. In addition, boys' achievement, especially in mathematics and science, was encouraged, while that of girls, even if they demonstrated a special aptitude in these areas, was not encouraged.[29] Raising teacher consciousness about gender bias and other forms of sexual discrimination has been part of a general effort of teacher education programs to make American schooling more inclusive and equitable.

Bilingual Education Controversies

Since the 1970s, bilingual education programs have been established in schools throughout the country, especially in states and most often in large cities with large populations of students whose first language was other than English. Typically, the largest language group enrolled in bilingual programs has been Spanish-speaking, but the programs serve many other language groups as well.

The 1990s saw controversy over bilingual education programs. Although some reactions to the controversy were at the national level, most of the debate took place at state and local levels. The 1990s' debates were not new to bilingual education, which often had been at the center of a controversy that focused on the continuation of bilingual education programs. While there were educational questions involved in bilingual education, the greatest issues were ideological and political. A long-standing educational issue was, should bilingual programs be for transitional or maintenance purposes? Proponents of transitional programs contended that instruction in both languages, the student's first language and English, should take place over a delimited time frame while students learn English. When the student reaches a level of English language proficiency that enables effective learning, the use of the non-English language as the medium of instruction should be phased out slowly.

Proponents of maintenance programs, often allied with multiculturalists, argued that bilingual programs should be continuous throughout the educational experience for students whose first language is one other than English. They contended that there is an important and enriched cultural dimension in knowing and using two languages. They further argued that those proficient in several languages would be better prepared for the interdependent global economy. Some proponents pointed out that there is an economic advantage to knowing two languages. For example, a study at the University of Miami suggests that facility in two languages, Spanish and English, positively affects family income. Using 1990's census statistics, this study suggests that Hispanic families who spoke only Spanish had an average income of $18,000; families who spoke only English earned $32,000; and those who spoke both Spanish and English, $50,378.[30] Opponents reject these claims, countering that maintenance programs encourage reliance on the non-English language and therefore retard or delay effective participation in a society where proficiency in standard English is needed for employment, socioeconomic mobility, and effective political participation.

Even more emotionally situated are the ideological and political issues surrounding bilingual education. On a comparative basis, it might be noted that, especially in education, language issues throughout the world tend to be impacted by ideological and political factors as is the case in Canada, where language issues create political tensions between those who speak English and those who speak French. In the United States the issue centers on how the national past is interpreted and how the nation is defined. Opponents of bilingual education tend to value a strong national cultural core that rests on the English language. They argue that immigrant groups in the past successfully learned English and as a result were able to move upward educationally, socially, economically, and politically. Based on this interpretation of the American educational history, they assert that recent immigrants should follow the historical example of those in the past. Those who favor bilingual programs contend that the United States, a culturally pluralistic rather than monocultural society, is comprised of many language as well as racial and ethnic groups. For them, the nation's educational history needs to be reinterpreted to include the contributions of groups in addition to the dominant English-speaking one. Also, they argue that the nation's character has not been permanently defined but remains in an ongoing process of redefinition. A more accurate definition of the American past and character, they assert, will be a multilingual and multicultural one.

In the 1990s, issues related to bilingual education that were somewhat latent in earlier decades surfaced in some states and local school districts where there were political movements that advocated declaring English as the official language. The debate over continuing bilingual programs was most intense in California, a state with large enrollments in bilingual programs. In 1997, approximately 1.3 million of California's five million students were participating in some kind of bilingual education program.[31] California, which permits voter-initiated referenda, passed a ballot initiative in 1997, eliminating bilingual education in public schools. The effects of this action on education in California remain to be seen. There is also the possibility that opponents of bilingual education may launch similar movements in other states in the future.

At the local district level, the use of Ebonics created a controversy in Oakland, California. The Oakland Board of Education, in 1996, recognized Ebonics, a form of black English, as a language to be used in instruction. The decision, which was debated in Oakland, also stimulated national comments. Proponents claimed that Ebonics, a genuine language used in the local community, should be used in the schools. Opponents questioned the board's decision, claiming that it was a local dialect whose use would impede economic success. On January 15, 1997, the board revised its policy, removing statements that suggested that some students would be taught in Ebonics rather than standard English.

Violence and Schools

Incidences of school violence had been increasing throughout the 1970s and 1980s. By the 1990s, violence near and in schools had become a national concern. Despite extensive commentary from television and other media newspersons and analysis by academic experts, the explanations of the cause of school violence and prescriptions on how to end it were couched by uncertainty. Some analysts attributed the increase in violence to the absence of effective gun controls in the United States. For example, a *Time* magazine article, "Childhood's End," condemning America's "gun culture," compared it to a cancer that had "metastasized" among the young, who believe that possessing a gun, a weapon of "impulse and rough justice," was a "rite of passage."[32] Other commentators saw the epidemic of violence as being stimulated by motion pictures, videos, and recordings that featured violence. Still others claimed it was a product of weak parental supervision and indifference to children. In dealing with such a contemporary and serious situation, it is difficult to provide distanced historical commentary. There is, however, one historically generated generalization that is applicable: schools are not disconnected but are part of society. As social institutions, schools will reflect the malaise and disorders present in the larger society as well as its positive achievements. Alex Molnar, commenting on school violence, said, "Our world is awash in violence. And no one is suffering more than our children." Some psychologists believe affected children are afflicted by a "post-traumatic stress disorder." Some sociologists refer to a "lost generation" of children growing up in fear for their lives.[33]

Gang Violence

Youth gangs, while not a new phenomenon in the sociology and history of American education, became so pervasive in the 1980s and 1990s that they tended to threaten the safety of neighborhoods and their schools. Although teen gangs were found throughout the country, most reported incidents of gang-related violence occurred in large cities, such as New York, Detroit, Boston, Atlanta, Los Angeles and Chicago. In Los Angeles County, for example, police sources estimated that some six hundred teen gangs, involving some 70,000 young people, were operative. In 1990, Los Angeles police records indicated that gangs were responsible for 374 murders.[34] Although the highest incidence of gang activity still occurred in large urban areas, gangs and gang-related and other kinds of violence were occurring in America's suburbs, small towns, and rural areas.

Historically, large cities have been the location of some type of gang, which was typically ethnically or racially based. Attracting alienated or disadvantaged youth, gangs formed to defend a group's turf, or "neighborhood," from outsiders, particularly members of other racial or ethnic groups. Gang violence in the 1980s and 1990s became increasingly menacing because of gang members' use of deadly weapons such as guns and rifles. According to commentators on urban America, the congruence of the teen gang and the easy availability of guns represented a deadly mixture for society and schools.[35] Teenage gang violence has taken the form of deliberate shootouts or gunfights between rival gang members or as random violence—"drive-by" shootings, where gang members cruise in cars, randomly firing at victims in rival territory. In some cases, the activities of teen gangs have been tied to the lucrative drug trade and have been identified as a link between the "drug" and "gun" cultures.

The social and educational response to gang violence has resulted in measures that range from the presence of police and metal detectors in schools to the creation of educational programs that alert students, teachers, and parents to the threat of gangs and gang violence. Some schools require students to wear uniforms to avoid the display of gang colors. Some communities have established curfews for youth. Although these are immediate responses, some sociological and criminal justice commentators argue that underlying pervasive causative factors, such as drug abuse, endemic poverty, high unemployment among inner-city minority youth, and the easy availability of guns need to be addressed if the problem is to be solved.[36]

In-School Violence

Somewhat different from gang-related violence has been the occurrence of acts of violence by students against their classmates in schools. The 1990s were plagued by a series of incidents of violence in which students, armed with guns, attacked and killed other students and teachers in several of the country's public schools. Unlike the gang-related violence in larger cities, the pattern of in-school violence, perpetrated by students against their classmates, appeared to be taking place in the country's small towns and suburbs. For example, on February 2, 1996, a sixteen-year-old boy killed two students and a teacher in Moses Lake, Washington. In 1997, there were three incidents of in-school shootings: (1) on February 19, a sixteen-year-old boy killed a classmate and the school principal in Bethel, Arkansas; (2) on

October 1, a sixteen-year-old boy killed two students in Pearl, Mississippi; (3) on December 1, a fourteen-year-old boy killed three students in West Paducah, Kentucky. In 1998, there were two incidents of serious school violence: two boys, aged eleven and thirteen, killed four students and a teacher at a middle school in Jonesboro, Arkansas, and a fifteen-year-old boy killed two students in Springfield, Oregon.[37]

One of the most tragic of the cases of in-school violence occurred on April 20, 1999, at Columbine High School in Littleton, Colorado, where two male students, using guns and homemade bombs, killed twelve of their classmates and a teacher. The perpetrators of the crime then committed suicide. Despite efforts by experts to analyze the cause of the massacre of students at Columbine High School, the horror of the event exceeded psychological and sociological explanation. The two assailants, members of an apparently socially alienated small group called the "Trench Coat Mafia," went on a terror rampage. The events were carried by national television, which broadcast live coverage of the anguished faces of students and parents, rescue efforts by paramedics, and SWAT teams and police surrounding the school.[38]

Youth Hate Crimes

Both internationally and nationally, there has been an increase in the incidence and reporting of hate crimes—violence directed against people because of their race, religion, ethnicity, or sexual orientation. Often, teenagers and youth are the perpetrators of this kind of violence. Group hatred based on stereotyping has long been studied, and a large body of literature has been developed on the phenomenon. Indeed, the rise of and emphasis on multicultural education in the United States and other countries is part of an effort to develop intercultural understanding, reduce group conflict, and encourage peaceful conflict resolution.

Despite efforts at multiculturalism and intercultural education, the post–cold war era has witnessed a rising tide of nationalistic and ethnically based violence. In the former Yugoslavia, ethnic warfare and ethnic cleansing have been taking place since 1990. Religious identification remains the basis for much of the terrorism and violence in Northern Ireland. There is rising anti-Semitism and anti-Gypsy activity in Eastern Europe. In Western Europe, especially in the reunited Germany, there have been demonstrations and violence directed against guest workers, foreign students, and refugees. These incidents of hate crimes and violence have occurred despite the remorse over the Holocaust in which more than six million Jews perished as victims of the racist Nazi regime. The explosion of hate crimes makes the commitment of "Never Again" ring as hollow rhetoric.

The United States has not escaped the revival of hate crimes. Indeed, the United States, too, has a long history in which members of minority groups, particularly African Americans and Hispanics, were the victims of violence based on race and ethnic origin. In the 1990s, almost all minority groups reported an increase in "bias" crimes. In particular occurrences of violence increased against African Americans, Jews, Arab Americans, Asian Americans, and Hispanics. The number of violent acts against homosexuals also increased. For example, in New York City, the number of bias-related hate crimes is reported to have risen 80 percent between 1986 and 1990. What is most disturbing is that 70 percent of those arrested as perpetrators of hate crimes were under the age of nineteen.[39] Although some of these hate crimes can be attributed to neo-Nazi groups or to "skinheads," the majority of them are perpetrated by teenagers who are not affiliated with any particular group but who manifest their anger at outsiders or at those who appear to be different for some reason, such as race, ethnicity, religion, or sexual preference.

Bullying

While reports of gang and group hate violence are increasing, there also are signs of increasing incidents of bullying among young people. Bullying, a feature of school life that has long been recorded in reminiscences and novels, is the act of a larger individual "picking on" one who is weaker, smaller, or simply different in some way. Recent studies of bullying in the United States, Norway, Australia, Finland, Poland, and Israel, countries with similar school systems, found that one of every ten pupils has experienced bullying.[40]

In American popular folklore, there is a mythical element in the response to bullying that is found in popular culture. In the popular account often found in motion pictures, a child, almost always a boy, will be the victim of bullying until he gets the courage to fight back. The bullied child eventually will "take on" his tormenter. Surrounded by a ring of boys, the two will fight it out. In the popular myth, the victim will beat his tormenter, vanquishing him, demonstrating his emergent masculinity and ending the reign of school terror. Contrary to the popular depiction of how bullying ends, Ronald Stephens, executive director of the National School Safety Center, stated that "schoolyard bullying is the most enduring and underrated safety problem in U.S. schools." It generates an "environment of terror" that endangers students and disturbs the peace needed for teaching and learning.[41] The schools' failure to address the prevalent problem of school bullying leads only to more extreme forms of violent behavior.

The victims of bullying often divert energy to devise strategies to escape the bully by avoiding potentially unsafe areas, such as the playground, restrooms, and certain routes to and from school. Dreading school, some may withdraw from school activities and become overly quiet isolates and underachievers. Others may harbor the frustration, fear, and rage within them until it explodes, sometimes in acts of violent retribution.

Programs of conflict resolution have been developed to deal with bullying as a form of violence. These programs emphasize the need for teachers to rid themselves of the mythic stereotype of bullying conveyed by motion pictures and novels in which the victim suddenly stands up, faces the bully, and overcomes the tormentor. They emphasize the need to disabuse such notions that "boys will be boys" and that bullying is part of the growing up process. Bullying-preventative programs include: (1) identifying aggressive children and counseling them in strategies to cooperate with other children in a more constructive way; (2) developing, communicating, and fairly enforcing clear standards of behavior and expectations; (3) monitoring playground activity by an alert adult supervisor who is visible to all students; (4) being alert for victim symptoms, such as withdrawal, crying, declining study habits and academic achievement, anxiety, cuts and bruises, or torn clothing.[42]

Sexual Harassment

An important trend in the 1980s and 1990s was a growing awareness of the problems of sexual harassment in the workplace and in educational institutions, including schools, colleges, and universities. On May 25, 1999, the U.S. Supreme Court, in a close five-to-four decision, ruled in *Davis v. Monroe County Board of Education* that schools are liable for sexual harassment in classrooms and on school premises. The case involved a fifth-grade girl's claims that school officials had not intervened to stop the sexual harassment by a boy in the class. The Court ruled that school districts can be held liable for damages under federal law, Title IX of the Education Amendments of 1972, for failing to stop a student from subjecting another student to severe and pervasive sexual harassment. Justice Sandra Day O'Connor, in presenting the majority decision, described the Court's ruling as a statutory weapon against behavior that is so severe that it negatively impacts a victim's ability to learn. A strongly phrased minority dissent by Justice Anthony Kennedy called the decision an unwarranted federal intrusion into "day-to-day classroom logistics and interactions" and an overreaction to "the routine problems of adolescence."[43]

Dating Violence

There has been increased dating violence among high school and college students. Teen dating violence has been defined as a situation in which someone uses physical or emotional abuse to assault, control, or intimidate another person. Actual physical abuse may be preceded by warning signals involving emotional intimidation, such as yelling, humiliating, or threatening a person. Physical abuse can include slapping, shoving, holding a person down against his or her will, and rape. In instances of dating violence, the perpetrators are almost always males, and the situations often involves boyfriends abusing their girlfriends. A survey of students from three Midwestern suburban, rural, and inner-city high schools revealed that 15.7 percent of females had experienced sexual dating violence.[44]

Male violence inflicted on females may be learned from fathers or male guardians; it is also reinforced by the "macho" syndrome conveyed informally by popular culture and the media in which masculinity is confused with male dominance of those who are physically weaker, particularly women. In situations where a boyfriend is abusing his girlfriend, abusive treatment may occur repeatedly because the girl hopes that her boyfriend's behavior will change and does nothing to stop it; she then falls into a pattern of recurrent victimization. For example, in the study cited above, 45.1 percent of the females who reported physical or sexual violence also reported repeat physical violence.[45] Teen dating violence, like the battered wife syndrome, tends to escalate and be repetitive unless intervention occurs. The majority of the victims of teen dating violence do not report its occurrence and tend to feel helpless in their victimization and isolated from helping resources. When they did discuss their problem with another person, it was usually with another teenager rather than an adult.

Although educators became increasingly aware of the problems of dating violence and other types of interpersonal violence between students, their response tended to be limited. It was more developed in colleges and universities than in secondary schools. However, efforts were being made in high schools to address the issues. The general response was that programs addressing sexual harassment and dating violence need to be multifaceted, involving specific information about the problem and providing counseling and therapy for victims. A key element in treating this kind of violence is in aiding the victim, most frequently a girl or young woman who is experiencing fear, shame, and low self-esteem. Counseling and therapy involve a process of developing self-esteem, breaking the cycle of dependency and abuse, and encouraging self-empowerment. According to educators who work with victims, the problem of sexual harassment needs to be part of an antiviolence curriculum that includes: (1) information about violence and sexual harassment as a form of violence; (2) providing a safe setting for students to discuss their experiences; (3) providing needed counseling services; and (4) encouraging students to make realistic decisions about their relationships and choices.[46] Experts in the field see support-group therapy that focuses on assertiveness, anger control, and responsive communication as an important tool in helping victims and perpetrators to end victimization and to develop healthy relationships.

Educational Responses to Violence

School districts and school administrators responded to violence with immediate and long-term measures. For many districts, immediate measures were initiated to increase safety and security through policing efforts. Twenty-five percent of the nation's largest school districts were using metal detectors to prevent students from bringing guns and other weapons into schools. A trend in the 1990s was to add police to the school staff. For example, 245 school districts had police or security departments in 1992, of which 156 districts had uniformed officers. In 102 districts, school security officers were armed.[47]

A long-term response to violence was the development of conflict resolution and violence prevention education. Some educators advocated that education to prevent violence needs to begin early in a child's life, with parents and other adults role-modeling appropriate behavior or employing other effective methods to teach children nonviolent responses. Children at an early age need to develop a readiness for nonviolent behavior by being exposed to nonviolent methods of dealing with frustration, anger, and hostility. Just as violent behavior is learned, alternatives to violence can also be learned. Some curricular experts believe that a curriculum that shows children how to resolve disputes peacefully should begin as early as the preschool level.

The Child Development Project, a comprehensive school-based program, was designed to encourage positive social behavior. Beginning with kindergarten, teachers and children work collaboratively in organizing the classroom and in dealing with behavior problems in a way that reinforces positive values such as caring for and helping others. Children are exposed to stories and plays whose characters face moral dilemmas and deal with these dilemmas in nonviolent ways. Seeking to build relationships between home and school, children are encouraged to share their stories and activities with their parents. The program uses a buddy system that pairs younger and older students for tutoring and school outings and field trips. Just as education about personal and social problems has been infused into the curriculum, so too can learning about violence and violence prevention.

Recent Trends in Higher Education

As indicated in earlier chapters, higher education in the United States after World War II experienced phenomenal and unprecedented growth. Colleges and universities became more inclusive of the general population, enrolling students from racial, ethnic, and socioeconomic groups that generally had not attended college in the past. A key development of the expansion of higher education was the Servicemen's Readjustment Act of 1944, the GI Bill. From 1944 through 1951, over two million veterans attended colleges or universities, aided by the GI Bill. The post–World War II years was a time of steady growth for colleges and universities. (For the impact of the GI Bill, see chapter 1.)

In the 1970s, it was predicted by some experts that enrollments in higher education would level off and grow at a slower rate than in the previous two decades. However, the student enrollments continued to climb due to the enrollment of more persons from racial, ethnic, gender, and age groups that previously were underrepresented. More members of minority groups, more women, and more older people were attending colleges and universities. Enrollments in two-year community colleges, a sector of higher education that experienced strong growth in the post–World War II era, kept increasing significantly. Currently, there are 437 private two-year junior colleges and 1,036 public community colleges in the United States.[48]

By the mid-1990s, 14,278,790 students were enrolled in colleges and universities: 5,825,213 in public four-year institutions, 5,308,467 in public two-year institutions, 2,923,867 in private four-year institutions, and 221,243 in private two-year institutions. Of these, 12,262,606 were undergraduate, 1,721,469 were graduate, and 294,713 were professional students. Projections for the year 2004 indicate increasing total enrollments of 16,078,000 (an 11 percent increase), with 12,531,000 in public and 3,547,000 in private institutions.[49]

In the academic year 1993–94, 542,449 associate's degrees, 1,169,275 bachelor's degrees, 387,070 master's degrees, 43,185 doctorate, and 75,418 professional degrees were awarded in the United States. Projections for the year 2004 indicate that the number of degrees awarded will increase by 10 percent. It is expected that 576,000 associate, 1,288,000 bachelor, 452,000 master, 44,400, and 90,200 professional degrees will be awarded.[50]

Curricular Modifications

The 1990s saw some modifications in typical undergraduate bachelor's degree programs. Most programs required that students complete an academic concentration of courses, a major, in a particular field such as history, biology, mathematics, business, or computer science. There was also a trend to develop interdisciplinary programs in which students take courses from a number of fields. For example, students who major in international programs may take courses from history, economics, political science, and other fields. Other programs that were added to the undergraduate curriculum were environmental studies, women's studies, African-American studies, peace studies, and ethnic studies. The 1990s also saw a reemphasis on academic minors. Some students, to improve employment opportunities after graduation, also completed two majors. Additionally, supervised internships in which a student receives clinical or "on-the-job" experience were required in many fields. Another addition to many programs and courses was a community service project. For example, students assist as volunteers in clinics or in reading programs in elementary and secondary schools.

In addition to the modifications discussed above, there was a general but inconclusive debate in higher education over the nature and scope of the core requirements in the general education component required in most undergraduate degree programs. Though there were several related issues, the major area of contention was whether the core should reflect the Western cultural tradition or be revised to include works reflecting Hispanic, African, Asian, and "third world" perspectives. Divergent opinions resulted in what have been called the culture wars. Recall from the section on multiculturalism that proponents of a more multicultural orientation alleged that the traditional Western-oriented core rested on Eurocentric works, or canons. In turn, defenders of the Western-oriented curricular core charged that their opponents were using new canons of "political correctness" to base the curriculum on their own particular ideological orientation.

Campus Climate

As discussed in chapter 9, colleges and universities experienced a climate of pronounced student political activism between 1965 and 1972. Students at the University of California at Berkeley organized the Free Speech Movement to protest what they regarded as unjustified limitations on their freedom of speech and right to organize. The Students for a Democratic Society, SDS, organized demonstrations, teach-ins, and sit-ins against involvement in the war in Vietnam at many colleges and universities. The event that shocked the United States occurred at Kent State University in Ohio in 1970, when four students were killed by National Guard troops who fired into a crowd of student demonstrators and bystanders. Since the 1970s, the higher education climate has not exhibited concerted movements of social and political protest. Rather, students seem more concerned with earning degrees and finding jobs that offer financial security.

In higher education, the cultural wars, the decade-long debates over multiculturalism in the curriculum, continued. Gender also remained an issue in higher education. The U.S. Supreme Court ruled that the Virginia Military Institute's all-male enrollment policy was unconstitutional. Following this decision, the Citadel, in Charleston, South Carolina, announced it would admit women cadets. This ended the all-male policy at the only two public institutions of higher education that did not admit women.

In the 1990s, colleges and universities faced many of the same problems that the larger society encountered, such as alcohol, drugs, and sexual abuse and violence. Drawing on their experience during the 1960s, institutions during the 1970s, 1980s, and 1990s developed policies to address these problems. Many developed policies that provide students with protection from sexual harassment by faculty and other students. There was concern about "date rape," sexual attacks on female students who are under the influence of drugs or alcohol. Though not unique to the 1990s, there also was concern about alcohol consumption by students, especially "binge drinking."

The Increasing Cost of Higher Education

The cost of a higher education, which dramatically increased during the 1980s, rose to new heights in the 1990s. To meet increased expenditures for faculty and staff salaries, construction, and operations, institutions raised tuition. Because of rising costs for health care, highways, and prisons, some states reduced the amount of state funding for higher education. However, private institutions had the highest increases in tuition and fees. The average tuition and room and board at a four-year public college for in-state residents during the 1978–79 school year was $1,994. By the mid-1990s, the cost increased to $6,252. At private four-year schools, tuition and room and board increased from an average of $4,514 in 1978–79 to an average of $17,207 in 1995–96.[51]

In the late 1980s and the 1990s, the patterns of financing a college education changed. More financial aid came from loans rather than grants. For example, in 1981–82, federal grants made up 54.6 percent of student financial aid and federal loans made up 41.4 percent. By the mid-1990s, federal grants had decreased to 39.7 percent and federal loans had increased to 58.9 percent. The average debt, in 1997, for student borrowers who attended public four-year institutions was $13,000, compared with $17,500 for those attending private colleges. For attending graduate school, the average debt was $24,500, and for those attending professional schools $48,500.[52] A tendency in the late 1990s was for some states to establish programs that allowed families to prepay college tuition years in advance by purchasing special contracts or tax-exempt bonds.

Affirmative Action

As a result of the Civil Rights movement of the 1960s, by the 1990s most colleges and universities had established affirmative action, equal-employment-opportunity guidelines that gave some preference in hiring new faculty and in student admissions to generally underrepresented minority groups. However, in the 1990s, some states (such as California) reduced their affirmative action programs and enacted legislation that restricted using race-based preferences in college admissions, financial aid, or hiring.

Institutional Restructuring, Faculty Compensation

As student enrollment rose in the post–World War II period, so did the number and salaries of faculty, administrators, and other staff involved in higher education. By the mid-1990s, the average salary for faculty was $53,444 at public universities, $47,294 at other four-year public institutions, $42,101 at public two-year institutions, $63,280 at private universities, and $43,196 at other private four-year institutions.[53] While faculty salaries are only one part of the cost of higher education, trustees and administrators developed plans (a process called strategic planning) to restructure their institutions. For example, some institutions looked into ways of changing tenure requirements to reduce the large numbers of tenured, older, and higher salaried professors. Additionally some institutions replaced retired, full-time faculty with less expensive, nontenured, part-time faculty.

By the mid-1990s, approximately one-third of the college and university instructors were in the part-time category. Critics of this restructuring feel that a heavy reliance on part-time faculty may decrease the quality of instruction. While part-time faculty often add special expertise to their teaching because they are also practitioners, such as in the fields of business, medicine, or law, many others, especially in the liberal arts and humanities, have earned Ph.D.s but are unable to find full-time, tenure track, teaching positions. These "roving scholars" may teach at several institutions. Additionally, the 1990s saw the continued practice of employing graduate students as teaching assistants to instruct students in undergraduate courses while the graduate students complete their doctoral degree programs. In the late 1990s, some graduate teaching assistants were attempting to organize unions to improve their pay and status.

Information Technology

As was true with elementary and secondary schools, colleges and universities in the 1990s continued to use more of the new electronic information technology—computers and the Internet—in instruction. For example, many college students were now required to have their own computers to access the Internet and other electronic data sources, to retrieve information from libraries, and to communicate with their professors via e-mail. Some professors have developed Web sites as a part of their courses that include overviews, excerpts from primary sources, discussion questions, and bibliographies. Professors communicate with each other and with students via e-mail. Course syllabi and assignments may also be conveyed via e-mail or Web sites. Many college textbooks have added sections on Web and Internet links to the topics they cover. The widely read *Chronicle of Higher Education* features a regular section on information technology that examines trends and available resources. A challenge of the future is to train faculty in these new modes of instructional technology. There is also the larger issue of how this new source of information is to be integrated with the knowledge conveyed by the more traditional scholarly article and book.

In the 1990s, colleges and universities expanded their distance education program and course offerings. Distance education was the new name for programs of off-campus instruction. Since the late nineteenth century colleges and universities, especially public institutions offered correspondence courses in which students mailed their lessons to professors for comment and evaluation. Courses were also offered by radio and television, often in conjunction with some kind of correspondence arrangement. Conventional off-campus courses were usually taken by part-time students who lived some distance from college or university campuses. These modes of off-campus instruction gained a new dimension in the contemporary distance education programs with the development of electronic data retrieval made possible by computers. While they continue to serve students who live a distance from the campus, the new distance education programs are attracting students both on- and off-campus. Some students find taking courses by e-mail to be more convenient in that they can log on at any time to send e-mail messages, join a continuing discussion, or refer to lecture notes and assignments.[54]

While the use of electronic data retrieval and the Internet has brought significant change to instruction, some professors are wary of students' over- or exclusive reliance on them. Though the information is often less dated than that which appears in journals and books, it often is presented in a highly generalized, encyclopedia-like format. The Web contains some solid scholarship but, unlike the more scholarly journal and book sources, it also contains unfounded, undocumented claims and, in some cases, a mixture of advertising.[55]

Conclusion

The 1990s not only comprised the last decade of the post–World War II era that began in 1945, but also marked the end of the twentieth century. During the decade, much political and educational rhetoric was devoted to preparing for and "building a bridge" to the new millennium of the twenty-first century. Like all historic periods, the 1990s harbored both optimistic as well as pessimistic trends for the coming century.

The 1990s showed signs of educational growth and progress. The information society was well advanced; the new computer-generated electronic sources of information and data retrieval were changing education throughout the country. Further, American education had become increasingly more inclusive of groups that had been neglected or underrepresented in the past. The curriculum, too, had grown increasingly enriched by multiculturalist and feminist perspectives.

While there were signs of progress, the 1990s also revealed areas of the dark side, both internationally, such as in the former Yugoslavia, and at home. Problems of drug addiction and violence continued. The late 1990s witnessed violence in schools—students killing classmates. Some of the incidents of violence stemmed from a strong anger and bias toward others, especially toward those who were ethnically, racially, or religiously different or those who did not fit a certain profile of sexual orientation. The problem of violence in the larger society and in schools remained a fearsome issue.

Specifically, the 1990s saw such the trends as: (1) efforts to establish national standards and tests to assess students' academic progress; (2) the development of alternative forms of educational organization, such as charter schools; (3) concerns over the deterioration of schools' physical plants; (4) increasing higher education costs; (5) determined efforts to infuse information technology into schools; (6) character education programs; (7) efforts to end violence in schools.

Notes

[1] *The National Education Goals* (Washington, DC: U.S. Department of Education, 1994).

[2] For a historical perspective on the computer revolution, see Michael E. Hobart and Zachary S. Schiffman, *Information Ages: Literacy, Numeracy, and the Computer Revolution* (Baltimore: Johns Hopkins University Press, 1998).

[3] Stephen Burd, "Republicans Take a Conservative Stance on Education," *The Chronicle of Higher Education* (September 6, 1996), p. A46.

[4] Douglas Lederman, "Democrats Vow to Make Education a Key in Their Drive to Keep the White House," *The Chronicle of Higher Education* (September 6, 1996), pp. A47–A48.

5 National Center for Education Statistics, *Digest of Education Statistics 1996* (Washington, DC: US Department of Education, 1996), pp. 1–2.

6 Joe Nathan, "Possibilities, Problems, and Progress: Early Lessons from the Charter Movement," *Phi Delta Kappan* (September 1996), pp. 18–23.

7 Pat Belanoff, "Portfolios and Literacy: Why?," in Laurel Black, Donald A. Deiker, Jeffrey Sommers, and Gail Stygall, eds., *New Directions in Portfolio Assessment* (Portsmouth, NH: Heinemann, 1994), pp. 13–24.

8 Edward M. White, "Portfolios as an Assessment Concept," in Laurel Black et al., pp. 25–39.

9 Gene J. Maeroff, "Assessing Alternative Assessment," *Phi Delta Kappan*, 73, No. 4 (December 1991), pp. 273–81.

10 The issues of multiculturalism, elimination of sexism, and bilingualism in education were not confined specifically to the 1990s but spanned the post–World War II decades, especially after the 1950s. They are included for discussion with the 1990s because they represent long-standing issues that are likely to continue into the twenty-first century.

11 Lawrence A. Cremin, ed., *The Republic and the School: Horace Mann on the Education of Free Man* (New York: Teachers College Press, Columbia University, 1957).

12 Claude M. Steele, "Race and the Schooling of Black Americans," *The Atlantic Monthly* (April 1992), p. 68.

13 Ibid., p. 78.

14 James Davison Hunter, *Culture Wars: The Struggle to Define America* (New York: Basic Books, HarperCollins, 1991).

15 For the issues of multiculturalism, Michael Kammen, *Contested Values: Democracy and Diversity in American Culture* (New York: St. Martin's Press, 1995); James A. Banks, *Multiethnic Education: Theory and Practice* (Boston: Allyn and Bacon, 1994).

16 Ronald Takaki, *A Different Mirror: A History of Multicultural America* (Boston: Little, Brown, and Co., 1993).

17 Arthur M. Schlesinger Jr. *The Disuniting of America* (New York: W. W. Norton and Co., 1992), pp. 16–17.

18 Ibid., p. 18.

19 Toni Marie Massaro, *Constitutional Literacy: A Core Curriculum for a Multicultural Nation* (Durham, NC: Duke University Press, 1993).

20 Ibid., p. 73.

21 Ibid., p. 129.

22 Hunter, *Culture Wars*, pp. 197–224.

23 Beverly A. Stitt, *Building Gender Fairness in Schools* (Carbondale: Southern Illinois University Press, 1988), p. 3.

24 Thorsten Husen and T. Neville Postlethwaite, eds. *The International Encyclopedia of Education: Research and Studies* (New York: Pergamon Press, 1985), p. 4558.

25 Janice Pottker and Andrew Fishel, *Sex Bias in the Schools: The Research Evidence* (Cranbury, NJ: Associated University Presses, 1977), p. 92.

26 Jay M. Shafritz, Richard P. Koeppe, and Elizabeth W. Sopher, *The Facts on File Dictionary of Education* (New York: Oxford University Press, 1988), p. 430.

27 Marcelain Wininger Rovana, "Preparing for a Firefighter's World: How to Teach Nonsexist Language," *English Journal* (December 1991), p. 62.

28 Husen and Postlethwaite, p. 4558.

29 Stitt, p. 4.

[30] Domenico Maceri, "Spanish for All? The Case for Bilingual Ed," *Chicago Tribune*, Sect. 1 (April 15, 1999), p. 27.

[31] Vincent J. Schololski, "Drive Is on to Eliminate Bilingual Education in California," *Chicago Tribune* (September 23, 1997), p. 5.

[32] Lance Morrow, "Childhood's End," *Time* (March 9, 1992), p. 23.

[33] Alex Molnar, "Too Many Kids Are Getting Killed," *Educational Leadership* (September 1992), p. 4.

[34] James Earl Hardy, "Violent Gang Warfare," *Scholastic Update* (April 5, 1991), p. 6.

[35] Sarah Glazier, "Violence in Schools," *CQ Researcher* (September 11, 1992), p. 788.

[36] Hardy, p. 6.

[37] Rachel Sauer, "In Towns of Tragedy, Pain Doesn't Go Away," *Chicago Tribune*, Sect. 1 (April 21, 1999), p. 10.

[38] Tim Jones and Steven Johnson, "Colorado School Shooting: 'Adrenaline Television' Dramatizes the Horror, while It's Happening," *Chicago Tribune*, Sect. 1 (April 21, 1999), p. 10.

[39] Katie Managle, "When Teens Hate," *Scholastic Update* (April 5, 1991), p. 7.

[40] Ronald D. Stephens, "Bullies and Victims: Protecting Our Schoolchildren," *USA Today* (September 1991), p. 72.

[41] Ibid., p. 72.

[42] Ibid., p. 73.

[43] Linda Greenhouse, "Sex Harassment in Class Is Ruled School's Liability," *New York Times* (May 25, 1999), pp. 1, 24.

[44] Libby Bergman, "Dating Violence among High School Students," *Social Work* 37, No.1 (January 1992), p. 21.

[45] Ibid., p. 23.

[46] Ibid., p. 25.

[47] Sarah Glazier, p. 790.

[48] *The Chronicle of Higher Education Almanac* (September 2, 1996), p. 8.

[49] Ibid., pp. 9, 18.

[50] Ibid., pp. 8, 18.

[51] Frederick K. Lowe, "Tuition Aid Lets Students MAP Futures," *Chicago Sun Times* (November 11, 1997), p. 3A.

[52] "Debt Burden Growing for College Graduates: Survey," *Chicago Sun Times* (November 11, 1997), p. 14A.

[53] *Chronicle of Higher Education Almanac*, p. 8.

[54] Lisa Guernsey, "Distance Education for the Not-So-Distant," *The Chronicle of Higher Education* (March 27, 1998), pp. A29–30.

[55] Kari Boyd McBride and Ruth Dickstein, "The Web Demands Critical Reading by Students," *The Chronicle of Higher Education* (March 20, 1998), p. B6.

Further Reading

Askew, Sue. *Boys Don't Cry: Boys and Sexism in Education*. Philadelphia: Open University Press, 1988.

Ban, John R. *Violence and Vandalism in Public Education: Problems and Prospects*. Danville, IL: Interstate Printers & Publishers, 1977.

Baron, Dennis. *Grammar and Gender*. New Haven: Yale University Press, 1986.

Besag, Valerie E. *Bullies and Victims in Schools: A Guide to Understanding and Management*. Philadelphia: Open University Press, 1989.

Black, Laurel, Donald A. Deiker, Jeffrey Sommers, and Gail Stygall, eds. *New Directions in Portfolio Assessment*. Portsmouth, NH: Heinemann, 1994.

Blauvelt, Peter D. *Effective Strategies for School Security*. Reston, VA: National Association of Secondary School Principals, 1981.

Bodinger-DeUriarte, Cristina. *Hate Crime: Sourcebook for Schools*. Los Alamitos: CA: Center for Educational Equity, Southwest Regional Laboratory, 1992.

Bybee, Roger W. *Violence, Values, and Justice in the Schools*. Boston, MA: Allyn and Bacon, 1981.

Cohen, Arthur M., and Florence B. Brawer and Associates. *Managing Community Colleges: A Handbook for Effective Practice*. San Francisco: Jossey-Bass, 1994.

Cutcliffe, Stephen H., and Terry S. Reynolds, eds. *Technology and American History: A Historical Anthology from Technology and Culture*. Chicago: University of Chicago Press, 1997.

Figueroa, Peter M. *Education and the Social Construction of "Race."* New York: Routledge, 1991.

Fisher, James L., and Martha Tack. *Leaders on Leadership: The College Presidency*. San Francisco: Jossey-Bass, 1988.

Ford, Peter, et al., *Managing Change in Higher Education: A Learning Environment Architecture*. Buckingham, UK: Society for Research into Higher Education & Open University Press, 1996.

Goldstein, Arnold F. *School Violence*. Englewood Cliffs, NJ: Prentice-Hall, 1984.

Gottfredson, Gary D. *Victimization in Schools*. New York: Plenum Press, 1985.

Gutek, Gerald L. *Education in the United States: An Historical Perspective*. Englewood Cliffs, NJ: Prentice-Hall, 1986.

Hobart, Michael E., and Zachary S. Schiffman. *Information Ages: Literacy, Numeracy, and the Computer Revolution*. Baltimore: Johns Hopkins University Press, 1998.

Ingram, Richard T. and Associates. *Governing Public Colleges and Universities: A Handbook for Trustees, Chief Executives, and Other Campus Leaders*. San Francisco: Jossey-Bass Publishers, 1993.

King, Edith W. *Teaching Ethnic and Gender Awareness: Methods and Materials for the Elementary School*. Dubuque, IA: Kendall/Hunt Publishing Co., 1990.

Kinnear, M. *Daughters of Time: Women in the Western Tradition*. Ann Arbor: University of Michigan Press, 1982.

Martin, James, James E. Samels and Associates. *Merging Colleges for Mutual Growth: A New Strategy for Academic Mergers*. Baltimore: Johns Hopkins Press, 1994.

Mowery, David C., and Nathan Rosenberg. *Paths of Innovation: Technological Change in 20th-Century America*. New York: Cambridge University Press, 1998.

Noddings, Nel. *Caring: A Feminine Approach to Ethics and Moral Education*. Berkeley: University of California Press, 1984.

Noddings, Nel. *Women and Evil*. Berkeley and Los Angeles: University of California Press, 1989.

Riley, Kevin W. *Street Gangs and the Schools: A Blueprint for Intervention.* Bloomington, IN: Phi Delta Kappa Educational Foundation, 1991.

Rippa, S. Alexander. *Education in a Free Society: An American History.* New York: Longman, 1992.

Ruddick, S. *Maternal Thinking: Towards a Politics of Peace.* Boston: Beacon Press, 1989.

Sadker, Myra Pollack, and David Miller Sadker. *Sex Equity for Schools.* New York: Longman Inc., 1982.

Schlesinger, Arthur M. *The Disuniting of America.* New York: W.W. Norton & Co., 1992.

Schostak, John F. *Schooling the Violent Imagination.* New York: Routledge & Kegan Paul, 1986.

Shapiro, June. *Equal Their Chances: Children's Activities for Non-Sexist Learning.* Englewood Cliffs, NJ: Prentice-Hall, 1981.

Sprung, Barbara. *Non-Sexist Education for Young Children: A Practical Guide.* New York: Citation Press, 1975.

Stacey, Judith. *And Jill Came Tumbling After: Sexism in American Education.* New York: Dell Publishing Co., 1978.

Stitt, Beverly A. *Building Gender Fairness in Schools.* Carbondale: Southern Illinois University Press, 1988.

Takaki, Ronald. *A Different Mirror: A History of Multicultural America.* Boston: Little, Brown, and Co., 1993.

Thelen, David. *Becoming Citizens in the Age of Television.* Chicago: University of Chicago Press, 1996.

Tucker, Allan, and Robert A. Bryan. *The Academic Dean: Dove, Dragon, and Diplomat.* New York: Macmillan Publishing Co., 1991.

Tyack, David, and Elisabeth Hansot. *Learning Together: A History of Coeducation in American Public Schools.* New Haven, CT: Yale University Press, 1990.

Warner, David, and David Palfreyman. *Higher Education Management: The Key Elements.* Buckingham, UK: Society for Research into Higher Education & Open University Press, 1996.

Winston, Roger B., Jr., Williams R. Nettles, and John H. Opper Jr. *Fraternities and Sororities on the Contemporary College Campus.* San Francisco: Jossey-Bass, 1987.

Index

AAUP. *See* American Association of University Professors

Abolitionism, 119–20

Academic freedom, 111, 113–14

ACLU. *See* American Civil Liberties Union

Action for Excellence, 280–81

ACT scores, 273

Adams, James Luther, 109

Addams, Jane, 65

Administration, school, 298

Adolescence, 69–70

Affirmative action, 320

AFL. *See* American Federation of Labor

African Americans

  Black Muslims, 227-28

  Black Panthers, 227, 233, 239

  black separatism, 236

  black studies, 223–24, 228–29, 238–39, 243, 302, 318

  Brown v. the Board of Education of Topeka, 8, 29, 57, 119, 121, 124–28, 136, 139, 142, 148–49, 251, 260–61, 274

  civil rights, 119–20, 148, 221–22, 227–28

  compensatory education, 143n46

  Ebonics, 309n10

  education of, 6, 8, 26, 28–29, 228, 260, 302

  hate crimes, 313

  King, Jr., Martin Luther, 139, 227, 236

  National Association for the Advancement of Colored People, 29, 76, 121–27, 139, 227, 258

  Organization of Afro-American Unity, 228

  Plessy v. Ferguson, 3, 28, 120–23, 126

  quota system in higher education, 14

  school integration, 6, 119, 136–38, 248, 250-51, 257

  segregated schools, 3, 6, 8, 28–29, 46

  Social Darwinism, 120

  Southern Christian Leadership Conference, 139–40, 227

  Swann v. Charlotte-Mecklenburg Board of Education, 139

  Urban League, 29, 139

  voters, 29, 129

AFT. *See* American Federation of Teachers

Agency for International Development, 164–65

Agnew, Spiro, 241, 254

AIDs education, 284–85

Air raid drills, school, 51–55

Allen, Raymond J., 103–4

Allied Health Professional Personnel Training Act, 181

Alternative education, 203, 209–10

Amendments, constitutional. *See* Constitution, U.S

American Association of Community and Junior Colleges, 265

American Association of Junior Colleges, 71

American Association of School Administrators, 71, 265

American Association of Universities, 113–14

327

Faubus, Orval E., 131–35
FBI. *See* Federal Bureau of Investigation
Featherstone, Joseph, 203–4
  Schools Where Children Learn, 203
Federal aid to education, 6, 9, 25–38, 162, 175
  Barden Bill, 36–37
  Clinton, William J., 293–97, 301
  Eisenhower, Dwight D., 44, 46, 154
  Ford, Gerald, 255–57, 259–60, 262–63
  GI Bill, 2, 8–15, 23, 27, 175, 222, 317
  Johnson, Lyndon, 170–83, 249–50, 253–54, 256
  Kennedy, John F., 154–62, 175–76, 181, 183
  Lanham Act, 1941, 27
  Morrill Land Grant Act of 1867, 9–10
  National Defense Education Act, 38, 46–47
  Nixon, Richard M., 157, 250–54, 262
  Northwest Ordinance of 1785, 26
  Northwest Ordinance of 1787, 26
  private and parochial schools, 9, 29–37
  Reagan, Ronald, 272, 274–77, 284
  Smith-Hughes Act, 1917, 26–27
  Taft-Thomas Bill for Federal Aid to Education, 34
  Truman, Harry S., 31–32, 49
Federal Bureau of Investigation, 85, 96
Federal Civil Defense Administration, 49
Federal Emergency Relief Funds, 27
Federally Affected Areas Act, 181
Federal Security Administration, 264
Feinberg Law, 105
Fellowships, graduate, 15
Feminist studies, 243, 248
Fisher, Frederick, 101
Ford, Gerald, 47, 182, 254, 263, 275–76, 285

busing, 255–58
educational policies, 255–59
federal aid to education, 255–57, 259–60, 262–63
Ford Foundation, 197
Fund for the Advancement of Education, 197
School Improvement Program, 197
Franco, Francisco, 90
Fredericksen and Schrader study, 13
Free schools, 209–10
Free Speech Movement, 231–33, 318
Freire, Paulo, 202, 213
Freud, Sigmund, 304
Fuchs, Claude, 86
Fundamentalist Protestants and education, 273–74
Fund for the Improvement of Post-secondary Education, 284

Gaines, Lloyd Lionel, 122–23
Galbraith, John, 177
  Affluent Society, 177
Gangs, youth, 273, 310–11
Garbarino, Joseph, 232
Gardner, David L., 277
Gardner, John, 157, 173, 176
Garfield, James A., 264
Gay and lesbian studies, 243
Gender roles, 305–8, 318–19
German Democratic Republic (East Germany), 17–18
German Federal Republic (West Germany), 17
Germany, 2, 16–18, 89–90
GI Bill (Servicemen's Readjustment Act of 1944), 2, 8–15, 23, 27, 175, 222, 317
Goals 2000: Educate America Act, 293–94
Goldwater, Barry, 77, 173, 176, 225, 234
Goodman, Paul, 203
Gore, Al, 294
Gramsci, Antonio, 202
Green, Edith, 158, 161, 178
Green v. New Kent County School Board, 138